Macbeth

Texts and Contexts

William Shakespeare, *The First Part of King Henry the Fourth: Texts and Contexts*
(The Bedford Shakespeare Series)
EDITED BY BARBARA HODGDON,
DRAKE UNIVERSITY

William Shakespeare,
A Midsummer Night's Dream: Texts and Contexts
(The Bedford Shakespeare Series)
EDITED BY GAIL KERN PASTER,
GEORGE WASHINGTON UNIVERSITY
AND
SKILES HOWARD,
RUTGERS UNIVERSITY AT NEW BRUNSWICK

William Shakespeare, *The Taming of the Shrew: Texts and Contexts*
(The Bedford Shakespeare Series)
EDITED BY FRANCES E. DOLAN,
MIAMI UNIVERSITY

The Bedford Companion to Shakespeare: An Introduction with Documents
BY RUSS MCDONALD,
UNIVERSITY OF NORTH CAROLINA AT GREENSBORO

William Shakespeare, *Hamlet*
(Case Studies in Contemporary Criticism)
EDITED BY SUSANNE L. WOFFORD,
UNIVERSITY OF WISCONSIN—MADISON

WILLIAM SHAKESPEARE

Macbeth

Texts and Contexts

—————————————— ✤ ——————————————

Edited by

WILLIAM C. CARROLL

Boston University

Bedford/St. Martin's   BOSTON ◆ NEW YORK

For Bedford/St. Martin's
Executive Editor: Karen S. Henry
Editorial Assistant: Nicole Simonsen
Production Supervisor: Dennis Conroy
Project Management: Stratford Publishing Services, Inc.
Marketing Manager: Charles Cavaliere
Text Design: Claire Seng-Niemoeller
Cover Design: Donna Lee Dennison
Cover Art: Details from *The Field of the Cloth of Gold*, c. 1545 (oil on canvas) English School. The Royal Collection © 2011 Her Majesty Queen Elizabeth II/The Bridgeman Art Library.
Composition: Stratford Publishing Services, Inc.
Printing and Binding: R. R. Donnelley & Sons Company

President: Charles H. Christensen
Editorial Director: Joan E. Feinberg
Director of Editing, Design, and Production: Marcia Cohen
Manager, Publishing Services: Emily Berleth

Library of Congress Catalog Card Number: 98–87542

For information, write: Bedford/St. Martin's, 75 Arlington Street, Boston, MA 02116 (617–399–4000)
ISBN-10: 0–312–14454–7 (paperback)
0–312–21068–X (hardcover)
ISBN-10: 978-0-312-14454-8

Published and distributed outside North America by
MACMILLAN PRESS LTD
Houndmills, Basingstoke, Hampshire RG21 2XS and London
Companies and representatives throughout the world.
ISBN: 0–333–73076–3

For Carol and David

About the Series

Shakespeare wrote his plays in a culture unlike, though related to, the culture of the emerging twenty-first century. The Bedford Shakespeare Series resituates Shakespeare within the sometimes alien context of the sixteenth and seventeenth centuries while inviting students to explore ways in which Shakespeare, as text and as cultural icon, continues to be part of contemporary life. Each volume frames a Shakespearean play with a wide range of written and visual material from the early modern period, such as homilies, polemical literature, emblem books, facsimiles of early modern documents, maps, woodcut prints, court records, other plays, medical tracts, ballads, chronicle histories, and travel narratives. Selected to reveal the many ways in which Shakespeare's plays were connected to the events, discourses, and social structures of his time, these documents and illustrations also show the contradictions and the social divisions in Shakespeare's culture and in the plays he wrote. Engaging critical introductions and headnotes to the primary materials help students identify some of the issues they can explore by reading these texts with and against one another, setting up a two-way traffic between the Shakespearean text and the social world these documents help to construct.

Jean E. Howard
Columbia University
Series Editor

About This Volume

This edition of *Macbeth* begins, above all, with the text of the play from David Bevington's superb edition of Shakespeare's complete works. This volume attempts to provide the historical, cultural, and political contexts in which Shakespeare's play appeared, probably in 1606. The texts I have included here are not simply those that have been identified as "sources" or "influences," though they are present as well. Some of these selections, we can be certain, Shakespeare never read; others were written after his death. These texts constitute the various discourses of the culture within which *Macbeth* was seen and understood, and which *Macbeth* in turn affected. Many writers other than Shakespeare and Holinshed (his main source) wrote about the historical figure of Macbeth, for example; the story of his reign was narrated, revised, and appropriated by many writers, often on opposite sides of various political and cultural debates, for their own purposes. The range of texts printed here reflects, I hope, the wide range of opinion and belief on many issues raised by the play, from the authority of the sovereign and the duty of the subject, through the idea of Scotland, to the nature of the female body.

As extensive as these selections may seem, of course, no single book could ever describe the full context of a period as distant and as complex as Shakespeare's. The very fact of a *selection* from among many texts means that there are underlying theories or interpretations of the play and its historical moment; beyond this inevitable bias, however, I believe the volume will enable readers to decide for themselves what is relevant to an understanding of the play. The introductions and notes to the various topics and selections are intended not to be definitive, but to provide the reader sufficient information to read the selection, and to describe some possible points of contact with the play.

The texts selected for inclusion here were written over a period of approximately seventy-five years on either side of *Macbeth*'s composition, ranging from John Major's history of Britain in 1521, to Thomas Duffet's parody of the witches in 1674; the chronological frame could have been widened considerably in both directions, especially into the present. The continuing conversation about the play is a testament to its power as a work of literature, and the appropriation of parts of the play into popular culture and the vernacular vocabulary (e.g., washing the blood off one's hands; the advertisement for a luxury car that announces, "Something wicked this way comes") reflects not only its striking originality, but also the historical process in which works or authors with great cultural capital, like Shakespeare, provide a rich source for later borrowers. This volume cannot represent the entire story of *Macbeth*, but has focused primarily on what is usually called the early modern period — the sixteenth and seventeenth centuries.

These documents have been divided and organized into six chapters, each taking up a different set of issues arising from the play. While the categories have considerable validity, I think, it will quickly become obvious to the reader that the selections are interconnected in a number of ways. Jacobean theories of sovereign power, for example, assume certain narrative elements of the story of Macbeth; the very existence of Banquo — a "fact" contested by some histories — takes on major significance in the succession struggle in which James stakes his claim to the throne. Similarly, questions about the nature of women cannot be confined to Chapter 6, but cross over into each of the other sections. The interconnectedness of these different discourses is reflected as well in the textual richness of and, often, self-contradictions in *Macbeth* itself.

EDITORIAL POLICY

I have used the earliest editions available to me in the original, on microfilm, or in facsimile throughout this volume. In the case of works originally published in Latin, I have used the earliest published English translations available. In glossing words and phrases, I have relied on the *Oxford English*

Dictionary. Much, but not all, of the biographical information used in the introductions has come from the *Dictionary of National Biography.*

The following editorial principles have been followed:

1. Spelling has been modernized and regularized, and reflects American usage in most cases. Exceptions: archaic verb endings (e.g., *-eth*) have been retained; archaic words have also been retained but glossed.

2. Punctuation has been very lightly modernized.

3. Italics and capitalizations in the original texts have not been retained, except where meaning is affected, or when the reference is to the title of a specific individual.

4. The titles of sixteenth- and seventeenth-century texts have been modernized, according to the above principles. The (more or less) full title of each work appears in a footnote to the selection; shortened titles are used elsewhere.

5. In citing sixteenth- and seventeenth-century texts, page numbers have been given where they exist. In some cases, however, the signature number is given. Signature numbers reflect how a book was printed: a large sheet of paper was folded into two, to create a *folio,* or *F,* volume; into four, to create a *quarto,* or *Q,* volume; or into eight, to create an *octavo,* or *O,* volume. The various large sheets were gathered and stitched together to form a book. The signature number begins with a letter, which identifies all the pages printed on that sheet; the letters, in alphabetical order, reflect the order of the gathered sheets. Thus, B3 is the second gathering, third page; D1 (or just D) is the fourth gathering, first page. The front side of a page is either unmarked or marked "r" (for *recto*); the back side of the page is marked "v" (for *verso*). Thus, B2v is the back side of the second page of the second gathering.

6. All calendar dates are given according to the Gregorian calendar, which makes January 1 the official first day of the year. England followed the Julian calendar until 1752; in this calendar system, the new year began on March 25 (the Feast of the Annunciation). Some documents, therefore, can present confusion to modern readers: March 24, 1602, the date of Queen Elizabeth's death as recorded in seventeenth-century documents, for example, is actually the year 1603 by our current (Gregorian) calendar.

I have glossed documents that reflect so-called New Style time as well. Much of the rest of Europe adopted the Gregorian calendar in the late sixteenth and early seventeenth centuries and, along with the different start of the new year, adopted the calendrical correction by which ten days were added so that the new calendar was astronomically correct. (By contrast, we now often add only a fraction of a single second every few years.) Thus, a document such as Nicolo Molin's report on the Gunpowder Plot, dated November 16, was actually November 6 in England. All dates in the texts selected here reflect the English calendar, or are glossed appropriately.

7. James reigned in Scotland as King James VI from 1567 to 1625; in 1603, he assumed the English crown, and reigned as King James VI and I, until his death in 1625. For the sake of simplicity, he is referred to throughout as either James, or King James I (as in the bibliography).

ACKNOWLEDGMENTS

Many individuals have been of great assistance in the preparation of this volume. I would certainly like to thank Russ McDonald, Fran Dolan, and Barbara Hodgdon, the editors of the first three volumes in this series. Their editions are models of scholarship and intelligence, and I learned much from them; each of them also provided valuable personal advice on a number of occasions. I also received some extremely useful commentary, at an early stage of the project, from Michael Bristol, Fran Dolan, Richard Halpern, Richard Strier, and Virginia Mason Vaughan. The general editor of the series, Jean Howard, read the manuscript with great care, sympathy, and intelligence; her comments and suggestions have been invaluable. The highly professional staff of the Folger Library also made the entire process pleasurable as well as efficient.

At Bedford/St. Martin's I would like to offer special thanks to Emily Berleth, the expert project coordinator; Donna Dennison, who designed the cover; Nicole Simonsen; Lorna Notsch; and Charles H. Christensen, the creative publisher of Bedford Books who supported this series from the beginning. At Stratford Publishing Services, I owe thanks to Linda Ayres-DeMasi, Laura S. Livingston, and Kate Cohen, a superbly attentive and helpful copyeditor.

In Boston, I want to thank several groups of excellent graduate students who took part in seminars in Jacobean culture where some of the ideas in this volume were first tested. I also want to thank the fifteen members of the *Teachers as Scholars* seminar at Harvard, who worked through some of these texts with me and offered much stimulating commentary. The plan of the whole volume received much useful criticism and support from the members of a Shakespeare Association workshop on "Contexts for Teaching Shakespeare and Contemporaries," ably directed by Ann C. Christensen and Barbara Sebek. Finally, my colleagues in Renaissance studies — Christopher Martin, William Riggs, and James R. Siemon — have provided friendship and intellectual stimulation for which I continue to be profoundly grateful.

Certainly the person most responsible for this volume is Karen Henry of Bedford/St. Martin's — an ideal editor in every way: professionally knowledgeable about the subject, supportive, imaginative, meticulous — and, thankfully, patient. Her ideas for the series, and for this specific volume, were always on target, wise, and helpful.

My greatest debt, as ever, is to my family, and this book is gratefully dedicated to them.

Contents

>‹‹

Prophecy 330

➔ *6. Discourses of the Feminine*   *344*

Illustrations

><

Introduction

>-<

Playgoers and readers have always recognized the power of *Macbeth*, from its first performances in Shakespeare's lifetime to its current critical status as one of Shakespeare's greatest plays. The play has invariably attracted each generation's leading actors and actresses to the parts of Macbeth and Lady Macbeth, beginning with Thomas Betterton in Sir William Davenant's production in the later seventeenth century (see p. 162), and David Garrick and Sarah Siddons (still considered one of the greatest Lady Macbeths ever) in the eighteenth century, to Laurence Olivier, Paul Scofield, Vivien Leigh, and Janet Suzman in the twentieth century, among many others.[1] The popularity of *Macbeth* derives not just from its magnificent title parts, however, but also from its total impact — of terror, horror, sublimity, grandeur, violence, perversion, claustrophobia, and the grotesque. It is an extraordinary mix: one of Shakespeare's shortest, most concentrated plays, yet one of his most complex and penetrating.

Macbeth's popularity on the stage has been matched by the esteem accorded to it by critics and scholars over nearly four centuries. In his influential book, *Shakespearean Tragedy* (1904), the distinguished critic A. C. Bradley

---

[1] See Bartholomeusz, Kliman, and Rosenberg for the stage history of *Macbeth*.

I

enshrined *Macbeth* as one of the "four great tragedies," along with *Hamlet, Othello,* and *King Lear.* The play has received enormous critical and scholarly attention throughout the twentieth century, but the commentary has been divided in its treatment of the various elements of the play. The witches, for example, have been described as everything from simply incarnations of evil, to representations of Fate or Destiny, to emblems of maternal malevolence (Adelman), and even to "the heroines of the piece . . . the most fertile force in the play" (Eagleton 2–3). Their inclusion in the play has been variously attributed to Shakespeare's desire to please King James, who had a personal and a scholarly interest in witchcraft; to Shakespeare's misogyny, in representing the feminine as demonic, and vice versa; and to Shakespeare's grasp of psychological projection, in which these malevolent external figures really symbolize the dark inner mental state of Macbeth himself.

A powerful work of theater and a complex work of literature, *Macbeth* had its own role to play in the history and culture of early modern England. The play has particular significance in reference to King James I, who had, as King James VI of Scotland, succeeded to the English throne upon the death of Queen Elizabeth I in 1603, three years before the play was written. *Macbeth* concerns not only Scotland and Scottish kings, but the specific line of Scottish kings from which King James traced his own descent. The relevance of this royal connection could hardly be clearer, and yet the exact nature of this relevance has been a subject of much scholarly dispute, especially in the twentieth century. Some scholars, such as H. N. Paul, have argued that *Macbeth* was written essentially to please King James, who was, after all, the patron of Shakespeare's theater company. Other readers, though, such as David Norbrook and Peter Stallybrass, have argued that this "King James version" of the play misreads both the historical and the theatrical evidence; they find the play to be far more ambivalent about, and even subversive of, James's ideological interests.

Politics and royal authority are not the only contexts in which the play is situated, of course. One danger inherent in such approaches to the play is that criticism can become too James-centered, too obsessed with the personal taste, actions, and political theories of the monarch. As important as these are to understanding *Macbeth* in its time, so too are other discourses, such as the larger fate of England itself, which was in the process of absorbing Scotland, and itself being absorbed by the new Scottish court. The union of the two monarchies in the person of King James also meant the union of these two nations; although legally it would not occur for another century, in practice it was already beginning. To many people in England in 1603, Scotland was not the friendly partner of England many see today, but a distinctly foreign nation, with a very different culture, history, and until recently, religion. For some, Scotland was not even a nation, but a collection of warring clans, with a historically weak and unstable monarchy, marked in its history by assassinations and savagery.

So too the subject of witchcraft should not be focused completely on King James, who wrote a treatise on witchcraft published in 1597, and presided over witchcraft trials in Scotland in the 1590s. Even given James's known interest in witchcraft, it is difficult to know precisely his thinking in 1606, which may have turned much more skeptical. English interest in witchcraft, in any event, preceded James's arrival in 1603, and was itself related to a much larger controversy about the nature and rights of women at the time. Roughly coinciding with Queen Elizabeth's ascent to the throne of England in 1558, this controversy about women included declarations of women's inferiority and defenses of their rights, advice books on how women were supposed to behave, disputes about cross-dressing, and new scientific inquiries into the nature of the female body. It is no coincidence that such powerful female characters as Lady Macbeth, Cleopatra, and the Duchess of Malfi, in John Webster's play of that name, all appeared on the London stage within a period of five or six years. Ironically, though — and this fact is also part of the controversy over women — all of these women's parts were performed by boy actors, because of the general prohibition against women appearing on the stage (though they were welcome enough in the audience). The standard cultural definitions of male and female gender roles and identities were being undermined by a number of forces, from the forty-five-year reign of a powerful female monarch, to evolving conceptions of marriage. The very different female characters in *Macbeth,* no less than the complex relationships between Macbeth and Lady Macbeth, and Macduff and Lady Macduff, occur not in a vacuum, but rather at a particular historical and cultural moment. The primary purpose of this edition is to provide the contemporary texts — some of which Shakespeare had read, many of which he had not — that constitute the political and cultural context of the day, so that readers may make their own judgments.

The Crisis of Sovereignty

In *Macbeth,* Shakespeare depicts four different kings, three of Scotland — Duncan, Macbeth, and Malcolm — and one of England — Edward the Confessor. Each of their histories is different (see Figure 1):

1. Duncan *inherited* the throne from his grandfather, Malcolm II; the line of descent bypassed the female altogether, just the opposite of what had happened in the cases of Elizabeth of England, daughter of Henry VIII,

	The Scottish Line		The English Line	
80	Kenneth II	976–1000		
81	Constantine III	1000–1002		
82	Kenneth III	1002–1005		
83	Malcolm II	1005–1034		
84	Duncan	1034–1040		
85	Macbeth	1040–1057	Edward the Confessor	1042–1066
86	Malcolm III (Malcolm Canmore)	1057–1093	William the Conqueror	1066–1087

FIGURE 1 *This comparative genealogy shows the kings of England and Scotland at the time of the play. The numbers on the left refer to the numerical order of the Scottish monarchy — thus Macbeth was the 85th king. The Scots prided themselves on their unbroken line of kings.*

and Mary of Scotland, daughter of James V. (This information is not in Shakespeare's play, but was in all the histories of the period.)

2. Macbeth secretly killed Duncan and was then *elected* king: *Ross*: "Then 'tis most like / The sovereignty will fall upon Macbeth." *Macduff*: "He is already named and gone to Scone / To be invested" (2.4.29–32).

3. Malcolm seems to both be elected *and* to inherit the throne. A key hurdle for Macbeth's ambition before he murders the king — "in my way it lies" (1.4.50) — occurs when Duncan gathers his court together after the defeat of the rebels:

> Sons, kinsmen, thanes,
> And you whose places are the nearest, know
> We will establish our estate upon
> Our eldest, Malcolm, whom we name hereafter
> The Prince of Cumberland. (1.4.35–39)

This act of *naming* suggests that Malcolm's succession through inheritance is not necessarily inevitable; thus, Macbeth might have legitimately achieved the crown through election, as the worthiest thane. Moreover, Macbeth was, according to Holinshed's *Chronicles* (Shakespeare's source for the plot), Duncan's first cousin, and so had some blood claim as well. But after Macbeth becomes king, and Malcolm flees, it is reported that "The son of Duncan, / From whom this tyrant [Macbeth] holds the due of birth, / Lives in the English court" (3.6.24–26). Thus Malcolm, in addition to being named heir to the throne, also seems to hold the "due of birth," or natural right to the crown. His ascent to the throne at the end of the play comes about through the killing of the current king of Scotland, who had achieved the throne through a legitimate means of succession, even though, of course, he had murdered Duncan. The play never suggests that Macbeth is overthrown as king because he had murdered his predecessor, however, but because he had become a "tyrant" (a key word in contemporary political discourse, as we will see). Thus Malcolm becomes king through an act of regicide, as well as by election and inheritance.

4. Edward the Confessor, just offstage in act 4, scene 3, is the holy, powerful, and legitimate English king to whom Malcolm has fled for safety. Unlike any of the Scottish kings, Edward is marked by his holiness, his power to heal rather than to destroy, and his grace. The mechanism of succession in England, moreover, does not seem ambiguous at all, but both natural and sanctified: Edward's power to heal the sick symbolizes the power of the kingship itself, for even this power, it is said, is inherited: "To the succeeding royalty he leaves / The healing benediction" (4.3.156–57). And Edward will die a peaceful, spiritual death, unlike the Scottish kings.

To this list of four we should perhaps also add the great procession of kings which the ghost of Banquo shows to Macbeth in the second apparition scene: "What, will the line stretch out to th' crack of doom?" (4.1.117). This vision represents the fulfillment of the witches' earlier prophecy, and the defeat of Macbeth's greater desires: Banquo is to be "father to a line of kings," while the witches have given Macbeth only "a fruitless crown / And put a barren scepter in my grip, / Thence to be wrenched with an unlineal hand, / No son of mine succeeding" (3.1.61–65). Thus Macbeth has apparently dreamed of establishing a legitimate line of inheritance, father to son, even as he has disrupted that principle and achieved the crown through a different principle himself. And beyond the four kings in the play, and the line of Banquo in the apparition scene, there was also in the audience, perhaps, King James himself,[2] the royal spectator of a royal bloodbath, whose own right of succession to the English throne was, as we shall see, questioned.

The character of sovereign power also varies considerably among the different kings of the play, ranging from Duncan's passivity, through Macbeth's "tyranny" and Malcolm's wily self-preservation, to Edward the Confessor's unclouded goodness. The origin of monarchical power, the nature of mo-

---

[2] Court records show that Shakespeare's company was paid "for three plays before His Majesty and the King of Denmark" (Queen Anne's father) in August 1606 at the royal residence of Hampton Court (Chambers, *Shakespeare* 2:333). It has sometimes been argued, based on this entry, that *Macbeth* was one of the plays performed, and it is a logical enough deduction, but there is no hard evidence to support such a conclusion. For critics such as Paul, it is essential to find *some* venue in which James, whom the play was supposed to please, could actually see the play.

narchical power, the principle of royal succession, and the manner of royal death — are all different, in some cases radically different, for each of the kings in the play. The kingship in *Macbeth* is by turns elected or inherited, unnatural or holy, legitimate or tyrannical.

I rehearse these features of the play in order to stress that the older view of *Macbeth*, supposedly written as a way to please King James with a drama of Scottish history and his own ancestors, tells only a small part of the story. Rather than clarifying and reinforcing the theories of kingship and sovereign power that James proposed in his writings and speeches, the play seems to go out of its way to mystify and undermine those theories, and in doing this, Shakespeare's play powerfully reproduces some of the major political controversies of his day.

Macbeth was written in 1606 (see the discussion of dating in the section on Middleton's *The Witch*, p. 155), and presumably performed in that same year. The writing and performance of the play occur in a key period in English history, which for our purposes here stretches from Henry VIII's break with the Catholic church in Rome in the 1520s over the subject of his divorce from his first wife, Catherine of Aragon, to the execution of Charles I, King James's son and heir, in 1649 by the Parliamentary forces led by Oliver Cromwell (see Figure 2). Henry VIII sought a divorce in order to marry a woman who could produce a male heir; more than a century later, the legal male heir of the Stuart line was "divorced" from his kingdom in a solemn act of regicide. This period was marked by what one modern critic has called the "deconsecration of sovereignty"; the theater itself, Franco Moretti has argued, was "in fact one of the decisive influences in the creation of a 'public' that for the first time in history assumed the right to bring a king to justice" (7). Tragedy, and especially plays such as *Macbeth*, "disentitled the absolute monarch to all ethical and rational legitimation. Having deconsecrated the king, it thus made it possible to decapitate him" (7–8). The Stuart monarchs, James I and Charles I, had argued strongly (James even before he was king of England) that they had an absolute, indefeasible right to the throne through the principle of blood inheritance, and that the rule of the monarch preceded and therefore superseded any rule of Parliament or other government, because kings were established by God alone, not by man. (See Chapter 2 for a more thorough discussion of these arguments.) The populace — whether through Parliament or through mob

FIGURE 2 *This is the standard genealogy of the English descent from Henry VII to the* ➤ *Stuart line; much has been left out (compare Figure 10, p. 193). James could trace his lineage back to the English line, through the female, to Margaret, the daughter of Henry VII.*

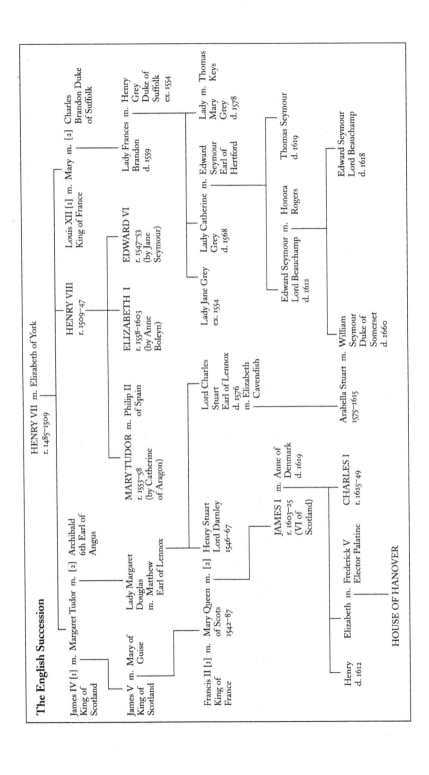

The English Succession

HENRY VII m. Elizabeth of York
r. 1485–1509

James IV [1] m. Margaret Tudor m. [2] Archibald 6th Earl of Angus — King of Scotland

HENRY VIII r. 1509–47

Louis XII [1] m. Mary m. [2] Charles Brandon Duke of Suffolk — King of France

James V m. Mary of Guise — King of Scotland

Lady Margaret Douglas m. Matthew Earl of Lennox

MARY TUDOR m. Philip II of Spain r. 1553–58 (by Catherine of Aragon)

EDWARD VI r. 1547–53 (by Jane Seymour)

ELIZABETH I r. 1558–1603 (by Anne Boleyn)

Lady Frances Brandon d. 1559 m. Henry Grey Duke of Suffolk ex. 1554

Lady Jane Grey ex. 1554

Lady Catherine Grey d. 1568 m. Edward Seymour Earl of Hertford

Lady Mary Grey d. 1578 m. Thomas Keys

Francis II [1] m. Mary Queen of Scots 1542–87 — King of France

Henry Stuart Lord Darnley 1546–67

Lord Charles Stuart Earl of Lennox d. 1576 m. Elizabeth Cavendish

Edward Seymour Lord Beauchamp d. 1612 m. Honora Rogers

Thomas Seymour d. 1619

JAMES I r. 1603–25 (VI of Scotland) m. Anne of Denmark d. 1619

Arabella Stuart 1575–1615 m. William Seymour Duke of Somerset d. 1660

Edward Seymour Lord Beauchamp d. 1618

CHARLES I r. 1625–49

Henry d. 1612

Elizabeth m. Frederick V Elector Palatine

HOUSE OF HANOVER

rule — had no right, no justification at all, to overthrow the king, even if that king were a tyrant, a madman, an incompetent. Arguing against supporters of the theory of tyrannicide, such as George Buchanan, James insisted in his own writings that the king's moral and political status were irrelevant, that even the worst tyrant (the sort which Malcolm, for example, pretends to be in act 4, scene 3 of *Macbeth*) could not, must not be overthrown. He could hardly have imagined that his own son — a perfectly legitimate king — would suffer such a fate.

This theory of absolute, divine right was by no means supported by the entire populace; on the contrary, there was a long history of opposition to such claims of unbridled power and right (see Chapter 3). In fact, the more insecure the actual powers of James I and Charles I became, the more insistently and dogmatically they and their supporters made claims to authority and divine right, as if asserting them would make them true. If they truly wielded such power, they would not have had to claim it so insistently. In *Macbeth*, Shakespeare presents a wide range of attitudes toward such contentions of sovereign power. When Macduff returns from discovering Duncan's dead body, for example, he says that "Most sacrilegious murder hath broke ope / The Lord's anointed temple and stole thence / The life o' the building!" (58–60). On the one hand, the king's body is the "Lord's anointed temple," something sacred and, one would think, untouchable; on the other hand, this body has suffered a ghastly mutilation and assault. The royal blood that ought to guarantee succession turns out to be just a bodily fluid that seems to flow inexhaustibly throughout the play; another royal body, Macbeth's, suffers decapitation — the same fate as that of Charles I. Indeed, decapitation is itself a metaphor for regicide, for the king ruled over his people, according to the repeated analogies of the time, as a father over his family, or a head over the body.

The history of claims of sovereign power and right in the century and a half between Henry VIII and Charles I is exactly paralleled by and intertwined with controversies and confusion over the very bedrock of monarchical right, the principle(s) of royal succession Henry VIII had attempted to provide for his descendants both through patrilineal (that is, the son of the father) inheritance, and through a kind of election by an Act of Parliament, through which he denied his elder sister Margaret (from whom James I was descended) any rights of succession should his own children die without issue (as in fact happened). Queen Elizabeth I not only refused to

FIGURE 3 *This is the standard genealogy of the Scottish descent. Of James's seven children, only three — Henry, Charles, and Elizabeth — survived infancy, and his great hope, Henry, died prematurely.* ➤

The Scottish Succession

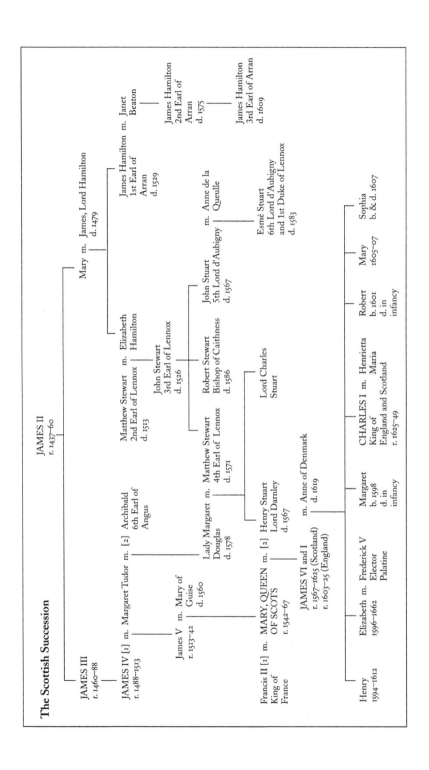

JAMES II
r. 1437–60

Mary m. James, Lord Hamilton
d. 1479

James Hamilton m. Janet Beaton
1st Earl of Arran
d. 1529

James Hamilton
2nd Earl of Arran
d. 1575

James Hamilton
3rd Earl of Arran
d. 1609

JAMES III
r. 1460–88

JAMES IV [1] m. Margaret Tudor m. [2] Archibald 6th Earl of Angus
r. 1488–1513

James V m. Mary of Guise
r. 1513–42   d. 1560

Matthew Stewart m. Elizabeth Hamilton
2nd Earl of Lennox
d. 1513

John Stewart
3rd Earl of Lennox
d. 1526

Robert Stewart
Bishop of Caithness
d. 1586

John Stuart m. Anne de la Queulle
5th Lord d'Aubigny
d. 1567

Esmé Stuart
6th Lord d'Aubigny
and 1st Duke of Lennox
d. 1583

Lady Margaret m. Matthew Stewart
Douglas   4th Earl of Lennox
d. 1578   d. 1571

Lord Charles Stuart

Francis II [1] m. MARY, QUEEN m. [2] Henry Stuart
King of   OF SCOTS   Lord Darnley
France   r. 1542–67   d. 1567

JAMES VI and I m. Anne of Denmark
r. 1567–1625 (Scotland)   d. 1619
r. 1603–25 (England)

Elizabeth m. Frederick V
1596–1662   Elector Palatine

Henry
1594–1612

Margaret
b. 1598
d. in
infancy

CHARLES I m. Henrietta Maria
King of England and Scotland
r. 1625–49

Robert
b. 1601
d. in
infancy

Mary
1605–07

Sophia
b. & d. 1607

marry, and thus remained childless, but she also refused to name her heir (though she relented on her deathbed, indicating with a nod of her nearly lifeless head that James should succeed her, according to reports of those whose interests coincided with James's). James based his own claims to the throne of England entirely on the principle of blood inheritance, though even that was disputed by some (see Chapter 2 for a more detailed discussion of these issues).

It is not an exaggeration to say that, along with England's relation with its enemy Spain, the major political question in England in the 1590s was that of royal succession.[3] Shakespeare wrote eight history plays in the 1590s on just this question, going back to the reign of Richard II, the rightful king deposed and murdered, and bringing the story forward until 1485, the founding of the Tudor reign in Henry Tudor's defeat of Richard III. The Tudor claim on the throne of England thus began from yet another principle of succession, the right of seizure and possession; blood relation claims were also made, though they were not at all strong ones. Shakespeare's history plays of the 1590s had registered all the tensions inherent in this earlier history, which seemed clearly to mirror his own contemporary history; but after 1600, it is Shakespeare's tragedies that most intensely represent these crises in sovereign power and succession, from *Hamlet* (in which the Danish monarchy seems to be both elected and with the strong expectation of patrilineal inheritance, yet finally succumbs to seizure by a foreign prince) to *King Lear* (in which the king disastrously abdicates and divides the kingdom, and in which royal succession at the end of the play is unclear, with different people in the two different versions of the play[4] offering the final speech of apparent order). *Macbeth* plays its part in this debate by representing the principles of succession to the Scottish kingship as uncertain, often arbitrary, and the powers of the kingship as by turns weak, violent, imperial, and parasitical. If the kingship becomes deconsecrated, as Moretti argues, then it becomes like any other institution, subject to change, violent or otherwise. *Macbeth* does not present the image of a purely secular kingship; on the contrary, the bodies at least of Duncan and of Edward the Confessor contain a royal charisma, a power, which is beyond their mere flesh and blood. But *Macbeth* does reproduce, in its plot, imagery, and structure, some of the contradictory claims of sovereign power and right that were disputed in early modern England.

---

[3] For thorough discussions of the succession issue for both Elizabeth and James, see Axton, Hurstfield, Levine, and Nenner.

[4] In the 1608 Quarto version of *King Lear*, Albany speaks the final four lines, but in the 1623 Folio version of *King Lear*, Edgar speaks the final four lines.

Religious Controversy

One of the most powerful, agonizing, and insoluble problems in the England of Shakespeare's day was that of religion; conflicts over religion were inseparably intertwined with other political and cultural debates, including particularly the crisis of sovereign power described above. As many contemporary observers noted, there were three main religious factions in England at this time: Puritan, Protestant, and Catholic.[5] The Puritan faction was associated with the religious writings of John Calvin, and with a political stance that, in its purest form, supposedly did not recognize the authority of secular power, even the king's. The Protestant faction, primarily the Church of England, which had split off from the Catholic Church during the reign of Henry VIII, constituted the great majority of the people at this time. (It should be noted that many Protestants continued to call themselves "Catholic," and members of the true church, but they did not recognize the authority of the Pope in the political or even religious realms.) The Catholics, often called Papists by their enemies because of their obedience to the Pope's authority, were a persecuted minority, with few legal rights; they could not legally go to Mass, could not receive a college degree or hold certain offices unless they had publicly forsworn the Catholic Church, and suffered substantial fines as "recusants" if they failed to attend Protestant religious services on Sundays.

The fate and fortunes of the Catholic minority during the sixteenth century varied considerably, depending on the current monarch and the political climate. When Henry VIII broke with Rome, he proceeded to seize for the crown all the lands held by monasteries — a considerable amount of the land in England — and disperse the traditional Catholic monastic communities; various other restrictions on Catholics were developed, but there was

---

[5] The term "Puritan" is a particularly vexed one. Contemporaries as different as the Protestant King James and the Catholic Robert Parsons use the term "Puritan" to describe a kind of radical Protestant faction. In his *Basilikon Doron*, James admits that the term properly should refer to the "Anabaptists, called the Family of Love" — a small, very specific group — but he goes on to say that he uses it more generally to apply to those who agree with certain of their positions, particularly their "contempt of the civil Magistrate, and in leaning to their own dreams and revelations . . . and before that any of their grounds [i.e., principles] be impugned, let King, people, law, and all be trod under foot" (143). Modern readers should work hard to dispel the current image of the Puritan as wearing a tall hat and tight collar, obsessed with sexual purity, and in general a spoilsport. Some Puritans in Shakespeare's time may have had some of these characteristics, but their main distinction was political and religious. Some indication of the ambiguity of the term *Puritan* may be seen in the fact that Sir John Harington, the Protestant godson of Queen Elizabeth, once called the Catholic Robert Parsons "a Puritan Papist" (Harington 4), thus conflating two supposedly irreconcilable categories.

relatively little outright persecution. Upon Henry's death in 1547, however, his son Edward VI succeeded him, and he and his councillors began a campaign of often violent iconoclasm — literally shattering and destroying the images, including the church buildings themselves, of Catholic faith; the Protestantism of Edward and his councillors was often severe and persecutory.[6] Edward died prematurely young (age sixteen), and in 1553 his sister Mary succeeded him to the crown. Mary was a Catholic, married to Philip II of Spain, and she attempted to reverse the Protestant tide, at times by force. Now the Protestants felt the lash of religious intolerance, and a large number of so-called Marian martyrs were executed for their beliefs. But Mary, too, died within a few years of achieving the crown, and in 1558 her sister Elizabeth took the throne.

Queen Elizabeth I, even as a young woman and new queen, was canny enough to avoid the extremes of the previous decade. She was not a Catholic, yet she used aspects of Catholic imagery and belief for her own purposes; worship of the Virgin Mary was no longer permitted, for example, but Elizabeth appropriated much of the Virgin's imagery for herself, and was known as the Virgin Queen.[7] An announced Protestant, Elizabeth resisted the more radical, anti-Catholic elements that her brother Edward had unleashed during his reign. There was no official toleration of Catholics, and the laws did not change to their benefit, but persecutions of them were intermittent. In 1570, however, Pope Pius V issued a papal bull, or declaration, entitled *Regnans in excelsis,* which proclaimed Elizabeth's excommunication *and* deposition from the throne of England; it pronounced her only a "pretended" queen (in spite of the fact that Rome had been treating her as a monarch in its dealings with her for over a decade), called upon the faithful to remove her, and absolved all Englishmen from any oath of allegiance to the queen. Aside from the religious issues of this action, which were considerable, the political implications were extremely grave: the papal declaration made *every* Catholic a potential traitor in the eyes of the state. The vast majority of English Catholics were in fact loyal subjects; as strong as their religious beliefs might be, their nationalism — manifested in a hatred and fear of Spain, a distrust of things Italian — was often greater. After the papal bull, however, the stakes were raised on both sides. Fiercely anti-Catholic Protestants and Puritans pressed for greater control and sup-

---

[6] Edward VI was born in 1537 and became king when he was ten years old. When a monarch was underage upon his or her ascent to the throne, a protector was appointed by the Privy Council (the administrative body of private councillors that assisted the king in ruling) from the ranks of the nobility; he would run the country on behalf of the youthful monarch.

[7] Elizabeth's refusal to marry was in large part a self-conscious political strategy — she was not one to share power — but it also brought an end to the Tudor line, and led to the succession crisis.

pression of Catholics, while a new threat from the Catholics began to have an impact within England.

The Society of Jesus — the Jesuits — was founded in 1534 in Paris by Ignatius Loyola, and authorized by the pope in 1540. As the group grew in strength and organization, it became known, to Protestants at least, as a secret army of fanatical soldiers dedicated to overthrowing heretic (that is, non-Catholic) rule everywhere; to Catholics, the society was a monastic order, bound by vows of chastity, poverty, and obedience, dedicated to supporting the Roman church against the reformers and propagating the faith among the heathen. Yet their secrecy and power led to conflicts with authorities even in Catholic countries. Eventually, Jesuit priests began to enter England secretly and to move around the country in disguise, energizing the faithful; among the earliest and most notorious were Father Campion (eventually caught and executed) and Father Parsons (see p. 191). For the government of Elizabeth I — for any government in a similar situation — the existence of a secret underground of religious fanatics dedicated to its overthrow was intolerable; it devoted enormous efforts to finding and punishing these Jesuits. Early in the reign of King James, the equation of the Jesuits with treason was resoundingly and absolutely confirmed, for many, by the Jesuits' prior knowledge of, and alleged involvement in, the Gunpowder Plot, an attempt on James's life (see p. 249). The Jesuit doctrine of "equivocation" — a form of withholding the truth in testimony (see p. 263) — to which Shakespeare alludes in 2.3 of *Macbeth*, seemed to be the final link between Jesuits, lying, and treason (see Mullaney, Fraser).

What with the growing power of a zealous anti-Catholic minority, the beleaguered sense of the Protestant majority, the presence of Jesuit priests, and the official persecution of Catholics, the pot of religious controversy bubbled throughout Elizabeth's reign. Civil disorders based in religious conflict, individual persecutions, families divided against themselves along religious lines — it was a difficult time in which to rule, made even more difficult by two major events in the late 1580s that had religious implications. First, Mary, the queen of Scotland, mother of James VI, was forced to abdicate in favor of James because of various scandals in 1567; a strong Catholic, she was a legitimate contender for the crown of England, and, unlike Elizabeth, she had a male heir who could continue after her. Elizabeth recognized her as a dangerous rival, and imprisoned Mary for several years after she was implicated in a plot against her. Even as a prisoner, Mary was implicated in various attempts to regain her throne, and possibly even take Elizabeth's, and Elizabeth was finally convinced to have Mary executed for treason in 1587, an act that James would not forget. The next year, 1588, saw the attempted invasion of England by its most hated and dangerous Catholic enemy, Spain; many people — not just government propagandists — saw the destruction of the Spanish fleet, largely the result of a storm, as a sign of God's blessing on Elizabeth and the English nation, and as a punishment of those who opposed them. In the last years of Elizabeth's reign, the religious divisions in England continued to grow, further fostered by growing anxiety about who Elizabeth's successor might be, and of what religious persuasion. There were strong Catholic as well as Protestant claimants for her throne.

Into this volatile situation James VI came down from Scotland in 1603 to take the throne of England. He had already experienced similar religious conflicts in Scotland, which had broken with the Catholic church some years later than England had. James was personally tolerant of other religious beliefs, and he seems to have given private assurances to various ambassadors and Catholic leaders that they could expect some accommodation when he became king (though this was all publicly denied a few years later). Moreover James's wife, Queen Anne, had herself converted to Catholicism a few years earlier, and observed her faith in private; but Anne's Catholicism was well known to Catholic leaders in Europe, leading many to believe, or hope, that she would be able to convert James himself as well. All hope of James's conversion soon died, however, and within a few years, he would institute some of the harshest anti-Catholic measures yet known.

In a speech of March 19, 1604, on the first day of his first Parliament, James himself elucidated the religious situation as he found it upon his accession to the throne:

> At my first coming [to England], although I found but one religion [i.e., Protestant], and that which by my self is professed, publicly allowed, and by the law maintained, yet found I another sort of religion, besides a private sect, lurking within the bowels of this nation. The first is the true religion, which by me is professed, and by the law is established. The second is the falsely called Catholics, but truly Papists. The third, which I call a sect rather than religion, is the Puritans and Novelists,[8] who do not so far differ from us in points of religion, as in their confused form of policy and parity, being ever discontented with the present government, and impatient to suffer any superiority, which maketh their sect unable to be suffered in any well-governed commonwealth. (*Works* 490)

The problem with the Papists, James observes, is their doctrine of the

> arrogant and ambitious supremacy of their Head the Pope, whereby he not only claims to be spiritual head of all Christians, but also to have an imperial

[8] **Novelist**: one who makes innovations (not necessarily a positive thing).

civil power over all kings and emperors, dethroning and decrowning princes with his foot as pleaseth him, and dispensing and disposing of all kingdoms and empires at his appetite. The other point which they observe in continual practice, is the assassinations and murders of kings, thinking it no sin, but rather a matter of salvation, to do all actions of rebellion and hostility against their natural Sovereign Lord, if he be once cursed [i.e., excommunicated].

(492)

In less than a year and a half, James would be the target of just such an assassination attempt by a small group of disgruntled, radical Catholics, which became known as the Powder Treason, or the Gunpowder Plot. After the Plot failed, even James conceded the need for a harsh crackdown on Catholics in general and Jesuits in particular, and a new and stricter oath of allegiance (subjects had to swear allegiance to the King and forswear papal supremacy) was initiated, making life even more difficult for loyal Catholics in matters of conscience.

The religious discourse of the period was by no means entirely constituted by such high matters of state as described above. The offstage presence of King Edward the Confessor in *Macbeth*, for example, is marked by his ability to heal the sick through his touch (see p. 222). English monarchs had for generations appropriated to themselves the kind of semimagical, religious aura which was quite commonly possessed by "cunning women" and "doctors" in the villages and countryside of the kingdom. The belief in such charismatic powers usually arose and flourished in rural areas away from London, as a symptom of a particular set of social and religious issues. Magical healing, prophecy, and potent cursing are aspects of religious belief no less than the high doctrines of papal superiority and transubstantiation. Shakespeare's *Macbeth* registers all these energies, like a seismometer on the edge of a volcano.

Discourses of the Feminine

Among the most striking features of *Macbeth* are its women — the three witches, Hecate, Lady Macbeth, and Lady Macduff; it was chiefly their parts, already substantial, that Sir William Davenant expanded in his adaptation of the play in 1664. In none of the historical narratives of Macbeth, however, do women play as extensive a part as they do in Shakespeare's play. *Macbeth* registers many aspects of the period's rich discourse about women, especially the question of a woman's place in the world. There had been misogynist attacks on women for centuries prior to Shakespeare, in which male writers described women's inferiority to men as deriving from their very creation in the Garden of Eden, from Adam's rib; defenders of women would often take the same evidence and argue the contrary point: that Eve was created from Adam's rib, not his foot, which signifies that she was at the same level as Adam, and not literally and figuratively lower.[9]

With the Reformation in the sixteenth century came new ideas about the nature of marriage, and a woman's rights within it.[10] By law, married women had no legal right to own property, and were in effect legally subsumed into their husbands: man and woman become one flesh in marriage, the saying went, and that flesh was the male. In the usual analogies, moreover, just as God ruled his kingdom, as the king ruled his subjects, and as the head ruled the body, so the husband ruled the wife. The alleged theological and philosophical superiority of the male was enshrined in the law in many ways; according to some commentators, husbands had the right, even the duty, to beat their wives (though not to death) if they became unruly. But within this confining legal system, what has been described as the practice of "Protestant companionate marriage" developed. In this paradigm of marriage, the wife was by no means liberated, in our modern sense, but was granted, or came to possess, a greater autonomy of action and will, at least within the domestic sphere; moreover, marriages could take place for love, as well as through parental arrangement. As a social institution, marriage in this period was always understood as a mechanism for the transfer of property from one male (the father) to another (the husband); the wife herself was thus one kind of property. Hence the arranged or even enforced marriage was the rule, at least for the aristocracy, where issues of property and title were extremely important. The law had always stated that the parents could not technically force a woman to marry; she always had to give her consent, though it is easy to imagine the social and legal pressures to succumb to the parents' will. But marriage for love was increasingly justified.[11] Many of these issues of courtship and marriage are played out in Shakespeare's comedies, and the first scene of *King Lear* is virtually a guidebook to what can go wrong.

Macbeth depicts two paradigms of marriage. The Macbeths are a kind of anti-family; not only do they not have children — one fundamental purpose of marriage, according to the Bible, was to go forth and multiply — but also Lady Macbeth claims she would sacrifice whatever child she did

---

[9] For a solid discussion of the controversy over women in the English Renaissance, see Woodbridge.

[10] Among many recent works on this topic, see Amussen, Houlbrooke, Macfarlane, *Marriage,* and Stone, *Family.*

[11] See Cook for an analysis of courtship theory in the period.

have in the name of ambition. A great deal of critical argument has taken place over the question of Lady Macbeth's childlessness.[12] She does after all say, "I have given suck, and know / How tender 'tis to love the babe that milks me; / I would, while it was smiling in my face, / Have plucked my nipple from his boneless gums / And dashed the brains out, had I so sworn as you / Have done to this" (1.7.55–60). Macbeth, on the other hand, laments that while Banquo is hailed as father to a line of kings, "Upon my head they [the witches] placed a fruitless crown / And put a barren scepter in my grip, / Thence to be wrenched with an unlineal hand, / No son of mine succeeding" (3.1.62–65). Shakespeare seems to want us to see it both ways: Lady Macbeth seems to have experienced the maternal, but only as a perversion; but the Macbeths are also apparently sterile, incapable of procreation.[13] They can create only destruction.

The Macbeths differ from the supposed cultural norm of the family in another way: in his letter in act 1, scene 5, reporting on the witches' prophecies, Macbeth calls his wife "my dearest partner of greatness" (1.5.8), and to a great extent they are coequal in their crime. At the beginning of the murder plot, the husband's traditional dominance is absent. In one attempt to explain their relationship, the psychoanalyst Sigmund Freud described them as "two disunited parts of a single psychical individuality" (Wain 137), in the sense that their strengths and weaknesses seem inversely and profoundly related; as many observers have noted, when Lady Macbeth is strong, Macbeth is weak (as at the beginning of the murder plot), and when Macbeth is strong, Lady Macbeth becomes weak (as at the end of the play). "Strong" and "weak" are of course not simple terms here. Still, at the beginning of the play, as the murder is being plotted and carried out, Lady Macbeth is a strong, terrifying figure — linked with the witches in many ways, and associated particularly with conventionally unfeminine notions: she would destroy her child if necessary, as we saw in the quotation above, and she calls upon the "murdering ministers" to "unsex me here," to erase whatever in her is feminine, and therefore supposedly weak and sympathetic, and fill her instead with "direst cruelty" (1.5.37–39). From one point of view, then, her "greatness" is the antithesis of being "female," and so her strength, her ambition, her murderousness, her antimaternal feelings, all mark her as

---

[12] One famous essay by L. C. Knights was entitled "How Many Children Had Lady Macbeth?"; it was a response to A. C. Bradley's approach to the play, which focused on a close analysis of individual characters as if they were real people.

[13] In some of the earlier narrative histories, Lady Macbeth has a son, Lulach — often called "the simple," or said to be mentally defective — by a previous marriage, but Shakespeare makes no mention of him.

"unfemale," and therefore to be linked with the witches, whose gender also is not purely female.

Lady Macduff, by contrast, at first seems to be Lady Macbeth's antithesis: the good, dutiful wife, not barren but fruitful, with a brave little son; her fate is subsumed in her husband's. Yet all that her obedience, fertility, and maternal devotion finally gain her is a violent death: she is abandoned by her husband — left defenseless with her son, and both are slaughtered by the murderers Macbeth has sent. The lesson seems clear: if you are a strong, willful wife, like Lady Macbeth, you will die; if you are a helpless, obedient wife, like Lady Macduff, you will die. Lady Macbeth is ultimately reduced to a sleepwalker — literally lacking consciousness — and apparently commits suicide offstage in the fifth act; Lady Macduff and her family suffer for their husband and father ("Not for their own demerits, but for mine, / Fell slaughter on their souls," Macduff admits [4.3.228–29]). Bad or good, strong or weak, willful or obedient, the women in the play suffer the same fate. As Janet Adelman and others have shown, moreover, *Macbeth* registers a systematic demonization, then destruction, of the maternal presence. Throughout the play, images of the female body are conjured up, but these images are of rape, mutilation, and assault. Only Macduff, the man not of woman born, seems to escape the contaminating maternal presence, permitting him to slay Macbeth at the end and take his place in a world now made up entirely of men; his birth by caesarean section, to a seventeenth-century audience, would of course have meant the death of his mother.

In beseeching the "murdering ministers" to "unsex me here," Lady Macbeth sought to join the stereotypical male world of cruelty, violence, and lack of remorse — something like the code of the warrior that Macbeth exemplifies in the first scenes of the play, when his defeat of the rebels is couched in a language that masks an inhuman ferocity. He is covered in blood from disembowelling and decapitating his opponents, and receives the highest praise and honors for it. In seeking to emulate that violence, Lady Macbeth will only open herself up to the kind of guilt and remorse that Macbeth feels at the beginning of the murder plot.

The witches are clearly linked with Lady Macbeth in a variety of ways, yet they differ from her in that they already exist only on the boundaries — of the kingdom, of gender, of good and evil. When he first sees them, Banquo notes "You seem to understand me, / By each at once her choppy finger laying / Upon her skinny lips. You should be women, / And yet your beards forbid me to interpret / That you are so" (1.3.43–47). There are a variety of ways to account for the existence of these witches on Shakespeare's stage, as noted above. One way to think about the witches is to ask what social function they served in the society outside the theater. One scholar, Christina

Larner, has argued that "witches represented the most extreme form of deviance" (89), and hence served the community as "a negative standard of social behaviour and social acceptability" (91). In Shakespeare's culture, the typical accused witch was an independent woman who did not conform to cultural stereotypes of the ideal woman — chaste, silent, and obedient. (Although men could in theory be witches, the overwhelming majority of those accused were women.) Such women were assertive, vocal, often suspected of having mysterious powers to heal or harm; to *name* them as witches, then, is to define them as deviant, even criminal, by the standards of the dominant culture.[14]

We should see the witches in *Macbeth*, then, not simply as external symbols of evil: they are profoundly linked not only to what is already in Macbeth himself, but also to the violent, hierarchical, male order of culture itself. They are the inevitable antithetical product of that social formation. Virtually everything about them — their appearance, their riddling language, their ambiguous gender — represents some inversion of the personal and social values exhibited by the dominant culture. But as loathsome and frightening as the witches may seem, Shakespeare does not allow the audience fully to embrace their opposite in this play, the violent male warrior culture of the Scots, for *Macbeth* also undermines those values.

At the summit of the male warrior culture in *Macbeth* is the king, and so we return again to our earlier topic, the crisis of sovereign order in the period. "Sovereign order," in spite of the long rule of Queen Elizabeth, is the order of the male, especially in *Macbeth*, and the witches, "the most extreme form of deviance," in Larner's phrase, are the enemy of masculine order. Yet as *Macbeth* opens, the chief embodiment of authority in the play, King Duncan, seems completely removed from the violent warrior culture over which he rules. Described as good, innocent, and worthy, Duncan actually *does* nothing in the play: his thanes fight his battles, defeat his enemies, secure his throne; Duncan rewards them with titles and riches, though those are not enough for Macbeth. Duncan's passivity in one sense creates the vacuum of power that Macbeth eagerly fills, and will be reflected in his son Malcolm, who also does not fight his own battle, relying on Macduff to overthrow Macbeth and secure his succession to the throne. At the center of sovereign authority in the play, then, is a kind of emptiness, a hollow in the center of a vortex of violence and treason.

Finally, the presence of the witches exposes the violence inherent in the dominant cultural system of the play, the savage customs of the Scots

---

[14] For other accounts of the origins of witchcraft accusations, see Willis, Purkiss, and the discussion in "Discourses of Witchcraft" (p. 300).

whereby honors and titles derive directly (and, in the play, entirely) from murderous violence. How does one become thane of Cawdor? By his death. How does one become king? By killing him. How does one become an earl, as at the end of the play? By killing. After each killing, the victim is described as a traitor or a tyrant or a "dead butcher" (5.8.70), and the victor is described as thane, earl, or king. Such is the basis of kingship in the play. The witches lead us, as they led Macbeth, to the heart of kingship's darkness.

PART ONE

><

WILLIAM SHAKESPEARE
Macbeth

Edited by David Bevington

Macbeth

>←←

SIWARD, *Earl of Northumberland*
YOUNG SIWARD, *his son*
SEYTON, *an officer attending Macbeth*
Another LORD
ENGLISH DOCTOR
SCOTTISH DOCTOR
GENTLEWOMAN *attending Lady Macbeth*
CAPTAIN *serving Duncan*
PORTER
OLD MAN
Three MURDERERS *of Banquo*
FIRST MURDERER *at Macduff's castle*
MESSENGER *to Lady Macbeth*
MESSENGER *to Lady Macduff*
SERVANT *to Macbeth*
SERVANT *to Lady Macbeth*
Three WITCHES *or* WEIRD SISTERS
HECATE
Three APPARITIONS

Lords, Gentlemen, Officers, Soldiers, Murderers, and Attendants

SCENE: *Scotland; England*]

ACT I, SCENE I°

Thunder and lightning. Enter three Witches.

FIRST WITCH:
    When shall we three meet again?
    In thunder, lightning, or in rain?
SECOND WITCH:
    When the hurlyburly's° done,
    When the battle's lost and won.
THIRD WITCH:
    That will be ere the set of sun.   5
FIRST WITCH:
    Where the place?
SECOND WITCH: Upon the heath.
THIRD WITCH:
    There to meet with Macbeth.

___

ACT I, SCENE I. Location: An open place.   3. **hurlyburly:** tumult.

FIRST WITCH:
I come, Grimalkin!°
SECOND WITCH:
Paddock° calls.
THIRD WITCH:
Anon.°   10
ALL:
Fair is foul, and foul is fair.
Hover through the fog and filthy air.   *Exeunt.*

Act i, Scene 2°

Alarum° within. Enter King [Duncan], Malcolm, Donalbain, Lennox, with attendants,
meeting a bleeding Captain.

DUNCAN:
What bloody man is that? He can report,
As seemeth by his plight, of the revolt
The newest state.°
MALCOLM: This is the sergeant°
Who like a good and hardy soldier fought
'Gainst my captivity. Hail, brave friend!   5
Say to the King the knowledge of the broil°
As thou didst leave it.
CAPTAIN: Doubtful it stood,
As two spent° swimmers that do cling together
And choke their art.° The merciless Macdonwald —
Worthy to be a rebel, for to that°   10
The multiplying villainies of nature
Do swarm upon him° — from the Western Isles°
Of kerns° and gallowglasses° is supplied;
And Fortune, on his damnèd quarrel° smiling,

---

8. **Grimalkin:** i.e., gray cat, name of the witch's familiar — a demon or evil spirit supposed to
answer a witch's call and to allow him or her to perform black magic.   9. **Paddock:** toad; also
a familiar.   10. **Anon:** at once, right away.   ACT I, SCENE 2. **Location:** A camp near Forres.
s.d. *Alarum:* trumpet call to arms.   3. **newest state:** latest news.   **sergeant:** i.e., staff officer.
(There may be no inconsistency with his rank of "captain" in the stage direction and speech
prefixes in the Folio.)   6. **broil:** battle.   8. **spent:** tired out.   9. **choke their art:** render their
skill in swimming useless.   10. **to that:** as if to that end or purpose.   11–12. **The multiplying**
. . . him: ever increasing numbers of villainous rebels (or perhaps villainous qualities) swarm
about him like vermin.   12. **Western Isles:** islands to the west of Scotland — the Hebrides
and perhaps Ireland.   13. **Of kerns:** with light-armed Irish foot soldiers.   **gallowglasses:**
horsemen armed with axes.   14. **quarrel:** cause.

Showed° like a rebel's whore. But all's too weak;   15
For brave Macbeth — well he deserves that name° —
Disdaining Fortune, with his brandished steel,
Which smoked with bloody execution,
Like valor's minion° carved out his passage
Till he faced the slave,°   20
Which° ne'er shook hands nor bade farewell to him°
Till he unseamed him from the nave° to th' chops,°
And fixed his head upon our battlements.

DUNCAN:
O valiant cousin,° worthy gentleman!

CAPTAIN:
As whence° the sun 'gins his reflection°   25
Shipwrecking storms and direful thunders break,
So from that spring whence comfort seemed to come
Discomfort swells. Mark, King of Scotland, mark.
No sooner justice had, with valor armed,
Compelled these skipping° kerns to trust their heels   30
But the Norweyan lord, surveying vantage,°
With furbished arms and new supplies of men,
Began a fresh assault.

DUNCAN:
Dismayed not this our captains, Macbeth and Banquo?

CAPTAIN:
Yes, as sparrows eagles, or the hare the lion.   35
If I say sooth,° I must report they were
As cannons overcharged with double cracks,°
So they doubly redoubled strokes upon the foe.
Except° they meant to bathe in reeking wounds
Or memorize° another Golgotha,°   40
I cannot tell.
But I am faint. My gashes cry for help.

---

15. **Showed:** appeared. 16. **name:** i.e., "brave." 19. **minion:** darling. 20. **the slave:** i.e., Macdonwald. 21. **Which:** who, i.e., Macbeth. **ne'er . . . to him:** proffered no polite salutation or farewell, acted without ceremony. 22. **nave:** navel. **chops:** jaws. 24. **cousin:** kinsman. 25. **As whence:** just as from the place where. **'gins his reflection:** begins its turning back (from its southward progression during winter). 30. **skipping:** (1) lightly armed, quick at maneuvering (2) skittish. 31. **surveying vantage:** seeing an opportunity. 36. **say sooth:** tell the truth. 37. **cracks:** charges of explosive. 39. **Except:** unless. 40. **memorize:** make memorable or famous. **Golgotha:** "place of a skull," where Christ was crucified (Mark 15:22).

DUNCAN:
So well thy words become thee as thy wounds;
They smack of honor both. — Go get him surgeons.

[Exit Captain, attended.]

Enter Ross and Angus.

Who comes here?

MALCOLM: The worthy Thane° of Ross. 45

LENNOX:
What a haste looks through his eyes!
So should he look that seems to° speak things strange.

ROSS:
God save the King!

DUNCAN:
Whence cam'st thou, worthy thane?

ROSS:
From Fife, great King, 50
Where the Norweyan banners flout° the sky
And fan our people cold.°
Norway° himself, with terrible numbers,°
Assisted by that most disloyal traitor,
The Thane of Cawdor, began a dismal° conflict, 55
Till that Bellona's bridegroom, lapped in proof,°
Confronted him° with self-comparisons,°
Point against point, rebellious arm 'gainst arm,
Curbing his lavish spirit; and to conclude,
The victory fell on us.

DUNCAN: Great happiness! 60

ROSS:
That now
Sweno, the Norways'° king, craves composition;°
Nor would we deign him burial of his men
Till he disbursèd at Saint Colme's Inch°
Ten thousand dollars° to our general use. 65

---

45. Thane: Scottish title of honor, roughly equivalent to "Earl." **47. seems to:** seems about to. **51. flout:** mock, insult. **52. fan . . . cold:** fan cold fear into our troops. **53. Norway:** the King of Norway. **terrible numbers:** terrifying numbers of troops. **55. dismal:** ominous. **56. Till . . . proof:** i.e., until Macbeth, clad in well-tested armor. (Bellona was the Roman goddess of war.) **57. him:** i.e., the King of Norway. **self-comparisons:** i.e., matching counterthrusts. **62. Norways':** Norwegians'. **composition:** agreement, treaty of peace. **64. Saint Colme's Inch:** Inchcolm, the Isle of St. Columba in the Firth of Forth. **65. dollars:** Spanish or Dutch coins.

DUNCAN:
No more that Thane of Cawdor shall deceive
Our° bosom° interest. Go pronounce his present° death,
And with his former title greet Macbeth.

ROSS:
I'll see it done.

DUNCAN:
What he hath lost noble Macbeth hath won.   *Exeunt.*   70

ACT I, SCENE 3°

Thunder. Enter the three Witches.

FIRST WITCH:
Where hast thou been, sister?

SECOND WITCH:
Killing swine.

THIRD WITCH:
Sister, where thou?

FIRST WITCH:
A sailor's wife had chestnuts in her lap,
And munched, and munched, and munched. "Give me," quoth I.   5
"Aroint thee,° witch!" the rump-fed° runnion° cries.
Her husband's to Aleppo gone, master o' the *Tiger;*°
But in a sieve I'll thither sail,
And like a rat without a tail
I'll do,° I'll do, and I'll do.°   10

SECOND WITCH:
I'll give thee a wind.

FIRST WITCH:
Thou'rt kind.

THIRD WITCH:
And I another.

FIRST WITCH:
I myself have all the other,°
And the very ports they blow,°   15

---

67. **Our:** (The royal "we.")   **bosom:** close and affectionate.   **present:** immediate.   ACT I,
SCENE 3. **Location:** a heath near Forres.   6. **Aroint thee:** begone.   **rump-fed:** fed on refuse,
or fat-rumped.   **runnion:** mangy creature, scabby woman.   7. ***Tiger:*** (A ship's name.)
9–10. **like . . . do:** (Suggestive of the witches' deformity and sexual insatiability. Witches were
thought to seduce men sexually.)   10. **do:** (1) act (2) perform sexually.   14. **other:** others.
15. **And . . . blow:** (The witches can prevent a ship from entering port by causing the winds to
blow from land.)

All the quarters that they know
I' the shipman's card°
I'll drain him dry as hay.
Sleep shall neither night nor day
Hang upon his penthouse lid.°   20
He shall live a man forbid.°
Weary sev'nnights° nine times nine
Shall he dwindle, peak,° and pine.
Though his bark cannot be lost,
Yet it shall be tempest-tossed.   25
Look what I have.

SECOND WITCH:

Show me, show me.

FIRST WITCH:

Here I have a pilot's thumb,
Wrecked as homeward he did come.   *Drum within.*

THIRD WITCH:

A drum, a drum!   30
Macbeth doth come.

ALL [*dancing in a circle*]:

The Weird Sisters,° hand in hand,
Posters of° the sea and land,
Thus do go about, about,
Thrice to thine, and thrice to mine,   35
And thrice again, to make up nine.
Peace! The charm's wound up.

Enter Macbeth and Banquo.

MACBETH:

So foul and fair a day I have not seen.

BANQUO:

How far is 't called° to Forres? — What are these,
So withered and so wild in their attire,   40
That look not like th' inhabitants o' th' earth
And yet are on 't? — Live you? Or are you aught
That man may question? You seem to understand me
By each at once her chappy° finger laying

---

17. **shipman's card:** compass card.   20. **penthouse lid:** i.e., eyelid (which projects out over the eye like a *penthouse* or slope-roofed structure).   21. **forbid:** accursed.   22. **sev'nnights:** weeks.   23. **peak:** grow peaked or thin.   32. **Weird Sisters:** women connected with fate or destiny; also women having a mysterious or unearthly, uncanny appearance.   33. **Posters of:** swift travelers over.   39. **is 't called:** is it said to be.   44. **chappy:** chapped.

Upon her skinny lips. You should be women, 45
And yet your beards forbid me to interpret
That you are so.

MACBETH: Speak, if you can. What are you?

FIRST WITCH:
All hail, Macbeth! Hail to thee, Thane of Glamis!

SECOND WITCH:
All hail, Macbeth! Hail to thee, Thane of Cawdor!

THIRD WITCH:
All hail, Macbeth, that shalt be king hereafter! 50

BANQUO:
Good sir, why do you start and seem to fear
Things that do sound so fair? — I' the name of truth,
Are ye fantastical° or that indeed
Which outwardly ye show?° My noble partner
You greet with present grace° and great prediction 55
Of noble having and of royal hope,
That he seems rapt withal.° To me you speak not.
If you can look into the seeds of time
And say which grain will grow and which will not,
Speak then to me, who neither beg nor fear 60
Your favors nor your hate.°

FIRST WITCH:
Hail!

SECOND WITCH:
Hail!

THIRD WITCH:
Hail!

FIRST WITCH:
Lesser than Macbeth, and greater. 65

SECOND WITCH:
Not so happy,° yet much happier.

THIRD WITCH:
Thou shalt get° kings, though thou be none.
So all hail, Macbeth and Banquo!

FIRST WITCH:
Banquo and Macbeth, all hail!

---

53. **fantastical:** creatures of fantasy or imagination.   54. **show:** appear.   55. **grace:** honor.
57. **rapt withal:** carried out of himself, distracted by these predictions.   **withal:** with it, by it.
60–61. **beg . . . hate:** beg your favors nor fear your hate.   66. **happy:** fortunate.   67. **get:** beget.

MACBETH:

Stay, you imperfect° speakers, tell me more! 70
By Sinel's° death I know I am Thane of Glamis,
But how of Cawdor? The Thane of Cawdor lives
A prosperous gentleman; and to be king
Stands not within the prospect of belief,
No more than to be Cawdor. Say from whence 75
You owe this strange intelligence,° or why
Upon this blasted° heath you stop our way
With such prophetic greeting? Speak, I charge you.   *Witches vanish.*

BANQUO:

The earth hath bubbles, as the water has,
And these are of them. Whither are they vanished? 80

MACBETH:

Into the air; and what seemed corporal° melted,
As breath into the wind. Would they had stayed!

BANQUO:

Were such things here as we do speak about?
Or have we eaten on° the insane root°
That takes the reason prisoner? 85

MACBETH:

Your children shall be kings.

BANQUO: You shall be king.

MACBETH:

And Thane of Cawdor too. Went it not so?

BANQUO:

To th' selfsame tune and words. — Who's here?

Enter Ross and Angus.

ROSS:

The King hath happily received, Macbeth,
The news of thy success; and when he reads°
Thy personal venture in the rebels' fight,°
His wonders and his praises do contend
Which should be thine or his. Silenced with that,° 90

---

70. **imperfect:** cryptic. 71. **Sinel's:** (Sinel was Macbeth's father.) 75–76. **Say . . . intelligence:** say from what source you have this unusual information. 77. **blasted:** blighted. 81. **corporal:** bodily. 84. **on:** of. **insane root:** root causing insanity; variously identified. 90. **reads:** i.e., considers. 91. **Thy . . . fight:** your endangering yourself in fighting the rebels; or (reading *fight* as *sight*) your endangering yourself before the very eyes of the rebels. 92–93. **His . . . that:** i.e., your wondrous deeds so outdo any praise he could offer that he is silenced.

In viewing o'er the rest o' the selfsame day
He finds thee in the stout Norweyan ranks, 95
Nothing° afeard of what thyself didst make,
Strange images of death. As thick as tale
Came post with post,° and every one did bear
Thy praises in his kingdom's great defense,
And poured them down before him.

ANGUS: We are sent 100
To give thee from our royal master thanks,
Only to herald thee into his sight,
Not pay thee.

ROSS:
And, for an earnest° of a greater honor,
He bade me, from him, call thee Thane of Cawdor; 105
In which addition,° hail, most worthy thane,
For it is thine.

BANQUO: What, can the devil speak true?

MACBETH:
The Thane of Cawdor lives. Why do you dress me
In borrowed robes?

ANGUS: Who° was the thane lives yet,
But under heavy judgment bears that life 110
Which he deserves to lose. Whether he was combined°
With those of Norway, or did line° the rebel°
With hidden help and vantage, or that with both
He labored in his country's wrack,° I know not;
But treasons capital,° confessed and proved, 115
Have overthrown him.

MACBETH [aside]:   Glamis, and Thane of Cawdor!
The greatest is behind.° [To Ross and Angus.] Thanks for your pains.
[Aside to Banquo.] Do you not hope your children shall be kings
When those that gave the Thane of Cawdor to me
Promised no less to them?

BANQUO [to Macbeth]:   That, trusted home,° 120
Might yet enkindle you unto the crown,
Besides the Thane of Cawdor. But 'tis strange;

---

96. **Nothing:** not at all.   97–98. **As . . . with post:** as fast as could be told, i.e., counted, came messenger after messenger (unless the text should be amended to "As thick as hail").
104. **earnest:** token payment.   106. **addition:** title.   109. **Who:** he who.   111. **combined:** confederate.   112. **line:** reinforce.   **the rebel:** i.e., Macdonwald   114. **in . . . wrack:** to bring about his country's ruin.   115. **capital:** deserving death.   117. **behind:** to come.   120. **home:** all the way.

And oftentimes to win us to our harm
The instruments of darkness° tell us truths,
Win us with honest trifles, to betray 's   125
In deepest consequence.° —
Cousins,° a word, I pray you.   [*He converses apart with Ross and Angus.*]
MACBETH [*aside*]:
Two truths are told,
As happy prologues to the swelling act°
Of the imperial theme. — I thank you, gentlemen.   130
[*Aside.*] This supernatural soliciting°
Cannot be ill, cannot be good. If ill,
Why hath it given me earnest of success
Commencing in a truth? I am Thane of Cawdor.
If good, why do I yield to that suggestion   135
Whose horrid° image doth unfix my hair
And make my seated heart knock at my ribs,
Against the use° of nature? Present fears°
Are less than horrible imaginings.
My thought, whose° murder yet is but fantastical,°   140
Shakes so my single state of man°
That function° is smothered in surmise,°
And nothing is but what is not.°
BANQUO:
Look how our partner's rapt.
MACBETH [*aside*]:
If chance will have me king, why, chance may crown me   145
Without my stir.°
BANQUO: New honors come° upon him,
Like our strange garments, cleave not to their mold
But with the aid of use.°
MACBETH [*aside*]:   Come what come may,
Time and the hour runs through the roughest day. °

---

124. **darkness:** (Indicates the demonic beyond the witches.) 126. **In deepest consequence:** in the profoundly important sequel. 127. **Cousins:** i.e., fellow lords. 129. **swelling act:** stately drama. 131. **soliciting:** tempting. 136. **horrid:** literally, "bristling," like Macbeth's hair. 138. **use:** custom. **fears:** things feared. 140. **whose:** in which. **but fantastical:** merely imagined. 141. **single . . . man:** weak human condition. 142. **function:** normal power of action. **surmise:** speculation, imaginings. 143. **nothing . . . not:** only unreal imaginings have (for me) any reality. 146. **stir:** bestirring (myself). **come:** i.e., which have come. 147–148. **cleave . . . use:** do not take the shape of the wearer until often worn. (Macbeth is often connected in the text with clothes that don't really fit him.) 149. **Time . . . day:** i.e., what must happen will happen one way or another.

BANQUO:

Worthy Macbeth, we stay° upon your leisure.   150

MACBETH:

Give me your favor.° My dull brain was wrought°
With things forgotten. Kind gentlemen, your pains
Are registered° where every day I turn
The leaf to read them. Let us toward the King.
[*Aside to Banquo.*] Think upon what hath chanced, and at more time,°   155
The interim having weighed it, let us speak
Our free hearts° each to other.

BANQUO [*to Macbeth*]:

Very gladly.

MACBETH [*to Banquo*]:

Till then, enough. — Come, friends.

                                                             Exeunt.

Act i, Scene 4°

Flourish. Enter King [Duncan], Lennox, Malcolm, Donalbain, and attendants.

DUNCAN:

Is execution done on Cawdor? Are not
Those in commission° yet returned?

MALCOLM: My liege,
They are not yet come back. But I have spoke
With one that saw him die, who did report
That very frankly he confessed his treasons,   5
Implored Your Highness' pardon, and set forth
A deep repentance. Nothing in his life
Became him like the leaving it. He died
As one that had been studied° in his death
To throw away the dearest thing he owed°   10
As 'twere a careless° trifle.

DUNCAN: There's no art
To find the mind's construction in the face.
He was a gentleman on whom I built
An absolute trust.

---

150. **stay:** wait. 151. **favor:** pardon. **wrought:** shaped, preoccupied. 153. **registered:** recorded (in my memory). 155. **at more time:** at a time of greater leisure. 157. **Our free hearts:** our hearts freely. Act i, Scene 4. Location: Forres. The palace. 2. **in commission:** having warrant (to see to the execution of Cawdor). 9. **been studied:** made it his study. 10. **owed:** owned. 11. **careless:** uncared for.

Enter Macbeth, Banquo, Ross, and Angus.

              O worthiest cousin!
The sin of my ingratitude even now   15
Was heavy on me. Thou art so far before°
That swiftest wing of recompense is slow
To overtake thee. Would thou hadst less deserved,
That the proportion both of thanks and payment
Might have been mine!° Only I have left to say,   20
More is thy due than more than all can pay.

MACBETH:
The service and the loyalty I owe,
In doing it, pays itself. Your Highness' part
Is to receive our duties; and our duties
Are to your throne and state children and servants,°   25
Which do but what they should by doing everything
Safe toward your love and honor.°

DUNCAN: Welcome hither!
I have begun to plant thee, and will labor
To make thee full of growing. Noble Banquo,
That hast no less deserved, nor must be known   30
No less to have done so, let me infold thee
And hold thee to my heart.

BANQUO: There if I grow,
The harvest is your own.

DUNCAN: My plenteous joys,
Wanton° in fullness, seek to hide themselves
In drops of sorrow. — Sons, kinsmen, thanes,   35
And you whose places are the nearest, know
We° will establish our estate° upon
Our eldest, Malcolm, whom we name hereafter
The Prince of Cumberland;° which honor must
Not unaccompanied invest him only,°   40
But signs of nobleness, like stars, shall shine

---

16. **before:** ahead (in deserving). 19–20. **That . . . mine:** that I might have thanked and rewarded you in ample proportion to your worth. 25. **Are . . . servants:** are like children and servants in relation to your throne and dignity, existing only to serve you. 27. **Safe . . . honor:** to safeguard you whom we love and honor. 34. **Wanton:** unrestrained. 37. **We:** (The royal "we.") **establish our estate:** fix the succession of our state. 39. **Prince of Cumberland:** title of the heir apparent to the Scottish throne. 40. **Not . . . only:** not be bestowed on Malcolm alone; other deserving nobles are to share honors.

On all deservers. — From hence to Inverness,°
And bind us further to you.°

MACBETH:
The rest is labor which is not used for you.°
I'll be myself the harbinger° and make joyful   45
The hearing of my wife with your approach;
So humbly take my leave.

DUNCAN: My worthy Cawdor!

MACBETH [*aside*]:
The Prince of Cumberland! That is a step
On which I must fall down or else o'erleap,
For in my way it lies.° Stars, hide your fires;   50
Let not light see my black and deep desires.
The eye wink at the hand;° yet let that be°
Which the eye fears, when it is done, to see.   *Exit.*

DUNCAN:
True, worthy Banquo. He is full so valiant,°
And in his commendations° I am fed;   55
It is a banquet to me. Let's after him,
Whose care is gone before to bid us welcome.
It is a peerless kinsman.   *Flourish. Exeunt.*

ACT 1, SCENE 5°

Enter Macbeth's Wife, alone, with a letter.

LADY MACBETH [*reads*]:   "They met me in the day of success; and I have
learned by the perfect'st° report they have more in them than mortal
knowledge. When I burnt in desire to question them further, they made
themselves air, into which they vanished. Whiles I stood rapt in the
wonder of it came missives° from the King, who all-hailed me 'Thane of   5
Cawdor,' by which title, before, these Weird Sisters saluted me, and
referred me to the coming on of time with 'Hail, king that shalt be!' This

---

42. **Inverness:** the seat or location of Macbeth's castle, Dunsinane.   43. **bind . . . you:** put me
further in your (Macbeth's) obligation by your hospitality.   44. **The . . . you:** inactivity, not
being devoted to your service, becomes tedious and wearisome.   45. **harbinger:** forerunner,
messenger to arrange royal lodging.   50. **in my way it lies:** (The monarchy was not hereditary,
and Macbeth had a right to believe that he himself might be chosen as Duncan's successor; he
here questions whether he will interfere with the course of events.)   52. **wink . . . hand:** blind
itself to the hand's deed.   **let that be:** may that thing come to pass.   54. **full so valiant:** fully as
valiant as you say. (Apparently, Duncan and Banquo have been conversing privately on this
subject during Macbeth's soliloquy.)   55. **his commendations:** the praises given to him.
ACT 1, SCENE 5. Location: Inverness. Macbeth's castle.   2. **perfect'st:** most accurate.
5. **missives:** messengers.

have I thought good to deliver thee,° my dearest partner of greatness,
that thou mightst not lose the dues of rejoicing by being ignorant of what
greatness is promised thee. Lay it to thy heart, and farewell." 10
Glamis thou art, and Cawdor, and shalt be
What thou art promised. Yet do I fear° thy nature;
It is too full o' the milk of human kindness
To catch the nearest way. Thou wouldst be great,
Art not without ambition, but without 15
The illness° should attend it. What thou wouldst highly,°
That wouldst thou holily; wouldst not play false,
And yet wouldst wrongly win. Thou'dst have, great Glamis,
That which cries "Thus thou must do," if thou have° it,
And that which rather thou dost fear to do 20
Than wishest should be undone.° Hie° thee hither,
That I may pour my spirits in thine ear
And chastise with the valor of my tongue
All that impedes thee from the golden round°
Which fate and metaphysical° aid doth seem 25
To have thee crowned withal.°

Enter [a servant as] Messenger.

What is your tidings?

MESSENGER:
The King comes here tonight.

LADY MACBETH: Thou'rt mad to say it!
Is not thy master with him, who, were 't so,
Would have informed for preparation?°

MESSENGER:
So please you, it is true. Our thane is coming. 30
One of my fellows had the speed of° him,
Who, almost dead for breath, had scarcely more
Than would make up his message.

LADY MACBETH: Give him tending;°
He brings great news. *Exit Messenger.*
The raven himself is hoarse
That croaks the fatal entrance of Duncan 35

8. **deliver thee:** inform you of. 12. **do I fear:** I am anxious about, mistrust. 16. **illness:** evil (that). **highly:** greatly. 19. **have:** are to have, want to have. 20–21. **And that . . . undone:** i.e., and the thing you ambitiously crave frightens you more in terms of the means needed to achieve it than in the idea of having it; if you could have it without those means, you certainly wouldn't wish it undone. 21. **Hie:** hasten. 24. **round:** crown. 25. **metaphysical:** supernatural. 26. **withal:** with. 29. **informed for preparation:** i.e., sent me word so that I might get things ready. 31. **had . . . of:** outstripped. 33. **tending:** attendance.

Under my battlements. Come, you spirits
That tend on mortal thoughts,° unsex me here
And fill me from the crown to the toe top-full
Of direst cruelty! Make thick my blood;
Stop up th' access and passage to remorse,°   40
That no compunctious visitings of nature°
Shake my fell° purpose, nor keep peace° between
Th' effect and it!° Come to my woman's breasts
And take my milk for gall,° you murdering ministers,°
Wherever in your sightless° substances   45
You wait on° nature's mischief!° Come, thick night,
And pall° thee in the dunnest° smoke of hell,
That my keen knife see not the wound it makes,
Nor heaven peep through the blanket of the dark
To cry "Hold, hold!"

Enter Macbeth.

                Great Glamis! Worthy Cawdor!   50
Greater than both by the all-hail hereafter!
Thy letters have° transported me beyond
This ignorant present, and I feel now
The future in the instant.

MACBETH: My dearest love,
Duncan comes here tonight.

LADY MACBETH: And when goes hence?   55

MACBETH:
Tomorrow, as he purposes.

LADY MACBETH: O, never
Shall sun that morrow see!
Your face, my thane, is as a book where men
May read strange matters. To beguile the time,°
Look like the time;° bear welcome in your eye,   60
Your hand, your tongue. Look like th' innocent flower
But be the serpent under 't. He that's coming

---

37. **tend . . . thoughts:** attend on, act as the instruments of, deadly or murderous thoughts.
40. **remorse:** pity. 41. **nature:** natural feelings. 42. **fell:** fierce, cruel. **keep peace:** intervene. 43. **Th' effect and it:** i.e., my *fell purpose* and its accomplishment. 44. **for gall:** in exchange for gall, or perhaps *as* gall, with the milk itself being the gall. **ministers:** agents.
45. **sightless:** invisible. 46. **wait on:** attend, assist. **nature's mischief:** the kind of evil to which human nature is prone. 47. **pall:** envelop. **dunnest:** darkest. 52. **letters have:** i.e., letter has. 59. **beguile the time:** i.e., deceive all observers. 60. **Look like the time:** look the way people expect you to look.

Must be provided for; and you shall put
This night's great business into my dispatch,°
Which shall to all our nights and days to come   65
Give solely sovereign sway and masterdom.

MACBETH:
We will speak further.

LADY MACBETH: Only look up clear.°
To alter favor ever is to fear.°
Leave all the rest to me.   *Exeunt.*

ACT I, SCENE 6°

*Hautboys° and torches. Enter King [Duncan], Malcolm, Donalbain, Banquo, Lennox,
Macduff, Ross, Angus, and attendants.*

DUNCAN:
This castle hath a pleasant seat.° The air
Nimbly and sweetly recommends itself
Unto our gentle° senses.

BANQUO: This guest of summer,
The temple-haunting° martlet,° does approve°
By his loved mansionry° that the heaven's breath   5
Smells wooingly here. No jutty,° frieze,
Buttress, nor coign of vantage° but this bird
Hath made his pendent bed and procreant° cradle.
Where they most breed and haunt, I have observed
The air is delicate.

Enter Lady [Macbeth].

DUNCAN: See, see, our honored hostess!   10
The love that follows us sometimes is our trouble,
Which still we thank as love.° Herein I teach you

---

64. **dispatch:** management.   67. **look up clear:** give the appearance of being untroubled.
68. **To . . . fear:** i.e., to show a troubled countenance is to arouse suspicion.   ACT I, SCENE 6.
Location: Before Macbeth's castle.   **s.d.** *Hautboys:* oboelike instruments.   1. **seat:** site.
3. **gentle:** (1) noble (2) refined (by the delicate air).   4. **temple-haunting:** nesting in churches.
martlet: house martin.   **approve:** prove.   5. **mansionry:** nest building.   6. **jutty:** projection
of wall or building.   7. **coign of vantage:** convenient corner, i.e., for nesting.   8. **procreant:**
for breeding.   11–12. **The love . . . love:** the love that sometimes forces itself inconveniently
upon us we still appreciate, since it is meant as love. (Duncan is graciously suggesting that his
visit is a bother, but, he hopes, a welcome one.)

How you shall bid God 'ild° us for your pains,°
And thank us for your trouble.

LADY MACBETH: All our service
In every point twice done, and then done double,   15
Were poor and single° business to contend
Against° those honors deep and broad wherewith
Your Majesty loads our house. For those of old,°
And the late° dignities heaped up to° them,
We rest° your hermits.°

DUNCAN: Where's the Thane of Cawdor?   20
We coursed° him at the heels, and had a purpose
To be his purveyor;° but he rides well,
And his great love, sharp as his spur, hath holp° him
To his home before us. Fair and noble hostess,
We are your guest tonight.

LADY MACBETH: Your servants ever   25
Have theirs, themselves, and what is theirs in compt
To make their audit at Your Highness' pleasure,
Still to return your own.°

DUNCAN: Give me your hand.
Conduct me to mine host. We° love him highly,
And shall continue our graces towards him.   30
By your leave, hostess.   *Exeunt.*

Act i, Scene 7°

Hautboys. Torches. Enter a sewer,° and divers servants with dishes and service, [and pass] over the stage. Then enter Macbeth.

MACBETH:
If it were done when 'tis done, then 'twere well
It were done quickly. If th' assassination

---

13. **bid . . . pains:** ask God to reward me for the trouble I'm giving you. (This is said in the same gently jocose spirit as lines 11–12.) **'ild:** yield, repay.   16. **single:** small, inconsiderable.   16–17. **contend Against:** vie with.   18. **those of old:** i.e., honors formerly bestowed on us.   19. **late:** recent.   **to:** besides, in addition to.   20. **rest:** remain.   **hermits:** i.e., those who will pray for you like hermits or beadsmen.   21. **coursed:** followed (as in a hunt).   22. **purveyor:** an officer sent ahead to provide for entertainment; here, forerunner.   23. **holp:** helped.   25–28. **Your . . . own:** those who serve you hold their own servants, themselves, and all their possessions in trust from you, and can render an account whenever you wish, ready always to render back to you what is yours. (A feudal concept of obligation.)   29. **We:** (The royal "we.")   Act i, Scene 7. **Location:** Macbeth's castle; an inner courtyard.   s.d. *sewer:* chief waiter, butler.

Could trammel up the consequence,° and catch
With his surcease° success° — that but° this blow
Might be the be-all and the end-all! — here,°   5
But here, upon this bank and shoal of time,
We'd jump° the life to come. But in these cases
We still have judgment° here, that° we but teach
Bloody instructions,° which, being taught, return
To plague th' inventor. This evenhanded justice   10
Commends° th' ingredience° of our poisoned chalice
To our own lips. He's here in double trust:
First, as I am his kinsman and his subject,
Strong both against the deed; then, as his host,
Who should against his murderer shut the door,   15
Not bear the knife myself. Besides, this Duncan
Hath borne his faculties° so meek, hath been
So clear° in his great office, that his virtues
Will plead like angels, trumpet-tongued, against
The deep damnation of his taking-off;°   20
And Pity, like a naked newborn babe
Striding° the blast,° or heaven's cherubin, horsed
Upon the sightless couriers° of the air,
Shall blow the horrid deed in every eye,
That tears shall drown the wind.° I have no spur   25
To prick the sides of my intent, but only
Vaulting ambition, which o'erleaps itself
And falls on th' other° —

Enter Lady [Macbeth].

How now, what news?

LADY MACBETH:

He has almost supped. Why have you left the chamber?   30

3. **trammel . . . consequence:** entangle as in a net and prevent the consequences that follow
any action.   4. **his surcease:** cessation (of the assassination and of Duncan's life).   **success:**
what succeeds, follows. (If only the assassination itself were the end of the matter.)   **that but:**
so that only.   5. **here:** in this world.   7. **jump:** risk. (But imaging the physical act is characteristic of Macbeth; compare this with line 27.)   8. **still have judgment:** are invariably punished.   **that:** in that.   9. **instructions:** lessons.   11. **Commends:** presents.   **ingredience:**
contents of a mixture.   17. **faculties:** powers of office.   18. **clear:** free of taint.   20. **taking-
off:** murder.   22. **Striding:** bestriding.   **blast:** tempest (of compassionate horror).
23. **sightless couriers:** invisible steeds or runners, i.e., the winds.   25. **shall drown the wind:**
i.e., will be as heavy as a downpour of rain and thereby still the wind.   28. **other:** other side.
(The image is of a horseman vaulting into his saddle and ignominiously falling on the opposite
side.)

MACBETH:
Hath he asked for me?

LADY MACBETH: Know you not he has?

MACBETH:
We will proceed no further in this business.
He hath honored me of late, and I have bought°
Golden opinions from all sorts of people,
Which would° be worn now in their newest gloss,   35
Not cast aside so soon.

LADY MACBETH: Was the hope drunk
Wherein you dressed yourself? Hath it slept since?
And wakes it now, to look so green° and pale
At what it did so freely? From this time
Such I account thy love. Art thou afeard   40
To be the same in thine own act and valor
As thou art in desire? Wouldst thou have that
Which thou esteem'st the ornament of life,°
And live a coward in thine own esteem,
Letting "I dare not" wait upon° "I would,"   45
Like the poor cat i' th' adage?°

MACBETH: Prithee, peace!
I dare do all that may become a man;
Who dares do more is none.

LADY MACBETH: What beast was 't, then,
That made you break° this enterprise to me?
When you durst do it, then you were a man;   50
And, to be more than what you were, you would
Be so much more the man. Nor time nor place
Did then adhere,° and yet you would° make both.
They have made themselves, and that their fitness° now
Does unmake you. I have given suck, and know   55
How tender 'tis to love the babe that milks me;
I would, while it was smiling in my face,
Have plucked my nipple from his boneless gums

[Handwritten margin note: Tells him to be a man]

---

33. **bought:** acquired (by bravery in battle). 35. **would:** ought to, should. 38. **green:** sickly.
43. **the ornament of life:** i.e., the crown. 45. **wait upon:** accompany, always follow.
46. **adage:** (i.e., "The cat would eat fish but she will not wet her feet.") 49. **break:** broach.
53. **adhere:** agree, suit. **would:** wanted to. 54. **that their fitness:** that very suitability of
time and place.

And dashed the brains out, had I so sworn as you
Have done to this.

MACBETH: If we should fail?

LADY MACBETH: We fail?   60
But° screw your courage to the sticking place°
And we'll not fail. When Duncan is asleep —
Whereto the rather shall his day's hard journey
Soundly invite him — his two chamberlains°
Will I with wine and wassail° so convince°   65
That memory, the warder of the brain,
Shall be a fume, and the receipt° of reason
A limbeck° only.° When in swinish sleep
Their drenchèd natures lies as in a death,
What cannot you and I perform upon   70
Th' unguarded Duncan? What not put upon
His spongy° officers, who shall bear the guilt
Of our great quell?°

MACBETH: Bring forth men-children only!
For thy undaunted mettle° should compose
Nothing but males. Will it not be received,°   75
When we have marked with blood those sleepy two
Of his own chamber and used their very daggers,
That they have done 't?

LADY MACBETH: Who dares receive it other,°
As° we shall make our griefs and clamor roar
Upon his death?

MACBETH: I am settled, and bend up   80
Each corporal agent° to this terrible feat.
Away, and mock° the time with fairest show.
False face must hide what the false heart doth know.   *Exeunt.*

Handwritten margin notes: "Plotting Murder", "Lady Macbeth is more dominant"

61. **But:** only. **the sticking place:** the notch into which is fitted the string of a crossbow cranked taut for shooting. **64. chamberlains:** attendants on the bedchamber. **65. wassail:** carousal, drink. **convince:** overpower. **66–68. warder . . . only:** (The brain was thought to be divided into three ventricles: imagination in front, memory at the back, and between them the seat of reason. The fumes of wine, arising from the stomach, would deaden memory and judgment.) **67. receipt:** receptacle, ventricle. **68. limbeck:** device for distilling liquids. **72. spongy:** soaked, drunken. **73. quell:** murder. **74. mettle:** (The same word as *metal*): substance, temperament. **75. received:** i.e., as truth. **78. other:** otherwise. **79. As:** inasmuch as. **80–81. bend . . . agent:** strain every muscle. **82. mock:** deceive.

ACT 2, SCENE 1°

Enter Banquo, and Fleance, with a torch° before him.

BANQUO:
How goes the night, boy?
FLEANCE:
The moon is down. I have not heard the clock.
BANQUO:
And she goes down at twelve.
FLEANCE: I take 't, 'tis later, sir.
BANQUO:
Hold, take my sword. [*He gives him his sword.*] There's husbandry° in
    heaven;
Their candles are all out. Take thee that too.
                              [*He gives him his belt and dagger.*]   5
A heavy summons° lies like lead upon me,
And yet I would not° sleep. Merciful powers,°
Restrain in me the cursèd thoughts that nature
Gives way to in repose!

Enter Macbeth, and a Servant with a torch.

Give me my sword. Who's there?   [*He takes his sword.*]   10
MACBETH:
A friend.
BANQUO:
What, sir, not yet at rest? The King's abed.
He hath been in unusual pleasure,
And sent forth great largess° to your offices.°
This diamond he greets your wife withal,   15
By the name of most kind hostess, and shut up
In° measureless content.   [*He gives a diamond.*]
MACBETH: Being unprepared,
Our will became the servant to defect,°
Which else should free° have wrought.

ACT 2, SCENE 1. **Location:** Inner courtyard of Macbeth's castle. Time is virtually continuous from the previous scene. **s.d.** *torch:* (This may mean "torchbearer," although it does not at line 9 s.d.). 4. **husbandry:** economy. 6. **summons:** i.e., to sleep. 7. **would not:** am reluctant to (owing to my uneasy fears). **powers:** order of angels deputed by God to resist demons. 14. **largess:** gifts, gratuities. **offices:** quarters used for the household work. 16–17. **shut up In:** concluded what he had to say with expressions of, or, perhaps, he professes himself enclosed in. 18. **Our . . . defect:** our good will (to entertain the King handsomely) was limited by our meager means (at such short notice). 19. **free:** freely, unrestrainedly.

BANQUO:
  All's well. 20
  I dreamt last night of the three Weird Sisters.
  To you they have showed some truth.
MACBETH: I think not of them.
  Yet, when we can entreat an hour to serve,
  We would spend it in some words upon that business,
  If you would grant the time.
BANQUO: At your kind'st leisure. 25
MACBETH:
  If you shall cleave to my consent when 'tis,°
  It shall make honor for you.
BANQUO: So° I lose none
  In seeking to augment it, but still keep
  My bosom franchised° and allegiance clear,°
  I shall be counseled.°
MACBETH: Good repose the while! 30
BANQUO:
  Thanks, sir. The like to you.   *Exit Banquo [with Fleance].*
MACBETH: [*to Servant*]
  Go bid thy mistress, when my drink° is ready,
  She strike upon the bell. Get thee to bed.   *Exit [Servant].*
  Is this a dagger which I see before me,
  The handle toward my hand? Come, let me clutch thee. 35
  I have thee not, and yet I see thee still.
  Art thou not, fatal° vision, sensible°
  To feeling as to sight? Or art thou but
  A dagger of the mind, a false creation,
  Proceeding from the heat-oppressèd° brain? 40
  I see thee yet, in form as palpable
  As this which now I draw.   [*He draws a dagger.*]
  Thou marshall'st me the way that I was going,°
  And such an instrument I was to use.
  Mine eyes are made the fools o' th' other senses, 45
  Or else worth all the rest.° I see thee still,

---

26. **cleave . . . 'tis:** give me your support, adhere to my view, when the time comes.   27. **So:** provided.   29. **franchised:** free (from guilt).   **clear:** unstained.   30. **counseled:** receptive to suggestion.   32. **drink:** i.e., posset or bedtime drink of hot spiced milk curdled with ale or wine, as also in 2.2.6.   37. **fatal:** ominous.   **sensible:** perceivable by the senses.   40. **heat-oppressèd:** fevered.   43. **Thou . . . going:** you seem to guide me toward the destiny I intended, toward Duncan's chambers.   45–46. **Mine . . . rest:** i.e., either this is a fantasy, deceiving me with what my eyes seem to see, or else it is a true vision expressing something that is beyond ordinary sensory experience.

And on thy blade and dudgeon° gouts° of blood,
Which was not so before. There's no such thing.
It is the bloody business which informs°
Thus to mine eyes. Now o'er the one half world   50
Nature seems dead, and wicked dreams abuse°
The curtained° sleep. Witchcraft celebrates
Pale Hecate's offerings,° and withered Murder,
Alarumed° by his sentinel, the wolf,
Whose howl's his watch,° thus with his stealthy pace,   55
With Tarquin's° ravishing strides, towards his design
Moves like a ghost. Thou sure and firm-set earth,
Hear not my steps which way they walk, for fear
Thy very stones prate of my whereabouts
And take the present horror from the time   60
Which now suits with it.° Whiles I threat, he lives;
Words to the heat of deeds too cold breath gives.°   *A bell rings.*
I go, and it is done. The bell invites me.
Hear it not, Duncan, for it is a knell
That summons thee to heaven or to hell.   *Exit.* 65

Act 2, Scene 2°

Enter Lady [Macbeth].

LADY MACBETH:
That which hath made them drunk hath made me bold;
What hath quenched them hath given me fire. Hark! Peace!
It was the owl that shrieked, the fatal bellman,°
Which gives the stern'st good-night.° He is about it.
The doors are open; and the surfeited grooms°   5
Do mock their charge° with snores. I have drugged their possets,°

47. **dudgeon:** hilt of a dagger. **gouts:** drops. 49. **informs:** creates forms or impressions. 51. **abuse:** deceive. 52. **curtained:** (1) veiled by bed curtains (2) screened from rationality and consciousness. 53. **Pale Hecate's offerings:** sacrificial offerings to Hecate, the goddess of night and witchcraft. (She is *pale* because she is identified with the pale moon.) 54. **Alarumed:** given the signal to action. 55. **watch:** watchword, or cry like the hourly call of the night watchman. 56. **Tarquin's:** (Tarquin was a Roman tyrant who ravished Lucrece.) 60–61. **And take . . . with it:** and thus echo and augment the horror which is so suited to this evil hour, or, usurp the present horror by breaking the silence. 62. **Words . . . gives:** words give only lifeless expression to live deeds, are no substitute for deeds. **Act 2, Scene 2.** Location: Scene continues. 3. **bellman:** one who rings a bell to announce a death or to mark the hours of the night. 4. **stern'st good-night:** i.e., notice to condemned criminals that they are to be executed in the morning. 5. **grooms:** servants. 6. **mock their charge:** make a mockery of their guard duty. **possets:** hot bedtime drinks (as in 2.1.32).

That death and nature do contend about them
Whether they live or die.

MACBETH [*within*]:   Who's there? What, ho!

LADY MACBETH:
Alack, I am afraid they have awaked,
And 'tis not done. Th' attempt and not the deed   10
Confounds° us. Hark! I laid their daggers ready;
He could not miss 'em. Had he not resembled
My father as he slept, I had done 't.

Enter Macbeth [bearing bloody daggers].

My husband!

MACBETH:
I have done the deed. Didst thou not hear a noise?   15

LADY MACBETH:
I heard the owl scream and the crickets° cry.
Did not you speak?

MACBETH:
When?

LADY MACBETH:
Now.

MACBETH:
As I descended?   20

LADY MACBETH:
Ay.

MACBETH:
Hark! Who lies i' the second chamber?

LADY MACBETH:
Donalbain.

MACBETH [*looking at his hands*]:
This is a sorry sight.

LADY MACBETH:
A foolish thought, to say a sorry sight.   25

MACBETH:
There's one did laugh in 's sleep, and one cried "Murder!"
That they did wake each other. I stood and heard them.
But they did say their prayers, and addressed them°
Again to sleep.

LADY MACBETH: There are two° lodged together.

---

11. **Confounds:** ruins.   16. **owl, crickets:** (The sounds of both could be ominous and prophetic of death.)   28. **addressed them:** settled themselves.   29. **two:** i.e., Malcolm and Donalbain.

MACBETH:

> One cried "God bless us!" and "Amen!" the other,   30
> As° they had seen me with these hangman's hands.°
> List'ning their fear, I could not say "Amen"
> When they did say "God bless us!"

LADY MACBETH:

> Consider it not so deeply.

MACBETH:

> But wherefore could not I pronounce "Amen"?   35
> I had most need of blessing, and "Amen"
> Stuck in my throat.

LADY MACBETH: These deeds must not be thought°

> After these ways; so,° it will make us mad.

MACBETH:

> Methought I heard a voice cry "Sleep no more!
> Macbeth does murder sleep," the innocent sleep,   40
> Sleep that knits up the raveled sleave° of care,
> The death of each day's life, sore labor's bath,°
> Balm of hurt minds, great nature's second course,°
> Chief nourisher in life's feast —

LADY MACBETH: What do you mean?

MACBETH:

> Still it cried "Sleep no more!" to all the house;   45
> "Glamis hath murdered sleep, and therefore Cawdor
> Shall sleep no more; Macbeth shall sleep no more."

LADY MACBETH:

> Who was it that thus cried? Why, worthy thane,
> You do unbend° your noble strength to think
> So brainsickly of things. Go get some water   50
> And wash this filthy witness° from your hand.
> Why did you bring these daggers from the place?
> They must lie there. Go, carry them and smear
> The sleepy grooms with blood.

MACBETH: I'll go no more.

> I am afraid to think what I have done;   55
> Look on 't again I dare not.

---

31. As: as if.   **hangman's hands:** bloody hands (because the hangman would draw and quarter the condemned, and also executed with an ax).   **37. thought:** thought about.   **38. so:** if we do so.   **41. raveled sleave:** tangled skein.   **42. bath:** i.e., to relieve the soreness.   **43. second course:** (Ordinary feasts had two courses, of which the second was the *chief nourisher;* here, sleep is seen as following eating in a restorative process.)   **49. unbend:** slacken (as one would a bow; contrast with "bend up" in 1.7.80).   **51. witness:** evidence.

LADY MACBETH: Infirm of purpose!
　　Give me the daggers. The sleeping and the dead
　　Are but as pictures. 'Tis the eye of childhood
　　That fears a painted devil. If he do bleed,
　　I'll gild° the faces of the grooms withal,   60
　　For it must seem their guilt.   [*She takes the daggers, and*] *exit. Knock within.*
MACBETH: Whence is that knocking?
　　How is 't with me, when every noise appalls me?
　　What hands are here? Ha! They pluck out mine eyes.
　　Will all great Neptune's ocean wash this blood
　　Clean from my hand? No, this my hand will rather   65
　　The multitudinous° seas incarnadine,°
　　Making the green one red.°

Enter Lady [Macbeth].

LADY MACBETH:
　　My hands are of your color, but I shame
　　To wear a heart so white. (*Knock.*) I hear a knocking
　　At the south entry. Retire we to our chamber.   70
　　A little water clears us of this deed.
　　How easy is it, then! Your constancy
　　Hath left you unattended.° (*Knock.*) Hark! More knocking.
　　Get on your nightgown,° lest occasion call us
　　And show us to be watchers.° Be not lost   75
　　So poorly° in your thoughts.
MACBETH:
　　To know my deed, 'twere best not know myself.°   *Knock.*
　　Wake Duncan with thy knocking! I would thou couldst!   *Exeunt.*

ACT 2, SCENE 3°

Knocking within. Enter a Porter.

PORTER: Here's a knocking indeed! If a man were porter of hell gate, he
　　should have old° turning the key. (*Knock.*) Knock, knock, knock! Who's

---

60. gild: smear, coat, as if with a thin layer of gold. (Gold was ordinarily spoken of as red.) **66. multitudinous:** both multiform and teeming. **incarnadine:** make red. **67. one red:** one all-pervading red. **72–73. Your . . . unattended:** your firmness has deserted you. **74. nightgown:** dressing gown. **75. watchers:** those who have remained awake. **76. poorly:** dejectedly. **77. To . . . myself:** i.e., it were better to be lost in my thoughts than to have consciousness of my deed; if I am to live with myself, I will have to shut this out or be no longer the person I was. **ACT 2, SCENE 3. Location:** Scene continues. The knocking at the door has already been heard in 2.2. It is not necessary to assume literally, however, that Macbeth and Lady Macbeth have been talking near the *south entry* (2.2.70) where the knocking is heard. **2. old:** plenty of.

there, i' the name of Beelzebub?° Here's a farmer that hanged himself on
th' expectation of plenty.° Come in time!° Have napkins° enough about
you; here you'll sweat for 't (*Knock.*) Knock, knock! Who's there, in th' 5
other devil's name? Faith, here's an equivocator,° that could swear in both
the scales against either scale, who committed treason enough for God's
sake, yet could not equivocate to heaven. O, come in, equivocator.
(*Knock.*) Knock, knock, knock! Who's there? Faith, here's an English tailor come hither for stealing out of a French hose.° Come in, tailor. Here 10
you may roast your goose.° (*Knock.*) Knock, knock! Never at quiet! What
are you? But this place is too cold for hell. I'll devil-porter it no further. I
had thought to have let in some of all professions that go the primrose
way to th' everlasting bonfire. (*Knock.*) Anon, anon! [*He opens the gate.*] I
pray you, remember the porter. 15

Enter Macduff and Lennox.

MACDUFF:
Was it so late, friend, ere you went to bed,
That you do lie so late?
PORTER: Faith, sir, we were carousing till the second cock;° and drink, sir,
is a great provoker of three things.
MACDUFF: What three things does drink especially provoke? 20
PORTER: Marry,° sir, nose-painting,° sleep, and urine. Lechery, sir, it provokes and unprovokes: it provokes the desire but it takes away the performance. Therefore much drink may be said to be an equivocator with
lechery: it makes him and it mars him; it sets him on and it takes him off;
it persuades him and disheartens him, makes him stand to and not stand 25
to°; in conclusion, equivocates him in a sleep° and, giving him the lie,°
leaves him.°

---

3. **Beelzebub:** a devil.   3–4. **Here's . . . plenty:** i.e., here's a farmer who has hoarded in antic-
ipation of a scarcity and will be justly punished by a crop surplus and low prices.   4. **Come in
time:** i.e., you have come in good time.   **napkins:** handkerchiefs (to mop up the sweat).
6. **equivocator:** (This is regarded by many editors as an allusion to the trial of the Jesuit Henry
Garnet for treason in the spring of 1606 and to the doctrine of equivocation said to have been
presented in his defense; according to this doctrine, a lie was not a lie if the utterer had in his
mind a different meaning in which the utterance was true.)   10. **French hose:** very narrow
breeches of the sort that would easily reveal the tailor's attempt to skimp on the cloth supplied
him for their manufacture — as he evidently had done with impunity when the French style
ran to loose-fitting breeches.   11. **roast your goose:** heat your tailor's smoothing iron (with an
obvious pun on the sense, "cook your goose").   18. **second cock:** i.e., 3 A.M., when the cock
was thought to crow a second time.   21. **Marry:** (Originally, an oath, "by the Virgin Mary.")
nose-painting: i.e., reddening of the nose through drink.   25–26. **makes . . . stand to:** stimu-
lates him sexually but without sexual capability.   26. **equivocates . . . sleep:** (1) lulls him
asleep (2) gives him an erotic experience in dream only.   **giving him the lie:** (1) deceiving him
(2) laying him out flat.   27. **leaves him:** (1) dissipates as intoxication (2) is passed off as urine.

MACDUFF: I believe drink gave thee the lie° last night.

PORTER: That it did, sir, i' the very throat on me.° But I requited him for
his lie, and, I think, being too strong for him, though he took up my legs°   30
sometimes, yet I made a shift° to cast° him.

MACDUFF: Is thy master stirring?

Enter Macbeth.

Our knocking has awaked him. Here he comes.   [*Exit Porter.*]

LENNOX:

Good morrow, noble sir.

MACBETH: Good morrow, both.

MACDUFF:

Is the King stirring, worthy thane?

MACBETH: Not yet.   35

MACDUFF:

He did command me to call timely° on him.
I have almost slipped° the hour.

MACBETH: I'll bring you to him.

MACDUFF:

I know this is a joyful trouble to you,
But yet 'tis one.

MACBETH:

The labor we delight in physics pain.°   40
This is the door.

MACDUFF: I'll make so bold to call,
For 'tis my limited° service.   *Exit Macduff.*

LENNOX:

Goes the King hence today?

MACBETH: He does; he did appoint so.

LENNOX:

The night has been unruly. Where we lay,   45
Our chimneys were blown down, and, as they say,
Lamentings heard i' th' air, strange screams of death,
And prophesying with accents terrible°

---

28. **gave thee the lie:** (1) called you a liar (2) made you unable to stand and put you to sleep.
29. **i' the . . . me:** i.e., insulting me with a deliberate lie that requires a duel (with a pun on the
literal sense). **on:** of. 30. **took up my legs:** lifted me as a wrestler would (with a suggestion
of the drunkard's unsteadiness on his legs and perhaps also of lifting the leg as a dog might to
urinate). 31. **made a shift:** managed. **cast:** (1) throw, as in wrestling (2) vomit. 36. **timely:**
betimes, early. 37. **slipped:** let slip. 40. **physics pain:** i.e., cures that labor of its troublesome
aspect. 42. **limited:** appointed. 48. **accents terrible:** terrifying utterances.

Of dire combustion° and confused events
New hatched to the woeful time.° The obscure bird°   50
Clamored the livelong night. Some say the earth
Was feverous and did shake.

MACBETH: 'Twas a rough night.

LENNOX:

My young remembrance cannot parallel
A fellow to it.

Enter Macduff.

MACDUFF: O, horror, horror, horror!
Tongue nor heart cannot conceive nor name thee!   55

MACBETH AND LENNOX:

What's the matter?

MACDUFF:

Confusion° now hath made his masterpiece!
Most sacrilegious murder hath broke ope
The Lord's anointed temple and stole thence
The life o' the building!   60

MACBETH:

What is 't you say? The life?

LENNOX:

Mean you His Majesty?

MACDUFF:

Approach the chamber and destroy your sight
With a new Gorgon.° Do not bid me speak;
See, and then speak yourselves.   *Exeunt Macbeth and Lennox.*
                     Awake, awake!   65
Ring the alarum bell. Murder and treason!
Banquo and Donalbain, Malcolm, awake!
Shake off this downy sleep, death's counterfeit,
And look on death itself! Up, up, and see
The great doom's image!° Malcolm, Banquo,   70
As from your graves rise up° and walk like sprites°
To countenance° this horror! Ring the bell.   *Bell rings.*

Enter Lady [Macbeth].

---

49. **combustion:** tumult. 50. **New . . . time:** newly born to accompany the woeful nature of the time. **obscure bird:** owl, the bird of darkness. 57. **Confusion:** destruction. 64. **Gorgon:** one of three monsters with hideous faces (Medusa was a Gorgon), whose look turned the beholders to stone. 70. **great doom's image:** replica of Doomsday. 71. **As . . . rise up:** (At the Last Judgment, the dead will rise from their graves to be judged.) **sprites:** souls, ghosts. 72. **countenance:** (1) be in keeping with (2) behold.

LADY MACBETH:
    What's the business,
    That such a hideous trumpet° calls to parley
    The sleepers of the house? Speak, speak!   75
MACDUFF:
    O gentle lady,
    'Tis not for you to hear what I can speak.
    The repetition° in a woman's ear
    Would murder as it fell.

Enter Banquo.

                      O Banquo, Banquo,
    Our royal master's murdered!
LADY MACBETH: Woe, alas!   80
    What, in our house?
BANQUO: Too cruel anywhere.
    Dear Duff, I prithee, contradict thyself
    And say it is not so.

Enter Macbeth, Lennox, and Ross.

MACBETH:
    Had I but died an hour before this chance°
    I had lived a blessèd time; for from this instant   85
    There's nothing serious in mortality.°
    All is but toys.° Renown and grace is dead;
    The wine of life is drawn, and the mere lees°
    Is left this vault° to brag of.

Enter Malcolm and Donalbain.

DONALBAIN:
    What is amiss?
MACBETH: You are, and do not know 't.   90
    The spring, the head, the fountain of your blood
    Is stopped, the very source of it is stopped.
MACDUFF:
    Your royal father's murdered.
MALCOLM: O, by whom?

---

74. **trumpet:** (Another metaphorical suggestion of the Last Judgment; the *trumpet* here is the shouting and the bell.)   78. **repetition:** recital, report.   84. **chance:** occurrence (the murder of Duncan).   86. **serious in mortality:** worthwhile in mortal life.   87. **toys:** trifles. 88. **lees:** dregs.   89. **vault:** (1) wine-vault (2) earth, with its vaulted sky.

LENNOX:
> Those of his chamber, as it seemed, had done 't.
> Their hands and faces were all badged° with blood;   95
> So were their daggers, which unwiped we found
> Upon their pillows. They stared and were distracted;
> No man's life was to be trusted with them.

MACBETH:
> O, yet I do repent me of my fury,
> That I did kill them.

MACDUFF: Wherefore did you so?   100

MACBETH:
> Who can be wise, amazed,° temp'rate and furious,
> Loyal and neutral, in a moment? No man.
> Th' expedition° of my violent love
> Outran the pauser, reason. Here lay Duncan,
> His silver skin laced with his golden° blood,   105
> And his gashed stabs looked like a breach in nature°
> For ruin's wasteful° entrance; there the murderers,
> Steeped in the colors of their trade, their daggers
> Unmannerly breeched with gore.° Who could refrain
> That had a heart to love, and in that heart   110
> Courage to make 's love known?°

LADY MACBETH [*fainting*]:   Help me hence, ho!

MACDUFF:
> Look to the lady.

MALCOLM [*aside to Donalbain*]:
>   Why do we hold our tongues,
> That most may claim this argument° for ours?

DONALBAIN [*aside to Malcolm*]:
> What should be spoken here, where our fate,
> Hid in an auger hole,° may rush and seize us?   115
> Let's away. Our tears are not yet brewed.

MALCOLM [*aside to Donalbain*]:
> Nor our strong sorrow upon the foot of motion.°

---

95. **badged:** marked, as with a badge or emblem.   101. **amazed:** bewildered.   103. **expedition:** haste.   105. **golden:** (See the note for 2.2.60.)   106. **breach in nature:** gap in the defenses of life. (A metaphor of military siege.)   107. **wasteful:** destructive.   109. **breeched with gore:** covered (as with breeches) to the hilts with gore.   111. **make 's love known:** make manifest his love.   113. **argument:** topic, business.   115. **in an auger hole:** i.e., in some hiding place, in ambush.   117. **upon . . . motion:** yet in motion, ready to act.

BANQUO:

Look to the lady.   [*Lady Macbeth is helped out.*]

And when we have our naked frailties hid,°

That suffer in exposure, let us meet   120

And question° this most bloody piece of work

To know it further. Fears and scruples° shake us.

In the great hand of God I stand, and thence

Against the undivulged pretense° I fight

Of treasonous malice.°

MACDUFF: And so do I.

ALL: So all.   125

MACBETH:

Let's briefly° put on manly readiness°

And meet i' the hall together.

ALL: Well contented.

                    Exeunt [*all but Malcolm and Donalbain*].

MALCOLM:

What will you do? Let's not consort° with them.

To show an unfelt sorrow is an office

Which the false man does easy.° I'll to England.   130

DONALBAIN:

To Ireland, I. Our separated fortune

Shall keep us both the safer. Where we are,

There's daggers in men's smiles; the nea'er in blood,

The nearer bloody.°

MALCOLM: This murderous shaft that's shot

Hath not yet lighted,° and our safest way   135

Is to avoid the aim. Therefore to horse,

And let us not be dainty of° leave-taking,

But shift away.° There's warrant° in that theft

Which steals itself when there's no mercy left.   *Exeunt.*

---

119. **our naked frailties hid:** clothed our poor, shivering bodies (which remind us of our human frailty). 121. **question:** discuss. 122. **scruples:** doubts, suspicions. 123–25 **thence . . . malice:** with God's help, I will fight against the as-yet-unknown purpose that prompted this treason. 124. **pretense:** design. 125. **malice:** enmity. 126. **briefly:** quickly. **manly readiness:** men's clothing and resolute purpose. 128. **consort:** keep company, associate. 130. **easy:** easily. 133–34. **the nea'er . . . bloody:** the closer the kinship, the greater the danger of being murdered. 135. **lighted:** alighted, descended. 137. **dainty of:** particular about. 138. **shift away:** disappear by stealth. **warrant:** justification.

Act 2, Scene 4°

Enter Ross with an Old Man.

OLD MAN:
 Threescore and ten I can remember well,
 Within the volume of which time I have seen
 Hours dreadful and things strange, but this sore° night
 Hath trifled former knowings.°

ROSS: Ha, good father,°
 Thou seest the heavens,° as troubled with man's act,°   5
 Threatens his bloody stage.° By th' clock 'tis day,
 And yet dark night strangles the traveling lamp.°
 Is 't night's predominance° or the day's shame
 That darkness does the face of earth entomb
 When living light should kiss it?

OLD MAN: 'Tis unnatural,   10
 Even like the deed that's done. On Tuesday last
 A falcon, towering° in her pride of place,°
 Was by a mousing° owl hawked at and killed.

ROSS:
 And Duncan's horses — a thing most strange and certain —
 Beauteous and swift, the minions° of their race,   15
 Turned wild in nature, broke their stalls, flung out,
 Contending 'gainst obedience, as° they would
 Make war with mankind.

OLD MAN: 'Tis said they eat° each other.

ROSS:
 They did so, to th' amazement of mine eyes
 That looked upon 't.

Enter Macduff.

        Here comes the good Macduff —   20
 How goes the world, sir, now?

MACDUFF: Why, see you not?

ACT 2, SCENE 4. **Location:** Outside Macbeth's castle of Inverness.   3. **sore:** dreadful, grievous.   4. **trifled former knowings:** made trivial all former experiences.   **father:** old man.
5–6. **heavens, act, stage:** (A theatrical metaphor; the *heavens* refer to the decorated roof over
the *stage*.)   7. **traveling lamp:** i.e., sun.   8. **predominance:** ascendancy, superior influence (as
of a heavenly body).   12. **towering:** circling higher and higher. (A term in falconry.)   **place:**
pitch, highest point in the falcon's flight.   13. **mousing:** i.e., ordinarily preying on mice.
15. **minions:** darlings.   17. **as:** as if.   18. **eat:** ate. (Pronounced "et.")

ROSS:
Is't known who did this more than bloody deed?
MACDUFF:
Those that Macbeth hath slain.
ROSS: Alas the day,
What good could they pretend?°
MACDUFF: They were suborned.°
Malcolm and Donalbain, the King's two sons,   25
Are stol'n away and fled, which puts upon them
Suspicion of the deed.
ROSS: 'Gainst nature still!
Thriftless° ambition, that will ravin up°
Thine own life's means! Then 'tis most like°
The sovereignty will fall upon Macbeth.   30
MACDUFF:
He is already named° and gone to Scone°
To be invested.
ROSS: Where is Duncan's body?
MACDUFF:
Carried to Colmekill,°
The sacred storehouse of his predecessors
And guardian of their bones.
ROSS: Will you to Scone?   35
MACDUFF:
No, cousin, I'll to Fife.°
ROSS: Well, I will thither.
MACDUFF:
Well, may you see things well done there. Adieu,
Lest our old robes sit easier than our new!
ROSS:
Farewell, father.
OLD MAN:
God's benison° go with you, and with those   40
That would make good of bad, and friends of foes!   *Exeunt omnes.*

---

24. **What . . . pretend:** i.e., what could they hope to gain by it? **pretend:** intend. **suborned:** bribed, hired. 28. **Thriftless:** wasteful. **ravin up:** devour ravenously. 29. **like:** likely. 31. **named:** chosen. (See the note for 1.4.50.) **Scone:** ancient royal city of Scotland near Perth. 33. **Colmekill:** Icolmkill, i.e., Cell of St. Columba, the barren islet of Iona in the Western Islands, a sacred spot where the kings were buried; here, called a *storehouse.* 36. **Fife:** (Of which Macduff is Thane.) 40. **benison:** blessing.

ACT 3, SCENE 1°

Enter Banquo.

BANQUO:
Thou hast it now — King, Cawdor, Glamis, all
As the weird women promised, and I fear
Thou played'st most foully for 't. Yet it was said
It should not stand° in thy posterity,
But that myself should be the root and father   5
Of many kings. If there come truth from them —
As upon thee, Macbeth, their speeches shine° —
Why, by the verities on thee made good,
May they not be my oracles as well
And set me up in hope? But hush, no more.   10

Sennet° sounded. Enter Macbeth as King, Lady [Macbeth], Lennox, Ross, lords, and attendants.

MACBETH:
Here's our chief guest.
LADY MACBETH: If he had been forgotten,
It had been as a gap in our great feast
And all-thing° unbecoming.
MACBETH:
Tonight we hold a solemn° supper, sir,
And I'll request your presence.
BANQUO: Let Your Highness   15
Command° upon me, to the which my duties
Are with a most indissoluble tie
Forever knit.
MACBETH:
Ride you this afternoon?
BANQUO:
Ay, my good lord.   20
MACBETH:
We should have else desired your good advice,
Which still° hath been both grave° and prosperous,°
In this day's council; but we'll take tomorrow.
Is 't far you ride?

ACT 3, SCENE 1. **Location:** Forres. The palace. **4. stand:** stay, remain. **7. shine:** are brilliantly manifest. **s.d.** *Sennet:* trumpet call. **13. all-thing:** in every way. **14. solemn:** ceremonious. **16. Command:** lay your command. **22. still:** always. **grave:** weighty. **prosperous:** profitable.

BANQUO:

    As far, my lord, as will fill up the time   25

    Twixt this and supper. Go not my horse the better,°

    I must become a borrower of the night

    For a dark hour or twain.

MACBETH:

    Fail not our feast.

BANQUO:

    My lord, I will not.   30

MACBETH:

    We hear our bloody cousins are bestowed°

    In England and in Ireland, not confessing

    Their cruel parricide, filling their hearers

    With strange invention.° But of that tomorrow,

    When therewithal° we shall have cause of state   35

    Craving us jointly.° Hie you to horse. Adieu,

    Till you return at night. Goes Fleance with you?

BANQUO:

    Ay, my good lord. Our time does call upon 's.

MACBETH:

    I wish your horses swift and sure of foot,

    And so I do commend° you to their backs.   40

    Farewell.   *Exit Banquo.*

    Let every man be master of his time

    Till seven at night. To make society

    The sweeter welcome, we will keep ourself°

    Till suppertime alone. While° then, God be with you!   45

                  Exeunt Lords [and all but Macbeth and a Servant].

    Sirrah,° a word with you. Attend those men

    Our pleasure?

SERVANT:

    They are, my lord, without the palace gate.

MACBETH:

    Bring them before us.   *Exit Servant.*

              To be thus° is nothing,

    But° to be safely thus. — Our fears in° Banquo   50

---

26. **Go . . . better:** unless my horse makes better time than I expect.   31. **bestowed:** lodged.
34. **invention:** falsehood (i.e., that Macbeth was the murderer).   35. **therewithal:** besides
that.   35–36. **cause . . . jointly:** questions of state occupying our joint attention.   40. **commend:** commit, entrust.   44. **we . . . ourself:** I will keep to myself.   45. **While:** till.
46. **Sirrah:** (A form of address to a social inferior.)   49. **thus:** i.e., king.   50. **But:** unless.
in: concerning.

Stick deep, and in his royalty of nature°
Reigns that which would be° feared. 'Tis much he dares;
And to° that dauntless temper of his mind
He hath a wisdom that doth guide his valor
To act in safety. There is none but he   55
Whose being I do fear; and under him
My genius is rebuked,° as it is said
Mark Antony's was by Caesar.° He chid the sisters
When first they put the name of king upon me,
And bade them speak to him. Then, prophetlike,   60
They hailed him father to a line of kings.
Upon my head they placed a fruitless crown
And put a barren scepter in my grip,
Thence to be wrenched with° an unlineal° hand,
No son of mine succeeding. If 't be so,   65
For Banquo's issue have I filed° my mind;
For them the gracious Duncan have I murdered,
Put rancors° in the vessel of my peace
Only for them, and mine eternal jewel°
Given to the common enemy of man°   70
To make them kings, the seeds of Banquo kings.
Rather than so, come fate into the list,°
And champion me° to th' utterance!° — Who's there?

Enter Servant and two Murderers.

Now go to the door, and stay there till we call.   *Exit Servant.*
Was it not yesterday we spoke together?   75

MURDERERS:
It was, so please Your Highness.

MACBETH: Well then, now
Have you considered of my speeches? Know
That it was he in the times past which held you
So under fortune,° which you thought had been
Our innocent self. This I made good to you   80
In our last conference, passed in probation° with you

---

51. **royalty of nature:** natural kingly bearing.   52. **would be:** deserves to be.   53. **to:** added
to.   57. **My genius is rebuked:** my guardian spirit is daunted or abashed.   58. **Caesar:**
Octavius Caesar.   64. **with:** by.   **unlineal:** not of lineal descent from me.   66. **filed:** defiled.
68. **rancors:** malignant enemies (here visualized as a poison added to a vessel full of wholesome drink).   69. **eternal jewel:** i.e., soul.   70. **common . . . man:** i.e., devil.   72. **list:** lists,
place of combat.   73. **champion me:** fight with me in single combat.   **to th' utterance:** to the
last extremity (French, *à l'outrance*).   79. **under fortune:** down in your fortunes.   81. **passed
in probation:** went over the proof.

How you were borne in hand,° how crossed,° the instruments,°
Who wrought with them, and all things else that might
To half a soul° and to a notion° crazed
Say, "Thus did Banquo."

FIRST MURDERER: You made it known to us.   85

MACBETH:
I did so, and went further, which is now
Our point of second meeting. Do you find
Your patience so predominant in your nature
That you can let this go? Are you so gospeled°
To pray for this good man and for his issue,   90
Whose heavy hand hath bowed you to the grave
And beggared yours° forever?

FIRST MURDERER: We are men, my liege.

MACBETH:
Ay, in the catalogue ye go for° men,
As hounds and greyhounds, mongrels, spaniels, curs,
Shoughs,° water-rugs,° and demi-wolves° are clept°   95
All by the name of dogs. The valued file°
Distinguishes the swift, the slow, the subtle,
The housekeeper,° the hunter, every one
According to the gift which bounteous nature
Hath in him closed,° whereby he does receive   100
Particular addition from the bill
That writes them all alike;° and so of men.
Now, if you have a station in the file,°
Not i' the worst rank of manhood, say 't,
And I will put that business in your bosoms   105
Whose execution° takes your enemy off,
Grapples you to the heart and love of us,
Who wear our health but sickly in his life,°
Which in his death were perfect.

SECOND MURDERER: I am one, my liege,
Whom the vile blows and buffets of the world   110

---

82. **borne in hand:** deceived by false promises. **crossed:** thwarted. **instruments:** agents.
84. **To half a soul:** even to a half-wit. **notion:** mind. 89. **gospeled:** imbued with the gospel
spirit. 92. **yours:** your family. 93. **go for:** pass for, are entered for. 95. **Shoughs:** a kind of
shaggy dog. **water-rugs:** long-haired water dogs. **demi-wolves:** a crossbreed with the wolf.
clept: called. 96. **valued file:** list classified according to value. 98. **housekeeper:** watchdog.
100. **in him closed:** enclosed in him, set in him like a jewel. 101–02. **Particular . . . alike:**
particular qualification apart from the catalog that lists them all indiscriminately. 103. **file:**
military row, as in "rank and file"; see *rank* in line 104. 106. **Whose execution:** the doing of
which. 108. **in his life:** while he lives.

Hath so incensed that I am reckless what
I do to spite the world.

FIRST MURDERER: And I another,
So weary with disasters, tugged with° fortune,
That I would set° my life on any chance
To mend it or be rid on 't.

MACBETH: Both of you   115
Know Banquo was your enemy.

BOTH MURDERERS: True, my lord.

MACBETH:
So is he mine, and in such bloody distance°
That every minute of his being thrusts°
Against my near'st of life.° And though I could
With barefaced power° sweep him from my sight   120
And bid my will avouch it,° yet I must not,
For° certain friends that are both his and mine,
Whose loves I may not drop, but wail° his fall
Who° I myself struck down. And thence it is
That I to your assistance do make love,°   125
Masking the business from the common eye
For sundry weighty reasons.

SECOND MURDERER: We shall, my lord,
Perform what you command us.

FIRST MURDERER: Though our lives —

MACBETH:
Your spirits shine through you.° Within this hour at most
I will advise° you where to plant yourselves,   130
Acquaint you with the perfect spy° o' the time,
The moment on 't,° for 't must be done tonight,
And something from° the palace; always thought°
That I require a clearness.° And with him —
To leave no rubs° nor botches in the work —   135

---

113. **tugged with:** pulled about by (as in wrestling).   114. **set:** risk, stake.   117. **distance:** (1) hostility, enmity (2) interval of distance between fencers.   118. **thrusts:** (As in fencing.)   119. **near'st of life:** most vital part, the heart.   120. **With barefaced power:** by open use of my supreme royal authority.   121. **And . . . avouch it:** and use my mere wish as my justification.   122. **For:** because of, for the sake of.   123. **wail:** i.e., I must lament.   124. **Who:** whom.   125. **to . . . make love:** woo your aid.   129. **Your . . . you:** i.e., enough; I can see your determination in your faces.   130. **advise:** instruct.   131–32. **with . . . on 't:** with full and precise instructions as to when it is to be done.   **spy:** espial, observation.   133. **something from:** some distance removed from.   **thought:** being borne in mind.   134. **clearness:** freedom from suspicion.   135. **rubs:** defects, rough spots.

Fleance his son, that keeps him company,
Whose absence is no less material to me
Than is his father's, must embrace the fate
Of that dark hour. Resolve yourselves apart;°
I'll come to you anon.

BOTH MURDERERS: We are resolved, my lord.   140

MACBETH:
I'll call upon you straight. Abide within.   *Exeunt* [*Murderers*].
It is concluded. Banquo, thy soul's flight,
If it find heaven, must find it out tonight.   [*Exit.*]

ACT 3, SCENE 2°

Enter Macbeth's Lady and a Servant.

LADY MACBETH:
Is Banquo gone from court?

SERVANT:
Ay, madam, but returns again tonight.

LADY MACBETH:
Say to the King I would attend his leisure
For a few words.

SERVANT:
Madam, I will.   *Exit.* 5

LADY MACBETH:
Naught's had, all's spent,
Where our desire is got without content.°
'Tis safer to be that which we destroy
Than by destruction dwell in doubtful joy.°

Enter Macbeth.

How now, my lord? Why do you keep alone,   10
Of sorriest° fancies your companions making,
Using° those thoughts which should indeed have died
With them they think on? Things without° all remedy
Should be without regard.° What's done is done.

---

139. **Resolve yourselves apart:** make up your minds in private conference. **ACT 3, SCENE 2.**
Location: The palace. 7. **content:** contentedness. 9. **Than . . . joy:** than by destroying
achieve only an apprehensive joy. 11. **sorriest:** most despicable or wretched. 12. **Using:**
keeping company with, entertaining. 13. **without:** beyond. 14. **without regard:** not pon-
dered upon.

MACBETH:

 We have scorched° the snake, not killed it.   15
 She'll close° and be herself, whilst our poor malice°
 Remains in danger of her former tooth.°
 But let the frame of things disjoint, both the worlds suffer,°
 Ere we will eat our meal in fear and sleep
 In the affliction of these terrible dreams   20
 That shake us nightly. Better be with the dead,
 Whom we, to gain our peace, have sent to peace,°
 Than on the torture° of the mind to lie
 In restless ecstasy.° Duncan is in his grave;
 After life's fitful fever he sleeps well.   25
 Treason has done his worst; nor steel,° nor poison,
 Malice domestic,° foreign levy,° nothing
 Can touch him further.

LADY MACBETH:

 Come on,
 Gentle my lord, sleek o'er your rugged looks.°   30
 Be bright and jovial among your guests tonight.

MACBETH:

 So shall I, love, and so, I pray, be you.
 Let your remembrance apply° to Banquo;
 Present him eminence,° both with eye and tongue —
 Unsafe the while, that we   35
 Must lave our honors in these flattering streams°
 And make our faces vizards° to our hearts,
 Disguising what they are.

LADY MACBETH: You must leave this.

MACBETH:

 O, full of scorpions is my mind, dear wife!
 Thou know'st that Banquo and his Fleance lives.   40

---

15. **scorched:** slashed, cut. 16. **close:** heal, close up again. **poor malice:** feeble hostility.
17. **her former tooth:** her fang, just as before. 18. **let . . . suffer:** let the universe itself fall
apart, both heaven and earth perish. 22. **to gain . . . to peace:** to gain contentedness through
satisfied ambition, have sent to eternal rest. 23. **torture:** rack. 24. **ecstasy:** frenzy.
26. **nor steel:** neither steel. 27. **Malice domestic:** civil war. **foreign levy:** the levying of
troops abroad (against Scotland). 30. **Gentle . . . looks:** my noble lord, smooth over your
rough looks. 33. **Let . . . apply:** remember to pay special attention. 34. **eminence:** favor.
35–36. **Unsafe . . . streams:** i.e., we are unsafe at present and so must put on a show of flattering cordiality to make our reputation look clean, or, we are unsafe so long as we must flatter
thus. (*Lave* means "wash.") 37. **vizards:** masks.

LADY MACBETH:
But in them nature's copy's° not eterne.°
MACBETH:
There's° comfort yet; they are assailable.
Then be thou jocund. Ere the bat hath flown
His cloistered° flight, ere to black Hecate's° summons
The shard-borne° beetle with his drowsy hums   45
Hath rung night's yawning° peal, there shall be done
A deed of dreadful note.
LADY MACBETH: What's to be done?
MACBETH:
Be innocent of the knowledge, dearest chuck,°
Till thou applaud the deed. Come, seeling° night,
Scarf up° the tender eye of pitiful° day,   50
And with thy bloody and invisible hand
Cancel and tear to pieces that great bond°
Which keeps me pale!° Light thickens,°
And the crow° makes wing to th' rooky° wood;
Good things of day begin to droop and drowse,   55
Whiles night's black agents to their preys do rouse.°
Thou marvel'st at my words, but hold thee still.
Things bad begun make strong themselves by ill.
So, prithee, go with me.   *Exeunt.*

Act 3, Scene 3°

Enter three Murderers.

FIRST MURDERER:
But who did bid thee join with us?
THIRD MURDERER: Macbeth.

---

41. **nature's copy:** lease of life (i.e., by copyhold or lease subject to cancellation); also, the individual human being made from nature's mold.   **eterne:** perpetual.   42. **There's:** i.e., in that thought there is.   44. **cloistered:** i.e., in and among buildings.   **Hecate:** goddess of night and witchcraft, as in 2.1.53.   45. **shard-borne:** borne on shards, or horny wing cases, or, *shard-born,* bred in cow-droppings (shards).   46. **yawning:** drowsy.   48. **chuck:** (A term of endearment.)   49. **seeling:** eye-closing. (Night is pictured here as a falconer sewing up the eyes of day lest it should struggle against the deed that is to be done.)   50. **Scarf up:** blindfold.   **pitiful:** compassionate.   52. **bond:** i.e., bond by which Banquo and Fleance hold their lives from nature, or moral law against murder, or bond of prophecy.   53. **pale:** pallid from fear (with a suggestion perhaps of *paled,* "fenced in").   **thickens:** grows opaque and dim.   54. **crow:** rook.   **rooky:** full of rooks.   56. **to ... rouse:** bestir themselves to hunt their prey.   ACT 3, SCENE 3. **Location:** A park near the palace.

SECOND MURDERER: [*to the First Murderer*]
    He needs not our mistrust, since he delivers
    Our offices° and what we have to do
    To° the direction just.°
FIRST MURDERER: Then stand with us.
    The west yet glimmers with some streaks of day.   5
    Now spurs the lated° traveler apace
    To gain the timely° inn, and near approaches
    The subject of our watch.
THIRD MURDERER:
    Hark, I hear horses.
BANQUO (*within*):
    Give us a light there, ho!   10
SECOND MURDERER:
    Then 'tis he. The rest
    That are within the note of expectation°
    Already are i' the court.
FIRST MURDERER:
    His horses go about.°
THIRD MURDERER:
    Almost a mile; but he does usually —   15
    So all men do — from hence to th' palace gate
    Make it their walk.

Enter Banquo and Fleance, with a torch.

SECOND MURDERER:
    A light, a light!
THIRD MURDERER:
    'Tis he.
FIRST MURDERER:
    Stand to 't.   20
BANQUO:
    It will be rain tonight.
FIRST MURDERER:
    Let it come down! | [*They attack Banquo*]

2–3. **He . . . offices:** we need not mistrust this man, since he states exactly our duties (as told us by Macbeth). **4. To:** according to. **just:** exactly. (That is, one can tell he comes from Macbeth, since he has instructions identical to ours.) **6. lated:** belated. **7. timely:** arrived in good time. **12. within . . . expectation:** in the list of those expected. **14. go about:** i.e., can be heard as servants take them to the stables (while Banquo and Fleance, provided with a torch, walk from the palace gate to the castle).

BANQUO:
　O, treachery! Fly, good Fleance, fly, fly, fly!
　Thou mayst revenge. — O slave!　　　　　　　[*He dies. Fleance escapes.*]
THIRD MURDERER:
　Who did strike out the light?
FIRST MURDERER:　　　　　　　　Was 't not the way?°　　　　　　　25
THIRD MURDERER:
　There's but one down; the son is fled.
SECOND MURDERER:
　We have lost best half of our affair.
FIRST MURDERER:
　Well, let's away and say how much is done.　　　　　　*Exeunt.*°

ACT 3, SCENE 4°

Banquet prepared. Enter Macbeth, Lady [Macbeth], Ross, Lennox, Lords, and
attendants.

MACBETH:
　You know your own degrees;° sit down. At first
　And last,° the hearty welcome.　　　　　　　　　[*They sit.*]
LORDS:　　　　　　　　　　Thanks to Your Majesty.
MACBETH:
　Ourself will mingle with society°
　And play the humble host.
　Our hostess keeps her state,° but in best time°　　　　　　5
　We will require her welcome.°
LADY MACBETH:
　Pronounce it for me, sir, to all our friends,
　For my heart speaks they are welcome.

Enter First Murderer [to the door].

MACBETH:
　See, they encounter° thee with their hearts' thanks.
　Both sides are even.° Here I'll sit i' the midst.　　　　　　10

---

25. **way:** i.e., thing to do.　**s.d.** *Exeunt:* (Presumably, the murderers drag the body of Banquo offstage as they go.)　**ACT 3, SCENE 4. Location:** A room of state in the palace.　1. **degrees:** ranks (as a determinant of seating).　1–2. **At . . . last:** once for all.　3. **mingle with society:** i.e., leave the chair of state and circulate among the guests.　5. **keeps her state:** remains in her canopied chair of state.　**in best time:** when it is most appropriate.　6. **require her welcome:** call upon her to give the welcome.　9. **encounter:** respond to.　10. **even:** full, with equal numbers on both sides.

Be large° in mirth; anon we'll drink a measure°
The table round. [*He goes to the Murderer.*] There's blood upon thy face.

MURDERER:
'Tis Banquo's, then.

MACBETH:
'Tis better thee without than he within.°
Is he dispatched?   15

MURDERER:
My lord, his throat is cut. That I did for him.

MACBETH:
Thou art the best o' the cutthroats.
Yet he's good that did the like for Fleance;
If thou didst it, thou art the nonpareil.°

MURDERER:
Most royal sir, Fleance is scaped.   20

MACBETH:
Then comes my fit again. I had else been perfect,
Whole as the marble, founded° as the rock,
As broad and general° as the casing° air.
But now I am cabined, cribbed,° confined, bound in
To saucy° doubts and fears. But Banquo's safe?   25

MURDERER:
Ay, my good lord. Safe in a ditch he abides,
With twenty trenchèd gashes on his head,
The least a death to nature.

MACBETH: Thanks for that.
There the grown serpent lies; the worm° that's fled
Hath nature that in time will venom breed,   30
No teeth for th' present. Get thee gone. Tomorrow
We'll hear ourselves° again.   *Exit Murderer.*

LADY MACBETH: My royal lord,
You do not give the cheer.° The feast is sold
That is not often vouched, while 'tis a-making,
'Tis given with welcome.° To feed were best at home;°   35

---

11. **large:** liberal, free.   **measure:** i.e., cup filled to the brim for a toast.   14. **'Tis ... within:** it is better for you to have his blood on you than he to have it within him.   19. **the nonpareil:** without equal.   22. **founded:** firmly established.   23. **broad and general:** unconfined.   **casing:** encasing, enveloping.   24. **cribbed:** shut in.   25. **saucy:** sharp, impudent, importunate.   29. **worm:** small serpent.   32. **hear ourselves:** confer.   33. **give the cheer:** welcome your guests.   33–35. **is sold ... welcome:** seems grudgingly given, as if in return for money, unless it is often accompanied with assurances of welcome while it is in progress.   35. **To feed ... home:** mere eating is best done at home.

From thence,° the sauce to meat° is ceremony;
Meeting were bare° without it.

Enter the Ghost of Banquo, and sits in Macbeth's place.

MACBETH: Sweet remembrancer!
Now, good digestion wait on° appetite,
And health on both!
LENNOX: May 't please Your Highness sit?
MACBETH:
Here had we now our country's honor roofed°   40
Were the graced person of our Banquo present,
Who may I° rather challenge for° unkindness
Than pity for mischance.
ROSS: His absence, sir,
Lays blame upon his promise. Please 't Your Highness
To grace us with your royal company?   45
MACBETH: [*seeing his place occupied*]
The table's full.
LENNOX: Here is a place reserved, sir.
MACBETH:
Where?
LENNOX:
Here, my good lord. What is 't that moves Your Highness?
MACBETH:
Which of you have done this?
LORDS: What, my good lord?
MACBETH:
Thou canst not say I did it. Never shake   50
Thy gory locks at me.
ROSS:
Gentlemen, rise. His Highness is not well.   [*They start to rise.*]
LADY MACBETH:
Sit, worthy friends. My lord is often thus,
And hath been from his youth. Pray you, keep seat.
The fit is momentary; upon a thought°   55
He will again be well. If much you note him
You shall offend him° and extend° his passion.

---

36. **From thence:** away from home, dining in company.   **meat:** food.   37. **Meeting were
bare:** gatherings of friends would be unadorned.   38. **wait on:** attend.   40. **roofed:** under
one roof.   42. **Who may I:** whom I hope I may.   **challenge for:** reprove for.   55. **upon a
thought:** in a moment.   57. **offend him:** make him worse.   **extend:** prolong.

Feed, and regard him not. — [*She confers apart with Macbeth.*] Are you a
   man?

MACBETH:
   Ay, and a bold one, that dare look on that
   Which might appall the devil.

LADY MACBETH: O, proper stuff!°   60
   This is the very painting of your fear.
   This is the air-drawn° dagger which, you said,
   Led you to Duncan. O, these flaws° and starts,
   Impostors to° true fear, would well become°
   A woman's story at a winter's fire,   65
   Authorized by° her grandam. Shame itself!
   Why do you make such faces? When all's done,
   You look but on a stool.

MACBETH: Prithee, see there!
   Behold, look! Lo, how say you?
   Why, what care I? If thou canst nod, speak too.   70
   If charnel houses° and our graves must send
   Those that we bury back, our monuments
   Shall be the maws of kites.°   [*Exit Ghost.*]

LADY MACBETH:
   What, quite unmanned in folly?

MACBETH:
   If I stand here, I saw him.

LADY MACBETH: Fie, for shame!   75

MACBETH:
   Blood hath been shed ere now, i' th' olden time,
   Ere humane° statute purged the gentle weal;°
   Ay, and since too, murders have been performed
   Too terrible for the ear. The time has been
   That, when the brains were out, the man would die, 80
   And there an end; but now they rise again
   With twenty mortal murders° on their crowns,°

---

60. **O, proper stuff!** O, nonsense!   62. **air-drawn:** made of thin air, or floating disembodied in
space. 63. **flaws:** gusts, outbursts. 64. **to:** compared with. **become:** befit. 66. **Authorized by:** told on the authority of. 71. **charnel houses:** depositories for bones or bodies.
72–73. **our . . . kites:** i.e., we will have to leave the unburied bodies to scavenging birds of prey.
77. **Ere . . . weal:** before the institution of law cleansed the commonwealth of violence and
made it gentle. **humane:** (This spelling, interchangeable with *human,* carries both meanings:
"appertaining to humankind" and "befitting humanity.") 82. **mortal murders:** deadly
wounds. **crowns:** heads.

And push us from our stools.° This is more strange
Than such a murder is.
LADY MACBETH: My worthy lord,
Your noble friends do lack you.
MACBETH: I do forget.   85
Do not muse at me, my most worthy friends;
I have a strange infirmity, which is nothing
To those that know me. Come, love and health to all!
Then I'll sit down. Give me some wine. Fill full.   [*He is given wine.*]

Enter Ghost.

I drink to the general joy o' th' whole table,   90
And to our dear friend Banquo, whom we miss.
Would he were here! To all, and him, we thirst,°
And all to all.°
LORDS: Our duties and the pledge.°   [*They drink.*]
MACBETH: [*seeing the Ghost*]
Avaunt, and quit my sight! Let the earth hide thee!
Thy bones are marrowless, thy blood is cold;   95
Thou hast no speculation° in those eyes
Which thou dost glare with!
LADY MACBETH: Think of this, good peers,
But as a thing of custom. 'Tis no other;
Only it spoils the pleasure of the time.
MACBETH:
What man dare, I dare.   100
Approach thou like the rugged Russian bear,
The armed° rhinoceros, or th' Hyrcan° tiger;
Take any shape but that, and my firm nerves°
Shall never tremble. Or be alive again
And dare me to the desert° with thy sword.   105
If trembling I inhabit then,° protest° me
The baby of a girl.° Hence, horrible shadow!
Unreal mockery, hence! [*Exit Ghost.*] Why, so; being gone,
I am a man again. Pray you, sit still.

---

83. **push ... stools:** usurp our places at feasts (with a suggestion of usurpation of the throne.)
92. **thirst:** desire to drink.   93. **all to all:** all good wishes to all, or, let all drink to everyone
else.   **Our ... pledge:** in drinking the toast you just proposed, we offer our homage.
96. **speculation:** power of sight.   102. **armed:** armor-plated.   **Hyrcan:** of Hyrcania, in
ancient times a region near the Caspian Sea.   103. **nerves:** sinews.   105. **the desert:** some
solitary place.   106. **If ... then:** i.e., if then I tremble.   **protest:** proclaim.   107. **The baby
of a girl:** a baby girl, or, girl's doll.

LADY MACBETH:

You have displaced the mirth, broke the good meeting   110
With most admired° disorder.°

MACBETH: Can such things be,
And overcome° us like a summer's cloud,
Without our special wonder? You make me strange
Even to the disposition that I owe,°
When now I think you can behold such sights   115
And keep the natural ruby of your cheeks
When mine is blanched with fear.

ROSS: What sights, my lord?

LADY MACBETH:

I pray you, speak not. He grows worse and worse;
Question° enrages him. At once,° good night.
Stand not upon the order of your going,°   120
But go at once.°

LENNOX: Good night, and better health
Attend His Majesty!

LADY MACBETH: A kind good night to all!

Exeunt Lords [and attendants].

MACBETH:

It will have blood, they say; blood will have blood.
Stones have been known to move, and trees to speak;°
Augurs° and understood relations° have   125
By maggotpies and choughs° and rooks brought forth°
The secret'st man of blood.° What is the night?°

LADY MACBETH:

Almost at odds with morning, which is which.

MACBETH:

How sayst thou,° that Macduff denies his person
At our great bidding?

LADY MACBETH: Did you send to him, sir?   130

---

111. **admired:** wondered at.   **disorder:** lack of self-control.   112. **overcome:** come over.
113–14. **You make . . . owe:** you cause me to feel I do not know my own nature (which I had
presumed to be that of a brave man.)   119. **Question:** talk.   **At once:** to you all; now.
120. **Stand . . . going:** i.e., do not take the time to leave in ceremonious order of rank, as you
entered.   121. **at once:** all together and now.   124. **Stones . . . speak:** i.e., even inanimate
nature speaks in such a way as to reveal the unnatural act of murder.   125. **Augurs:** prophecies.
understood relations: reports able to be interpreted or understood, or the hidden ties that link
the parts of nature to one another.   126. **By . . . choughs:** by means of magpies and jackdaws.
brought forth: revealed.   127. **man of blood:** murderer.   **the night:** i.e., the time of night.
129. **How sayst thou:** what do you say to the fact.

MACBETH:
>I hear it by the way;° but I will send.
>There's not a one of them but in his house
>I keep a servant fee'd.° I will tomorrow —
>And betimes° I will — to the Weird Sisters.
>More shall they speak, for now I am bent° to know 135
>By the worst means the worst. For mine own good
>All causes° shall give way. I am in blood
>Stepped in so far that, should I wade no more,°
>Returning were° as tedious as go° o'er.
>Strange things I have in head, that will to hand, 140
>Which must be acted ere they may be scanned.°

LADY MACBETH:
>You lack the season° of all natures, sleep.

MACBETH:
>Come, we'll to sleep. My strange and self-abuse°
>Is the initiate fear° that wants hard use.°
>We are yet but young in deed. *Exeunt.* 145

Act 3, Scene 5°

Thunder. Enter the three Witches, meeting Hecate.

FIRST WITCH:
>Why, how now, Hecate? You look angerly.°

HECATE:
>Have I not reason, beldams° as you are?
>Saucy and overbold, how did you dare
>To trade and traffic with Macbeth
>In riddles and affairs of death, 5
>And I, the mistress of your charms,
>The close° contriver of all harms,
>Was never called to bear my part
>Or show the glory of our art?
>And, which is worse, all you have done 10

---

131. **by the way:** indirectly.   133. **fee'd:** i.e., paid to spy.   134. **betimes:** (1) early (2) while there is still time.   135. **bent:** determined.   137. **All causes:** all other considerations. 138. **should . . . more:** even if I were to wade no farther.   139. **were:** would be.   **go:** going. 141. **acted . . . scanned:** put into performance even before there is time to scrutinize them. 142. **season:** preservative.   143. **strange and self-abuse:** strange self-delusion.   144. **initiate fear:** fear experienced by a novice.   **wants hard use:** lacks toughening experience.   **ACT 3, SCENE 5. Location:** A heath. (This scene is probably by another author.)   1. **angerly:** angrily, angry.   2. **beldams:** hags.   7. **close:** secret.

Hath been but for a wayward son,
Spiteful and wrathful, who, as others do,
Loves for his own ends, not for you.
But make amends now. Get you gone,
And at the pit of Acheron°   15
Meet me i' the morning. Thither he
Will come to know his destiny.
Your vessels and your spells provide,
Your charms and everything beside.
I am for th' air. This night I'll spend   20
Unto a dismal° and a fatal end.
Great business must be wrought ere noon.
Upon the corner of the moon
There hangs a vaporous drop profound;°
I'll catch it ere it come to ground,   25
And that, distilled by magic sleights,
Shall raise such artificial sprites°
As by the strength of their illusion
Shall draw him on to his confusion.°
He shall spurn fate, scorn death, and bear   30
His hopes 'bove wisdom, grace, and fear.
And you all know, security°
Is mortals' chiefest enemy.   *Music and a song.*
Hark! I am called. My little spirit, see,
Sits in a foggy cloud and stays for me.   [*Exit.*]   35
                    Sing within, "Come away, come away,"° *etc.*

FIRST WITCH:
Come, let's make haste. She'll soon be back again.   *Exeunt.*

Act 3, Scene 6°

Enter Lennox and another Lord.

LENNOX:

My former speeches have but hit your thoughts,
Which can interpret farther.° Only I say

---

15. **Acheron:** the river of sorrows in Hades; here, hell itself. 21. **dismal:** disastrous, ill-
omened. 24. **profound:** i.e., heavily pendent, ready to drop off. 27. **artificial sprites:** spirits
produced by magical arts. 29. **confusion:** ruin. 32. **security:** overconfidence. s.d. **Come
away etc.:** (The song occurs in Thomas Middleton's *The Witch.*) **Act 3, Scene 6. Location:**
Somewhere in Scotland. 1–2. **My . . . farther:** what I've just said has coincided with your
own thought. I needn't say more; you can surmise the rest.

Things have been strangely borne.° The gracious Duncan
Was pitied of Macbeth; marry, he was dead.°
And the right valiant Banquo walked too late, 5
Whom you may say, if 't please you, Fleance killed,
For Fleance fled. Men must not walk too late.
Who cannot want the thought° how monstrous
It was for Malcolm and for Donalbain
To kill their gracious father? Damnèd fact!° 10
How it did grieve Macbeth! Did he not straight°
In pious° rage the two delinquents tear
That were the slaves of drink and thralls° of sleep?
Was not that nobly done? Ay, and wisely too;
For 'twould have angered any heart alive 15
To hear the men deny 't. So that I say
He has borne all things well;° and I do think
That had he Duncan's sons under his key —
As, an 't° please heaven, he shall not — they should° find
What 'twere to kill a father. So should Fleance. 20
But peace! For from broad words,° and 'cause he failed
His presence° at the tyrant's feast, I hear
Macduff lives in disgrace. Sir, can you tell
Where he bestows himself?°
LORD: The son of Duncan,
From whom this tyrant holds the due of birth,° 25
Lives in the English court, and is received
Of° the most pious Edward° with such grace
That the malevolence of fortune nothing
Takes from his high respect.° Thither Macduff
Is gone to pray the holy king, upon his aid,° 30
To wake Northumberland° and warlike Siward,
That by the help of these — with Him above
To ratify the work — we may again
Give to our tables meat,° sleep to our nights,

3. borne: carried on. 4. of: by. marry . . . dead: i.e., to be sure, this pity occurred after Duncan died, not before. 8. cannot . . . thought: can help thinking. 10. fact: deed, crime. 11. straight: straightway, at once. 12. pious: holy, loyal, sonlike. 13. thralls: slaves. 17. borne all things well: managed everything cleverly. 19. an 't: if it. should: would be sure to. 21. from broad words: on account of plain speech. 22. His presence: i.e., to be present. 24. bestows himself: is quartered, has taken refuge. 25. holds . . . birth: withholds the birthright (i.e., the Scottish crown). 27. Of: by. Edward: Edward the Confessor, King of England. 29. his high respect: the high respect paid to him. (Being out of fortune has not lessened the dignity with which Malcolm is received in England.) 30. upon his aid: in aid of Malcolm. 31. wake Northumberland: rouse the people of Northumberland. 34. meat: food.

Free from our feasts and banquets° bloody knives,   35
Do faithful homage, and receive free° honors —
All which we pine for now. And this report
Hath so exasperate the King° that he
Prepares for some attempt of war.

LENNOX:
Sent he to Macduff?   40

LORD:
He did; and with an absolute "Sir, not I,"°
The cloudy° messenger turns me° his back
And hums, as who should say,° "You'll rue the time
That clogs° me with this answer."

LENNOX: And that well might
Advise him to a caution, t' hold what distance   45
His wisdom can provide.° Some holy angel
Fly to the court of England and unfold
His message ere he come, that a swift blessing
May soon return to this our suffering country
Under° a hand accursed!   50

LORD:
I'll send my prayers with him.   *Exeunt.*

ACT 4, SCENE 1°

[*A cauldron.*] *Thunder. Enter the three Witches.*

FIRST WITCH:
Thrice the brinded° cat hath mewed.

SECOND WITCH:
Thrice, and once the hedgepig° whined.

THIRD WITCH:
Harpier° cries.° 'Tis time, 'tis time!

---

35. **Free . . . banquets:** free our feasts and banquets from.   36. **free:** freely bestowed, or, pertaining to freemen.   38. **exasperate the King:** exasperated Macbeth.   41. **with . . . I:** i.e., when Macduff answered the messenger curtly with a refusal.   42. **cloudy:** louring, scowling. **turns me:** i.e., turns. (*Me* is used colloquially for emphasis.)   43. **hums . . . say:** says "umph!" as if to say.   44. **clogs:** encumbers, loads.   45–46. **Advise . . . provide:** warn him (Macduff) to keep what safe distance he can (from Macbeth).   49–50. **suffering country Under:** country suffering under.   ACT 4, SCENE 1. **Location:** A cavern (see 3.5.15). In the middle, a boiling cauldron (provided presumably by means of the trapdoor, see 4.1.106. The trapdoor must also be used in this scene for the apparitions).   1. **brinded:** marked by streaks (as by fire), brindled.   2. **hedgepig.** hedgehog.   3. **Harpier:** (The name of a familiar spirit; probably derived from *harpy.*)   **cries:** i.e., gives the signal to begin.

FIRST WITCH:
Round about the cauldron go;
In the poisoned entrails throw.   5
Toad, that under cold stone
Days and nights has thirty-one
Sweltered venom, sleeping got,°
Boil thou first i' the charmèd pot.

ALL: [*as they dance round the cauldron*]
Double, double, toil and trouble;   10
Fire burn, and cauldron bubble.

SECOND WITCH:
Fillet° of a fenny° snake,
In the cauldron boil and bake;
Eye of newt and toe of frog,
Wool of bat and tongue of dog,   15
Adder's fork° and blindworm's° sting,
Lizard's leg and owlet's wing,
For a charm of powerful trouble,
Like a hell-broth boil and bubble.

ALL:
Double, double, toil and trouble;   20
Fire burn, and cauldron bubble.

THIRD WITCH:
Scale of dragon, tooth of wolf,
Witches' mummy,° maw and gulf°
Of the ravined° salt-sea shark,
Root of hemlock digged i' the dark,   25
Liver of blaspheming Jew,
Gall° of goat, and slips° of yew°
Slivered° in the moon's eclipse,
Nose of Turk and Tartar's lips,
Finger of birth-strangled babe   30
Ditch-delivered by a drab,°
Make the gruel thick and slab.°

7–8. **Days . . . got:** for thirty-one days and nights has exuded venom formed during sleep.
12. **Fillet:** slice. **fenny:** inhabiting fens or swamps. 16. **fork:** forked tongue. **blindworm:** slowworm, a harmless burrowing lizard. 23. **mummy:** mummified flesh made into a magical potion. **maw and gulf:** gullet and stomach. 24. **ravined:** ravenous, or glutted with prey (?). 27. **Gall:** the secretion of the liver, bile. **slips:** cuttings for grafting or planting. **yew:** (A tree often planted in churchyards and associated with mourning.) 28. **Slivered:** broken off (as a branch). 31. **Ditch . . . drab:** born in a ditch of a harlot. 32. **slab:** viscous.

Add thereto a tiger's chaudron°
For th' ingredience° of our cauldron.

ALL:

Double, double, toil and trouble;   35
Fire burn, and cauldron bubble.

SECOND WITCH:

Cool it with a baboon's blood,
Then the charm is firm and good.

Enter Hecate to the other° three Witches.

HECATE:

O, well done! I commend your pains,
And everyone shall share i' the gains.   40
And now about the cauldron sing
Like elves and fairies in a ring,
Enchanting all that you put in.°

> *Music and a song:* "Black spirits,"° *etc.*
> [*Exit Hecate.*]

SECOND WITCH:

By the pricking of my thumbs,
Something wicked this way comes.   45
    Open, locks,
    Whoever knocks!

Enter Macbeth.

MACBETH:

How how, you secret, black,° and midnight hags?
What is 't you do?

ALL: A deed without a name.

MACBETH:

I conjure you, by that which you profess,   50
Howe'er you come to know it, answer me.
Though you untie the winds and let them fight
Against the churches, though the yeasty° waves
Confound° and swallow navigation up,
Though bladed corn° be lodged° and trees blown down,   55

---

33. **chaudron:** entrails.   34. **ingredience:** contents of a mixture.   **s.d.** *other:* (Said because Hecate is a witch, too, not because more witches enter.)   **39–43. O . . . in:** (These lines are universally regarded as non-Shakespearean.)   **s.d. Black spirits etc.:** (This song is found in Middleton's *The Witch.*)   **48. black:** i.e., dealing in black magic.   **53. yeasty:** foamy.   **54. Confound:** destroy.   **55. bladed corn:** grain that is enclosed in the blade, not yet in full ear.   **lodged:** thrown down, laid flat.

Though castles topple on their warders' heads,
Though palaces and pyramids do slope°
Their heads to their foundations, though the treasure
Of nature's germens° tumble all together,
Even till destruction sicken,° answer me   60
To what I ask you.
FIRST WITCH: Speak.
SECOND WITCH: Demand.
THIRD WITCH: We'll answer.
FIRST WITCH:
Say if thou'dst rather hear it from our mouths
Or from our masters?
MACBETH: Call 'em. Let me see 'em.
FIRST WITCH:
Pour in sow's blood, that hath eaten
Her nine farrow;° grease that's sweaten°   65
From the murderer's gibbet° throw
Into the flame.
ALL: Come high or low,°
Thyself and office° deftly show!

Thunder. First Apparition, an armed Head.°

MACBETH:
Tell me, thou unknown power —
FIRST WITCH: He knows thy thought.
Hear his speech, but say thou naught.   70
FIRST APPARITION:
Macbeth! Macbeth! Macbeth! Beware Macduff,
Beware the Thane of Fife. Dismiss me. Enough.   *He descends.*°
MACBETH:
Whate'er thou art, for thy good caution, thanks;
Thou hast harped° my fear aright. But one word more —
FIRST WITCH:
He will not be commanded. Here's another,   75
More potent than the first.

---

57. **slope**: bend.   59. **nature's germens**: seed or elements from which all nature operates.
60. **sicken**: be surfeited, grow faint with horror and nausea at its own excess.   65. **nine far-row**: litter of nine.   **sweaten**: sweated.   66. **gibbet**: gallows.   67. **high or low**: of the upper
or lower air, from under the earth or in hell; or, of whatever rank.   68. **office**: function.   s.d.
armed Head: (Perhaps symbolizes the head of Macbeth cut off by Macduff and presented by
him to Malcolm, or else the head of Macduff, armed in rebellion against Macbeth.)   s.d. *He
descends:* (i.e., by means of the trapdoor.)   74. **harped**: hit, touched (as in touching a harp to
make it sound.)

Thunder. Second Apparition, a bloody Child.°

SECOND APPARITION: Macbeth! Macbeth! Macbeth!
MACBETH: Had I three ears, I'd hear thee.
SECOND APPARITION:
  Be bloody, bold, and resolute; laugh to scorn
  The power of man, for none of woman born   80
  Shall harm Macbeth.   *Descends.*
MACBETH:
  Then live, Macduff; what need I fear of thee?
  But yet I'll make assurance double sure,
  And take a bond of° fate. Thou shalt not live,
  That I may tell pale-hearted fear it lies,   85
  And sleep in spite of thunder.

Thunder. Third Apparition, a Child crowned, with a tree in his hand.°

                      What is this
  That rises like° the issue of a king
  And wears upon his baby brow the round
  And top° of sovereignty?
ALL: Listen, but speak not to 't.
THIRD APPARITION:
  Be lion-mettled, proud, and take no care   90
  Who chafes, who frets, or where conspirers are.
  Macbeth shall never vanquished be until
  Great Birnam Wood to high Dunsinane Hill
  Shall come against him.   *Descends.*
MACBETH: That will never be.
  Who can impress° the forest, bid the tree   95
  Unfix his earthbound root? Sweet bodements,° good!
  Rebellious dead,° rise never till the wood
  Of Birnam rise, and our high-placed Macbeth
  Shall live the lease of nature,° pay his breath
  To time and mortal custom.° Yet my heart   100

---

s.d. *bloody Child:* (Symbolizes Macduff untimely ripped from his mother's womb; see
5.8.15–16.)   84. **take a bond of:** get a guarantee from (i.e., by killing Macduff, to make doubly
sure he can do no harm).   s.d. *Child . . . hand:* (Symbolizes Malcolm, the royal child; the tree
anticipates the cutting of boughs in Birnam Wood, 5.4.)   87. **like:** in the likeness of.
88–89. **round And top:** crown.   95. **impress:** press into service, like soldiers.   96. **bodements:** prophecies.   97. **Rebellious dead!** i.e., Banquo and his lineage (?).   99. **lease of
nature:** natural period, full life span.   100. **mortal custom:** death, the common lot of humanity.

Throbs to know one thing. Tell me, if your art
Can tell so much: shall Banquo's issue ever
Reign in this kingdom?

ALL: Seek to know no more.

MACBETH:
I will be satisfied. Deny me this,
And an eternal curse fall on you! Let me know.   105

[The cauldron descends.] Hautboys.
Why sinks that cauldron? And what noise° is this?

FIRST WITCH:
Show!

SECOND WITCH:
Show!

THIRD WITCH:
Show!

ALL:
Show his eyes, and grieve his heart;   110
Come like shadows, so depart!

A show of eight Kings° and Banquo last; [the eighth King] with a glass° in his hand.

MACBETH:
Thou art too like the spirit of Banquo. Down!
Thy crown does sear mine eyeballs. And thy hair,
Thou other° gold-bound brow, is like the first.
A third is like the former. Filthy hags,   115
Why do you show me this? A fourth? Start,° eyes!
What, will the line stretch out to th' crack of doom?°
Another yet? A seventh? I'll see no more.
And yet the eighth appears, who bears a glass
Which shows me many more; and some I see   120
That twofold balls° and treble scepters° carry.
Horrible sight! Now I see 'tis true,
For the blood-boltered° Banquo smiles upon me
And points at them for his.° *[The apparitions vanish.]* What, is this so?

---

106. **noise:** music. **s.d.** *eight Kings:* (Banquo was the supposed ancestor of the Stuart dynasty, ending in King James VI of Scotland and James I of England, the *eighth King* here.) *glass:* (magic) mirror (also in line 119). 114. **other:** i.e., second. 116. **Start:** bulge from their sockets. 117. **th' crack of doom:** the thunder-peal of Doomsday at the end of time. 121. **twofold balls:** (A probable reference to the double coronation of James at Scone and Westminster, as King of England and Scotland.) **treble scepters:** (Probably refers to James's assumed title as King of Great Britain, France, and Ireland.) 123. **blood-boltered:** having his hair matted with blood. 124. **for his:** as his descendants.

FIRST WITCH:
Ay, sir, all this is so. But why   125
Stands Macbeth thus amazedly?°
Come, sisters, cheer we up his sprites°
And show the best of our delights.
I'll charm the air to give a sound,
While you perform your antic round,°   130
That this great king may kindly say
Our duties did his welcome pay.°

Music. The Witches dance, and vanish.

MACBETH:
Where are they? Gone? Let this pernicious hour
Stand aye accursèd in the calendar!
Come in, without there!

Enter Lennox.

LENNOX: What's Your Grace's will?   135
MACBETH:
Saw you the Weird Sisters?
LENNOX: No, my lord.
MACBETH:
Came they not by you?
                              No, indeed, my lord.
MACBETH:
Infected be the air whereon they ride,
And damned all those that trust them! I did hear
The galloping of horse.° Who was 't came by?   140
LENNOX:
'Tis two or three, my lord, that bring you word
Macduff is fled to England.
MACBETH: Fled to England!
LENNOX:
Ay, my good lord.
MACBETH: [*aside*]
Time, thou anticipat'st° my dread exploits.
The flighty° purpose never is o'ertook   145

125–32. Ay . . . pay: (These lines are assumed to have been written by someone other than Shakespeare.) 126. amazedly: stunned. 127. sprites: spirits. 130. antic round: grotesque dance in a circle. 132. pay: repay. 140. horse: horses. 144. thou anticipat'st: you forestall (since, by allowing time to pass without my acting, I have lost an opportunity). 145. flighty: fleeting.

Unless the deed go with it.° From this moment
The very firstlings of my heart shall be
The firstlings of my hand.° And even now,
To crown my thoughts with acts, be it thought and done:
The castle of Macduff I will surprise,°   150
Seize upon Fife, give to th' edge o' the sword
His wife, his babes, and all unfortunate souls
That trace him in his line.° No boasting like a fool;
This deed I'll do before this purpose cool.
But no more sights! — Where are these gentlemen?   155
Come, bring me where they are.   *Exeunt.*

ACT 4, SCENE 2°

Enter Macduff's Wife, her Son, and Ross.

LADY MACDUFF:
  What had he done to make him fly the land?
ROSS:
  You must have patience, madam.
LADY MACDUFF: He had none.
  His flight was madness. When our actions do not,
  Our fears do make us traitors.°
ROSS: You know not
  Whether it was his wisdom or his fear.   5
LADY MACDUFF:
  Wisdom? To leave his wife, to leave his babes,
  His mansion, and his titles° in a place
  From whence himself does fly? He loves us not,
  He wants the natural touch;° for the poor wren,
  The most diminutive of birds, will fight,   10
  Her young ones in her nest,° against the owl.
  All is the fear and nothing is the love,
  As little is the wisdom, where the flight
  So runs against all reason.

146. Unless . . . it: unless the execution of the deed accompanies the conception of it immediately.   147–48. The very . . . hand: the first-born promptings of my heart will be the purposes I will first act upon.   150. surprise: seize without warning.   153. trace . . . line: follow him in the line of inheritance.   ACT 4, SCENE 2. Location: Fife. Macduff's castle.   3–4. When . . . traitors: even when we have committed no treasonous act, our fearful responses make us look guilty (since fleeing to the English court is in itself treasonous).   7. titles: possessions to which he has title.   9. wants . . . touch: lacks the natural instinct (to protect one's family).   11. Her . . . nest: when her young ones are in the nest.

ROSS: My dearest coz,°
I pray you, school° yourself. But, for° your husband,   15
He is noble, wise, judicious, and best knows
The fits o' the season.° I dare not speak much further,
But cruel are the times when we are traitors
And do not know ourselves,° when we hold rumor
From what we fear,° yet know not what we fear,   20
But float upon a wild and violent sea
Each way and none.° I take my leave of you;
Shall° not be long but° I'll be here again.
Things at the worst will cease, or else climb upward
To what they were before. — My pretty cousin,   25
Blessing upon you!

LADY MACDUFF:
Fathered he is, and yet he's fatherless.

ROSS:
I am so much a fool, should I stay longer
It would be my disgrace and your discomfort.°
I take my leave at once.   *Exit Ross.*   30

LADY MACDUFF:
Sirrah,° your father's dead;
And what will you do now? How will you live?

SON:
As birds do, Mother.

LADY MACDUFF: What, with worms and flies?

SON:
With what I get, I mean; and so do they.

LADY MACDUFF:
Poor bird! Thou'dst never fear   35
The net nor lime,° the pitfall nor the gin.°

SON:
Why should I, Mother? Poor birds they are not set for.°
My father is not dead, for all your saying.

---

14. **coz:** kinswoman.   15. **school:** control.   **for:** as for.   17. **fits o' the season:** violent convulsions of the time.   18–19. **are traitors . . . ourselves:** are accused of treason without recognizing ourselves as such, or are alienated from one another by a climate of fear and suspected treason.   19–20. **hold . . . From what we fear:** believe every fearful rumor on the basis of what we fear might be.   22. **Each . . . none:** being tossed this way and that without any real progress.   23. **Shall:** it shall.   **but:** before.   29. **It . . . discomfort:** I should disgrace my manhood by weeping and cause you distress.   31. **Sirrah:** (Here, an affectionate form of address to a child.)   36. **lime:** birdlime (a sticky substance put on branches to snare birds). **gin:** snare.   37. **Poor . . . for:** i.e., traps are not set for *poor* birds, as you call me.

LADY MACDUFF:
Yes, he is dead. How wilt thou do for a father?

SON:
Nay, how will you do for a husband?   40

LADY MACDUFF:
Why, I can buy me twenty at any market.

SON:
Then you'll buy 'em to sell again.

LADY MACDUFF:
Thou speak'st with all thy wit,
And yet, i' faith, with wit enough for thee.

SON:
Was my father a traitor, Mother?   45

LADY MACDUFF:
Ay, that he was.

SON:
What is a traitor?

LADY MACDUFF:
Why, one that swears and lies.°

SON:
And be all traitors that do so?

LADY MACDUFF:
Every one that does so is a traitor,   50
And must be hanged.

SON:
And must they all be hanged that swear and lie?

LADY MACDUFF:
Every one.

SON:
Who must hang them?

LADY MACDUFF:
Why, the honest men.   55

SON: Then the liars and swearers are fools, for there are liars and swearers
enough to beat the honest men and hang up them.

LADY MACDUFF: Now, God help thee, poor monkey! But how wilt thou
do for a father?

SON: If he were dead, you'd weep for him; if you would not, it were a good   60
sign that I should quickly have a new father.

LADY MACDUFF: Poor prattler, how thou talk'st!

---

48. **swears and lies:** swears an oath and breaks it (though the boy may understand *swears* to
mean "uses profanity").

Enter a Messenger.

MESSENGER:
    Bless you, fair dame! I am not to you known,
    Though in your state of honor° I am perfect.°
    I doubt° some danger does approach you nearly.   65
    If you will take a homely° man's advice,
    Be not found here. Hence with your little ones!
    To fright you thus, methinks, I am too savage;
    To do worse° to you were fell° cruelty,
    Which is too nigh your person.° Heaven preserve you!   70
    I dare abide no longer.   *Exit Messenger.*
LADY MACDUFF: Whither should I fly?
    I have done no harm. But I remember now
    I am in this earthly world, where to do harm
    Is often laudable, to do good sometimes
    Accounted dangerous folly. Why then, alas,   75
    Do I put up that womanly defense
    To say I have done no harm?

Enter Murderers.

                 What are these faces?
FIRST MURDERER: Where is your husband?
LADY MACDUFF:
    I hope in no place so unsanctified
    Where such as thou mayst find him.
FIRST MURDERER: He's a traitor.   80
SON:
    Thou liest, thou shag-haired villain!
FIRST MURDERER: What, you egg?   *[He stabs him.]*
    Young fry° of treachery!
SON: He has killed me, Mother.
    Run away, I pray you!   *[He dies.]*
               Exit [Lady Macduff] crying "Murder!"
           [followed by the Murderers with the Son's body].

---

64. **in . . . honor:** with your honorable state. **perfect:** perfectly acquainted. **65. doubt:** fear. **66. homely:** plain. **69. To do worse:** i.e., actually to harm you. **fell:** savage. **70. Which . . . person:** i.e., which savage cruelty is all too near at hand. **82. fry:** spawn, progeny.

ACT 4, SCENE 3°

Enter Malcolm and Macduff.

MALCOLM:
Let us seek out some desolate shade, and there
Weep our sad bosoms empty.

MACDUFF: Let us rather
Hold fast the mortal° sword, and like good men
Bestride° our downfall'n birthdom.° Each new morn
New widows howl, new orphans cry, new sorrows   5
Strike heaven on the face, that it resounds°
As if it felt with Scotland and yelled out
Like syllable of dolor.°

MALCOLM: What I believe, I'll wail;
What know, believe;° and what I can redress,
As I shall find the time to friend,° I will.   10
What you have spoke it may be so, perchance.
This tyrant, whose sole° name blisters our tongues,
Was once thought honest. You have loved him well;
He hath not touched you yet.° I am young;° but something
You may deserve of him through me,° and wisdom°   15
To offer up a weak, poor, innocent lamb
T' appease an angry god.

MACDUFF:
I am not treacherous.

MALCOLM:
But Macbeth is.
A good and virtuous nature may recoil°   20
In an imperial charge.° But I shall crave your pardon.
That which you are my thoughts cannot transpose;°

ACT 4, SCENE 3. **Location:** England. Before King Edward the Confessor's palace.   3. **mortal:** deadly.   4. **Bestride:** stand over in defense.   **birthdom:** native land.   6. **that it resounds:** so that it echoes.   7–8. **As . . . dolor:** as if heaven, feeling itself the blow delivered to Scotland, cried out with a similar cry of pain.   8–9. **What . . . believe:** i.e., what I believe to be amiss in Scotland I will grieve for, and anything I am certain to be true I will believe. (But one must be cautious in these duplicitous times.)   10. **to friend:** opportune, congenial.   12. **sole:** mere.   14. **He . . . yet:** i.e., the fact that Macbeth hasn't hurt you yet makes me suspicious of your loyalties.   **young:** i.e., inexperienced.   14–15. **something . . . me:** i.e., you may win favor with Macbeth by delivering me to him.   15. **wisdom:** i.e., it would be worldly-wise.   20. **recoil:** give way, fall back (as in the firing of a gun).   21. **In . . . charge:** under pressure from royal command. (*Charge* puns on the idea of a quantity of powder and shot for a gun, as in *recoil.*)   22. **That . . . transpose:** my suspicious thoughts cannot change you from what you are, cannot make you evil.

Angels are bright still, though the brightest° fell.
Though all things foul would wear the brows of grace,
Yet grace must still look so.°

MACDUFF: I have lost my hopes.°   25

MALCOLM:
Perchance even there° where I did find my doubts.°
Why in that rawness° left you wife and child,
Those precious motives,° those strong knots of love,
Without leave-taking? I pray you,
Let not my jealousies be your dishonors,   30
But mine own safeties.° You may be rightly just,
Whatever I shall think.

MACDUFF: Bleed, bleed, poor country!
Great tyranny, lay thou thy basis° sure,
For goodness dare not check° thee; wear thou thy wrongs,°
The title is affeered!° Fare thee well, lord.   35
I would not be the villain that thou think'st
For the whole space that's in the tyrant's grasp,
And the rich East to boot.°

MALCOLM: Be not offended.
I speak not as in absolute fear° of you.
I think our country sinks beneath the yoke;   40
It weeps, it bleeds, and each new day a gash
Is added to her wounds. I think withal°
There would be hands uplifted in my right;°
And here from gracious England° have I offer
Of goodly thousands. But, for all this,   45
When I shall tread upon the tyrant's head,
Or wear it on my sword, yet my poor country
Shall have more vices than it had before,

23. **the brightest:** i.e., Lucifer.   24–25. **Though . . . so:** even though evil puts on the appearance of good so often as to cast that appearance into deep suspicion, yet goodness must go on looking and acting like itself.   25. **hopes:** i.e., hopes of persuading Malcolm to lead the cause against Macbeth.   26. **Perchance even there:** i.e., perhaps in that same mistrustful frame of mind.   **doubts:** i.e., fears such as that Macduff may covertly be on Macbeth's side.   27. **rawness:** unprotected condition. (Malcolm suggests that Macduff's leaving his family unprotected could be construed as more evidence of his not having anything to fear from Macbeth.)   28. **motives:** persons inspiring you to cherish and protect them; incentives to offer strong protection.   30–31. **Let . . . safeties:** may it be true that my suspicions of your lack of honor are founded only in my own wariness.   33. **basis:** foundation.   34. **check:** rebuke, call to account.   **wear . . . wrongs:** continue to enjoy your wrongfully gained powers.   35. **affeered:** confirmed, certified.   38. **to boot:** in addition.   39. **absolute fear:** complete mistrust.   42. **withal:** in addition.   43. **right:** cause.   44. **England:** i.e., the King of England.

More suffer, and more sundry° ways than ever,
By him that shall succeed.

MACDUFF: What should he be?°   50

MALCOLM:
It is myself I mean, in whom I know
All the particulars of vice so grafted°
That, when they shall be opened,° black Macbeth
Will seem as pure as snow, and the poor state
Esteem him as a lamb, being compared   55
With my confineless harms.°

MACDUFF: Not in the legions
Of horrid hell can come a devil more damned
In evils to top° Macbeth.

MALCOLM: I grant him bloody,
Luxurious,° avaricious, false, deceitful,
Sudden,° malicious, smacking of every sin   60
That has a name. But there's no bottom, none,
In my voluptuousness. Your wives, your daughters,
Your matrons, and your maids could not fill up
The cistern of my lust, and my desire
All continent° impediments would o'erbear   65
That did oppose my will.° Better Macbeth
Than such an one to reign.

MACDUFF: Boundless intemperance
In nature° is a tyranny; it hath been
Th' untimely emptying of the happy throne
And fall of many kings. But fear not yet°   70
To take upon you what is yours. You may
Convey° your pleasures in a spacious plenty,
And yet seem cold;° the time you may so hoodwink.°
We have willing dames enough. There cannot be
That vulture in you to devour so many   75
As will to greatness dedicate themselves,
Finding it so inclined.

---

49. **more sundry:** in more various. 50. **What . . . be?:** whom could you possibly mean? 52. **grafted:** (1) engrafted, indissolubly mixed (2) grafted like a plant that will then *open* or unfold. 53. **opened:** unfolded (like a bud). 56. **my confineless harms:** the boundless injuries I shall inflict. 58. **top:** surpass. 59. **Luxurious:** lecherous. 60. **Sudden:** violent, passionate. 65. **continent:** (1) chaste (2) restraining, containing. 66. **will:** lust (also in line 89). 68. **nature:** human nature. 70. **yet:** nevertheless. 72. **Convey:** manage with secrecy. 73. **cold:** chaste. **the time . . . hoodwink:** you may thus deceive the age. **hoodwink:** blindfold.

MALCOLM: With this there grows
In my most ill-composed affection° such
A stanchless° avarice that, were I king,
I should cut off the nobles for their lands,   80
Desire his° jewels and this other's° house,
And my more-having would be as a sauce
To make me hunger more, that° I should forge
Quarrels unjust against the good and loyal,
Destroying them for wealth.
MACDUFF: This avarice   85
Sticks deeper, grows with more pernicious root
Than summer-seeming° lust, and it hath been
The sword° of our slain kings. Yet do not fear;
Scotland hath foisons° to fill up your will
Of your mere own.° All these are portable,°   90
With other graces weighed.°
MALCOLM:
But I have none. The king-becoming graces,
As justice, verity, temperance, stableness,
Bounty, perseverance, mercy, lowliness,°
Devotion, patience, courage, fortitude,   95
I have no relish° of them, but abound
In the division° of each several° crime,
Acting it many ways. Nay, had I power, I should
Pour the sweet milk of concord into hell,
Uproar° the universal peace, confound   100
All unity on earth.
MACDUFF: O Scotland, Scotland!
MALCOLM:
If such a one be fit to govern, speak.
I am as I have spoken.
MACDUFF: Fit to govern?
No, not to live. O nation miserable,
With an untitled° tyrant bloody-sceptered,   105

---

78. **ill-composed affection:** evil disposition.   79. **stanchless:** insatiable.   81. **his:** one man's. **this other's:** another's.   83. **that:** so that.   87. **summer-seeming:** appropriate to youth (and lessening in later years).   88. **sword:** i.e., cause of overthrow.   89. **foisons:** resources, plenty. 90. **Of . . . own:** out of your own royal estates alone.   **portable:** bearable.   91. **weighed:** counterbalanced.   94. **lowliness:** humility.   96. **relish:** flavor or trace.   97. **division:** subdivisions, various possible forms.   **several:** separate.   100. **Uproar:** throw into an uproar. 105. **untitled:** lacking rightful title, usurping.

When shalt thou see thy wholesome days again,
Since that the truest issue of thy throne
By his own interdiction° stands accurst
And does blaspheme his breed?° Thy royal father
Was a most sainted king; the queen that bore thee,   110
Oft'ner upon her knees than on her feet,
Died every day she lived.° Fare thee well.
These evils thou repeat'st upon thyself
Hath banished me from Scotland. O my breast,°
Thy hope ends here!
MALCOLM: Macduff, this noble passion,   115
Child of integrity,° hath from my soul
Wiped the black scruples, reconciled my thoughts
To thy good truth and honor. Devilish Macbeth
By many of these trains° hath sought to win me
Into his power, and modest wisdom plucks me°   120
From overcredulous haste. But God above
Deal between thee and me! For even now
I put myself to thy direction and
Unspeak my own detraction,° here abjure
The taints and blames I laid upon myself   125
For° strangers to my nature. I am yet
Unknown to woman,° never was forsworn,
Scarcely have coveted what was mine own,
At no time broke my faith, would not betray
The devil to his fellow, and delight   130
No less in truth than life. My first false speaking
Was this upon° myself. What I am truly
Is thine and my poor country's to command —
Whither indeed, before thy here-approach,
Old Siward with ten thousand warlike men,   135
Already at a point,° was setting forth.
Now we'll together; and the chance of goodness
Be like our warranted quarrel!° — Why are you silent?

---

108. **interdiction:** debarring of self.   109. **does blaspheme his breed:** defames his breeding, i.e., is a disgrace to his royal lineage.   112. **Died . . . lived:** lived a life of daily mortification.   114. **breast:** heart.   116. **Child of integrity:** a product of your integrity of spirit.   119. **trains:** plots, artifices.   120. **modest . . . me:** wise prudence holds me back.   124. **mine own detraction:** my detraction of myself.   126. **For:** as.   127. **Unknown to woman:** a virgin.   132. **upon:** against.   136. **at a point:** prepared.   137–38. **the chance . . . quarrel:** may the chance of success be proportionate to the justice of our cause.

MACDUFF:
Such welcome and unwelcome things at once
'Tis hard to reconcile.   140

Enter a Doctor.

MALCOLM:
Well, more anon. — Comes the King forth, I pray you?
DOCTOR:
Ay, sir. There are a crew of wretched souls
That stay° his cure. Their malady convinces°
The great essay of art;° but at his touch —
Such sanctity hath heaven given his hand —   145
They presently° amend.
MALCOLM: I thank you, Doctor.   *Exit [Doctor].*
MACDUFF:
What's the disease he means?
MALCOLM: 'Tis called the evil.°
A most miraculous work in this good king,
Which often, since my here-remain° in England,
I have seen him do. How he solicits° heaven   150
Himself best knows; but strangely-visited° people,
All swoll'n and ulcerous, pitiful to the eye,
The mere° despair of surgery, he cures,
Hanging a golden stamp° about their necks
Put on with holy prayers; and 'tis spoken,   155
To the succeeding royalty he leaves
The healing benediction.° With this strange virtue°
He hath a heavenly gift of prophecy,
And sundry blessings hang about his throne
That speak him full of grace.

Enter Ross.

MACDUFF: See who comes here.   160
MALCOLM:
My countryman,° but yet I know° him not.

---

143. **stay:** wait for. **convinces:** conquers.   144. **essay of art:** efforts of medical skill.
146. **presently:** immediately.   147. **evil:** i.e., scrofula, supposedly cured by the royal touch;
James I claimed this power.   149. **here-remain:** stay.   150. **solicits:** prevails by prayer with.
151. **strangely-visited:** afflicted by strange diseases.   153. **mere:** utter.   154. **stamp:** minted
coin.   156–57. **To . . . benediction:** to his royal successors he bequeathes this healing blessedness.   157. **virtue:** healing power.   161. **My countryman:** (So identified by his dress.)   **know:**
recognize.

MACDUFF:

My ever-gentle° cousin, welcome hither.

MALCOLM:

I know him now. Good God betimes° remove
The means that makes us strangers!

ROSS: Sir, amen.

MACDUFF:

Stands Scotland where it did?

ROSS: Alas, poor country   165
Almost afraid to know itself. It cannot
Be called our mother, but our grave; where nothing
But who° knows nothing is once° seen to smile;
Where sighs and groans and shrieks that rend the air
Are made, not marked;° where violent sorrow seems   170
A modern ecstasy.° The dead man's knell
Is there scarce asked for who, and good men's lives
Expire before the flowers° in their caps,
Dying or ere they sicken.°

MACDUFF: O, relation°
Too nice,° and yet too true!

MALCOLM: What's the newest grief?   175

ROSS:

That of an hour's age doth hiss° the speaker;
Each minute teems° a new one.

MACDUFF: How does my wife?

ROSS:

Why, well.°

MACDUFF: And all my children?

ROSS: Well too.

MACDUFF:

The tyrant has not battered at their peace?

ROSS:

No, they were well at peace when I did leave 'em.   180

MACDUFF:

Be not niggard of your speech. How goes 't?

---

162. **gentle:** noble.   163. **betimes:** speedily.   167–68. **nothing But who:** nobody except a person who.   168. **once:** ever.   170. **marked:** noticed (because they are so common).   171. **modern ecstasy:** commonplace emotion.   173. **flowers:** (Often worn in Elizabethan caps.)   174. **or ere they sicken:** before they have had time to fall ill.   **relation:** report.   175. **nice:** minutely accurate, elaborately phrased.   176. **hiss:** cause to be hissed (for repeating stale news).   177. **teems:** teems with, yields.   178. **well:** (Ross quibbles, in his reluctance to tell the bad news, on the saying that "the dead are well," i.e., at rest.)

ROSS:

When I came hither to transport the tidings
Which I have heavily° borne, there ran a rumor
Of many worthy fellows that were out,°
Which was to my belief witnessed the rather°   185
For that° I saw the tyrant's power° afoot.
Now is the time of help. [*To Malcolm.*] Your eye in Scotland
Would create soldiers, make our women fight,
To doff° their dire distresses.

MALCOLM: Be 't their comfort
We are coming thither. Gracious England° hath   190
Lent us good Siward and ten thousand men;
An older and a better soldier none°
That Christendom gives out.°

ROSS: Would I could answer
This comfort with the like! But I have words
That would° be howled out in the desert air,   195
Where hearing should not latch° them.

MACDUFF: What concern they?
The general cause? Or is it a fee-grief°
Due to° some single breast?

ROSS: No mind that's honest
But in it shares some woe, though the main part
Pertains to you alone.

MACDUFF: If it be mine,   200
Keep it not from me; quickly let me have it.

ROSS:

Let not your ears despise my tongue forever,
Which shall possess them with° the heaviest sound
That ever yet they heard.

MACDUFF: Hum! I guess at it.

ROSS:

Your castle is surprised, your wife and babes   205
Savagely slaughtered. To relate the manner

---

183. **heavily:** sadly.   184. **Of . . . out:** i.e., that many worthy Scots had taken up arms in rebellion against tyranny.   185. **witnessed the rather:** made the more believable.   186. **For that:** because, in that.   **power:** army.   189. **doff:** put off, get rid of.   190. **Gracious England:** i.e., Edward the Confessor.   192. **none:** there is none.   193. **gives out:** tells of, proclaims.   195. **would:** should.   196. **latch:** catch (the sound of).   197. **fee-grief:** a grief with an individual owner, having absolute ownership.   198. **Due to:** i.e., owned by.   203. **possess them with:** put them in possession of.

Were, on the quarry° of these murdered deer,
To add the death of you.

MALCOLM: Merciful heaven!
What, man, ne'er pull your hat° upon your brows;
Give sorrow words. The grief that does not speak   210
Whispers° the o'erfraught° heart and bids it break.

MACDUFF:
My children too?

ROSS: Wife, children, servants, all
That could be found.

MACDUFF: And I must° be from thence!
My wife killed too?

ROSS: I have said.

MALCOLM: Be comforted.
Let's make us medicines of our great revenge   215
To cure this deadly grief.

MACDUFF:
He has no children.° All my pretty ones?
Did you say all? O hell-kite! All?
What, all my pretty chickens and their dam
At one fell swoop?°   220

MALCOLM:
Dispute it° like a man.

MACDUFF:
I shall do so;
But I must also feel it as a man.
I cannot but remember such things were,
That were most precious to me. Did heaven look on   225
And would not take their part? Sinful Macduff,
They were all struck for thee!° Naught° that I am,
Not for their own demerits, but for mine,
Fell slaughter on their souls. Heaven rest them now!

MALCOLM:
Be this the whetstone of your sword. Let grief   230
Convert° to anger; blunt not the heart, enrage it.

---

207. **quarry:** heap of slaughtered deer at a hunt (with a pun on *dear, deer*).   209. **pull your hat:**
(A conventional gesture of grief.)   211. **Whispers:** whispers to.   **o'erfraught:** overburdened.
213. **must:** had to.   217. **He has no children:** (Referring either to Macbeth, who must not be
a father if he can do such a thing, or, to Malcolm, who speaks comfortingly without knowing what such a loss feels like to a father.)   220. **fell swoop:** cruel swoop of the *hell-kite,*
bird of prey from hell (with a suggestion too of swoopstake, sweepstake).   221. **Dispute it:**
struggle against.   227. **for thee:** i.e., as divine punishment for your sins.   **Naught:** wicked.
231. **Convert:** change.

MACDUFF:
O, I could play the woman with mine eyes
And braggart with my tongue! But, gentle heavens,
Cut short all intermission.° Front to front°
Bring thou this fiend of Scotland and myself;   235
Within my sword's length set him. If he scape,
Heaven forgive him too!°

MALCOLM: This tune goes manly.
Come, go we to the King. Our power° is ready;
Our lack is nothing but our leave.° Macbeth
Is ripe for shaking, and the powers above   240
Put on their instruments.° Receive what cheer you may.
The night is long that never finds the day.   *Exeunt.*

ACT 5, SCENE 1°

Enter a Doctor of Physic and a Waiting-Gentlewoman.

DOCTOR: I have two nights watched with you, but can perceive no truth in
your report. When was it she last walked?

GENTLEWOMAN: Since His Majesty went into the field, I have seen her
rise from her bed, throw her nightgown upon her, unlock her closet,° take
forth paper, fold it, write upon 't, read it, afterwards seal it, and again   5
return to bed; yet all this while in a most fast sleep.

DOCTOR: A great perturbation in nature, to receive at once the benefit of
sleep and do the effects of watching!° In this slumbery agitation,° besides
her walking and other actual performances, what, at any time, have you
heard her say?   10

GENTLEWOMAN: That, sir, which I will not report after her.

DOCTOR: You may to me, and 'tis most meet° you should.

GENTLEWOMAN: Neither to you nor anyone, having no witness to confirm
my speech.

Enter Lady [Macbeth], with a taper.

---

234. **intermission:** delay, interval.   **Front to front:** face to face.   236–37. **If . . . too:** if I let
him escape, may he find forgiveness not only from me but from Heaven itself! (This is a condition that Macbeth will not allow to happen.)   238. **power:** army.   239. **Our . . . leave:** we
need only to take our leave (of the English King).   241. **Put . . . instruments:** Set us on as
their agents, or, arm themselves.   ACT 5, SCENE 1. **Location:** Dunsinane. Macbeth's castle.
4. **closet:** chest or desk.   8. **effects of watching:** deeds characteristic of waking.   **agitation:**
activity.   12. **meet:** suitable.

Lo you, here she comes! This is her very guise, and, upon my life, fast 15
asleep. Observe her. Stand close.° [*They stand aside.*]

DOCTOR: How came she by that light?

GENTLEWOMAN: Why, it stood by her. She has light by her continually.
'Tis her command.

DOCTOR: You see her eyes are open. 20

GENTLEWOMAN: Ay, but their sense are shut.

DOCTOR: What is it she does now? Look how she rubs her hands.

GENTLEWOMAN: It is an accustomed action with her to seem thus washing
her hands. I have known her continue in this a quarter of an hour.

LADY MACBETH: Yet here's a spot. 25

DOCTOR: Hark, she speaks. I will set down what comes from her, to satisfy°
my remembrance the more strongly.

LADY MACBETH: Out, damned spot! Out, I say! One — two — why then,
'tis time to do 't. Hell is murky. — Fie, my lord, fie, a soldier, and afeard?
What need we fear who knows it, when none can call our power to 30
account? Yet who would have thought the old man to have had so much
blood in him?

DOCTOR: Do you mark that?

LADY MACBETH: The Thane of Fife had a wife. Where is she now? —
What, will these hands ne'er be clean? — No more o' that, my lord, no 35
more o' that; you mar all with this starting.°

DOCTOR: Go to,° go to. You have known what you should not.

GENTLEWOMAN: She has spoke what she should not, I
am sure of that. Heaven knows what she has known.

LADY MACBETH: Here's the smell of the blood still. All the perfumes of 40
Arabia will not sweeten this little hand. O, o, o!

DOCTOR: What a sigh is there! The heart is sorely charged.°

GENTLEWOMAN: I would not have such a heart in my bosom for the
dignity° of the whole body.

DOCTOR: Well, well, well. 45

GENTLEWOMAN: Pray God it be, sir.°

DOCTOR: This disease is beyond my practice. Yet I have known those
which have walked in their sleep who have died holily in their beds.

LADY MACBETH: Wash your hands, put on your nightgown; look not so
pale! I tell you yet again, Banquo's buried. He cannot come out on 's° 50
grave.

---

16. **close:** concealed.   26. **satisfy:** confirm, support.   36. **this starting:** these startled movements.   37. **Go to:** (An exclamation of reproof, directed at Lady Macbeth.)   42. **sorely
charged:** heavily burdened.   44. **dignity:** worth, value.   46. **Pray . . . sir:** pray God it will turn
out well, as you say, sir (playing on the Doctor's "*Well, well,*" i.e., "dear, dear").   50. **on 's:** of his.

DOCTOR: Even so?

LADY MACBETH: To bed, to bed! There's knocking at the gate. Come,
come, come, come, give me your hand. What's done cannot be undone.
To bed, to bed, to bed!   *Exit Lady.*   55

DOCTOR: Will she go now to bed?

GENTLEWOMAN: Directly.

DOCTOR:

Foul whisperings are abroad. Unnatural deeds
Do breed unnatural troubles. Infected minds
To their deaf pillows will discharge their secrets.   60
More needs she the divine than the physician.
God, God forgive us all! Look after her;
Remove from her the means of all annoyance,°
And still° keep eyes upon her. So, good night.
My mind she has mated,° and amazed my sight.   65
I think, but dare not speak.

GENTLEWOMAN: Good night, good Doctor.   *Exeunt.*

ACT 5, SCENE 2°

Drum and colors. Enter Menteith, Caithness, Angus, Lennox, [and] soldiers.

MENTEITH:

The English power is near, led on by Malcolm,
His uncle Siward, and the good Macduff.
Revenges burn in them, for their dear causes
Would to the bleeding and the grim alarm
Excite the mortified man.°

ANGUS: Near Birnam Wood   5
Shall we well° meet them; that way are they coming.

CAITHNESS:

Who knows if Donalbain be with his brother?

LENNOX:

For certain, sir, he is not. I have a file°
Of all the gentry. There is Siward's son,
And many unrough° youths that even now   10
Protest° their first of manhood.

MENTEITH: What does the tyrant?

---

63. **annoyance:** i.e., harming herself.   64. **still:** constantly.   65. **mated:** bewildered, stupe-
fied.   ACT 5, SCENE 2. **Location:** The country near Dunsinane.   3–5. **their . . . man:** their
grievous wrongs would awaken even the dead to answer the bloody and grim call to battle.
6. **well:** no doubt.   8. **file:** list, roster.   10. **unrough:** beardless.   11. **Protest:** assert publicly.

CAITHNESS:
Great Dunsinane he strongly fortifies.
Some say he's mad, others that lesser hate him
Do call it valiant fury; but for certain
He cannot unbuckle his distempered° cause   15
Within the belt of rule.
ANGUS: Now does he feel
His secret murders sticking on his hands;
Now minutely° revolts upbraid° his faith-breach.°
Those he commands move only in command,°
Nothing in love. Now does he feel his title   20
Hang loose about him, like a giant's robe
Upon a dwarfish thief.
MENTEITH: Who then shall blame
His pestered° senses to recoil and start,
When all that is within him does condemn
Itself for being there?
CAITHNESS: Well, march we on   25
To give obedience where 'tis truly owed.
Meet we the med'cine of the sickly weal,°
And with him pour we in our country's purge
Each drop of us.°
LENNOX: Or so much as it needs
To dew° the sovereign° flower and drown the weeds.   30
Make we our march towards Birnam.   *Exeunt, marching.*

Act 5, Scene 3°

Enter Macbeth, Doctor, and attendants.

MACBETH:
Bring me no more reports. Let them° fly° all!
Till Birnam Wood remove to Dunsinane,
I cannot taint with° fear. What's the boy Malcolm?
Was he not born of woman? The spirits that know

---

15. **distempered:** disease-swollen, dropsical.   18. **minutely:** every minute.   **upbraid:** censure.   **faith-breach:** violation of all trust and sacred vows.   19. **in command:** under orders.   23. **pestered:** troubled, tormented.   27. **Meet we . . . weal:** i.e., let us join forces with Malcolm, the physician of our sick land.   28–29. **pour . . . of us:** i.e., let us shed all our blood as a bloodletting or *purge* of our country.   30. **dew:** bedew, water.   **sovereign:** (1) royal (2) medically efficacious.   **Act 5, Scene 3. Location:** Dunsinane. Macbeth's castle.   1. **them:** i.e., the thanes.   **fly:** desert.   3. **taint with:** become imbued or infected with, weakened by.

All mortal consequences° have pronounced me thus: 5
"Fear not, Macbeth. No man that's born of woman
Shall e'er have power upon thee." Then fly, false thanes,
And mingle with the English epicures!°
The mind I sway° by and the heart I bear
Shall never sag with doubt nor shake with fear.   10

Enter Servant.

The devil damn thee black, thou cream-faced loon!°
Where gott'st thou that goose look?

SERVANT:
There is ten thousand —

MACBETH: Geese, villain?

SERVANT: Soldiers, sir.

MACBETH:
Go prick thy face and over-red thy fear,°
Thou lily-livered boy. What soldiers, patch?°   15
Death of thy° soul! Those linen cheeks of thine
Are counselors to fear.° What soldiers, whey-face?

SERVANT:
The English force, so please you.

MACBETH:
Take thy face hence. [*Exit Servant.*] Seyton! — I am sick at heart
When I behold° — Seyton, I say! — This push°   20
Will cheer° me ever, or disseat° me now.
I have lived long enough. My way° of life
Is fall'n into the sere,° the yellow leaf,
And that which should accompany old age,
As° honor, love, obedience, troops of friends,   25
I must not look to have, but in their stead
Curses, not loud but deep, mouth-honor, breath
Which the poor heart would fain deny and dare not.
Seyton!

---

5. **mortal consequences:** what befalls humanity.   8. **English epicures:** luxury-loving English-men (as seen from the Scottish point of view).   9. **sway:** rule myself.   11. **loon:** stupid fellow.   14. **Go prick . . . fear:** i.e., go prick or pinch your pale cheeks to bring some color into them. (The servant's blood has all retired into his lower abdomen on account of his fear, so that he is very pale and there is no blood in his liver, where his courage should have resided — hence, *lily-livered,* line 15.)   15. **patch:** domestic fool.   16. **of thy:** on your.   17. **Are . . . fear:** i.e., teach others to fear.   20. **behold:** (Macbeth does not finish this thought.)   **push:** effort, crisis.   21. **cheer:** (With a suggestion of "chair.")   **disseat:** dethrone.   22. **way:** course.   23. **sere:** dry and withered.   25. **As:** such as.

Enter Seyton.

SEYTON:
  What's your gracious pleasure?
MACBETH: What news more?   30
SEYTON:
  All is confirmed, my lord, which was reported.
MACBETH:
  I'll fight till from my bones my flesh be hacked.
  Give me my armor.
SEYTON:
  'Tis not needed yet.
MACBETH:
  I'll put it on.   35
  Send out more horses. Skirr° the country round.
  Hang those that talk of fear. Give me mine armor.
  How does your patient, Doctor?
DOCTOR:
  Not so sick, my lord,
  As she is troubled with thick-coming fancies   40
  That keep her from her rest.
MACBETH: Cure her of that.
  Canst thou not minister to a mind diseased,
  Pluck from the memory a rooted sorrow,
  Raze° out the written troubles of° the brain,
  And with some sweet oblivious° antidote   45
  Cleanse the stuffed bosom of that perilous stuff
  Which weighs upon the heart?
DOCTOR: Therein the patient
  Must minister to himself.
MACBETH:
  Throw physic° to the dogs! I'll none of it.
  Come, put mine armor on. Give me my staff.°   [*Attendants arm him.*] 50
  Seyton, send out. Doctor, the thanes fly from me. —
  Come, sir, dispatch.° — If thou couldst, Doctor, cast
  The water° of my land, find her disease,
  And purge it to a sound and pristine health,
  I would applaud thee to the very echo,   55

---

36. **Skirr:** scour. 44. **Raze:** (Suggesting also *race,* "erase, obliterate.") **written troubles of:**
troubles written on. 45. **oblivious:** causing forgetfulness. 49. **physic:** medicine. 50. **staff:**
lance or baton of office. 52. **dispatch:** hurry. 52–53. **cast The water:** diagnose disease by
the inspection of urine.

That should applaud again. — Pull 't off,° I say. —
What rhubarb, senna,° or what purgative drug
Would scour° these English hence? Hear'st thou of them?

DOCTOR:
Ay, my good lord. Your royal preparation
Makes us hear something.

MACBETH: Bring it° after me. —   60
I will not be afraid of death and bane,
Till Birnam Forest comes to Dunsinane.   *Exeunt [all but the Doctor].*

DOCTOR:
Were I from Dunsinane away and clear,
Profit again should hardly draw me here.   *[Exit.]*

ACT 5, SCENE 4°

Drum and colors. Enter Malcolm, Siward, Macduff, Siward's Son, Menteith, Caithness, Angus, [Lennox, Ross,] and soldiers, marching.

MALCOLM:
Cousins, I hope the days are near at hand
That chambers will be safe.°

MENTEITH: We doubt it nothing.°

SIWARD:
What wood is this before us?

MENTEITH: The wood of Birnam.

MALCOLM:
Let every soldier hew him down a bough
And bear 't before him. Thereby shall we shadow   5
The numbers of our host and make discovery°
Err in report of us.

SOLDIERS: It shall be done.

SIWARD:
We learn no other but° the confident tyrant
Keeps° still in Dunsinane and will endure°
Our setting down before° 't.

MALCOLM: 'Tis his main hope;   10

---

56. **Pull 't off:** (Refers to some part of the armor not properly put on.)   57. **senna:** a purgative drug.   58. **scour:** purge, cleanse, rid.   60. **it:** i.e., the armor not yet put on Macbeth. **ACT 5, SCENE 4.** Location: Country near Birnam Wood.   2. **chambers . . . safe:** i.e., we may sleep safely in our bedchambers.   **nothing:** not at all.   6. **discovery:** scouting reports. 8. **no other but:** no other news but that.   9. **Keeps:** remains.   **endure:** allow, not attempt to prevent.   10. **setting down before:** laying siege to.

For where there is advantage° to be given,
Both more and less° have given him the revolt,
And none serve with him but constrainèd things
Whose hearts are absent too.

MACDUFF: Let our just censures
Attend the true event,° and put we on   15
Industrious soldiership.

SIWARD: The time approaches
That will with due decision make us know
What we shall say we have and what we owe.°
Thoughts speculative their unsure hopes relate,
But certain issue strokes must arbitrate° —   20
Towards which advance the war.°   *Exeunt, marching.*

ACT 5, SCENE 5°

Enter Macbeth, Seyton, and soldiers, with drum and colors.

MACBETH:
Hang out our banners on the outward walls.
The cry is still, "They come!" Our castle's strength
Will laugh a siege to scorn. Here let them lie
Till famine and the ague eat them up.
Were they not forced° with those that should be ours,   5
We might have met them dareful,° beard to beard,
And beat them backward home.   *A cry within of women.*
                    What is that noise?

SEYTON:
It is the cry of women, my good lord.   [*He goes to the door.*]

MACBETH:
I have almost forgot the taste of fears.
The time has been my senses would have cooled°   10
To hear a night-shriek, and my fell of hair°
Would at a dismal treatise° rouse and stir

11. **advantage:** opportunity (i.e., in military operations outside Macbeth's castle in which it is possible for would-be deserters to slip away; in a siege, his forces will be more confined to the castle and under his watchful eye). 12. **more and less:** high and low. 14–15. **Let . . . event:** let us postpone judgment about these uncertain matters until we've achieved our goal. 18. **What . . . owe:** what we only claim to have, as distinguished from what we actually have (or perhaps what we *owe* as duty). **owe:** own. 19–20. **Thoughts . . . arbitrate:** speculating can only convey our sense of hope; blows must decide the actual outcome. 21. **war:** army. ACT 5, SCENE 5. Location: Dunsinane. Macbeth's castle. 5. **forced:** reinforced. 6. **dareful:** boldly, in open battle. 10. **cooled:** felt the chill of terror. 11. **my fell of hair:** the hair of my scalp. 12. **dismal treatise:** sinister story.

As° life were in 't. I have supped full with horrors;
Direness, familiar to my slaughterous thoughts,
Cannot once start me.°

[*Seyton returns.*]

              Wherefore was that cry?   15

SEYTON:
  The Queen, my lord, is dead.

MACBETH:
  She should have died hereafter;°
  There would have been a time for such a word.
  Tomorrow, and tomorrow, and tomorrow
  Creeps in this° petty pace from day to day   20
  To the last syllable of recorded time,
  And all our yesterdays have lighted° fools
  The way to dusty° death. Out, out, brief candle!
  Life's but a walking shadow, a poor player
  That struts and frets his hour upon the stage   25
  And then is heard no more. It is a tale
  Told by an idiot, full of sound and fury,
  Signifying nothing.°

Enter a Messenger.

  Thou com'st to use thy tongue; thy story quickly.

MESSENGER:
  Gracious my lord,   30
  I should report that which I say I saw,
  But know not how to do 't.

MACBETH: Well, say, sir.

MESSENGER:
  As I did stand my watch upon the hill,
  I looked toward Birnam, and anon, methought,
  The wood began to move.

MACBETH: Liar and slave!   35

MESSENGER:
  Let me endure your wrath if 't be not so.

---

13. **As:** as if.   15. **start me:** make me start.   17. **She . . . hereafter:** she would have died someday, or, she should have died at some more appropriate time, freed from the relentless pressures of the moment.   19–28. **Tomorrow . . . nothing:** (For biblical echoes in this speech, see Psalms 18:28, 22:15, 90:9; Job 8:9, 14:1–2, 18:6.)   20. **this:** at this.   22. **lighted:** (The metaphor is of a candle used to light one to bed, just as life is a brief transit for wretched mortals to their deathbeds.)   23. **dusty:** (Since life, made out of dust, returns to dust.)

Within this three mile may you see it coming;
I say, a moving grove.
MACBETH: If thou speak'st false,
Upon the next tree shall thou hang alive
Till famine cling° thee. If thy speech be sooth,°   40
I care not if thou dost for me as much.
I pull in resolution,° and begin
To doubt th' equivocation of the fiend
That lies like truth. "Fear not, till Birnam Wood
Do come to Dunsinane," and now a wood   45
Comes toward Dunsinane. Arm, arm, and out!
If this which he avouches does appear,
There is nor flying hence nor tarrying here.
I 'gin to be aweary of the sun,
And wish th' estate° o' the world were now undone.   50
Ring the alarum bell! Blow wind, come wrack,°
At least we'll die with harness° on our back.   *Exeunt.*

ACT 5, SCENE 6°

Drum and colors. Enter Malcolm, Siward, Macduff, and their army, with boughs.

MALCOLM:
Now near enough. Your leafy screens throw down,
And show° like those you are. You, worthy uncle,°
Shall with my cousin, your right noble son,
Lead our first battle.° Worthy Macduff and we
Shall take upon 's what else remains to do,   5
According to our order.°
SIWARD: Fare you well.
Do we° but find the tyrant's power° tonight,
Let us be beaten, if we cannot fight.
MACDUFF:
Make all our trumpets speak! Give them all breath,
Those clamorous harbingers° of blood and death.   10
                    Exeunt. Alarums continued.

---

40. **cling:** cause to shrivel.   **sooth:** truth.   42. **pull in resolution:** can no longer give free rein to my self-confident determination.   50. **estate:** settled order.   51. **wrack:** ruin.   52. **harness:** armor.   ACT 5, SCENE 6. **Location:** Dunsinane. Before Macbeth's castle.   2. **show:** appear.   **uncle:** i.e., Siward.   4. **battle:** battalion.   6. **order:** plan of battle.   7. **Do we:** if we do.   **power:** army.   10. **harbingers:** forerunners.

ACT 5, SCENE 7°

Enter Macbeth.

MACBETH:
They have tied me to a stake. I cannot fly,
But bearlike I must fight the course.° What's he
That was not born of woman? Such a one
Am I to fear, or none.

Enter young Siward.

YOUNG SIWARD:
What is thy name?   5
MACBETH:
Thou'lt be afraid to hear it.
YOUNG SIWARD:
No, though thou call'st thyself a hotter name
Than any is in hell.
MACBETH: My name's Macbeth.
YOUNG SIWARD:
The devil himself could not pronounce a title
More hateful to mine ear.
MACBETH: No, nor more fearful.   10
YOUNG SIWARD:
Thou liest, abhorrèd tyrant! With my sword
I'll prove the lie thou speak'st.   *Fight, and young Siward slain.°*
MACBETH: Thou wast born of woman.
But swords I smile at, weapons laugh to scorn,
Brandished by man that's of a woman born.   *Exit.*

Alarums. Enter Macduff.

MACDUFF:
That way the noise is. Tyrant, show thy face!   15
If thou be'st slain, and with no stroke of mine,
My wife and children's ghosts will haunt me still.
I cannot strike at wretched kerns,° whose arms

ACT 5, SCENE 7. **Location:** Before Macbeth's castle; the battle action is continuous here.
2. course: bout or round of bearbaiting, in which the bear was tied to a stake and dogs were set upon him.   **s.d.** *young Siward slain:* (In some unspecified way, young Siward's body must be removed from the stage; his own father enters at line 24 and perceives nothing amiss, and in 5.8.38 young Siward is reported *missing* in action. Perhaps Macbeth drags off the body, or perhaps it is removed by soldiers during the alarums.)   **18. kerns:** (Properly, Irish foot soldiers; here, applied contemptuously to the rank and file.)

Are hired to bear their staves.° Either thou,° Macbeth,
Or else my sword with an unbattered edge   20
I sheathe again undeeded.° There thou shouldst be;°
By this great clatter one of greatest note
Seems bruited.° Let me find him, Fortune,
And more I beg not.   *Exit. Alarums.*

Enter Malcolm and Siward.

SIWARD:
    This way, my lord. The castle's gently rendered:°   25
    The tyrant's people on both sides do fight,
    The noble thanes do bravely in the war,
    The day almost itself professes° yours,
    And little is to do.
MALCOLM: We have met with foes
    That strike beside us.°
SIWARD: Enter, sir, the castle.   *Exeunt. Alarum.*   30

ACT 5, SCENE 8°

Enter Macbeth.

MACBETH:
    Why should I play the Roman fool° and die
    On mine own sword? Whiles I see lives,° the gashes
    Do better upon them.

Enter Macduff.

MACDUFF: Turn, hellhound, turn!
MACBETH:
    Of all men else I have avoided thee.
    But get thee back! My soul is too much charged   5
    With blood of thine already.
MACDUFF: I have no words;
    My voice is in my sword, thou bloodier villain
    Than terms can give thee out!°   *Fight. Alarum.*

19. **staves:** spears. **Either thou:** i.e., either I find you.   21. **undeeded:** having seen no action.
shouldst be: ought to be (judging by the noise).   23. **bruited:** announced   25. **gently ren-**
dered: surrendered without fighting.   28. **professes:** declares itself.   30. **strike beside us:**
fight on our side, or miss us deliberately.   **ACT 5, SCENE 8.   Location:** Before Macbeth's castle,
as the battle continues; after line 34, within the castle.   1. **Roman fool:** i.e., suicide, like Brutus, Mark Antony, and others.   2. **Whiles . . . lives:** i.e., as long as I see any enemy living.
8. **give thee out:** name you, describe you.

MACBETH: Thou losest labor.
  As easy mayst thou the intrenchant° air
  With thy keen sword impress° as make me bleed.   10
  Let fall thy blade on vulnerable crests;
  I bear a charmèd life, which must not yield
  To one of woman born.
MACDUFF: Despair° thy charm,
  And let the angel° whom thou still° hast served
  Tell thee, Macduff was from his mother's womb   15
  Untimely° ripped.
MACBETH:
  Accursèd be that tongue that tells me so,
  For it hath cowed my better part of man!°
  And be these juggling° fiends no more believed
  That palter with us in a double sense,°   20
  That keep the word of promise to our ear
  And break it to our hope. I'll not fight with thee.
MACDUFF:
  Then yield thee, coward,
  And live to be the show and gaze o' the time!°
  We'll have thee, as our rarer monsters are,   25
  Painted upon a pole,° and underwrit,
  "Here may you see the tyrant."
MACBETH: I will not yield
  To kiss the ground before young Malcolm's feet
  And to be baited with the rabble's curse.
  Though Birnam Wood be come to Dunsinane,   30
  And thou opposed, being of no woman born,
  Yet I will try the last.° Before my body
  I throw my warlike shield. Lay on, Macduff,
  And damned be him that first cries, "Hold, enough!"

                              Exeunt, fighting. Alarums.

---

9. **intrenchant:** that cannot be cut, indivisible.   10. **impress:** make an impression on.   13. **Despair:** despair of.   14. **angel:** evil angel, Macbeth's genius.   **still:** always.   16. **Untimely:** prematurely, i.e., by caesarean delivery.   18. **better . . . man:** i.e., courage.   19. **juggling:** deceiving.   20. **palter . . . sense:** equivocate with us.   24. **gaze o' the time:** spectacle or sideshow of the age.   26. **Painted . . . pole:** i.e., painted on a board or cloth and suspended on a pole.   32. **the last:** i.e., my last resort; my own strength and resolution.

*Enter fighting, and Macbeth slain. [Exit Macduff with Macbeth's body.] Retreat,°
and flourish. Enter, with drum and colors,° Malcolm, Siward, Ross, thanes, and soldiers.*

MALCOLM:
I would the friends we miss were safe arrived.   35
SIWARD:
Some must go off;° and yet, by these° I see
So great a day as this is cheaply bought.
MALCOLM:
Macduff is missing, and your noble son.
ROSS:
Your son, my lord, has paid a soldier's debt.
He only lived but till he was a man,   40
The which no sooner had his prowess confirmed
In the unshrinking station° where he fought,
But like a man he died.
SIWARD: Then he is dead?
ROSS:
Ay, and brought off the field. Your cause of sorrow
Must not be measured by his worth, for then   45
It hath no end.
SIWARD: Had he his hurts before?
ROSS:
Ay, on the front.
SIWARD: Why then, God's soldier be he!
Had I as many sons as I have hairs
I would not wish them to a fairer death.
And so, his knell is knolled.
MALCOLM: He's worth more sorrow,   50
And that I'll spend for him.
SIWARD: He's worth no more.
They say he parted° well and paid his score,°
And so, God be with him! Here comes newer comfort.

Enter Macduff, with Macbeth's head.

---

s.d. *Retreat:* a trumpet call ordering an end to the fighting.   ***Enter, with drum and colors,* etc.:**
(The remainder of the play is perhaps imagined as taking place in Macbeth's castle and could be
marked as a separate scene. In Shakespeare's theater, however, the shift is so nonrepresentational
and without scenic alteration that the action is virtually continuous.)   **36. go off:** die.   **by
these:** to judge by these (assembled).   **42. unshrinking station:** post from which he did not
shrink.   **52. parted:** departed, died.   **score:** reckoning.

MACDUFF:

Hail, King! For so thou art. Behold where stands°
Th' usurper's cursèd head. The time is free.°   55
I see thee compassed with thy kingdom's pearl,°
That speak my salutation in their minds,
Whose voices I desire aloud with mine:
Hail, King of Scotland!

ALL:

Hail, King of Scotland!   *Flourish.* 60

MALCOLM:

We shall not spend a large expense of time
Before we reckon° with your several° loves
And make us even with you.° My thanes and kinsmen,
Henceforth be earls, the first that ever Scotland
In such an honor named. What's more to do   65
Which would be planted newly with the time,°
As calling home our exiled friends abroad
That fled the snares of watchful tyranny,
Producing forth° the cruel ministers°
Of this dead butcher and his fiendlike queen —   70
Who, as 'tis thought, by self and violent° hands
Took off her life — this, and what needful else
That calls upon us, by the grace of Grace
We will perform in measure, time, and place.
So, thanks to all at once and to each one,   75
Whom we invite to see us crowned at Scone.   *Flourish. Exeunt omnes.*

---

54. **stands:** i.e., on a pole.   55. **free:** released from tyranny.   56. **compassed . . . pearl:** surrounded by the nobles of your kingdom (literally, the pearls encircling a crown).   62. **reckon:** come to a reckoning.   **several:** individual.   63. **make . . . you:** i.e., repay your worthiness.   66. **would . . . time:** should be established at the commencement of this new era.   69. **Producing forth:** bringing forward to trial.   **ministers:** agents.   71. **self and violent:** her own violent.

Textual Notes for Macbeth

Copy text: the First Folio. The act and scene divisions follow the Folio text, except that 5.8 is not marked in the Folio.

Act 1, Scene 1. 9. s.p. Second Witch: *All.* 10. s.p. Third witch: [not in F]. 11. s.p. All: [at line 9 in F].

Act 1, Scene 2. 1. s.p. [and elsewhere] Duncan: *King.* 13. gallowglasses: Gallow-grosses. 14. quarrel: Quarry. 21. ne'er: neu'r. 26. thunders break: Thunders.

Act 1, Scene 3. 32. Weird: weyward [elsewhere in F spelled "weyward" or "weyard"]. 39. Forres: Soris. 97. death. As: death, as. 98. Came: Can. 111. lose: loose.

Act 1, Scene 4. 1. Are: Or.

Act 1, Scene 5. 1. s.p. [and elsewhere] Lady Macbeth: Lady. 9. lose: *loose.* 43. it: hit.

Act 1, Scene 6. 4. martlet: Barlet. 9. most: must.

Act 1, Scene 7. 6. shoal: Schoole. 48. do: no.

Act 2, Scene 1. 56. strides: sides. 57. sure: sowre. 58. way they: they may.

Act 2, Scene 2. 13. s.d.: [at line 8 in F, after "die"].

Act 2, Scene 3. 32. s.d.: [after line 31 in F]. 133. nea'er: neere.

Act 3, Scene 1. 76. s.p. Murderers: *Murth.* 116. s.p. Both Murderers: *Murth.* [also at line 140]. 141. s.d. *Exeunt:* [at line 143 in F].

Act 3, Scene 3. 7. and: end.

Act 3, Scene 4. 79. time: times. 122. s.d. *Exeunt: Exit.*

Act 3, Scene 6. 24. son: Sonnes. 38. the: their.

Act 4, Scene 1. 34. cauldron: Cawdron. 38. s.d. *to: and.* 59. germens: Germaine. 93. Dunsinane: Dunsmane. 94. s.d. *Descends: Descend.* 98. Birnam: Byrnan [also spelled "Birnan," "Byrnane," and "Birnane" in act 5]. 119. eighth: eight.

Act 4, Scene 2. 1. s.p. [and throughout] Lady Macduff: *Wife.* 22. none: moue. 67–68. ones ... methinks,: ones / To fright you thus. Me thinkes. 77. s.d. *Enter Murderers:* [after "What are these faces" in F]. 78. s.p. [and throughout scene] First Murderer: *Mur.* 81. shag-haired: shagge-ear'd.

Act 4, Scene 3. 4. downfall'n: downfall. 15. deserve: discerne. 35. Fare: Far. 108. accurst: accust. 124. detraction, here: detraction. Heere. 134. thy: they. 144. essay: assay. 146. s.d.: [after "amend" in F]. 161. not: nor. 237. tune: time.

Act 5, Scene 1. 30. fear who: feare? who.

Act 5, Scene 3. 41. Cure her: Cure. 54. pristine: pristiue. 57. senna: Cyme. 62. s.d.: [at line 64 in F].

Act 5, Scene 4. 16. s.p. Siward: *Sey.*

PART TWO

><

Cultural Contexts

CHAPTER I

Representations of Macbeth

$\leftrightarrow\!\!\prec$

Early Narratives

Macbeth was the eighty-fifth King of Scotland, ruling from 1040–1057 C.E. He killed his predecessor, King Duncan, was himself killed, and was succeeded by Malcolm III, Duncan's son — on that much, the early chroniclers of Scottish history agreed. These minimal facts seem clear enough, but the *legend* of Macbeth grew ever more complex and elaborate over the century before Shakespeare's play was written. The three sixteenth-century histories excerpted in this section — those by John Major (1521), George Buchanan (1582), and Raphael Holinshed (1587, but essentially a translation of Hector Boece, 1526) — represent significantly different stages in the development of the Macbeth narrative. Of the three histories, we can say with certainty only that Holinshed's was known to Shakespeare, though it is very likely that he knew Buchanan's version as well. The point of reading these particular texts, however, is not so much that they were or were not clear "sources" of Shakespeare's play, in the sense that he knew and used them for aspects of his plot, character, and language, but that, taken together, these histories reveal the *uses* to which the story of Macbeth was put — the ways in which political, religious, and patriotic concerns amplified and shaped the historical record.

The reign of Macbeth was of special interest throughout the reign of the Stuarts, and particularly in the later sixteenth century, as James VI, King of Scotland, pressed his claim to the English crown. Even before James came to the throne or Shakespeare wrote his play, various popular versions of this period of Scottish history circulated. A play called *The King of Scots* was given at court in 1567–68 (Chambers *Elizabethan* 4: 144). In his *Nine Days Wonder* of 1600, Will Kempe — until 1599 the leading comic actor in Shakespeare's company — refers to a now lost ballad on the subject: "I met a proper upright youth . . . a penny Poet, whose first making was the miserable stolen story of Macdoel, or Macdobeth, or Macsomewhat, for I am sure a Mac it was, though I never had the maw to see it" (Kempe 21). Two years later (in April 1602), Philip Henslowe, the manager of the rival theatrical company, refers in his diary to a play called *Malcolm, Kyng of Scottes,* which is also unfortunately now lost (Chambers 2: 179); whether this Malcolm was Malcolm III, Macbeth's successor, or Malcolm II, Duncan's grandfather and predecessor on the throne, is unclear, but all the events of this period of royal history held special relevance for popular audiences around 1600.

Three aspects of this period of Scottish history particularly linked it to the concerns of Shakespeare's contemporaries, including his monarch. (See Figure 1, p. 4.) First, it was the period when the Scottish crown ceased to be an *elective* monarchy, and became one of *inheritance.* King Kenneth II, Malcolm II's grandfather, had secured the passage of a new law, that "for the creation of the Scottish kings in time to come . . . The eldest heir male of the deceased king, whether the same were son or nephew, of what age soever he should be, yea though he should be in the mother's womb at the time of the father's decease, should from thenceforth succeed in the kingdom of Scotland" (Holinshed 5: 247). When, after much struggle, Malcolm II was ready to become king, "he utterly refused to receive the crown, except the law established by his [grand]father Kenneth for the succession thereof were first confirmed and approved" (Holinshed 5: 255). When Duncan (Malcolm II's grandson) became king, his own son, who would be Malcolm III, was understood to succeed him through inheritance, but this new principle of royal succession was broken by Macbeth's murder of Duncan and usurpation of the crown. As we shall see later in more detail, the principle of royal succession through *patrilineal inheritance* was absolutely essential to James VI's claim to the crown of England; to his chagrin, some political and religious theorists had in the 1590s raised questions about whether the principle of inheritance was in fact possible or even desirable in his case, and argued that some degree of election — by Parliament, or by the people — was required. Thus, eleventh-century Scottish history foregrounded the contemporary political issues that were coming to a head.

A second reason why the reign of Macbeth seemed especially significant is that the Stuart kings, from James V on, had traced their lineage back from the undoubted founder of the line, Walter Steward, to the mythical Banquo; according to these histories, Banquo's son Fleance flees to Wales and impregnates the Welsh princess with a son, Walter. This myth of lineal continuity appears in no history prior to Boece's, in the reign of James V. The significance of the supposed link between Banquo and Walter Steward was clear — by it, the Scottish king also had a claim on the Welsh crown, and ultimately the English; moreover, *both* sides of the Steward line were therefore of royal blood. (Again, we will discuss the uses of this myth of lineage in more detail later.)

A third and final reason for the relevance of the reign of Macbeth to contemporary audiences is that Macbeth's reign overlapped with that of Edward the Confessor in England (1042–1066), the last king before William the Conqueror, whose name would usually top all future English royal genealogies. But Edward the Confessor's heritage was itself highly significant, as Sir Thomas Craig, a Scottish historian and political leader wrote in 1603: "The throne of England was restored to its native kings, however, in the person of Edward the Confessor, whose heir was his nephew the Etheling Edgar, son of his brother Edmund (known as "Ironside" for his valor). In the event of his dying without heirs, as actually happened, Edgar's title passed to his sister Margaret, who was already the wife of Malcolm, king of Scots [Malcolm III, who succeeded Macbeth]. Through her, therefore, not only the title to the English crown, but almost every title of nobility in England, passed to Scotland . . . in the descendant of that line, our most gracious sovereign [James VI]" (Craig 267). Thus, James VI claimed not only the Scottish but also the Welsh and English crowns, based on the narratives of early Scottish history — all centered on the period of the reign of Macbeth.

Beyond these issues of succession, however, the development of the Macbeth narrative suggests how other cultural forces as well impinged on and shaped the story. In Major's version, for example, there is no Lady Macbeth — one of the most celebrated aspects of Shakespeare's play — and Buchanan and Holinshed mention her only briefly; and in Holinshed alone are there witches, or prophetesses. What for John Major is a tale of political aggression, "opposing faction," and clannish violence turns into a case of demonic subversion and temptation in Holinshed's account. Shakespeare may have found more of his inspiration for Lady Macbeth in other accounts of ambitious wives in Holinshed's history, such as that of a Captain Donwald, who was "kindled in wrath by the words of his wife, determined to follow her advice in the execution of so heinous an act [i.e., regicide]"

(Holinshed 5: 234). In Shakespeare's play, Macbeth, like Captain Donwald, is tempted by, and succumbs to, various representations of the demonized feminine. In Chapter 6 we will examine further the significance of Shakespeare's turn toward such issues.

The historical narrative of Macbeth also gradually takes on multiple elements of supernatural prophecy. John Major's account is simply one of Macbeth's political will — "to gain a kingdom many a wicked act is done" — while George Buchanan, who had read Boece's description of the witches, remains skeptical, allowing his Macbeth only a dream of "three women, whose beauty was more august and surprising than bare women's useth to be" (in contrast to the usual loathliness of witches); while these dream-women pronounce the famous prophecies, still Macbeth had already "conceived a secret hope of the kingdom in his mind, [and] was further encouraged in his ambitious thoughts" by this dream. (Buchanan thus offers a pre-Freudian explanation of the dream as wish-fulfillment.) In stories about other kings, moreover, Buchanan expresses a dry irony about the historical truth of supernatural interventions in human affairs: "These things I deliver, as I receiv'd them from our ancestors: what to think of this sort of witchcraft, I leave to the judgment of the reader, only minding him, that this story [of the bewitching of King Duff] is found amongst our ancient archives and records" (Buchanan bk. 6, 183). Among those records is Boece's history, which, via Holinshed, develops the full-blown account of the three Weird Sisters who confront Macbeth — and also, the royal progenitor, Banquo — with their prophecies. The crime described in all these accounts of course remains the same — regicide — but many other aspects of the crime vary among the different versions. Even the basic facts of the Macbeth narrative become contested, such as how and where Duncan was murdered, for example, or who kills Macbeth and under what conditions. Finally, in the succeeding accounts, the role of Edward the Confessor becomes ever larger, and more politically pointed — from that of the host who simply provides refuge to Malcolm, to the holy man and supplier (through Siward, Earl of Northumberland) of a ten-thousand-man invading army.

The development of the Macbeth narrative also reveals an increasing emphasis on Macbeth's motivation(s) and on the consequences of his crime — in effect, an interiorization of the story, turning attention to Macbeth's psychology. By the time of Shakespeare's play, his powerful feelings of guilt — completely absent from earlier narratives — will become prominent. At the same time, the routine of Scottish clan violence is reshaped into more purposive historical structures — thus the elaborate symmetries in

Shakespeare's play, which ends as it began, with a victorious warrior-thane decapitating the rebellious thane whose place he has taken.

One episode in the Macbeth narrative, however, remains more or less the same in each of these versions — the scene between Macduff and Malcolm in England, when Macduff urges Malcolm to return to Scotland to help overthrow Macbeth, and Malcolm tests Macduff's loyalty by accusing himself of various unkingly crimes. There is little fundamental change in this scene from version to version, and it is proportionately a major part of the narrative, especially in Major's version. Even the crimes of which Malcolm accuses himself — lechery, avarice, deceit — remain the same. Literary critics have always found it one of the most puzzling moments in Shakespeare's *Macbeth* and have stressed its deliberately unnaturalistic psychology. While Shakespeare links the scene to the rest of the play through a dense web of repeated words and images, it is by no means certain why this inverted loyalty test — in which the "suitor" is told not how good, but how bad, his subject is — is so central to the story of Macbeth. The issues of loyalty involved in the test, however — kingly rectitude, justified resistance to tyrants, the implications of inheritance — are central not only to the Macbeth narrative, but to early Scottish history in general.

SCOTTISH HISTORIOGRAPHY

Nations are constituted by ideas as well as by geography and population. The "idea" of America, what the word stands for, is very different from the "idea" of, for example, Israel; the ideas of these nations are certainly connected to their radically distinct geographies and ethnic heritages, but their extremely different histories also profoundly shape their current identities. For a young nation, the writing of its history is always a decisive process in its self-creation. Scotland in the sixteenth century already had an ancient heritage, but in many ways it was still less a nation than a collection of warring clan factions; until the adult reign of James VI, moreover, the Scottish monarch possessed considerably less power than his or her English counterpart. Even with his centralization of power, James himself experienced a considerable amount of violence directed against himself and his family. The historians of early modern Scotland stressed, however, the undoubted length and continuity of the line of the Scottish monarchy, which had never succumbed to foreign invasion, as England had done. Scottish historians and royal propagandists invariably traced the Stuart line back at least as far as Fergus in the fourth century B.C.E.; some writers even traced the line back to the Greeks — to a noble Athenian named Gathelus who supposedly married the pharaoh's daughter, Scota (hence, Scotia, or Scotland); others traced the kingship back to the biblical tribes of Israel, or to King Arthur (supposed to have ruled in the sixth century C.E.).

The Scottish nation was thus represented, to a considerable extent, by the story of its monarchy, and that royal line was a long — perhaps unbelievably long — and heroic one; it was also, as some English emphasized, a violent and bloody line. In a famous outburst during a 1607 Parliamentary debate over union with Scotland, the English member of Parliament Sir Christopher Piggott said that the Scots "have not suffered above two kings to die in their beds, these two hundred years. Our king [James] hath hardly escaped them; they have attempted [to murder] him" (Galloway 104). For this breach of decorum (though his statement was largely true) Piggott was expelled from the House of Commons and imprisoned in the Tower. The historians of early modern Scotland certainly did not ignore or downplay the violence inherent in their tradition; nine of the ten kings who preceded Macbeth had been assassinated. But this historical violence and instability, now largely controlled, became further proof of the greatness of James VI. Moreover, one of the turning points in Scottish royal history, as we saw above, was the shift from an elective to an inherited monarchy — the principle of succession James and his supporters were invoking on behalf of his claim to the English crown.

John Major (1469–1550), a great patriot and scholar, was the first of the "modern" Scottish historians, in contrast to the fourteenth- and fifteenth-century chroniclers such as John of Fordun (died circa 1384) and Andrew Wyntoun (circa 1350–1428). Major studied briefly at Cambridge University, but he spent much more time at universities in France, particularly Paris, where he went in 1493. As an ally of Scotland, France was a hospitable place for generations of Scottish students at this time; many of the greatest scholars in Europe, moreover, studied in Paris in the early sixteenth century. Major eventually became a distinguished professor of theology in Paris, writing and lecturing widely on scholastic philosophy and theology. He returned to Scotland in 1518, first to Glasgow, then to St. Andrews as a senior professor in 1522. Among Major's students in Glasgow was John Knox, the most famous religious reformer of sixteenth-century Scotland, and among his students at St. Andrews was George Buchanan, to whom we will turn in a moment. Major returned to the Sorbonne in 1525, and Buchanan either accompanied him or followed shortly thereafter. Major published a number of significant works in the next several years — on Aristotle's *Logic* and *Ethics*, on theology, and a commentary on the four Gospels — and in 1531 returned to St. Andrews, where he held various positions until his death. Major published no significant works after 1530.

Major published his history of Scotland in 1521, in Latin: *Historia Majoris Britanniae, tam Angliae quam Scotiae, per Joannem Majorem, nomine quidem Scotum, professione autem theologum* (A history of Greater Britain as well of England as of Scotland by John Major, by name a Scot but by profession a theologian). The choice of Latin, rather than vernacular Scots, was not inevitable, even for an expert in Scholastic philosophy and theology such as Major; writing in Latin did, however, guarantee that a wider, European audience would read of the greatness of Scotland. The Latin title is interesting for two other reasons. First, there is a pun in it: John Major's History of Major (greater) Britain. Second, there is the prophetic name, Greater Britain. When James VI became James I of England in 1603, uniting the kingdoms of Scotland and England in himself, he began to employ the name *Great Britain* for this new empire (the use of this term aroused great opposition among the English, however, who wanted little to do with the Scots). Major was also ahead of his time in believing that unifying the two kingdoms was desirable. In lamenting the failure of the Scots in the thirteenth century to marry the heiress of their kingdom to the English king, for example, he observed that "For thus [by such marriage], and only thus, could two intensely hostile peoples, inhabitants of the same island, of which neither can conquer the other, have been brought together under one and the same king. And what although the name and kingdom of the Scots had disappeared — so too would the name and kingdom of the English no more have had a place among men — for in the place of both we should have had a king of Britain" (Major 189).

Major's history preceded by six years that of Hector Boece (circa 1465–1536), who had also studied at the College of Montaigu in France during Major's time there. Boece's history was also written in Latin, but it was translated into Scots around 1535, by command of King James V. Major was a critical and scrupulous historian by the standards of his day; Boece, by contrast, repeated or invented many stories and myths that had no historical foundation — most important, for our purposes, the legend of Walter Stewart's descent from Banquo, which makes its first appearance in Boece. One English contemporary, John Leland, wrote that everything written in Boece's history was a lie.

George Buchanan (1506–1582) was one of the major scholars of Europe in the sixteenth century. The French essayist Michel de Montaigne referred to him as "that famous Scottish Poet" (bk. 1, 85) for his literary works, and his *De jure regni apud Scotos* (The powers of the crown in Scotland) has been widely recognized as one of the most influential political essays of the sixteenth century. Buchanan was educated in Paris and at St. Andrews, where he studied under John Major; Buchanan's intellectual interests soon diverged from those of his master, however, for Buchanan was more skeptical, more steeped in humanist texts, as well as Protestant in his beliefs. Buchanan became a teacher in Paris for a decade and then returned to Scotland, where he was a tutor to one of James V's sons. Buchanan became a professor of Latin at the College of Guienne, in Bordeaux, where Montaigne was one of his students. There Buchanan wrote his two major plays, *Baptistes* and *Jephthes* (both on biblical themes). When he went to teach in Portugal in 1547, he was tried for heresy by the Inquisition and imprisoned for several months. Eventually, after more teaching in Paris, he returned to St. Andrews in 1561. Though a Protestant and a leader in the reformed Church of Scotland, Buchanan found some favor with Mary, Queen of Scots, in the next few years, when he was reported to be instructing her in Livy, the Roman historian.

The turning point in Buchanan's career, and indeed in early modern Scottish and English history, came in a brief period in 1566–67. Mary's son, James, was born June 19, 1566; the following February, Mary's husband, Lord Darnley, was murdered. Just three months later, Mary married the Earl of Bothwell, the man widely believed responsible for Darnley's murder. Resentment and outrage ran so high that Mary was forced to abdicate the crown, and her thirteen-month-old son was crowned James VI on July 29, 1567. Buchanan was appointed one of the commissioners to investigate Mary's actions. His political essay, *De jure regni*, argued that the Scots had indeed been justified, by the laws of nature and of God, in forcing the abdication of a lawful monarch. Buchanan harshly condemned the alleged actions of Mary: no person, even the monarch, was above the law authorized by the people. (Buchanan's arguments justifying the overthrow of tyrants would become very well known, as we shall see.) Near the end of his life, Buchanan began writing his history of Scotland, the *Rerum Scoticarum historia* ("History of Scotland"); some saw its interpretation of Scottish history as the historical illustration of the political theories expounded in his *De jure regni*. Although Buchanan repeated Boece's history of the largely mythical first forty kings of Scotland, his account was, he said, purged of "vain fables" (Buchanan bk. 1, 1), and became a series of illustrations of the righteous overthrow of tyrannical kings by the people, and positive instances of the election of kings by councils of the nobility. Buchanan died in 1582, just as his history was being printed.

Among Buchanan's other students in the 1570s was the young king, James VI, to whom Buchanan had, perhaps naïvely, dedicated the *De jure regni*, the attack on his mother! Buchanan's efforts to instruct James met with mixed success, as became evident after Buchanan's death: On the one hand, James praised Buchanan for bringing him to an excellence in Latin — "All the world knows . . . that my master Mr. George Buchanan was a great master in that faculty. I follow his pronunciation both of the Latin and the Greek, and am sorry that my people of England do not the like" (McFarlane 447n.). On the other hand, James worked to discredit and destroy Buchanan's major political works. In 1584, the Scottish Parliament passed an act to punish authors of slanderous works against the monarchy, specifying by name only two works: "the books of the *Chronicle* and *De jure regni apud Scotos* made by umquhile [now deceased] Mr. George Buchanan" (Gatherer 6). In his own *Basilikon Doron*, James urged his son to be well versed in history, but went on, "I mean not of such infamous invectives, as Buchanan's or Knox's Chronicles." James later supervised William Camden in the writing of his history, and urged other historians to revise Buchanan's "invective" against his mother, and to refute the argument supporting the deposition of tyrannical kings.

James succeeded in suppressing Buchanan's work in the short run, but Buchanan ultimately triumphed. Buchanan's ideas were quoted in support of those who deposed and executed James's son and heir, Charles I; in his *Tenure of Kings and Magistrates* (1649), for example, which justified the deposition, John Milton quotes Buchanan's history approvingly several times; in his *Defensio pro populo Anglicano* (A defence of the English people, 1651), Milton replied to those who questioned the legality of a limited government, "For Scotland I refer you to Buchanan" (Milton 4: 481). Buchanan had his posthumous revenge on James in more personal ways, too, for James reported many years after Buchanan's death that when someone "in high place" approached him, "he trembled at his approach, it minded him so of his pedagogue" (McFarlane 449), and near the end of his life, James said that he had been visited in a nightmare by Buchanan, "who seemed to check him severely, as he used to do; and his majesty, in his dream, seemed desirous to pacify him" (Birch 2: 301). Thus Buchanan, and his political legacy, haunted James and the Stuart line in several ways.

One other Scottish historian deserves notice here: John Leslie (or Lesley), Bishop of Ross (1527?–1596), published his *De origine, moribus, et rebus gestis Scotorum* ("Of the Origin, Customs, and Deeds of the Scots") in 1578. Leslie was a very active Catholic partisan of Mary, Queen of Scots: his 1569 tract, *A Defense of the Honour of the Right High, Mighty and Noble Princess Mary* defended her from the criminal charges brought against her, and even asserted her right to the English succession; he himself played no small role in various intrigues designed to restore her to the throne she had been forced to abdicate. Leslie's history also proclaimed the ancient heritage of the Stuart line; as an illustration, Leslie produced the famous family tree (Figure 4) that represents James's supposed descent from Banquo.

Raphael Holinshed (?–1580?) was English, but has a major place in this discussion because he reproduced Hector Boece's history of Scotland in the English language, for English readers, and the overall popular success of his work meant that Boece's history, rather than Major's or Buchanan's, became the best known among them; it was the history of Scotland that Shakespeare most closely followed.

Little is known about Holinshed's life. He was not a scholar, at least in comparison to Major or Buchanan, but worked as a translator for a London printer named Reginald Wolfe. For twenty-five years, Wolfe worked on a universal history and cosmography, and Holinshed worked under his direction. When Wolfe died in 1573, however, none of it had yet been published. Holinshed and some of his colleagues determined to press on only with the histories and descriptions of England, Ireland, and Scotland; the first edition, *The Chronicles of England, Ireland, and Scotland*, was published in London in 1577. The sections on England and Ireland relied on many different authorities, but the section on Scotland was almost entirely a translation into English from Bellenden's Scots translation of Hector Boece's Latin history. The sense of a popular English reading audience is clear in the dedication: "Wherefore since the learned read him in his own style [Latin], and his countrymen in their natural language [Scots], why should not we borrow his description, and read the same in English likewise [?]" (Holinshed 5: A3v).

Holinshed died about 1580, but the editorial team, with new members, continued, and produced a second edition in 1587. The second edition did not include the illustrations from the first edition, and a few parts of it were immediately censored by the government because they dealt with events as recent as the late 1570s, including actions by the still-reigning Queen Elizabeth. It is this second edition of Holinshed's *Chronicles* that Shakespeare read, and from which our text is taken, but the four illustrations are from the 1577 edition.

FIGURE 4 *The genealogy of the Scottish descent from Banquo produced by the* ➤ *Scottish historian John Leslie in* De origine, moribus, et rebus gestis Scotorum *(1578). A supporter of Mary, Leslie shows James (in the Latin, "Jacobus") at the top, but only as "princeps" or prince, not king. This tree also reinforces the foundational myth of the Stuart line — that it began with Banquo, at the root of the tree.*

→ JOHN MAJOR

From A History of Greater Britain   *1521*

This Duncan was secretly put to death by the faction which had been till then in opposition. He was mortally wounded by one Macbeth[1] at Lochgowane, and was thence carried to Elgin, where he died. He was buried by the side of his fathers in Iona. Now those kings showed a grave want of foresight, in that they found no way of union and friendship with the opposing faction: for either they should have banished them from the land of their fathers as disturbers of the common peace and welfare; or, if this opposite faction was carrying on its designs in secret, and was unknown to the king, he should not at least have taken measures against it without a large army at his back: for to gain a kingdom many a wicked act is done — following that saying always in the mouth of Cæsar: 'If the law must be violated, let it be violated at least for empire; in all else follow after piety.' Give them but the chance — and those men are few indeed who will not risk their all for a crown — though their title to it may be far from clear. This Machabeus, or Macbeth as some speak it, when Duncan had been thus betrayed to his end, assumed the sceptre of sovereignty, usurper fashion, to himself, and would have pursued the sons of dead Duncan to their destruction. For Duncan had two sons: to wit, Malcolm Canmore, that is Malcolm of the big head,[2] and Donald Bane. . . . For two years [the] two brothers stayed in their own country, hoping for victory; and when they could strive no more, Donald took his course to the Isles and Malcolm to Cumbria. . . .

This Malcolm Canmore, though he had a just right to the kingdom of Scotland, remained in England during fourteen years, till at length his friends alike and his rivals called him back to the paternal home: his rivals, indeed, to the end they might destroy him; and his friends that he might put to the test his chance of sovereignty. . . . This Macbeth afflicted with divers punishments those who favoured Malcolm Canmore: some he despoiled; some he cast into loathsome dungeons; others again he not only stripped of all that they had, but drove them exiles from the kingdom, and there were not wanting some that he beheaded. Among the remnant was Macduff,

---

[1] **Macbeth:** "Machabeda" in the original; Macbeth's name is spelled in a number of ways in the various historical narratives.   [2] **big head:** the name "Canmore" derives from Gaelic *ceann* ("chief" or "leader") and *mor* ("great" or "important"); the phrase "big head" or "great head" therefore refers to his rank, not his physical appearance.

Selection from John Major, *A History of Greater Britain*, translated from the original Latin and edited with notes by Archibald Constable (Edinburgh: Printed at the University Press by T. and A. Constable for the Scottish History Society, 1892) 120–23.

Thane of Fife, one of the chief men of the kingdom. Now Macbeth mistrusted this man sorely, and insulted him with these words — saying that he would soon bring him under the yoke, even as an ox in the plough. But Macduff feigned to take this as said in jest, as if he were innocent of what was meant, and so turned aside the rage of the king; and, withdrawing himself in secret from the court, took ship for England. Macbeth thereupon seized upon all his possessions for the royal treasury, and declared him at the horn an enemy of the commonweal, banishing him too in perpetuity from the kingdom. But this action displeased the rest of the nobles greatly, inasmuch as the king on his own authority only, without summons of the supreme council, had proscribed[3] a man of this quality.

Now when Macduff was come to the presence of Malcolm Canmore, and was urging him to return to the land of his fathers, promising him that the nobles and the common people too would welcome his arrival — he, desiring to put Macduff's good faith to the test, declared that for three reasons he should prove himself an unserviceable king: first of all, that he was by nature voluptuous, and by consequence would deal wantonly with the daughters and (what is a much greater wrong) the wives of the nobility; secondly, that he was avaricious, and would covet all men's goods. To these two objections Macduff makes answer: 'In the kingdom of Scotland, all northern and cold though it be, you shall find a wife, the fairest you will, who shall alone suffice for your needs. There is no prince, whether in England or Scotland, who will not readily give you his daughter in marriage. And for avarice, you shall use as your own the whole possessions of the realm; and there is naught that the people will deny you if you but ask it in the way of love and with no desire for strife.' To all this Malcolm then made yet a third objection, saying: 'I am a liar, a man of deceit, unstable in all my ways.' And then to him Macduff is said to have made this answer: 'Dregs of the race of man, begone; begone, thou monster among men — fit neither to reign nor live.' Now Malcolm, when he had thus proved the honesty and good faith of Macduff, declared to him the true reason wherefore he had made these objections, and bade him be of good courage — promising him that if, as he trusted, God should restore the sceptre to his hands, he would make double restitution whereof Macduff had been despoiled. Yet he was unwilling to take his departure from England, where already he had been an exile fifteen years, till he had come to speech of Edward, king of the English, and had received the king's gracious consent that he should depart. And Edward received him with all kindness — for all men were sure of the kindest reception from him — and granted him support both of money and men.

---

[3] **proscribed:** banished

Meanwhile arise mutterings of revolt in Scotland against Macbeth, and on the first arrival of Malcolm and Macduff the princes and people welcomed them gladly, and met their king with tokens of joy; which when Macbeth the usurper came to know, he fled to the northern parts of Scotland. Thither Malcolm pursued him, making no delay, and after a short struggle, Macbeth, who was much inferior in his forces, was at Lumphanan slain. Meanwhile, however, when news of his death was brought to the followers of Macbeth, they carry to Scone one Lulach,[4] his cousin, nicknamed the simpleton, and there crown him, judging that some part of the nobles and the common people would be with them; but when they found he had no following, they fled. When Malcolm came to know what had happened he sends men in search of Lulach, whom they find and put to death at Strathbogie, and the few who had still clung to him hid themselves as best they could. On the final overthrow of this evil faction, Malcolm was brought to Scone, and there, in the year of our Lord one thousand and fifty-seven, was solemnly crowned.

[4] **Lulach**: Macbeth's stepson by his wife, Queen Gruoch, not his "cousin" (although this term could generally apply to almost any relative).

→ GEORGE BUCHANAN

From History of Scotland   1582

[D]uncan welcomed Macbeth's aid against the rebels; Macbeth promised] that, if the command or generalship were bestowed on him and Bancho, who was well acquainted with that country, he would quickly subdue all, and quiet things. This Mackbeth was of a sharp wit, and of a very lofty spirit; and, if moderation had accompanied it, he had been worthy of a command, though an eminent one. But, in punishing offenders, he was so severe, that having no respect to the laws, he seemed soon likely to degenerate into cruelty. When the chief command of the army was conferred upon him, many were so terrified, that, casting aside their hopes, which they had conceived by reason of the king's slothful temper, they hid themselves in holes and corners. The Islanders and the Irish, their flight being stopp'd, were driven into great despair, and in a fierce fight were every one of them slain; Macduald himself, with a few others flying into a neighbor castle,

George Buchanan, *Rerum Scoticarum historia,* translated by T. Page (London, 1690), from bk. 7.

being past all hopes of pardon, redeemed himself and his from the opprobri-
ousness of his enemies, by a voluntary death. Mackbeth, not content with
that punishment, cut off his head, and sent it to the King at Perth, and hung
up the rest of his body, for all to behold, in a conspicuous place. Those of the
Redshanks,[1] which he took, he caused to be hanged.

This domestic sedition being appeased, a far greater terror succeeded,
and seized on him, occasioned by the Danes. For Sueno, the powerful King
of the Danes, dying, left three kingdoms to his three sons; England to
Harold; Norway to Sueno; and Denmark to Canutus. Harold dying soon
after, Canutus succeeded him in the realm of England. Sueno, (or Swain)
King of Norway, being emulous of his brother's glory, crossed the seas with a
great navy, and landed in Fife; upon the bruit[2] of his coming, Mackbeth was
sent to levy an army; Bancho, the other general, staying in the interim, with
the King. Duncanus, or Donald, as if he had been roused from a fit of slug-
gishness, was forced to go meet the enemy. They fought near Culross, with
such obstinate courage, that as one party was scarce able to fly, so the other
had no heart to pursue. The Scots, who look'd upon themselves as overcome,
rather by the incommodiousness of the place, than by the valor of their enemies, retreated to Perth; and there stayed with the relicts of their conquered
forces, waiting for the motions[3] of the enemy.

[Duncan offers to send food to the Norwegian troops during a period of
negotiation.] . . .

Whereupon, a great deal of bread and wine was sent, both wine pressed
out of the grape, and also strong drink made of barly-malt, mixed with the
juice of a poisonous herb, whereof abundance grows in Scotland, called,
Somniferous Night-shade. The stalk of it is above two foot long, and in its
upper part spreads into branches, the leaves are broadish, accuminated[4] on
the outside, and faintly green. The berries are great and of a black color
when they are ripe, which proceed out of the stalk under the bottom of the
leaves. Their taste is sweetish, and almost insipid. It hath a very small seed,
as little as the grains of a fig. The virtue[5] of the fruit, root, and especially of
the seed, is soporiferous;[6] and will make men mad, if they be taken in too
great quantities. With this herb all the provision was infected, and they that
carried it, to prevent all suspicion of fraud, tasted of it before, and invited the
Danes to drink huge draughts thereof. Sueno himself, in token of good will,

---

[1] **Redshanks**: Celtic inhabitants of the Scottish Highlands or Ireland ("red legs," from their
exposure to the sun).   [2] **bruit**: noise, sound.   [3] **motions**: movements of the army.   [4] **accuminated**: brought to a sharp point.   [5] **virtue**: power, operative influence.   [6] **soporiferous**: inducing an unnatural or excessive sleep.

did the same, according to the custom of his nation. But Duncan, knowing that the force of the potion would reach to their very vitals,[7] whilst they were asleep, had in great silence admitted Mackbeth, with his forces into the city, by a gate which was furthest off from the enemy's camp; and, understanding by his spies, that the enemy was fast asleep and full of wine, he sent Bancho before, who well knew all the avenues both of that place, and of the enemy's camp too, with the greatest part of the army; placing the rest in ambush. He, entering their camp, and making a great shout, found all things in a greater posture of negligence than he imagined, before. There were a few raised up at the noise, who running up and down, like madmen, were slain as they were met; the others were killed, sleeping. . . .

'Tis reported, that the Danes, having made so many unlucky expeditions into Scotland, bound themselves by a solemn oath, never to return, as enemies, thither, any more. When matters thus prosperously succeeded with the Scots, both at home and abroad, and all things flourished in peace, Mackbeth, who had always a disgust at the unactive slothfulness of his cousin; and thereupon had conceived a secret hope of the kingdom in his mind, was further encouraged in his ambitious thoughts, by a dream which he had: For one night, when he was far distant from the King, he seemed to see three women, whose beauty was more august and surprising than bare women's useth to be, of which, one saluted him, Thane of Angus; another, Thane of Murray; and a third, King of Scotland. His mind, which was before sick betwixt hope and desire, was mightily encouraged by this dream, so that he contrived all possible ways, by which he might obtain the kingdom; in order to which, a just occasion was offered him, as he thought. Duncan begat two sons on the daughter of Sibert, a petty King of Northumberland; Malcolm, surnamed Cammorus, (which is as much as *jolt-head,*) and Donaldus, surnamed Banus, i.e., *white:* of these, he made Malcolm, scarce yet out of his childhood, Governor of Cumberland. Mackbeth took this matter mighty heinously;[8] in regard, he look'd upon it as obstacle of delay to him, in his obtaining the kingdom; for, having arrived at the enjoyment of his other honors, promised him by his dream; by this means, he thought, that either he should be secluded altogether from the kingdom; or else, should be much retarded in the enjoyment thereof; in regard the government of Cumberland was always look'd upon, as the first step to the kingdom of Scotland. Besides, his mind, which was fierce enough of itself, was spurred on, by the daily importunities of his wife, (who

---

[7] **vitals:** essential organs of the body.   [8] **heinously:** hatefully.

was privy[9] to all his counsels.) Whereupon, communicating the matter to his most intimate friends, amongst whom Bancho was one, he got a fit opportunity, at Inverness, to way-lay the King, and so slew him in the seventh year of his reign; and gathering a company together, went to Scone, and under the shelter of popular favor, made himself King. Duncan's children were astonished at this sudden disaster. They saw their father was slain, the author of the murder in the throne, and snares laid for them, to take away their lives; that so, by their deaths, the kingdom might be confirmed to Mackbeth: Whereupon, they shifted up and down, and hid themselves, and thus, for a time, escaped his fury. But perceiving that no place could long secure them from his rage; and that, being of a fierce nature, there was no hope of clemency to be expected from him, they fled several ways; Malcolm, into Cumberland, and Donald, to the kindred of his father, in the Hebrides Islands.[10]

MACKBETH, THE EIGHTY-FIFTH KING

Mackbeth, to confirm the ill-gotten kingdom to himself, procured the favor of the nobles by great gifts, being secure of the king's children because of their age, and of his neighboring princes, in regard of their mutual animosities, and discords. Thus having engaged the great men, he determined to procure the favor of the vulgar by justice and equity, and to retain it by severity, if nothing else would do. Whereupon, he determined with himself to punish the free-booters[11] or thieves, who had taken courage from the lenity of Duncan. . . . The public peace being thus restored, he applied his mind to make laws, (a thing almost wholly neglected by former kings) and indeed, he enacted many good and useful ones, which now are either wholly unknown, or else lie unobserved, to the great damage of the public. In a word, he so managed the government for ten years, that, if he had not obtained it by violence, he might have been accounted inferior to none of the former kings. But when he had so strengthened himself with the aid and favor of the multitude, that he feared no force to disturb him, the murder of the king (as 'tis very probable) hurried his mind into dangerous precipices, so that he converted his government, got by treachery, into a cruel tyranny. He vented the first shock of his inhumanity upon Bancho, who was his companion in the King's parricide. Some ill men had spread a kind of prophecy abroad among the vulgar, *That hereafter his posterity should enjoy the*

---

[9] **privy**: has knowledge of a secret.   [10] **Hebrides Islands**: islands to the west of Scotland.
[11] **free-booters**: those who go about in search of plunder.

kingdom; whereupon, fearing lest he, being a powerful and active man, and also of the blood royal,[12] should imitate the example proposed by himself, he courteously invited him and his son to supper, but, in his return, he caused him to be slain, as if a sudden fray and tumult had arisen. His son Fleance, being not known in the dark, escaped the ambush, and, being informed by his friends how his father was treacherously slain by the King, and that his life was also sought after, he fled secretly into Wales. Upon that murder, so cruelly and perfidiously committed, the nobles were afraid of themselves, insomuch, that they all departed to their own homes, and came but few of them, and those very seldom, to court. So that the King's cruelty being partly discovered by some, and partly vehemently suspected by all, mutual fear and hatred sprung up betwixt him and the nobility. Whereupon, seeing the matter could no longer be concealed, he broke forth into open tyranny, and the rich and powerful for light, frivolous, and, many times, but pretended, causes, were put to death. Their confiscated goods helped to maintain a band of debauchees, which he had about him under the name of a guard. And yet, he thought, that his life was not sufficiently secured by them neither, so that he resolved to build a castle on the top of the hill Dunsinane, where there was a large prospect all over the country; which work proceeding but slowly on, by reason of the difficulty of carriage of materials thither, he commanded in all the thanes of the whole kingdom, and so dividing the task amongst them, they themselves were to oversee, that the laborers did their duty. At that time Mackduff was the Thane of Fife, a very powerful man in his country;[13] he, being loth to commit his life unto the King's hands, went not himself, but sent thither many workmen, and some of them his intimate friends, to press on the work. The King, either out of a desire (as was pretended) to see how the building proceeded, or else to apprehend Mackduff, (as he himself feared) came to view the structure, and by chance spying a team of Mackduff's oxen, not able to draw up their load against a steep hill, he took thence a willing occasion to vent his passion against the Thane, saying, *That he knew well enough, before, his disobedient temper, and therefore was resolved to punish it; and, to make him an example, he threatened to lay the yoke upon his own neck, instead of his oxen.* Mackduff, hearing of it, commended the care of his family to his wife, and, without any delay, fitted up a small vessel, as well as the straits[14] of time permitted, and so passed over into Lothian, and from thence into England. The King hearing that he intended to fly, made haste into Fife, with a strong band of men to prevent him; but, he being departed before, the King was

---

[12] **blood royal:** i.e., he too is stained with the King's blood through regicide.   [13] **country:** home area.   [14] **straits:** limited amount.

presently admitted into his castle, where he poured out all his fury upon the Thane's wife and children, who were there present. His goods were confiscated, he himself was proclaimed traitor, and a grievous punishment was threatened to any, who dared to converse with, or entertain, him. He exercised also great cruelty against others, if they were either noble or rich, without distinction. For now the nobility was despised by him, and he managed the government by domestic counsels. In the meantime, Macduff, arriving in England, found Malcolm there, royally treated by King Edward. For Edward, when the Dane's power was broken in England, being recalled from banishment, did favor Malcolm. . . .

[Macduff tries to persuade Malcolm to raise an army against Macbeth.]

Besides, he told him, that King Edward was so gracious a prince, that he would not be wanting to him, his friend, and suppliant; that the people did also favor him and hated the tyrant; in fine,[15] *That God's favor would attend the good, against the impious, if he were not wanting*[16] *to himself.* But Malcolm, who had often before been persuaded, and solicited to return, by messengers secretly sent to him from Mackbeth; that he might not be ensnared, before he committed so great a concern to fortune, resolved to try the faithfulness of Mackduff.

[Malcolm accuses himself of horrible, unkingly vices; Macduff in despair is about to leave him when Malcolm tells him he was only testing his loyalty.]

Thus they, plighting their faith one to another, consulted concerning the destruction of the tyrant, and advised their friends of it, by secret messages. King Edward assisted him with ten thousand men. . . . At the report of this army's march, there was a great combustion in Scotland, and many flock'd in daily to the new King; Mackbeth being deserted by almost all his men, in so sudden a revolt, not knowing what better course to take, shut up himself in the castle of Dunsinnan, and sent his friends into the Hebrides, and into Ireland, with money to hire soldiers. Malcolm understanding his design, makes up directly towards him, the people praying for him all along as he went, and, with joyful acclamations, wishing him good success. His soldiers took this as an omen of victory, and thereupon stuck up green boughs in their helmets, representing an army triumphing, rather than going to fight. Mackbeth being terrified at the confidence of his enemy, immediately fled; and his soldiers, forsaken by their leader, surrendered themselves up to Malcolm. Some of our writers do here record many fables, which are like Milesian[17] tales, and fitter for the stage, than an history; and therefore I

---

[15] **in fine:** in short. [16] **wanting:** lacking. [17] **Milesian tales:** "Milesian fables or nonsensical;

omit them.[18] Mackbeth reigned seventeen years. In the first ten, he performed the duty of a very good king; in the last seven, he equalled the cruelty of the worst of tyrants.

MALCOLM, III. THE EIGHTY-SIXTH KING.

Malcolm, having thus recovered his father's kingdom, was declared King at Scone, the 25th day of April, in the year of our redemption, 1057. At the entrance of his reign, he convened an assembly of the estates at Forfar; where the first thing he did, was, to restore to the children their father's estates, who had been put to death by Mackbeth. He is thought by some to have been the first, that introduced new and foreign names, as distinguishments of degrees in honor, which he borrowed from his neighbor-nations, and are no less barbarous than the former were: such as are Dukes, Marquesses, Earls, Barons, Riders or Knights. Mackduff, the Thane of Fife, was the first who had the title of Earl, conferred upon him, and many others afterwards, according to their respective merits, were honored with new titles. . . .

[After a peace with England was established, various factions within Scotland fought against King Malcolm.]

Walter, the nephew[19] of Bancho by his son Fleance, who was before received into favor with the King, was sent against the Galway-men; and Mackduff, against the other rebels; whilst the King himself was gathering greater forces. Walter slew the head of that faction, and so quell'd the common soldiers, that the King at his return, made him Lord Steward of all Scotland, for his good service.

This magistrate was to gather in all the King's revenues; also, he had a jurisdiction, such as the sheriffs of counties have; and he is the same with that, which our ancestors called a Thane. But nowadays, the English speech getting the better of our country language, the Thanes of counties are in many places called Stewards; and he, which was anciently called Abthane, is now the Lord High Steward of Scotland. Yet, in some few places, the name

---

for the inhabitants of Miletum in Ionia were infamous for telling tales, so far from being true, that they had not the least shadow of truth in them" (note to another usage of term in Page's translation).   [18] Buchanan is referring to the more spectacular, and less believable, stories about Macbeth, such as supernatural visitations by witches and mysterious prophecies. His explanations are more down-to-earth: instead of witches, Macbeth has a dream; and instead of the witches prophesying Banquo's line, "some ill men" (enemies of Banquo) spread a rumor designed to engage Macbeth's cruelty.   [19] **nephew**: Walter is actually Banquo's grandson.

of Thane doth yet remain. From this Walter, the family of the Stewarts, who have so long reigned over Scotland, took its beginning.

→ RAPHAEL HOLINSHED

From The Chronicles of England, Scotland, and Ireland 1587

After Malcolm succeeded his nephew Duncan, the son of his daughter Beatrice: for Malcolm had two daughters, the one which was this Beatrice, being given in marriage unto one Abbanath Crinen, a man of great nobility, and thane of the isles and west parts of Scotland, bare of that marriage the foresaid Duncan; the other called Doada, was married unto Sinell the thane of Glammis, by whom she had issue one Macbeth a valiant gentleman, and one that if he had not been somewhat cruel of nature, might have been thought most worthy the government of a realm. On the other part, Duncan was so soft and gentle of nature, that the people wished the inclinations and manners of these two cousins to have been so tempered and interchangeably bestowed betwixt them, that where the one had too much of clemency, and the other of cruelty, the mean vertue betwixt these two extremities might have reigned by indifferent[1] partition in them both, so should Duncan have proved a worthy king, and Macbeth an excellent captain. The beginning of Duncan's reign was very quiet and peaceable, without any notable trouble; but after it was perceived how negligent he was in punishing offendors, many misruled persons took occasion thereof to trouble the peace and quiet state of the commonwealth, by seditious commotions which first had their beginnings in this wise.[2]

Banquo the thane of Lochaber, of whom the house of the Stewards[3] is descended, the which by order of lineage hath now for a long time enjoyed the crown of Scotland, even till these our days, as he gathered the finances due to the king, and further punished somewhat sharply such as were notorious offendors, being assailed by a number of rebels inhabiting in that country, and spoiled[4] of the money and all other things, had much ado to get away with life, after he had received sundry[5] grievous wounds amongst

---

[1] **indifferent:** not definitely possessing either of two opposite qualities.   [2] **wise:** way, manner.
[3] **Stewards:** i.e., the Stuarts.   [4] **spoiled:** robbed.   [5] **sundry:** various.

Raphael Holinshed, *The Chronicles of England, Scotland, and Ireland* (1587; this text from the London, 1808 edition), 5:264–77.

FIGURE 5 *"A sergeant at arms, slain by the rebels," from Raphael Holinshed's* The Chronicles of England, Scotland, and Ireland *(1577). Like many illustrations in Holinshed's 1577 edition, this woodcut was used several times in different histories. The 1587 edition did not reprint the illustrations.*

them. Yet escaping their hands, after he was somewhat recovered of his hurts and was able to ride, he repaired to the court, where making his complaint to the King in most earnest wise, he purchased at length that the offendors were sent for by a sergeant at arms, to appear to make answer unto such matters as should be laid to their charge: but they augmenting their mischievous act with a more wicked deed, after they had misused the messenger with sundry kinds of reproaches, they finally slew him also.

Then, doubting not but for such contemptuous demeanor against the King's regal authority, they should be invaded with all the power the king could make, Macdonwald one of great estimation among them, making first a confederacy with his nearest friends and kinsmen, took upon him to be chief captain of all such rebels, as would stand against the king, in maintenance of their grievous offences lately committed against him. Many slanderous words also, and railing taunts this Macdonwald uttered against his prince, calling him a faint-hearted milksop, more meet[6] to govern a sort of idle monks in some cloister, than to have the rule of such valiant and hardy men of war as the Scots were. He used also such subtle persuasions and forged allurements, that in a small time he had gotten together a mighty

[6] **meet:** fit.

power of men: for out of the western isles there came unto him a great multitude of people, offering themselves to assist him in that rebellious quarrel, and out of Ireland in hope of the spoil came no small number of kerns and gallowglasses,[7] offering gladly to serve under him, whither it should please him to lead them.

Macdonwald thus having a mighty puissance[8] about him, encountered with such of the King's people as were sent against him into Lochaber, and discomfiting[9] them, by mere force took their captain Malcolm,[10] and after the end of the battle smote off his head. This overthrow being notified to the King, did put him in wonderful fear, by reason of his small skill in warlike affairs. Calling therefore his nobles to a council, he asked of them their best advice for the subduing of Macdonwald and other the rebels. Here, in sundry heads (as ever it happeneth) were sundry opinions, which they uttered according to every man his skill. At length Macbeth speaking much against the King's softness, and overmuch slackness in punishing offendors, whereby they had such time to assemble together, he promised notwithstanding, if the charge were committed unto him and unto Banquo, so to order the matter, that the rebels should be shortly vanquished and quite put down, and that not so much as one of them should be found to make resistance within the country.

And even so it came to pass: for being sent forth with a new power, at his entering into Lochaber, the fame of his coming put the enemies in such fear, that a great number of them stole secretly away from their captain Macdonwald, who nevertheless enforced thereto, gave battle unto Macbeth, with the residue which remained with him: but being overcome, and fleeing for refuge into a castle (within the which his wife and children were enclosed) at length when he saw how he could neither defend the hold[11] any longer against his enemies, nor yet upon surrender be suffered to depart with life saved, he first slew his wife and children, and lastly himself, lest if he had yielded simply, he should have been executed in most cruel wise for an example to other. Macbeth entering into the castle by the gates, as then set open, found the carcass of Macdonwald lying dead there amongst the residue of the slain bodies, which when he beheld, remitting no piece of his cruel nature with that pitiful sight, he caused the head to be cut off, and set upon a pole's end, and so sent it as a present to the King who as then lay at Bertha. The headless trunk he commanded to be hung up upon an high pair of gallows.

---

[7] **kerns and gallowglasses**: "kerns" were lightly armed foot soldiers, while "gallowglasses" were well-trained and heavily armed soldiers; both terms were applied to Irish or Scottish (i.e., non-English) soldiers. Shakespeare borrows this phrase in the play (1.2.13). [8] **puissance**: power, force. [9] **discomfiting**: overcoming, defeating. [10] **Malcolm**: a captain in the army, not the Malcolm who is the son of Duncan. [11] **hold**: fortress.

FIGURE 6 *"Macdonwald slayeth his wife and children, and lastly himself," from Raphael Holinshed's* The Chronicles of England, Scotland, and Ireland *(1577). This image was also recycled in other stories within the* Chronicles.

Them of the western isles suing for pardon, in that they had aided Macdonwald in his traitorous enterprise, he fined at great sums of money: and those whom he took in Lochaber, being come thither to bear armor against the king, he put to execution. Hereupon the islandmen conceived a deadly grudge towards him, calling him a covenant-breaker, a bloody tyrant, and a cruel murderer of them whom the King's mercy had pardoned. With which reproachful words Macbeth being kindled in wrathful ire against them, had passed over with an army into the isles, to have taken revenge upon them for their liberal talk, had he not been otherwise persuaded by some of his friends, and partly pacified by gifts presented unto him on the behalf of the islandmen, seeking to avoid his displeasure. Thus was justice and law restored again to the old accustomed course, by the diligent means of Macbeth. Immediately whereupon word came that Sueno King of Norway was arrived in Fife with a puissant[12] army, to subdue the whole realm of Scotland. . . . the pretense of his coming was to avenge the slaughter of his uncle Camus, and other of the Danish nations slain at Barre, Crierdane and Cernmer.

The cruelty of this Sueno was such, that he neither spared man, woman, nor child, of what age, condition or degree soever they were. Whereof when

---

[12] **puissant:** powerful.

King Duncan was certified, he set all slothful and lingering delays apart, and began to assemble an army in most speedy wise, like a very valiant captain: for oftentimes it happeneth, that a dull coward and slothful person, constrained by necessity, becometh very hardy and active. Therefore when his whole power was come together, he divided the same into three battles.[13] The first was led by Macbeth, the second by Banquo, and the King himself governed in the main battle or middle ward, wherein were appointed to attend and wait upon his person the most part of all the residue of the Scottish nobility.

The army of Scottishmen being thus ordered, came unto Culros, where encountering with the enemies, after a sore and cruel fought battle, Sueno remained victorious, and Duncan with his Scots discomfited.[14] Howbeit the Danes were so broken by this battle, that they were not able to make long chase on their enemies, but kept themselves all night in order of battle, for doubt lest the Scots assembling together again, might have set upon them at some advantage. On the morrow, when the fields were discovered,[15] and that it was perceived how no enemies were to be found abroad, they gathered the spoil,[16] which they divided amongst them, according to the law of arms. Then was it ordained by commandment of Sueno, that such no soldier should hurt either man, woman, or child except as were found with weapon in hand ready to make resistance, for he hoped now to conquer the realm without further bloodshed.

But when knowledge was given how Duncan was fled to the castle of Perth and that Macbeth was gathering a new power to withstand the incursions of the Danes, Sueno raised his tents and coming to the said castle, laid a strong siege round about it. Duncan seeing himself thus environed by his enemies, sent a secret message by counsel of Banquo to Macbeth, commanding him to abide at Inchcuthill, till he heard from him some other news. In the meantime Duncan fell in feigned[17] communication with Sueno, as though he would have yielded up the castle into his hands, under certain conditions, and this did he to drive time, and to put his enemies out of all suspicion of any enterprise meant against them, till all things were brought to pass that might serve for the purpose. At length, when they were fallen at a point for rendering up the hold, Duncan offered to send forth of the castle into the camp great provision of victuals[18] to refresh the army, which offer was gladly accepted of the Danes, for they had been in great penury[19] of sustenance many days before.

---

[13] **battles**: a body or line of troops (as in "battalion").   [14] **discomfited**: defeated.   [15] **discovered**: revealed.   [16] **spoil**: the plunder.   [17] **feigned**: pretended.   [18] **victuals**: food, supplies.   [19] **penury**: scarcity.

The Scots hereupon took the juice of mekilwoort berries,[20] and mixed the same in their ale and bread, sending it thus spiced and confectioned, in great abundance unto their enemies. They rejoicing that they had got meat and drink sufficient to satisfy their bellies, fell to eating and drinking after such greedy wise, that it seemed they strove who might devour and swallow up most, till the operation of the berries spread in such sort through all the parts of their bodies, that they were in the end brought into a fast[21] dead sleep, that in manner it was impossible to awake them. Then forthwith Duncan sent unto Macbeth, commanding him with all diligence to come and set upon the enemies, being in easy point to be overcome. Macbeth making no delay, came with his people to the place, where his enemies were lodged, and first killing the watch, afterwards entered the camp, and made such slaughter on all sides without any resistance, that it was a wonderful[22] matter to behold, for the Danes were so heavy of sleep, that the most part of them were slain and never stirred: other that were awakened either by the noise or other ways forth, were so amazed and dizzy headed upon their wakening, that they were not able to make any defense: so that of the whole number there escaped no more but only Sueno himself and ten other persons, by whose help he got to his ships lying at rode[23] in the mouth of Taie. . . .

The Scots having won so notable a victory, after they had gathered and divided the spoil of the field, caused solemn processions to be made in all places of the realm, and thanks to be given to almighty God, that had sent them so fair a day over their enemies. But whilst the people were thus at their processions, word was brought that a new fleet of Danes was arrived at Kingcorn, sent thither by Canute King of England, in revenge of his brother Sueno's overthrow. To resist these enemies, which were already landed, and busy in spoiling the country, Macbeth and Banquo were sent with the King's authority, who having with them a convenient[24] power, encountered the enemies, slew part of them, and chased the other to their ships. They that escaped and got once to their ships, obtained of Macbeth for a great sum of gold, that such of their friends as were slain at this last bickering, might be buried in Saint Colmes Inch. In memory whereof, many old sepultures[25] are yet in the said Inch, there to be seen graven with the arms of the Danes, as the manner of burying noble men still is, and heretofore hath been used.

A peace was also concluded at the same time betwixt the Danes and Scottishmen, ratified (as some have written) in this wise: That from thenceforth the Danes should never come into Scotland to make any war against

---

[20] **mekilwoort berries:** the nightshade plant, which has poisonous juice.   [21] **fast:** deep, sound.
[22] **wonderful:** astonishing, amazing.   [23] **rode:** boat-anchor.   [24] **convenient:** suitable, appropriate.   [25] **sepultures:** graves, tombs.

FIGURE 7 *"Macbeth, Banquo, and the Three Weird Sisters," from Raphael Holinshed's* The Chronicles of England, Scotland, and Ireland *(1577). This woodcut, justly famous, is the only image of the four in Holinshed's history of Macbeth that was not used elsewhere in the book. The three women are not dressed according to modern notions of witchcraft. They may be distinguished by age — old, middle, and young.*

the Scots by any manner of means. And these were the wars that Duncan had with foreign enemies, in the seventh year of his reign. Shortly after happened a strange and uncouth[26] wonder, which afterward was the cause of much trouble in the realm of Scotland, as ye shall after hear. It fortuned as Macbeth and Banquo journeyed towards Forres, where the King then lay, they went sporting by the way together without other company, save only themselves, passing through the woods and fields, when suddenly in the midst of a laund,[27] there met them three women in strange and wild apparel, resembling creatures of elder world,[28] whom when they attentively beheld, wondering much at the sight, the first of them spake and said, "All hail Macbeth, Thane of Glammis" (for he had lately entered into that dignity and office by the death of his father Sinell.) The second of them said, "Hail Macbeth, Thane of Cawdor." But the third said, "All hail Macbeth, that hereafter shalt be King of Scotland."

Then Banquo, "What manner of women (saith he) are you, that seem so little favorable unto me, whereas to my fellow here, besides high offices, ye

---

[26] **uncouth**: strange, marvelous.   [27] **laund**: glade.   [28] **elder world**: i.e., ancient times.

assign also the kingdom, appointing forth nothing for me at all?" "Yes" (saith the first of them) "we promise greater benefits unto thee, than unto him, for he shall reign in deed, but with an unlucky end: neither shall he leave any issue[29] behind him to succeed in his place, where contrarily thou in deed shalt not reign at all, but of thee those shall be born which shall govern the Scottish kingdom by long order of continual descent." Herewith the foresaid women vanished immediately out of their sight. This was reputed at the first but some vain fantastical[30] illusion by Macbeth and Banquo, insomuch that Banquo would call Macbeth in jest, King of Scotland; and Macbeth again would call him in sport likewise, the father of many kings. But afterwards the common opinion was, that these women were either the Weird Sisters, that is (as ye would say) the goddesses of destiny, or else some nymphs or fairies, indued with knowledge of prophecy by their necromantical[31] science, because everything came to pass as they had spoken. For shortly after, the Thane of Cawdor being condemned at Forres of treason against the King committed, his lands, livings, and offices were given of the King's liberality to Macbeth.

The same night after, at supper, Banquo jested with him and said, "Now Macbeth thou hast obtained those things which the two former sisters prophesied, there remaineth only for thee to purchase that which the third said should come to pass." Whereupon Macbeth revolving the thing in his mind, began even then to devise how he might attain to the kingdom: but yet he thought with himself that he must tarry a time, which should advance him thereto (by the divine providence) as it had come to pass in his former preferment. But shortly after, it chanced that King Duncan, having two sons by his wife which was the daughter of Siward Earl of Northumberland, he made the elder of them called Malcolm Prince of Cumberland, as it were thereby to appoint him his successor in the kingdom, immediately after his decease. Macbeth, sore troubled herewith, for that he saw by this means his hope sore hindered (where, by the old laws of the realm, the ordinance was, that if he that should succeed were not of able age to take the charge upon himself, he that was next of blood unto him should be admitted) he began to take counsel how he might usurp the kingdom by force, having a just quarrel so to do (as he took the matter) for that Duncan did what in him lay to defraud him of all manner of title and claim, which he might in time to come, pretend unto[32] the crown.

The words of the three sisters also (of whom before ye have heard) greatly encouraged him hereunto, but specially his wife lay sore upon him to

---

[29] **issue**: children.   [30] **fantastical**: imaginary.   [31] **necromantical**: black magic, sorcery; the art of prophecy.   [32] **pretend unto**: claim.

FIGURE 8 *"Macbeth usurpeth the crown," from Raphael Holinshed's* The Chronicles of England, Scotland, and Ireland *(1577). Even this woodcut was used in several different histories.*

attempt the thing, as she that was very ambitious, burning in unquenchable desire to bear the name of a queen. At length therefore, communicating his purposed intent with his trusty friends, amongst whom Banquo was the chiefest, upon confidence of their promised aid, he slew the King at Inverness, or (as some say) at Botgosuane, in the sixth year of his reign. Then having a company about him of such as he had made privy[33] to his enterprise, he caused himself to be proclaimed King, and forthwith went unto Scone where (by common consent) he received the investure of the kingdom according to the accustomed manner. The body of Duncan was first conveyed unto Elgin, and there buried in kingly wise; but afterwards it was removed and conveyed unto Colmekill, and there laid in a sepulture amongst his predecessors, in the year after the birth of our Savior, 1046.

Malcolm Canmore and Donald Bane the sons of King Duncan, for fear of their lives (which they might well know that Macbeth would seek to bring to end for his more sure confirmation in the estate) fled into Cumberland, where Malcolm remained, till time that Saint Edward[34] the son of Etheldred recovered the dominion of England from the Danish power, the which Edward received Malcolm by way of most friendly entertainment:

---

[33] **privy:** having knowledge of a secret.   [34] **Saint Edward:** i.e., Edward the Confessor, King of England 1042–1066 C.E.

but Donald passed over into Ireland, where he was tenderly cherished by the king of that land. Macbeth, after the departure thus of Duncan's sons, used great liberality towards the nobles of the realm, thereby to win their favor, and when he saw that no man went about to trouble him, he set his whole intention to maintain justice, and to punish all enormities and abuses, which had chanced through the feeble and slothful administration of Duncan . . . that many years after all theft and reiffings[35] were little heard of, the people enjoying the blissful benefit of good peace and tranquility. Macbeth . . . was accounted the sure defense and buckler[36] of innocent people; and hereto he also applied his whole endeavor, to cause young men to exercise themselves in virtuous manners, and men of the church to attend their divine service according to their vocations. . . . He made many wholesome laws and statutes for the public weal[37] of his subjects. . . .

These . . . laws Macbeth caused to be put as then in use, governing the realm for the space of ten years in equal justice. But this was but a counterfeit zeal of equity[38] shown by him, partly against his natural inclination to purchase thereby the favor of the people. Shortly after, he began to show what he was, instead of equity practicing cruelty. For the prick of conscience (as it chanceth ever in tyrants, and such as attain to any estate by unrighteous means) caused him ever to fear, lest he should be served of the same cup as he had ministered to his predecessor. The words also of the three Weird Sisters, would not out of his mind, which as they promised him the kingdom, so likewise did they promise it at the same time unto the posterity of Banquo. He willed therefore the same Banquo with his son named Fleance, to come to a supper that he had prepared for them, which was indeed, as he had devised, present death at the hands of certain murderers, whom he hired to execute that deed, appointing them to meet with the same Banquo and his son without[39] the palace, as they returned to their lodgings, and there to slay them, so that he would not have his house slandered, but that in time to come he might clear himself, if anything were laid to his charge upon any suspicion that might arise.

It chanced yet by the benefit of the dark night, that though the father were slain, the son yet by the help of almighty God reserving him to better fortune, escaped that danger: and afterwards having some inkling (by the admonition of some friends which he had in the court) how his life was sought no less than his father's, who was slain not by chancemedly[40] (as by the handling of the matter Macbeth would have had it to appear) but even

---

[35] **reiffings**: robberies.   [36] **buckler**: protector (literally, a small, round shield).   [37] **weal**: well-being.   [38] **equity**: fairness, impartiality.   [39] **without**: outside of.   [40] **chancemedley**: by accident, haphazardly.

upon a prepensed[41] device: whereupon to avoid further peril he fled into Wales.[42] . . .

. . . [A]fter the contrived slaughter of Banquo, nothing prospered with the foresaid Macbeth: for in manner every man began to doubt[43] his own life, and durst unneth[44] appear in the King's presence; and even as there were many that stood in fear of him, so likewise stood he in fear of many, in such sort that he began to make those away by one surmised cavillation[45] or other, whom he thought most able to work him any displeasure.

At length he found such sweetness by putting his nobles thus to death, that his earnest thirst after blood in this behalf might in no wise be satisfied: for ye must consider he won double profit (as he thought) hereby: for first they were rid out of the way whom he feared, and then again his coffers were enriched by their goods which were forfeited to his use, whereby he might the better maintain a guard of armed men about him to defend his person from injury of them whom he had in any suspicion. Further, to the end he might the more cruelly oppress his subjects with all tyrant-like wrongs, he built a strong castle on the top of an high hill called Dunsinane, situated in Gowry,[46] ten miles from Perth, on such a proud height, that standing there aloft, a man might behold well near all the countries[47] of Angus, Fife, Stermond, and Ernedale, as it were lying underneath him. This castle then being founded on the top of that high hill, put the realm to great charges[48] before it was finished, for all the stuff necessary to the building, could not be brought up without much toil and business. But Macbeth being once determined to have the work go forward, caused the thanes of each shire within the realm, to come and help towards that building, each man his course about.

At the last, when the turn fell unto Macduff Thane of Fife to build his part, he sent workmen with all needful provision, and commanded them to show such diligence in every behalf, that no occasion might be given for the King to find fault with him, in that he came not himself as other had done, which he refused to do, for doubt lest the king bearing him (as he partly understood) no great good will, would lay violent hands upon him, as he had done upon diverse other. Shortly after, Macbeth coming to behold how the work went forward, and because he found not Macduff there, he was sore offended, and said, "I perceive this man will never obey my commandments, till he be ridden with a snaffle:[49] but I shall provide well enough for him."

---

[41] **prepensed:** premeditated. [42] At this point Holinshed describes, at length, the succession of Scottish kings from Banquo to King James. [43] **doubt:** fear for. [44] **unneth:** scarcely. [45] **cavillation:** unfair legal trickery. [46] **Gowrie:** Shakespeare does not include this reference in his play; the Earl of Gowrie had allegedly attempted to assassinate King James in 1600. [47] **countries:** i.e., shires or counties. [48] **great charges:** great expense. [49] **snaffle:** bridle.

Neither could he afterwards abide to look upon the said Macduff, either for that he thought his puissance over great; either else for that he had learned of certain wizards, in whose words he put great confidence (for that the prophecy had happened so right, which the three fairies or Weird Sisters had declared unto him) how that he ought to take heed of Macduff, who in time to come should seek to destroy him.

And surely hereupon had he put Macduff to death, but that a certain witch, whom he had in great trust, had told that he should never be slain with man born of any woman, nor vanquished till the wood of Birnam came to the castle of Dunsinane. By this prophecy Macbeth put all fear out of his heart, supposing he might do what he would, without any fear to be punished for the same, for by the one prophecy he believed it was impossible for any man to vanquish him, and by the other impossible to slay him. This vain hope caused him to do many outrageous things, to the grievous oppression of his subjects. At length Macduff, to avoid peril of life, purposed with himself to pass into England, to procure Malcolm Canmore to claim the crown of Scotland. But this was not so secretly devised by Macduff, but that Macbeth had knowledge given him thereof: for kings (as is said) have sharp sight like unto lynx, and long ears like unto Midas.[50] For Macbeth had in every noble man's house one sly fellow or other in fee[51] with him, to reveal all that was said or done within the same, by which slight he oppressed the most part of the nobles of his realm.

Immediately then, being advertised whereabout Macduff went, he came hastily with a great power into Fife, and forthwith besieged the castle where Macduff dwelled, trusting to have found him therein. They that kept the house, without any resistance opened the gates, and suffered him to enter, mistrusting none evil. But nevertheless Macbeth most cruelly caused the wife and children of Macduff, with all other whom he found in that castle, to be slain. Also he confiscated the goods of Macduff, proclaimed him traitor, and confined him out of all the parts of his realm; but Macduff was already escaped out of danger, and gotten into England unto Malcolm Canmore, to try what purchase he might make by means of his support to revenge the slaughter so cruelly executed on his wife, his children, and other friends. At his coming unto Malcolm, he declared into what great misery the estate of Scotland was brought, by the detestable cruelties exercised by the tyrant Macbeth, having committed many horrible slaughters and murders, both as well of the nobles as commons, for the which he was hated right mortally of all his liege people, desiring nothing more than to be deliv-

---

[50] **Midas:** fabled king whose ears were turned into ass's ears.   [51] **in fee:** on the payroll.

ered of that intolerable and most heavy yoke of thralldom,[52] which they sustained at such a caitiff's[53] hands.

Malcolm hearing Macduff's words, which he uttered in very lamentable sort, for mere compassion and very ruth[54] that pierced his sorrowful heart, bewailing the miserable state of his country, he fetched a deep sigh; which Macduff perceiving, began to fall most earnestly in hand with him, to enterprise the delivering of the Scottish people out of the hands of so cruel and bloody a tyrant, as Macbeth by too many plain experiments did show himself to be: which was an easy matter for him to bring to pass, considering not only the good title he had, but also the earnest desire of the people to have some occasion ministered, whereby they might be revenged of those notable injuries, which they daily sustained by the outrageous cruelty of Macbeth's misgovernance. Though Malcolm was very sorrowful for the oppression of his countrymen the Scots, in manner as Macduff had declared; yet doubting whether he were come as one that meant unfeignedly[55] as he spake, or else as sent from Macbeth to betray him, he thought to have some further trial, and thereupon dissembling his mind at the first, he answered as followeth.

"I am truly very sorry for the misery chanced to my country of Scotland, but though I have never so great affection to relieve the same, yet by reason of certain incurable vices, which reign in me, I am nothing meet thereto. First, such immoderate lust and voluptuous sensuality (the abominable fountain of all vices) followeth me, that if I were made King of Scots, I should seek to deflower your maids and matrons, in such wise that mine intemperancy should be more importable[56] unto you than the bloody tyranny of Macbeth now is." Hereunto Macduff answered: "This surely is a very evil fault, for many noble princes and kings have lost both lives and kingdoms for the same; nevertheless there are women enough in Scotland, and therefore follow my counsel, make thyself king, and I shall convey the matter so wisely, that thou shalt be so satisfied at thy pleasure in such secret wise, that no man shall be aware thereof."

Then said Malcolm, "I am also the most avaricious creature on the earth, so that if I were king, I should seek so many ways to get lands and goods, that I would slay the most part of all the nobles of Scotland by surmised[57] accusations, to the end I might enjoy their lands, goods, and possessions; and therefore to show you what mischief may ensue on you through mine unsatiable covetousness, I will rehearse unto you a fable. There was a fox having a sore place on him overset with a swarm of flies, that continually sucked out her blood: and when one that came by and saw this manner,

---

[52] **thralldom**: servitude, bondage. [53] **caitiff**: base coward, wretch. [54] **ruth**: pity. [55] **unfeignedly**: honestly. [56] **importable**: unbearable. [57] **surmised**: false.

demanded whether she would have the flies driven beside[58] her, she answered no: for if these flies that are already full, and by reason thereof suck not very eagerly, should be chased away, other that are empty and felly[59] and hungered, should light in their places, and suck out the residue of my blood far more to my grievance than these, which now being satisfied do not much annoy me. Therefore," saith Malcolm, "Suffer me to remain where I am, lest if I attain to the regiment of your realm, mine unequenchable avarice may prove such, that ye would think the displeasures which now grieve you, should seem easy in respect of the unmeasurable outrage, which might ensue through my coming amongst you."

Macduff to this made answer, how "It was a far worse fault than the other: for avarice is the root of all mischief, and for that crime the most part of our kings have been slain and brought to their final end. Yet notwithstanding follow my counsel, and take upon thee the crown. There is gold and riches enough in Scotland to satisfy thy greedy desire." Then said Malcolm again, "I am furthermore inclined to dissimulation, telling of leasings,[60] and all other kinds of deceit, so that I naturally rejoice in nothing so much, as to betray and deceive such as put any trust or confidence in my words. Then sith[61] there is nothing that more becometh a prince than constancy, verity, truth, and justice, with the other laudable fellowship of those fair and noble virtues which are comprehended only in soothfastness,[62] and that lying utterly overthroweth the same; you see how unable I am to govern any province or region: and therefore sith you have remedies to cloak and hide all the rest of my other vices, I pray you find shift to cloak this vice amongst the residue."

Then said Macduff: "This yet is the worst of all, and there I leave thee, and therefore say; Oh ye unhappy and miserable Scottishmen, which are thus scourged with so many and sundry calamities, each one above other! Ye have one cursed and wicked tyrant that now reigneth over you, without any right or title, oppressing you with his most bloody cruelty. This other that hath the right to the crown, is so replete with the inconstant behavior and manifest vices of Englishmen, that he is nothing worthy to enjoy it: for by his own confession he is not only avaricious, and given to unsatiable lust, but so false a traitor withal, that no trust is to be had unto any word he speaketh. Adieu Scotland, for now I account myself a banished man for ever, without comfort or consolation:" and with those words the brackish tears trickled down his cheeks very abundantly.

At the last, when he was ready to depart, Malcolm took him by the

---

[58] **beside:** away from.   [59] **felly:** fierce, cruel.   [60] **leasings:** lies.   [61] **sith:** since.   [62] **soothfast-ness:** truthfulness.

sleeve, and said: "Be of good comfort, Macduff, for I have none of these vices before remembered, but have jested with thee in this manner, only to prove thy mind: for diverse times heretofore hath Macbeth sought by this manner of means to bring me into his hands, but the more slow I have showed myself to condescend to[63] thy motion and request, the more diligence shall I use in accomplishing the same." Incontinently[64] hereupon they embraced each other, and promising to be faithful the one to the other, they fell in consultation how they might best provide for all their business, to bring the same to good effect. Soon after, Macduff repairing to the borders of Scotland, addressed his letters with secret dispatch unto the nobles of the realm, declaring how Malcolm was confederate with him, to come hastily into Scotland to claim the crown, and therefore he required them, sith he was right inheritor thereto, to assist him with their powers to recover the same out of the hands of the wrongful usurper.

In the meantime, Malcolm purchased such favor at King Edward's hands, that old Siward Earl of Northumberland, was appointed with ten thousand men to go with him into Scotland, to support him in this enterprise, for recovery of his right. After these news were spread abroad in Scotland, the nobles drew into two several[65] factions, the one taking part with Macbeth, and the other with Malcolm. Hereupon ensued oftentimes sundry bickerings, and diverse light skirmishes: for those that were of Malcolm's side, would not jeopard[66] to join with their enemies in a pight[67] field, till his coming out of England to their support. But after that Macbeth perceived his enemy's power to increase, by such aid as came to them forth of England with his adversary Malcolm, he recoiled back into Fife, there purposing to abide in camp fortified, at the castle of Dunsinane, and to fight with his enemies, if they meant to pursue him; howbeit some of his friends advised him, that it should be best for him, either to make some agreement with Malcolm, or else to flee with all speed into the isles, and to take his treasure with him, to the end he might wage sundry great princes of the realm to take his part, and retain strangers,[68] in whom he might better trust than in his own subjects, which stole daily from him: but he had such confidence in his prophecies, that he believed he should never be vanquished, till Birnam wood were brought to Dunsinane; nor yet to be slain with any man, that should be or was born of any woman.

Malcolm following hastily after Macbeth, came the night before the battle into Birnam wood, and when his army had rested for a while there to refresh them, he commanded every man to get a bough of some tree or

---

[63] **condescend to**: agree to. [64] **Incontinently**: instantly. [65] **several**: separate. [66] **jeopard**: risk. [67] **pight**: pitched (i.e., in combat). [68] **strangers**: foreigners (i.e., mercenaries).

other of that wood in his hand, as big as he might bear, and to march forth therewith in such wise, that on the next morrow they might come closely and without sight in this manner within view of his enemies. On the morrow when Macbeth beheld them coming in this sort, he first marveled what the matter meant, but in the end remembered himself that the prophecy which he had heard long before that time, of the coming of Birnam wood to Dunsinane castle, was likely to be now fulfilled. Nevertheless, he brought his men in order of battle, and exhorted them to do valiantly, howbeit his enemies had scarcely cast from them their boughs, when Macbeth perceiving their numbers, betook him straight to flight, whom Macduff pursued with great hatred even till he came into Lunphanan, where Macbeth perceiving that Macduff was hard at his back, leapt beside his horse, saying, "Thou traitor, what meaneth it that thou shouldst thus in vain follow me that am not appointed to be slain by any creature that is born of a woman, come on therefore, and receive thy reward which thou hast deserved for thy pains," and therewithal he lifted up his sword thinking to have slain him.

But Macduff quickly avoiding from his horse, yet he came at him, answered (with his naked sword in his hand) saying: "It is true Macbeth, and now shall thine insatiable cruelty have an end, for I am even he that thy wizards have told thee of, who was never born of my mother, but ripped out of her womb." Therewithal he stepped unto him, and slew him in the place. Then cutting his head from his shoulders, he set it upon a pole, and brought it unto Malcolm. This was the end of Macbeth, after he had reigned 17 years over the Scottishmen. In the beginning of his reign he accomplished many worthy acts, very profitable to the commonwealth, (as ye have heard) but afterward by illusion of the Devil, he defamed the same with most terrible cruelty. He was slain in the year of the Incarnation 1057, and in the 16. year of King Edward's reign over the Englishmen.

Malcolm Canmore thus recovering the realm (as ye have heard), by support of King Edward, in the 16. year of the same Edward's reign, he was crowned at Scone the 25 day of April, in the year of our Lord 1057. Immediately after his coronation he called a Parliament at Forfair, in the which he rewarded them with lands and livings that had assisted him against Macbeth, advancing them to fees and offices as he saw cause, and commanded that specially those that bare the surname of any offices or lands, should have and enjoy the same. He created many earls, lords, barons, and knights. Many of them that before were thanes, were at this time made earls, as Fife, Menteith, Atholl, Lennox, Murray, Caithness, Ross, and Angus. These were the first earls that have been heard of amongst the Scottishmen (as their histories do make mention).

The Cultural Afterlife of Shakespeare's *Macbeth*

Written in 1606 but not published until 1623, Shakespeare's *Macbeth* nevertheless quickly made an impact on his contemporaries. In his play *The Knight of the Burning Pestle*, usually dated 1607–08 (Beaumont xi–xiii), Francis Beaumont seems to be parodying the ghost of Banquo scene, when he has Jasper the apprentice pretend to be his own ghost to frighten Venturewell:

> And never shalt thou sit or be alone
> In any place, but I will visit thee
> With ghastly looks, and put into thy mind
> The great offences which thou didst to me.
> When thou art at thy table with thy friends,
> Merry in heart, and fill'd with swelling wine,
> I'll come in midst of all thy pride and mirth,
> Invisible to all men but thyself,
> And whisper such a sad tale in thine ear
> Shall make thee let the cup fall from thy hand,
> And stand as mute and pale as Death itself. (5.1.18–28)

Beaumont's appropriation of this scene — the same one mentioned by Simon Forman in 1611 (see below) — is perhaps the first of four centuries' worth of quotations, adaptations, parodies, and imitations of famous scenes in the play. Thomas Duffett's parody of 1674 (see p. 178) mocks not only individual lines of Shakespeare's play, but also many of the innovations — stagecraft and the songs particularly — of Sir William Davenant's version (p. 162).

The witches, Banquo's ghost, Lady Macbeth's sleepwalking, trying to wash blood off guilty hands — these and other such moments have entered our culture in many forms and now exist independently of the play itself. The lines "Double, double, toil and trouble, / Fire burn and cauldron bubble," "Out damned spot!," and "Tomorrow, and tomorrow, and tomorrow," while not quite as famous as "To be or not to be," have nevertheless entered the lexicon of popular culture, and are as likely to be heard as questions on a television game show or tags on an advertisement as on the stage of the Royal Shakespeare Theatre in Stratford-upon-Avon. In the movie *Dead Poets Society* (1989), set at a prep school, the English teacher (played by Robin Williams) tries to enliven Shakespeare for his students by mimicking John Wayne as *he* would try to say, "Is this a dagger I see before me?" In a more serious vein, the great Japanese film director, Akira Kurosawa, transformed *Macbeth* to a medieval Japanese setting in his brilliant film *Throne of*

Blood (1957). The noted directors Orson Welles (1948), Roman Polanski (1971), and Trevor Nunn (1979) have also made powerful film interpretations of the play. Today, *Macbeth* is also accessible through a thirty-minute animated film and an "illustrated" classic comic-book version, and as an interactive CD-ROM. The "Karaoke Macbeth" CD-ROM is also available.

Macbeth has also become famous — or notorious — among actors and directors as a specially difficult, even dangerous play. It is said to be very bad luck for an actor or director even to pronounce the *name* of the play, and as a result they usually refer to it as the "Scottish play." There are many theatrical legends about accidents and bad luck afflicting those associated with productions of the play; whether all, or even most, are true is another question. The play's legend of bad luck may have begun with two seventeenth-century accounts of tragic accidents at productions. On August 20, 1673, Thomas Isham made this entry in his journal: "It is reported that Harris has killed his associate actor, in a scene on the stage, by accident. It was the tragedy called 'Macbeth,' in which Harris performed the part of Macduff, and ought to have slain his fellow-actor, Macbeth; but during the fence [i.e., fencing] it happened that Macduff pierced Macbeth in the eye, by which thrust he fell lifeless, and could not bring out the last words of his part" (Munro 2: 193). (This would have been Davenant's production of *Macbeth*, with Thomas Betterton acting the part of Macbeth; but it is possible another actor had substituted for him. It is also possibly only a rumor.) In 1691, Gerard Langbaine offered a similar story about the audience, one that he claimed to have witnessed: "At the acting of this tragedy, on the stage, I saw a real one acted in the pit; I mean the death of Mr. Scroop, who received his death's wound from the late Sir Thomas Armstrong, and died presently after he was remov'd to a house opposite to the theater in Dorset-Garden" (Munro 2: 365–66).

The five examples of the afterlife of *Macbeth* that follow are confined to the period of approximately sixty years after the play was first written and performed. The first two selections were written during Shakespeare's lifetime, and while he was still active in his theater company, the King's Men — one by a playgoer (Forman), the other by a fellow dramatist (Middleton). The last three selections were written after the English Civil War, which began in 1642. In that same year, a Parliamentary majority ordered that all the theaters be closed. The reigning Stuart monarch, Charles I, was imprisoned and, in 1649, executed, in one of the more shocking political acts of the past century. Oliver Cromwell led a nonmonarchical form of government, sometimes called the Protectorate; the theaters remained officially closed throughout this period. Charles I's son, Charles II, was restored to the throne in 1660, and the theaters were allowed to reopen. Many things in the

Restoration theater were now different from the period before 1642. The theater buildings themselves were now largely different ones — usually smaller and with a more expensive admission than Shakespeare's Globe Theatre, for example — actresses were now permitted on the stage, and plays *by* women, such as Aphra Behn (?1640–1689), were now performed. Given the lack of dramatic repertory since 1642, Restoration theater managers and playwrights frequently revived plays written before 1642, and Shakespeare's plays were among the favorites, including *Macbeth* (see the excerpt from Davenant, p. 162). While links to the earlier period of drama were strong, still a very different political and cultural world was in place in 1660, and many Restoration writers, highly sensitive to the resumption of the throne by a Stuart monarch, now saw the legend of Macbeth as itself a kind of prophecy of the reign of the Stuarts. Boece's myth of the line of Banquo/Fleance leading to Walter Stewart was taken as historical fact, as the anonymous selection, "The Story of Macbeth" reveals.

→ SIMON FORMAN

From Book of Plays   *1611*

Simon Forman (1552–1611) was a doctor, astrologer, and occasional playgoer. He made his name as a doctor by remaining in London and treating patients during the severe plague outbreaks of 1592 and 1594. He was accused, after his death, of providing Frances Howard, then Lady Essex, with a love potion for Robert Carr, with whom she was having an affair, and possibly other drugs to make her husband impotent. (This scandal constitutes part of the context of Thomas Middleton's *The Witch*; see the introduction to that excerpt below.)

In his *Book of Plays*, Forman recorded his attendance at, and his observations of, four plays performed at the Globe theater in April and May of 1611: Shakespeare's *Macbeth, Cymbeline,* and *The Winter's Tale,* as well as a *Richard II* that, as Forman reports it, so differs in its plot from Shakespeare's *Richard II* that it seems to be a different play. Forman's accounts of these plays are fascinating and extremely valuable in that they are eyewitness reports of the stagings of Shakespeare's plays during his lifetime. But his accounts are also frustrating, because he was an erratic observer. In his notes on seeing *The Winter's Tale* on May 15, 1611, for example, Forman spends almost a third of his account on Autolycus and the tricks he plays on the inhabitants of Bohemia, but he never even men-

Simon Forman, *The Book of Plays and Notes hereof and Formans for Common Policy* (no date; manuscript in Bodleian Library, Oxford). Modernized from the transcription in Chambers, *Shakespeare,* 2:337–38.

tions the notorious bear that eats Antigonus, or the great statue scene when Hermione returns to life — two of the most celebrated theatrical moments in all of Shakespeare's plays.

Similarly, Forman leaves much out of his notes on *Macbeth* — the second appearance of the witches, for example, or Hecate herself — and he either imagined scenes that did not exist on the stage or perhaps conflated the performance he saw with some written version he had read. It is highly unlikely that Forman saw Macbeth and Banquo "riding through a wood" on the Globe stage, for example, but he might have read this passage in Holinshed; and did Forman really *see* Macbeth and Lady Macbeth trying to wash the blood from their hands, or only imagine it, stimulated by the play's imagery and Lady Macbeth's comments? On the other hand, Forman gives a vivid description of the banquet scene and the appearance of Banquo's ghost, with a very specific aspect of the staging — that the ghost of Banquo "sat down in his chair *behind*" Macbeth (my emphasis). For all its peculiarities, Forman's account of seeing *Macbeth* in the Globe theater, some five years after it had been written and first staged, allows us a glimpse of what actually happened in Shakespeare's theater.

In *Macbeth* at the Globe, 1610,[1] the 20 of April Saturday, there was to be observed first how Macbeth and Banquo, two noblemen of Scotland, riding through a wood, there stood before them three women fairies or nymphs, and saluted Macbeth, saying three times unto him, "Hail Macbeth, King of Codon;[2] for thou shalt be a king, but shall beget no kings, etc." Then said Banquo, "What, all to Macbeth and nothing to me?" "Yes," said the nymphs, "Hail to thee, Banquo, thou shalt beget kings, yet be no king." And so they departed and came to the court of Scotland, to Duncan King of Scots, and it was in the days of Edward the Confessor. And Duncan bade them both kindly welcome, and made Macbeth forthwith Prince of Northumberland,[3] and sent him home to his own castle, and appointed Macbeth to provide for him, for he would sup with him the next day at night, and did so. And Macbeth contrived to kill Duncan, and through the persuasion of his wife did that night murder the King in his own castle, being his guest. And there were many prodigies seen that night and the day before. And when Macbeth had murdered the King, the blood on his hands could not be washed off by any means, nor from his wife's hands, which handled the bloody daggers in hiding them, by which means they became

---

[1] 1610: apparently an error for 1611 (April 20 was a Saturday in 1611, not 1610; performances of other plays correctly dated 1611 surround this entry).   [2] **Codon**: i.e., Cawdor (Forman collapses two separate prophecies into a single one here).   [3] **Northumberland**: i.e. Cumberland (see *Macbeth* 1.4.39; again, a likely misremembering on Forman's part).

much amazed and affronted. The murder being known, Duncan's two sons fled, the one to England, the other to Wales, to save themselves. They being fled, they were supposed guilty of the murder of their father, which was nothing so. Then was Macbeth crowned king, and then he for fear of Banquo, his old companion, that he should beget kings but be no king himself, he contrived the death of Banquo, and caused him to be murdered on the way as he rode. The next night, being at supper with his noblemen whom he had bid to a feast to the which also Banquo should have come, he began to speak of noble Banquo, and to wish that he were there. And as he thus did, standing up to drink a carouse to him, the ghost of Banquo came and sat down in his chair behind him. And he, turning about to sit down again, saw the ghost of Banquo, which fronted[4] him so, that he fell into a great passion of fear and fury, uttering many words about his murder, by which, when they heard that Banquo was murdered, they suspected Macbeth.

Then Macduff fled to England to the King's son, and so they raised an army, and came into Scotland, and at Dunsinane overthrew Macbeth. In the meantime, while Macduff was in England, Macbeth slew Macduff's wife and children, and after in the battle Macduff slew Macbeth.

Observe also how Macbeth's queen did rise in the night in her sleep, and walk, and talked and confessed all, and the doctor noted her words.

[4] fronted: frightened.

→ THOMAS MIDDLETON

From The Witch   *1615/16*

The playwright Thomas Middleton (1580–1627) is intimately connected to the text of Shakespeare's *Macbeth* as we have it today. It is clear that he revised Shakespeare's play, and some have gone so far as to term him virtually a coauthor. The story of the relationship among Shakespeare, Middleton, and the texts of their plays reveals much about how authorship was understood at the time, and how Shakespeare's *Macbeth* was transformed after its initial appearance. The following outline represents a consensus of current scholarly opinion, but not all scholars would necessarily agree.[1]

[1] See the discussions in the editions of *The Witch* by Esche, Greg, and Schafer, as well as in the editions of *Macbeth* by Braunmuller, Brooke, Muir, and Wells and Taylor.

This selection has been edited and modernized from the transcription in *The Witch*, ed. W. W. Greg and F. P. Wilson. Malone Society, 1950.

1. Shakespeare seems to have written *Macbeth* in 1606, perhaps as early as August, but a more precise dating is impossible.

2. *Macbeth* was revised about 1610–11 by Thomas Middleton, possibly even with Shakespeare, at which point the witches' songs in act 3, scene 5 and act 4, scene 1 were added; other lines may also have been added, but it is impossible to be certain which ones. In the printed text of *Macbeth*, only the first lines of the songs are given (such as the stage direction *"Sing within. Come away, come away, &c."*).

3. Thomas Middleton wrote *The Witch* probably between 1613 and 1616, and most likely around 1615–16; Middleton's play includes the full text of the witches' songs. The dating of Middleton's play rests in part on its extensive allusions to the Thomas Overbury affair: Frances Howard, daughter of the powerful Earl of Suffolk, married Robert Carr, the Earl of Essex, in 1613, after her previous marriage was annulled on the (dubious) grounds that it had never been consummated; Carr's secretary, Sir Thomas Overbury, who had opposed the marriage, was murdered at Frances Howard's instigation while he was a prisoner in the Tower. The crime eventually came to light, and Howard and Carr were found guilty at a scandalous trial in late 1615. (See p. 153 for Simon Forman's role in the case.)

4. Ralph Crane, a professional scrivener, or copyist, produced the manuscript of *The Witch* — the only existing copy of the play — sometime after 1619, when he seems to have begun working for the King's Men, Shakespeare's theater company.

5. The only contemporary text of Shakespeare's *Macbeth* was printed in 1623, in the First Folio, along with most of Shakespeare's other plays.

The dates of the revision of *Macbeth* and the writing of *The Witch* are by no means certain; it is even possible that Middleton wrote *The Witch* before he revised *Macbeth*. What *is* clear, though, is that the version of *Macbeth* that everyone has been reading and watching since 1623 was written not by Shakespeare alone, but by Shakespeare and/or with Thomas Middleton, for Middleton used the same songs in two different plays. Thus, the full context of Shakespeare's *Macbeth* includes the complex field of dramatic production and collaborative authorship in early modern England. The *Macbeth* we know today is a product of many different forces — aesthetic, economic, theatrical — at work in the period.

Printed below are edited versions of the full texts of the two songs as they appear in Middleton's *The Witch*; scholars assume that they would have been more or less the same when performed as part of *Macbeth*. (One line in the first song, spoken as an aside by another character, has been omitted because it has no connection to *Macbeth*.)

The Witch

FROM ACT 3, SCENE 3 (*MACBETH* 3.5.33FF)

[VOICES OF WITCHES] *in the air*[1]:
 Come away, come away;
 Hecate, Hecate, come away.
HECATE:
 I come, I come, I come, I come,
 With all the speed I may,
 With all the speed I may.   5
 Where's Stadlin?[2]
[STADLIN] *in the air*:
                    Here.
[HECATE:]
 Where's Puckle?
[PUCKLE] *in the air*:
                    Here,
 And Hoppo too and Hellwain too;
 We lack but you, we lack but you.
 Come away, make up the count.[3]   10
HECATE:
 I will but 'noint,[4] and then I mount.
[VOICES OF WITCHES] *above:*
 There's one comes down to fetch his dues:

[*Malkin*][5] *a spirit like a cat descends*[6]

 A kiss, a coll, a sip of blood,
 And why thou stay'st so long
    I muse, I muse,   15
 Since the air's so sweet and good.
HECATE:
 Oh, art thou come?
 What news, what news?

---

[1] **in the air**: presumably from the balcony above the stage.   [2] **Stadlin**: the names "Stadlin," "Puckle," "Hoppo," and "Hellwain" are taken from Reginald Scot, *The Discovery of Witchcraft* (1584); see the discussion of his work (p. 302).   [3] **count**: total.   [4] **'noint**: anoint.   [5] **Malkin**: typical name for a cat (see also Graymalkin, in *Macbeth* 1.1.8); also associated with female demons or sluttish women.   [6] **descends**: the Globe Theatre, and presumably also the New Globe (built in 1613), had a winch in the ceiling of the overhanging roof, above the stage; probably only one actor at a time could ascend or descend.

[MALKIN]:
  All goes still to our delight;
  Either come or else   20
    Refuse, refuse.
HECATE:
  Now I am furnished for the flight.

  . . . .

HECATE *going up* [*with Malkin*]:
  Now I go, now I fly,
  Malkin my sweet spirit, and I.
  Oh, what a dainty pleasure 'tis   25
    To ride in the air
      When the moon shines fair,
  And sing and dance, and toy[7] and kiss.
  Over woods, high rocks, and mountains,
  Over seas, our mistress'[8] fountains,   30
  Over steep towers,[9] and turrets,
  We fly by night, 'mongst troops of spirits.
  No ring of bells to our ears sounds,
  No howls of wolves, no yelps of hounds.
  No, not the noise of water's breach[10]   35
  Or cannon's throat our height can reach.
[VOICES] *above*:
  No ring of bells etc.

FROM ACT 5, SCENE 2 (*MACBETH* 4.1.43FF)

A charm[11] song about a vessel[12]

HECATE:
  Black spirits and white, red spirits and grey,
  Mingle, mingle, mingle, you that mingle may.
    Titty, Tiffin, keep it stiff in.
    Fire-drake, Puckey, make it lucky.
    Liard, Robin,[13] you must bob in.   5

---

[7] **toy**: to play (erotically).   [8] **our mistress'**: Diana, the moon, was another name for Hecate.
[9] **steep towers**: this is the manuscript reading; some editors emend this to "steeples, towers."
[10] **water's breach**: i.e., the roaring of the waves.   [11] **charm**: the "charm" is intended to seduce
the "younker," or young man.   [12] **vessel**: the witches' cauldron.   [13] **Robin**: the names of these
spirits apparently also come from Reginald Scot, *The Discovery of Witchcraft* (1584); "Robin" is
Robin Goodfellow, or Puck, as in Shakespeare's *A Midsummer Night's Dream*.

Round, around, around, about, about —
All ill come running in, all good keep out!
1. [WITCH]:
Here's the blood of a bat.
HECATE:
Put in that, oh put in that.
2. [WITCH]:
Here's libbard's bane.[14]   10
HECATE:
Put in again.
1. [WITCH]:
The juice of toad, the oil of adder.
2. [WITCH]:
Those will make the younker[15] madder.
HECATE:
Put in — there's all — and rid the stench.
FIRESTONE:
Nay, here's three ounces of the red-haired[16] wench.   15
ALL [THE WITCHES]:
Round, around, around, etc.

---

[14] **libbard's bane:** leopard's poison (a particular kind of plant).   [15] **younker:** a young nobleman
or gentleman.   [16] **red-haired:** red hair was sometimes considered poisonous; also associated
with lechery.

✦ From "The Story of Macbeth"
A Collection of Divers and Remarkable Stories   *1670*

This narrative version of Macbeth's story occurs in a handwritten, evidently personal little book, a collection of one hundred and fifty "remarkable stories,"
which is now in the Folger Shakespeare Library. "Macbeth" is the first story in
the collection; there is also a version of *Romeo and Juliet.* Among the other stories are accounts of history, magic, love, and classical myth.

There is nothing remarkable about this anonymous author's account of Macbeth, but it perfectly typifies a Stuart royalist perspective on the story; it is in fact
a close paraphrase from an account in a popular book called *Microcosmus,* by
Peter Heylyn, first printed in 1621, with seven further editions through 1639. It
seems indebted more to Holinshed than to Shakespeare; for example, there is no

---

From *A Collection of Divers and Remarkable Stories. Tragical and Comical* (Folger Shakespeare
Library, V.a.81).

Lady Macbeth present, and as we can see in Davenant's version of the play, she is certainly one of the most memorable elements of the play. Instead, there is an emphasis on Macbeth's immediate and irresistible ambition, stimulated by the prophecies. Macbeth also becomes an even purer form of the tyrant — the word is repeated frequently — and his ten years of good rule in Holinshed and others now vanishes into mere libidinousness and cruelty "for the space of eighteen years, for so long he tyrannously reigned."

The "story" of Macbeth can only be concluded, in this account, by its consequences for royal succession, as if the very purpose of Macbeth's life and death were to generate Fleance and the race of Stuart monarchs; we have come a long distance from John Major's history of 1521. For this anonymous writer, the story of Macbeth in 1670 (as for Heylyn fifty years earlier) exists primarily as a justification for the Stuart monarchy, restored to the throne ten years earlier.

When Duncan was King of Scotland, anno 1034, he had two principal noblemen whom he employed in all matters of importance, called Macbeth and Banquo; these two travelling together, through a forest, were met by three witches, or Weirds, as the Scots call them. The first whereof making obeisance to Macbeth, saluted him, "Thane of Glamis" (a title to which that of Earl succeeded afterward), the second, "Thane of Cawdor," the third, "King of all Scotland." "This," said Banquo to them, "is unequal dealing, to give all the honors to my friend, and none to me." To whom one of the Weirds in answer to him, said, "That he indeed should not be king, but out of his loins should come a race of kings, that should rule Scotland for ever"; and having said thus, they all three suddenly vanished. Upon their arrival at court, Macbeth was immediately created Thane of Glamis; and not long after, some new services of his requiring further recompense, he was honored with the title of Thane of Cawdor. Seeing then how happily the prediction of the three Weirds fell out, in the two former [prophecies], he was resolved not to be wanting to himself in fulfilling the third, and therefore he killed the King, and after by reason of his command among the soldiers, and the populace, he succeeded in his throne. Being scarce warm in his seat, he called to mind the prediction given to his companion Banquo, whom hereupon suspecting as his supplanter, he caused him, with his whole kindred, to be murdered, only one son he had, named Fleance, escaped with much difficulty into Wales.

King Macbeth freed of this fear, built Dunsinane Castle, making it his ordinary residence. But afterward on new fears, consulting with certain wizards, about his future estate, he was by one told, that he should never be overcome, till Birnam Wood (which was some few miles distant) did come to Dunsinane Castle; and by another, that he should never be slain, by any man born of a woman. Secure then, as he thought, he omitted no kind of libidinousness or cruelty, for the space of eighteen years, for so long he tyrannously reigned. At last Macduff, Governor of Fife, joining to himself some few patriots, which had not as yet felt the tyrant's sword, privately met one night in Birnam Wood, and early in the morning, marched toward Dunsinane Castle, every man bearing a bough in his hand before him, the better to keep themselves from discovery: by which stratagem, they presently took the castle by *scalado*.[1] Macbeth escaping, was pursued, overtaken, and urged to fight by Macduff; to whom the tyrant half in scorn replied, that in vain he attempted his death, for it was his destiny, never to be slain by any man born of a woman. "Now then," said Macduff, "is thy fatal hour come, for I was never born of a woman, but violently cut out of my mother's belly, she dying before her delivery." Which words so daunted the tyrant, that he was easily slain, and Malcolm Canmor, the true heir to the crown, was seated in the throne.

In the meantime Fleance the son of Banquo thrived so well in Wales, that falling in love with a Welsh Prince his daughter, and she not rejecting his affection, he begot a son on her named Walter. This Walter, flying out of Wales for a murder, was entertained in Scotland, and his descent once known, he was preferred to be Steward to King Edgar, anno 1100, from which office the name of Steward became as the surname of all his family. From this Walter descended that Robert Steward, who in right of his wife, that was the sister of David Bruce, King of Scotland, was king thereof, anno 1371, and this Robert, being descended from the princes of Wales that were of ancient times, thereby restored the British blood to the Scottish throne. Since which time, there hath been eleven[2] sovereigns of this name in Scotland, this present year of our Lord 1670 successively; which is answerable to the prediction of the Weird who told Banquo, that his race should rule Scotland for ever.

---

[1] **scalado:** climbing over with ladders; scaling. [2] **eleven:** James I was the ninth Stuart, Charles I the tenth, and Charles II, reigning in 1670, the eleventh.

→ SIR WILLIAM DAVENANT

From Macbeth, A Tragedy   *1663/64*

The dramatist and poet Sir William Davenant (1606–1668) was said to be Shakespeare's godson, and later would himself claim to be his natural, illegitimate son (Aubrey 85). Davenant was educated at Oxford and moved in courtly society during the reign of Charles I. In 1638, he was made England's Poet Laureate. An active supporter of the Royalist side during the Civil War, Davenant was imprisoned in the Tower from 1650 to 1652. Davenant was manager of the Drury Lane Theatre before and after the Civil War, and then manager of the Covent Garden Theatre. Drury Lane and Covent Garden were the only two "patent," or legally licensed, theaters after the Restoration of Charles II in 1660. Davenant wrote some thirty masques and plays, both before and after the Civil War, including the first English opera, *The Siege of Rhodes,* in 1656. Davenant was also among the first to employ actresses on the stage after 1660; before 1642, women's parts on the stage were almost always played by boy actors.

One of the important literary projects of Restoration dramatists was to recover — which usually meant, to rewrite — the plays of Shakespeare. He was widely recognized as the greatest of the pre–Civil War dramatists, but he was said to have lived in a "barbarous" age, relatively speaking, and hence there were certain flaws in his plays. The language, moral lessons, and stagecraft of Shakespeare's plays were therefore frequently "improved," or rewritten. The rewriting of Shakespeare could range from the individual word and image, to the great issues of plot. In his version of *King Lear,* for example, Nahum Tate (1652–1715) gave Shakespeare's great tragedy a happy ending, in which Cordelia does not die, but survives and marries Edgar! As bizarre as this transformation may seem to us now, Tate's version of *King Lear* was the only version *acted* in England for more than a century, from 1681 to 1838; while Shakespeare's text was always available in printed form, actors and audiences evidently preferred Tate's version. One widely praised adaptation of a Shakespearean text was John Dryden's *All for Love* (1678), a revision of *Antony and Cleopatra;* some readers think it is actually Dryden's best play.

Davenant's *Macbeth* is a fairly early instance of such Shakespearean revision. It was probably written in 1663–64, and Samuel Pepys saw it, according to an entry in his diary (Pepys 314), on November 5, 1664 (the anniversary of the Gunpowder Plot; see Chapter 3). It was published in 1674, in the text cited here. Davenant's version of the play was performed through 1751, though the great actor David Garrick produced his own version in the 1740s, in which he claimed to be restoring much of the Shakespearean text that Davenant had omitted. Still, Garrick made or retained substantial changes himself, including a death

---

William Davenant, *Macbeth, A Tragedy. With all the Alterations, Amendments, Additions, and New Songs* (London, 1674).

speech for Macbeth — he is not given one by Shakespeare — which must have reminded Garrick's audience of Marlowe's Dr. Faustus as he dies:

'Tis done! the scene of life will quickly close.
Ambition's vain, delusive dreams are fled,
And now I wake to darkness, guilt and horror.
I cannot bear it! let me shake it off —
'Two' not be; my soul is clogg'd with blood —
I cannot rise! I dare not ask for mercy —
It is too late, hell drags me down. I sink,
I sink — Oh! — my soul is lost forever!
Oh!   [*Dies.*]   (Garrick F5)

In his version of *Macbeth*, Davenant not only retained the songs added by Middleton earlier — it's likely that he took the entire Folio text as Shakespearean, in any event — but he also added others, in effect turning the play into a kind of opera. Davenant also "clarified" and "regularized" Shakespeare's verse in many places. Consider, as one example of such rewriting, Macbeth's lines after the murder, upon hearing the knocking at the gate:

Shakespeare	Davenant
Whence is that knocking?	What knocking's that?
How is't with me, when every noise appalls me?	How is't with me, when every noise affrights me?
What hands are here? Ha! They pluck out mine eyes.	What hands are here! can the sea afford
Will all great Neptune's ocean wash this blood	Water enough to wash away the stains?
Clean from my hand? No, this my hand will rather	No, they would sooner add a tincture to
The multitudinous seas incarnadine,	The sea, and turn the green into a
Making the green one red.	red. (2.2)
(2.2.61–67)	

Davenant's major changes to the play consist of the addition of five major passages (four of them whole new scenes), plus the return of Donalbain and Fleance at the end of the play. The main effects of Davenant's changes may be grouped into four categories: First, the roles of Macduff and Lady Macduff have been enormously expanded, until they are now virtually equal to those of the Macbeths; there are three entirely new scenes for them — act 2, scene 5, and act 3, scenes 2 and 6 — plus Lady Macduff's conversation with Lady Macbeth in act 1, scene 5. Second, there is a major new scene between Macbeth and Lady Macbeth (4.4); her role is also larger. Third, there is a major new encounter with the witches, in one of the Macduff scenes (2.5), with more songs and dances. Finally, Davenant tends to shift Shakespeare's intensely disturbing revelations of evil and perversion to the more comprehensible thematics of "ambition" and "tyranny" (themes of extreme relevance, no doubt, to someone who has barely survived the Civil War). The new Macduff scene, act 3, scene 2, is almost entirely about the relation between Macduff's personal ambition, balanced against the legitimate need to resist tyranny; it sounds like a typical political debate in the period. Macbeth, too, seems less extraordinary, and more conventionally motivated in these changes, as in the following revision of Macbeth's lines just before the murder of Duncan:

Shakespeare	Davenant
Whiles I threat, he lives;	But whilst I talk, he lives:
Words to the heat of deeds too cold breath gives.	*[A bell rings]*
A bell rings.	
I go, and it is done. The bell invites me.	hark, I am summon'd;
	O Duncan, hear it not, for 'tis a bell
Hear it not, Duncan, for it is a knell	That rings my coronation, and thy
That summons thee to heaven, or	knell. (2.1)
to hell. (2.1.61–65)	

Similarly, in one of the new scenes, Macbeth is made much more sentimental, and, strangely, still ambitious, as Malcolm's army approaches Scotland:

> The spur of my ambition prompts me to go
> And make my kingdom safe, but love which softens
> Me to pity her [Lady Macbeth] in her distress,
> Curbs my resolves.   (4.4)

In these and other changes, we can see how Shakespeare's *Macbeth*, just six decades after it was written, was substantially transformed through the different political, psychological, and dramatic imperatives of another age. In the case of Davenant himself — a playwright before and after the Civil War with real and perhaps imaginary ties to Shakespeare and his theater — his revision of *Macbeth* reveals a sympathetic but radically different artistic sensibility.

Macbeth, A Tragedy

ACT I, SCENE V

Enter Lady Macbeth, and Lady Macduff. Lady Macbeth having a letter in her hand.

LADY MACBETH:
Madam, I have observ'd since you came hither,
You have been still disconsolate. Pray tell me,
Are you in perfect health?

LADY MACDUFF: Alas! how can I?
My lord, when honor call'd him to the war,
Took with him half of my divided soul,   5
Which lodging in his bosom, lik'd so well
The place, that 'tis not yet return'd.
LADY MACBETH: Methinks
That should not disorder you: for, no doubt
The brave Macduff left half his soul behind him,
To make up the defect of yours.
LADY MACDUFF: Alas!   10
The part transplanted from his breast to mine,
(As 'twere by sympathy) still bore a share
In all the hazards which the other half
Incurr'd, and fill'd my bosom up with fears.
LADY MACBETH:
Those fears, methinks, should cease now he is safe.   15
LADY MACDUFF:
Ah, madam, dangers which have long prevail'd
Upon the fancy; even when they are dead
Live in the memory a-while.
LADY MACBETH:
Although his safety has not power enough to put
Your doubts to flight, yet the bright glories which   20
He gain'd in battle might dispel those clouds.
LADY MACDUFF:
The world mistakes the glories gain'd in war,
Thinking their lustre true: alas, they are
But comets, vapors! by some men exhal'd
From others' blood, and kindl'd in the region   25
Of popular applause, in which they live
A-while; then vanish: and the very breath
Which first inflam'd them, blows them out again.
LADY MACBETH [aside]:
I willingly would read this letter; but
Her presence hinders me; I must divert her.   30
[to Lady Macduff] If you are ill, repose may do you good;
Y'had best retire; and try if you can sleep.
LADY MACDUFF:
My doubtful thoughts too long have kept me waking,
Madam! I'll take your counsel. . . .   [Exit Lady Macduff.]

LADY MACBETH:
Now I have leisure, peruse this letter.   35
His last brought some imperfect news of things
Which in the shape of women greeted him
In a strange manner. This perhaps may give
More full intelligence   [*She reads the letter.*]

. . . .

ACT II, SCENE V

Scene An Heath. Enter Lady Macduff, Maid, and Servant.

LADY MACDUFF:
Art sure this is the place my lord appointed
Us to meet him?
SERVANT:
This is the entrance o'th' heath; and here
He order'd me to attend him with the chariot.
LADY MACDUFF:
How fondly[1] did my lord conceive that we   5
Should shun the place of danger by our flight
From Inverness? The darkness of the day
Makes the heath seem the gloomy walks of death.
We are in danger still: they who dare here
Trust Providence, may trust it anywhere.   10
MAID:
But this place, madam, is more free from terror:
Last night methoughts I heard a dismal noise
Of shrieks and groanings in the air.
LADY MACDUFF:
'Tis true, this is a place of greater silence;
Not so much troubled with the groans of those   15
That die; nor with the out-cries of the living.
MAID:
Yes, I have heard stories, how some men
Have in such lonely places been affrighted
With dreadful shapes and noises.   [*Macduff hollows.*[2]]

---

[1] **fondly**: foolishly.   [2] **hollows**: cries hello.

LADY MACDUFF:
But hark, my lord sure hollows;   20
'Tis he; answer him quickly.

SERVANT:
Illo, ho, ho, ho.

Enter Macduff.

LADY MACDUFF:
Now I begin to see him: are you on foot,
My lord?

MACDUFF:
Knowing the way to be both short and easy,   25
And that the chariot did attend me here,
I have adventur'd. Where are our children?

LADY MACDUFF:
They are securely sleeping in the chariot.

First Song by Witches.

I. WITCH:
Speak, sister, speak; is the deed done?

2. [WITCH]:
Long ago, long ago: 30
Above twelve glasses[3] since have run.

3. [WITCH]:
Ill deeds are seldom slow nor single:
Following crimes on former wait.
The worst of creatures fastest propagate.
Many more murders must this one ensue,   35
As if in death were propagation too.

2. [WITCH]:
He will.

I. [WITCH]:   He shall.

3. [WITCH]:   He must spill much more blood;
And become worse, to make his title good.

I. [WITCH]:
Now let's dance.

2. [WITCH]:   Agreed.

---

[3] **glasses**: presumably hourglasses; i.e., twelve hours.

3. [WITCH]:   Agreed.
4. [WITCH]:   Agreed.
CHORUS:
> We should rejoice when good kings bleed.   40
> When cattle die, about we go,
> What then, when monarchs perish, should we do?

MACDUFF:
> What can this be?

LADY MACDUFF:
> This is most strange: but why seem you afraid?
> Can you be capable of fears, who have   45
> So often caus'd it in your enemies?

MACDUFF:
> It was a hellish song: I cannot dread
> Ought[4] that is mortal; but this is something more.

Second Song.

> Let's have a dance upon the heath;
> We gain more life by Duncan's death.   50
> Sometimes like brinded[5] cats we shew,
> Having no musick but our mew.
> Sometimes we dance in some old mill,
> Upon the hopper, stones, and wheel,
> To some old saw, or bardish rhyme,   55
> Where still the mill-clack[6] does keep time.

> Sometimes about a hollow tree,
> Around, around, around dance we.
> Thither the chirping cricket comes,
> And beetle, singing drowsy hums.   60
> Sometimes we dance o're fens[7] and furze,[8]
> To howls of wolves, and barks of curs.
> And when with none of those we meet,
> We dance to th'echoes of our feet.

> At the night-raven's dismal voice,   65
> Whilst others tremble, we rejoice;

---

[4] **ought:** anything.   [5] **brinded:** streaked.   [6] **mill-clack:** "the clapper of a mill; an instrument which by striking the hopper causes the corn to be shaken into the mill-stones" (*Oxford English Dictionary*).   [7] **fens:** marsh, lowland.   [8] **furze:** spiny evergreen shrub that grows on waste land.

And nimbly, nimbly dance we still
To th'echoes from a hollow hill.

MACDUFF:
  I am glad you are not afraid.
LADY MACDUFF:
  I would not willingly to fear submit: 70
  None can fear ill, but those that merit it.
MACDUFF:
  Am I made bold by her? how strong a guard
  Is innocence? if anyone would be
  Reputed valiant, let him learn of you;
  Virtue both courage is, and safety too.   75

Enter Witches.   [*A dance of witches.*]

MACDUFF:
  These seem foul spirits; I'll speak to e'm.
  If you can anything by more than nature know;
  You may in those prodigious times foretell
  Some ill we may avoid.
I. WITCH:
  Saving thy blood will cause it to be shed.   80
2. [WITCH]:
  He'll bleed by thee, by whom thou first hast bled.
3. [WITCH]:
  Thy wife shall shunning danger, dangers find,
  And fatal be, to whom she most is kind.   [*Exeunt witches.*]
LADY MACDUFF:
  Why are you alter'd, sir? be not so thoughtful:
  The messengers of darkness never spake   85
  To men, but to deceive them.
MACDUFF:
  Their words seem to foretell some dire predictions.
LADY MACDUFF:
  He that believes ill news from such as these,
  Deserves to find it true. Their words are like
  Their shape; nothing but fiction.   90
  Let's hasten to our journey.
MACDUFF:
  I'll take your counsel; for to permit

Such thoughts upon our memories to dwell,
Will make our minds the registers of hell.   [*Exeunt omnes.*]

ACT III, SCENE II

Enter Macduff and Lady Macduff.

MACDUFF:
It must be so. Great Duncan's bloody death
Can have no other author but Macbeth.
His dagger now is to a scepter grown;
From Duncan's grave he has deriv'd his throne.
LADY MACDUFF:
Ambition urg'd him to that bloody deed: 5
May you be never by ambition led:
Forbid it, heav'n, that in revenge you should
Follow a copy that is writ in blood.
MACDUFF:
From Duncan's grave, methinks, I hear a groan
That calls aloud for justice.
LADY MACDUFF: If the throne   10
Was by Macbeth ill gain'd, heaven's justice may,
Without your sword, sufficient vengeance pay.
Usurpers' lives have but a short extent,
Nothing lives long in a strange element.
MACDUFF:
My country's dangers call for my defence   15
Against the bloody tyrant's violence.
LADY MACDUFF:
I am afraid you have some other end,
Than merely Scotland's freedom to defend.
You'd raise your self, whilst you would him dethrone;
And shake his greatness, to confirm your own.   20
That purpose will appear, when rightly scann'd,[9]
But usurpation at the second hand.
Good sir, recall your thoughts.
MACDUFF: What if I should
Assume the scepter for my country's good?

[9] **scann'd**: read, understood.

Is that an usurpation? can it be   25
Ambition to procure the liberty
Of this sad realm, which does by treason bleed?
That which provokes, will justify the deed.

LADY MACDUFF:

If the design should prosper, the event
May make us safe, but not you innocent: 30
For whilst to set your fellow subjects free
From present death, or future slavery,
You wear a crown, not by your title due,
Defence of them, is an offence in you;
That deed's unlawful though it cost no blood,   35
In which you'll be at best unjustly good.
You, by your pity which for us you plead,
Weave but ambition of a finer thread.

MACDUFF:

Ambition does the height of power affect,
My aim is not to govern, but protect: 40
And he is not ambitious that declares,
He nothing seeks of scepters but their cares.

LADY MACDUFF:

Can you so patiently yourself molest,
And lose your own, to give your country rest!
In plagues what sound physician would endure   45
To be infected for another's cure.

MACDUFF:

If by my troubles I could yours release,
My love would turn those torments to my ease:
I should at once be sick and healthy too,
Though sickly in my self, yet well in you.   50

LADY MACDUFF:

But then reflect upon the danger, sir,
Which you by your aspiring would incur.
From fortune's pinnacle, you will too late
Look down, when you are giddy with your height:
Whilst you with Fortune play to win a crown,   55
The people's stakes are greater than your own.

MACDUFF:

In hopes to have the common ills redrest,
Who would not venture single interest?

Enter Servant.

SERVANT:
  My lord, a gentleman, just now arriv'd
  From court, has brought a message from the King.   60
MACDUFF:
  One sent from him, can no good tidings bring?
LADY MACDUFF:
  What would the tyrant have?
MACDUFF: Go, I will hear
  The news, though it a dismal accent bear;
  Those who expect and do not fear their doom,
  May hear a message though from hell it come.   [*Exeunt.*]   65

ACT III, SCENE VI

Enter Macduff and Lady Macduff.

LADY MACDUFF:
  Are you resolv'd then to be gone?
MACDUFF: I am:
  I know my answer cannot but inflame
  The tyrant's fury to pronounce my death,
  My life will soon be blasted by his breath.
LADY MACDUFF:
  By why so far as England must you fly?   5
MACDUFF:
  The farthest part of Scotland is too nigh.[10]
LADY MACDUFF:
  Can you leave me, your daughter and your son,
  To perish by that tempest which you shun?
  When birds of stronger wing are fled away,
  The ravenous kite[11] does on the weaker prey.   10
MACDUFF:
  He will not injure you, he cannot be
  Possessed with such unmanly cruelty:
  You will your safety to your weakness owe
  As grass escapes the scyth by being low.
  Together we shall be too slow to fly: 15

---

[10] **nigh**: near.   [11] **Kite**: a bird of prey.

Single, we may outride the enemy.
I'll from the English King such succors[12] crave,
As shall revenge the dead, and living save.
My greatest misery is to remove,
With all the wings of haste from what I love.   20
LADY MACDUFF:
If to be gone seems misery to you,
Good sir, let us be miserable too.
MACDUFF:
Your sex which here is your security,
Will by the toils of flight your danger be.

Enter Messenger.

What fatal news does bring thee out of breath?   25
MESSENGER:
Sir, Banquo's kill'd.
MACDUFF: Then I am warn'd of death.
Farewell; our safety, us, a while must sever.
LADY MACDUFF:
Fly, fly, or we may bid farewell for ever.
MACDUFF:
Flying from Death, I am to life unkind,
For leaving you, I leave my life behind.   [*Exit.*] 30
LADY MACDUFF:
Oh my dear lord, I find now thou art gone,
I am more valiant when unsafe alone.
My heart feels manhood, it does death despise,
Yet I am still a woman in my eyes.
And of my tears thy absence is the cause,   35
So falls the dew when the bright sun withdraws.   [*Exeunt.*]

ACT IV, SCENE IV

Enter Macbeth and Seyton.

MACBETH:
Seyton, go bid the army march.
SEYTON:
The posture of affairs requires your presence.

---

[12] **succors**: means of relief.

MACBETH:
> But the indisposition of my wife
> Detains me here.

SEYTON:
> Th'enemy is upon our borders, Scotland's in danger.   5

MACBETH:
> So is my wife, and I am doubly so.
> I am sick in her, and in my kingdom too.
> Seyton.

SEYTON:
> Sir.

MACBETH:
> The spur of my ambition prompts me to go   10
> And make my kingdom safe, but love which softens
> Me to pity her in her distress,
> Curbs my resolves.

SEYTON [*aside*]:   He's strangely disorder'd.

MACBETH:
> Yet why should love since confin'd, desire
> To control ambition, for whose spreading hopes   15
> The world's too narrow. It shall not; great fires
> Put out the less; Seyton go bid my grooms
> Make ready; I'll not delay my going.

SEYTON:
> I go.

MACBETH:
> Stay Seyton, stay, compassion calls me back.   20

SEYTON [*aside*]:
> He looks and moves disorderly.

MACBETH: I'll not go yet.

Enter a Servant, who whispers [to] Macbeth.

SEYTON:
> Well, sir?

MACBETH: Is the Queen asleep?

SEYTON [*aside*]:
> What makes 'em whisper and his countenance change?
> Perhaps some new design has had ill success.

MACBETH:
> Seyton, go see what posture our affairs are in.   25

SEYTON:
I shall, and give you notice sir.   [*Exit Seyton.*]

Enter Lady Macbeth.

MACBETH:
How does my gentle love?
LADY MACBETH: Duncan is dead.
MACBETH:
No words of that.
LADY MACBETH: And yet to me he lives.
His fatal ghost is now my shadow, and pursues me
Where e're I go.
MACBETH: It cannot be, my dear,   30
Your fears have misinform'd your eyes.
LADY MACBETH:
See there; believe your own.
Why do you follow me? I did not do it.
MACBETH:
Methinks there's nothing.
LADY MACBETH:
If you have valor, force him hence.   35
Hold, hold, he's gone. Now you look strangely.
MACBETH:
'Tis the strange error of your eyes.
LADY MACBETH:
But the strange error of my eyes
Proceeds from the strange actions of your hands.
Distraction does by fits possess my head,   40
Because a crown unjustly covers it.
I stand so high that I am giddy[13] grown.
A mist does cover me, as clouds the tops
Of hills. Let us get down apace.
MACBETH:
If by your high ascent you giddy grow,   45
'Tis when you cast your eyes on things below.
LADY MACBETH:
You may in peace resign the ill-gain'd crown.
Why should you labor still to be unjust?

---

[13] **giddy**: dizzy.

There has been too much blood already spilt.
Make not the subjects victims to your guilt.   50
MACBETH:
Can you think that a crime, which you did once
Provoke me to commit? had not your breath
Blown my ambition up into a flame,
Duncan had yet been living.
LADY MACBETH: You were a man.
And by the charter of your sex you should   55
Have govern'd me, there was more crime in you
When you obey'd my counsels, than I contracted
By my giving it. Resign your kingdom now,
And with your crown put off your guilt.
MACBETH:
Resign the crown, and with it both our lives.   60
I must have better counsellors.
LADY MACBETH:
What, your witches?
Curse on your messengers of hell. Their breath
Infected first my breast. See me no more.
As King your crown sits heavy on your head,   65
But heavier on my Heart: I have had too much
Of kings already. See, the ghost again!   [*Ghost appears.*]
MACBETH:
Now she relapses.
LADY MACBETH [*to Macbeth*]:
                    Speak to him if thou canst.
[*to the ghost*] Thou look'st on me, and shew'st thy wounded breast.
Shew it the murderer.
MACBETH: Within there, ho!   70

Enter Women.

LADY MACBETH:
Am I taken prisoner? then the battle's lost.

                              [*Exit. Lady Macbeth led out by Women.*]

MACBETH:
She does from Duncan's death to sickness grieve,
And shall from Malcolm's death her health receive.
But her mind's weakness cannot now endure

To take the proper medicine for the cure.   75
When by a viper bitten, nothing's good
To cure the venom but the viper's blood.   [*Exit.*]

ACT V, SCENE II

Enter Donalbain and Fleance, met by Lennox.

LENNOX:
Is not that Donalbain and young Flean, Banquo's son?
DONALBAIN:
Who is this, my worthy friend?
LENNOX:
I by your presence feel my hopes full blown,
Which hitherto have been but in the bud.
What happy gale has brought you here to see   5
Your father's death reveng'd?
DONALBAIN:
Hearing of aid sent by the English king,
To check the tyrant's insolence, I'm come
From Ireland.
FLEANCE:
And I from France, we are but newly met.   10
DONALBAIN:
Where's my brother?
LENNOX:
He and the good Macduff are with the army
Behind the wood.
DONALBAIN: What does the tyrant now?
LENNOX:
He strongly fortifies in Dunsinane;
Some say he's mad, others who love him less,   15
Call it a valiant fury; but what e're
The matter is, there is a civil war
Within his bosom; which will hinder him
From waging this successfully. None can
Resist a foreign foe, who always has   20
An enemy within him. For each murder
He wears a dagger in his breast.
FLEANCE:
We heard that his own men deserted him.

LENNOX:
Those he commands move only in command
And not in love. He finds his crown sits loose: 25
His power grows less, his fears grow greater still.
Ambition is a tree whose roots are small,
Whose growth is high: whose shadow ever is
The blackness of the deed attending it,
Under which nothing prospers. All the fruit   30
It bears are doubts and troubles, with whose crown
The overburdened tree at last falls down.

DONALBAIN:
Let's haste and meet my brother, my interest
Is grafted into his, and cannot grow
Without it.   35

LENNOX:
So may you both outgrow unlucky chance,
And may the tyrant's fall that growth advance.   [*Exeunt.*]

→ THOMAS DUFFETT

Epilogue to *The Empress of Morocco*   *1674*

Thomas Duffett wrote a number of burlesques of contemporary plays by various playwrights in the 1670s; they are hardly great literature, but they help reveal
how his contemporaries saw these works. Perhaps his most famous play is *The
Mock Tempest* (1675), a parody of Dryden and Davenant's alteration of Shakespeare's *The Tempest*.

   The Empress of Morocco. A Farce is, to begin with, a parody of *The Empress of
Morocco* (1673), a heroic play by Elkanah Settle that received a great deal of notice.
To the end of this play, Duffett attached the parody of *Macbeth* as an Epilogue.
Here he was responding directly to Davenant's version of the play (see above),
with its elaborate stage machinery and songs. It is perhaps not surprising that
Duffett would mock some of Davenant's special effects — Hecate's "glorious
chariot" is only a "large wicker basket" — but he also parodies quite a bit of
Shakespeare. In Shakespeare's version, for example, the Second Witch utters
the famous lines, "By the pricking of my thumbs, / Something wicked this
way comes" (4.1.44–45); in Duffett's version they become, "By the itching of

Thomas Duffett, *Epilogue. Being a new Fancy after the old, and most surprising way of* Macbeth,
Perform'd with new and costly Machines. Epilogue to *The Empress of Morocco. A Farce* (London,
1674).

my bum, / Some wicked luck shou'd that way come." Nor do Shakespeare's witches — frightening, creepy, androgynous — escape mockery: in Duffett, they are simply prostitutes working the city, conning Templer, Shopkeeper, and even (it is implied by the frequent use of direct address) members of the audience; their songs celebrate their sister bawds, and the only prophecies they offer are insults directed to the audience — "Hail! hail! hail! you less than wits and greater! / Hail fop in corner!" The heroic, harrowing violence of Shakespeare's play, even in Davenant's muted version, is reduced here to a mercantile traffic in female flesh. Duffett's version suggests that some theatrical conventions and innovations are not universally valued, and that even some of the most celebrated features of Shakespeare's *Macbeth* can, from one point of view, be seen as comic.

An Epilogue spoken by Hecate and three witches, according to the famous mode of Macbeth. *The most renowned and melodious song of* John Dory, *being heard as it were in the air sung in parts by spirits, to raise the expectation, and charm the audience with thoughts sublime, and worthy of that heroic scene which follows.*

The scene opens. Thunder and lightning is discover'd, not behind painted tiffany[1] *to blind and amuse the senses, but openly, by the most excellent way of mustard-bowl, and saltpeter.*[2]

Three witches fly over the pit,[3] *riding upon beesoms.*[4] *Hecate descends over the stage in a glorious chariot, adorn'd with pictures of Hell and devils, and made of a large wicker basket.*

Hecate and three witches.

HECATE: What, you have been at hot cockles[5] I see, beldames![6] how dare you traffic thus, and not call me? 'Tis I must bear the brunt —
Where's W —— ?
[VOICE] *within*:   Here.
HECATE: Where's W —— ?   5
[VOICE] *within*:   Here.
HECATE:
Where's Mack'relback[7] and Jilting-Sue?[8]

---

[1] **tiffany:** a thin transparent gauze or silk.   [2] **saltpeter:** gunpowder; an explosive.   [3] **the pit:** where the audience stands in front of the stage.   [4] **beesoms:** a broom made out of sticks, heather, or broom (the plant).   [5] **hot cockles:** "a rustic game in which one player lay face downwards, or knelt down with his eyes covered, and being struck on the back by the others in turn, guessed who struck him" (*OED*). Also, an obscene pun that anticipates the witches' sexual activities.   [6] **beldames:** hags, witches; loathsome old women.   [7] **Mack'relback:** a "mackerel" was not only the name of a fish, but slang for a bawd or a pimp who provided for sexual debauchery. A bawd in John Marston's *The Malcontent* (1603) is named "Maquerelle."   [8] **Jilting-Sue:** a "jilt" was a woman who had lost her chastity, a slut.

ALL THE THREE WITCHES:
We want but you; we want but you.
HECATE:
You lazy hags! what mischief have you done?
1 WITCH:
I was with Templer⁹ lock'd from night till noon,   10
My case¹⁰ he open'd thrice and once
Actions he entered three and one,
But grown with study dull as dunce
His deeds I burnt,¹¹ his fees I spent;
And till next term or quarter's rent   15
I left him poor, and malcontent.
HECATE:
Thou shalt have a spirit. What hast thou done?
2 WITCH:
I pick'd Shopkeeper up, and went to th' sun.
He houncht — and houncht — and houncht;¹²
    And when h' had done,   20
    Pay me, quoth I,
Be damn'd, you whore! did fierce Mechanic cry,
And most unlike a true bred gentleman,
Drunk as a bitch he left me there in pawn.
HECATE:
His shop is in Fleetstreet —   25
2 WITCH:
In Hackney Coach, I'll thither sail,
Like wanton wife with sweeping tail;
    I'll do! I'll do! and I'll do!
3 WITCH:
A running nag I'll thee lend.
2 WITCH:
Thou art my friend.   30
1 WITCH:
I'll give thee chancre and bubo.¹³

---

⁹ **Templer**: one who works in the Inner Temple or the Middle Temple, i.e. a barrister or lawyer; also an ironic reference to a Templar, one of an order of medieval heroic knights.   ¹⁰ **case**: law case; sexual organs.   ¹¹ **His . . . burnt**: burned his legal documents; gave him a (burning) case of venereal disease.   ¹² **houncht**: rode the haunches, or pelvis; i.e. fornicated.   ¹³ **chancre and bubo**: the sores and infections of venereal disease.

2 WITCH:

I can have all the rest of friends below.   *Pointing to the pit.*
To sweating tub[14] I'll youth confine,
Where he shall dwindle, flux and pine,
Though white witch surgeon drench and 'noint.[15]   35
    I'll have at least a joint.

HECATE:

And what hast thou done?

3 WITCH:

With cock of game I fought a match,
While his —— my —— did catch,[16]
I stole his money and gold watch.   40

HECATE:

Thou shalt have an incubus;[17]
Come to our friends to make their charms more quicker,
Here's six go-downs of humming Stygian[18] liquor.

*Enter two spirits with brandy burning, which drink while it flames. Hecate and the
three witches sing. To the tune of, A Boat, a Boat, &c.*

HECATE:

A health, a health to Mother C——
From Moorfields fled to Millbank Castle,   45
She puts off rotten new rigg'd vessel.

I WITCH:

A health, a health to G—— that witch,
She needs must be in spite of fate rich,
Who sells tough hen for quail and partridge.

2 WITCH:

A health, a health to Sister T——   50
Her trade's chief beauty and example,
She'll serve the gallant, or the pimp, well.

3 WITCH:

A health, a health to Betty B——
Though she began the trade but newly,
Of country squires there's not a few lie.   55

---

[14] **sweating tub**: supposedly one of the cures for venereal disease.   [15] **'noint**: anoint.
[16] **While . . . catch**: the audience is supposed to fill in the easily guessed obscene words themselves.   [17] **incubus**: evil spirit supposed to descend on one in sleep, and especially to seek intercourse with women.   [18] **Stygian**: from the river Styx in Hell.

CHORUS:

> But of all the brisk bawds 'tis M—— for me.
> 'Tis M—— the best in her degree;
> She can serve from the lord, to the squire and clown,
> From a guinea[19] she'll fit ye to half a crown.[20]

I WITCH:

> Fie! Fah! Fum!   60
> By the itching of my bum,[21]
> Some wicked luck shou'd that way come.   *Pointing to the audience.*

HECATE:

> Stand still — by yonder dropping nose[22] I know,
> That we shall please them all before we go.

Hecate speaks to the audience.

HECATE:

> Hail! hail! hail! you less than wits and greater!   65
> Hail fop in corner! and the rest now met here,
> Though you'll ne'er be wits — from your loins shall spread,
> Diseases that shall reign when you are dead.
>> Deed is done!
>> War's begun!   70
>> Great Morocco's lost and won.
> Bankside Maulkin thrice hath mew'd, no matter;
> If Puss of t'other house will scratch, have at her.
> T'appease your spirits and keep our Farce from harm,
> Of strong ingredients we have powerful charm,   75
> To catch bully Critic whose wit but thin is:
> Yonder sits empty Cully stuffed with guineas,
> Then for the wary squeamish critic lover,
> A dainty virgin pullet[23] sits above there,
> And those two vizards[24] hide a brace[25] of Jinnies,[26]   80
> Enough to hamper all the critic ninnies.
> Besides all this, our charm is stronger made yet,
> With dock[27] of harlot hashed and grilliaded,[28]

---

[19] **guinea**: a gold coin, worth twenty-one shillings, first minted in 1663; also slang for a prostitute.   [20] **half a crown**: a coin worth two shillings and sixpence; to have "half a crown," or lose one's hair, was a symptom of venereal disease. Cf. "bald crown" *(King Lear* 1.4.160).   [21] **bum**: ass, rear end.   [22] **dropping nose**: a sign of veneral disease.   [23] **pullet**: young hen; i.e., young woman.   [24] **vizards**: masks.   [25] **brace**: a pair, couple.   [26] **Jinnies**: the female proper name, Jinny or Jenny; used especially for birds, i.e., sexual prey.   [27] **dock**: rump, buttocks.   [28] **hashed and grilliaded**: cut into small pieces and grilled.

Carcass of country girl that's fresh and wholesome,
Haunch of whitestone doe,[29] but that is fulsome.[30]   85
Moreover friends, in ev'ry place to fit ye,
Goose giblets, rumps, and kidneys for the city.
HECATE AND ALL THE THREE WITCHES:
Huff no more!   *A hellish noise is heard within.*
HECATE:
He that would damn this Farce does strive in vain,
This charm can never be o'ercome by man,   90
'Till Whetstones Park[31] remove to Distaff[32] Lane.

Within singing.

Hecate! Hecate! Come away.
HECATE:
Hark, I am call'd —

She sings.

I come; I come; Alack and well a-day
Alack and well a-day.   95

Within.

The pot boils over while you stay —
HECATE:
Vanish —
In basket chariot I will mount,
'Tis time I know it by my count.

Thunder and lightning. While they are flying up, Hecate sings.

The goose and the gander went over the green,   100
They flew in the corn that[33] they could not be seen.
CHORUS:
They flew, &c.

The three witches sing.

---

[29] **doe**: female deer; girl or young woman.   [30] **fulsome**: plentiful or abundant; offensive, nause-ating; in heat, in the act of breeding.   [31] **Whetstones Park**: a lane between Holborn and Lin-coln's Inn Fields in London, a notorious haunt for prostitutes.   [32] **Distaff**: figurative for "women"; also slang for the penis (a distaff is a cleft stick upon which either flax or wool is wound for hand-spinning).   [33] **that**: so that.

Rosemary's green, rosemary's green
   derry, derry, down.
When I am King, thou shalt be Queen,   105
   derry, derry, down.
If I have gold, thou shalt have part,
   derry, derry, down.
If I have none thou hast my heart.
   derry, derry, down.   110

FINIS.

CHAPTER 2

Discourses of Sovereignty

>‹

The Succession Controversy

The succession crisis of the 1590s exposed to public debate a number of complex issues relating to the concept of the monarchy, some of which the government and supporters of James believed not to be debatable at all. Similar debates, however, had existed since the reign of Henry VIII and had been particularly heated at the beginning of Elizabeth's reign (see Levine). Now, at the end of her reign, the same questions had surfaced again: On what grounds did or should the kingship pass from one person to another? Could there be a gap in time between a king and his or her successor? Did the people — the commonwealth or Parliament — have any voice in selecting or confirming their king? Was deposing a king ever justified? Sophisticated arguments were made on all sides of these questions.

Strictly speaking, however, the so-called Statute of Silence (the Second Treasons Act, 1571) had legally prohibited *any* debate on the topic of the queen's successor. Nevertheless, such discussions increased as Elizabeth grew older. Robert Parsons's *A Conference upon the Succession* of 1595 (excerpted below) was a bombshell lofted from the safety of France. Parsons's questioning of the principle of strict blood inheritance, and his advancement of a crowd of pretenders (among whom James VI of Scotland, Parsons argued, had an invalid claim), aroused a furious official reaction, but others — even the government itself, it seems — were saying the same thing. In one of the responses to Parsons in 1602, in fact, Elizabeth's own godson, Sir John Harington, reported that even before James had been born, "it was thought as fit that for a counterpoise to the Queen of Scots' pretense [to the English crown] some other titles should underhand[edly] be set on foot at home, and about that time Sir Nicholas Bacon[1] . . . wrote in defense of the house of Suffolk, and was perhaps for a color[2] chidden[3] for it, but immediately restored to favor" (Harington 41). Harington goes on to describe "the policy of the State" (42) in secretly promoting several other candidates, more recently the Infanta, daughter of Philip II of Spain, as a counterpoise to James. Thomas Wilson observed in 1601 that "there are 12 competitors that gape for the death of that good old Princess the now Queen" (Wilson 2). Whether Elizabeth brought it upon herself or not, there *was* a debate over succession caused by her failure to produce an heir; even if she had produced an heir, he or she would surely also have been challenged, judging by the polemics of the time.

In constructing their arguments about succession, writers tended to rely on four main kinds of evidence and argument. First, there was often an appeal to religious authority: Sir Thomas Craig, for example, a strong supporter of James, argued in 1603 that "It is clear that in instituting kings God ever preferred hereditary to elective succession. He gave it his countenance in the case of David and his posterity," and in several other biblical examples Craig summons, leading to the conclusion that "kings were first instituted by God; that monarchy was introduced from the beginning, and that it was settled on an hereditary basis in order that the ambition and strife of men might be stayed; for kingship is the fairest thing in heaven as on earth" (Craig 228–29). This was certainly James's position — one that strongly enhanced the authority and power of the kingship — as he expressed it in his own work, *The True Law of Free Monarchies* (1598):

> Monarchy is the true pattern of divinity . . . the lineal succession of crowns being begun among the people of God, and happily continued in divers Christian commonwealths: So as no objection either of heresy, or whatsoever private statute or law, may free the people from their oath-giving to their king, and his succession, established by the old fundamental laws of the kingdom. For, as he is their heritable over-lord, and so by birth, not by any

---

[1] The father of Francis Bacon. At the time, he was Lord Keeper of the Great Seal, a major position within the government (no document was authentic unless issued under the Great Seal of the kingdom).
[2] **for a color**: as a pretense.   [3] **chidden**: chided, reprimanded.

FIGURE 9 *A genealogy of the contemporary Scottish descent produced by the Scottish historian John Leslie in* De origine, moribus, et rebus gestis Scotorum *(1578). Leslie was a supporter of Mary, Queen of Scots. Here Mary is both larger than James and labelled as "Regina," or Queen, while James, aged 12, is labelled "Princeps," or Prince. In fact, James had already been King James VI for eleven years, but Leslie did not accept Mary's forced abdication.*

right in the coronation, cometh to his crown; it is alike unlawful (the crown ever standing full) to displace him that succeedeth thereto, as to eject the former: for at the very moment of the expiring of the king reigning, the nearest and lawful heir entereth in his place. (194, 209)

This is exactly the position against which Parsons argues in the excerpt below.

A second ground of argument, as indicated in another passage from the *True Law*, is an appeal to "natural law" — what a speaker would hope to be a universally agreed upon rule of behavior: "By the law of Nature the King becomes a natural Father to all his Lieges at his coronation. And as the Father, of his fatherly duty is bound to care for the nourishing, education, and virtuous government of his children; even so is the King bound to care for all his subjects" (195). This analogical argument, from natural law to political and social behavior, is a staple of discourse in the period; the analogies often went much further — as God rules over his faithful, so the King over his subjects, the father over his children, the husband over his wife, the head over the body, and so forth. Such appeals are always a move to naturalize one's own position by making it seem absolute, unchangeable, and inevitable. Needless to say, even those who accepted and made arguments based on natural law frequently disagreed on particular matters.

A third ground of argument is that of secular rather than religious history. Writers took the supposed tradition of the English or Scottish monarchies, as we saw in the section on early narratives, with the greatest seriousness, but different ones drew different lessons from that tradition. To take two Scots, for example, who consider exactly the same material: Sir Thomas Craig, in the passage above, finds succession by heredity to be God's plan, while George Buchanan — in telling the story of Malcolm II in his *Rerum Scoticarum historia* (*History of Scotland*) (see p. 128) — reaches just the opposite conclusion. Buchanan argues that the new law of patrilineal succession established by King Kenneth II, leading to Malcolm II's coronation, had unexpected consequences:

An universal good to all was pretended [by those who argued for succession by heredity], in thus settling the succession, that seditions, murders, and treacheries might be prevented amongst those of the blood; and also, that ambition, with the other mischiefs accompanying it, might be rooted out from amongst the nobles. But on the contrary, when I enquire into the causes of public grievances, and compare the old [law of election] with the modern [law of heredity], it seems to me, that all those mischiefs, which we would have avoided by this new law, are so far from being extinguished by the antiquating of the old, that they rather receive a great increase therefrom. For, not to speak of the plots of their kindred against those who are actually in the throne; nor of a present king's evil suspicions of those, whom Nature and the law would have accounted as most dear to him; I say, omitting these things . . . all the miseries of former ages may seem light and tolerable, if compared with those calamities which followed. (bk. 7, 205)

In arguing for this new law, kings aim to "perpetuate their name and stock," Buchanan concludes, but "how vain and fallacious that pretense is, the examples of the ancients, yea, even Nature itself, might inform them." A prime example, in the ultimate irony, is Malcolm II himself, who "left no male-child behind him" (206), thus leading to the rule of Duncan — and Macbeth.

A fourth ground of argument might be termed that of the mystique of blood — the belief that a blood relation was superior to any other connection or qualification for the kingship. In his *Treatise* on the succession (1598, written in 1595) — another of the responses to Robert Parsons's *Conference* — Peter Wentworth reviewed the shaky grounds upon which Richard III had taken the kingship:

> Rather than he would have been without some show of succession, how bare and weak soever, [Richard] did choose to cause proclaimed at Paul's Cross, his mother an harlot, and his brethren bastards. And thus he sought the kingdom no otherwise, than by right of succession [i.e. by heredity] . . . By which you see, that even in the conceit of the usurpers themselves, the most lying, infamous and falsely forged pretence of next and most lawful blood, is to be preferred before any Parliament, as being the ground and warrant for justifying and clearing the acts and doings of the same. And if the crown might be lawfully given at the pleasure of a Parliament, what reason is there to call Rich[ard] III or any such others, usurpers[?]   (Wentworth 55)

This primal belief in the efficacy of blood relation — even usurpers feel the need to claim it — could lead to tortured historical arguments, as we saw in the section on early narratives, where the Banquo-to-Fleance-to-Walter Steward myth quickly hardened into accepted historical fact. Long before James was born, the Stuart claim to the Scottish throne was reinforced by this legend. James's claim to the English throne was easily accepted in spite of the efforts of Parsons and others, yet even after he was crowned, still more "official" genealogies continued to be commissioned, indicating the absolute lineal sequence of James's heritage. In 1604, George Owen Harry published a heavily illustrated genealogy with the completely explanatory title (here unmodernized), *The Genealogy of the High and Mighty Monarch, James, by the grace of God, King of great Brittayne, &c. with his lineall descent from Noah, by divers direct lynes to Brutus, first Inhabiter of this Ile of Brittayne; and from him to Cadwalader, the last King of the Brittish bloud; and from thence, sundry wayes to his Maiesty: wherein is playnly shewed his rightfull Title, by lawfull descent from the said Cadwalader, as well to the Kingdome of Brittayne, as to the Principalities of Northwales and Southwales . . .* From Noah to Brutus to Fleance to James: such was the supposed unbroken line. Morgan Colman outdid Harry in 1608, however, with his *The Genealogies of King James I. and Queen Anne, his wife, from the Conquest,* with page after page of illustrations of tightly linked family trees.

Amid this unanimous chorus of *official* voices testifying to James's succession through an absolute, unbroken line of ancestors, however, a few contrary voices sounded through. In a long verse poem entitled *Daphnis Polystephanos* (1605) — a versified genealogy of James — Sir George Buc[4] hesitated at the Banquo legend, as tactfully as he could:

> But some derive your Majesty's British race from a nameless, and a good nameless daughter of Griffith ap Leolhin (a prince of Wales about the year 1051) upon whom (as they pretend) Fleance thane, or Steward of Abria, flying into Wales for succor, begot unlawfully a son, who should be ancestor to all the chief Stewards to this day. But this being not acknowledged by the best Scottish historiographers, and the thing not honorable, I may well pretermit it.[5] (Buc A4v)

The Fleance legend, depending as it does on murder, adultery, and bastardy, was not, Buc realized, an "honorable" history for a king, but Stuart mythographers had already erased most of the awkward spots in Fleance's story, and Buc's resistance to the legend was drowned out by all the other official versions.[6] The most authoritative and "official" voicing of the matter came in the Succession Act of 1604 (excerpted below), in which Parliament publicly and completely accepted all of James's claims — he is "lineally, rightfully, and lawfully descended" from Henry the Seventh's eldest daughter; and *immediately*, without a gap, upon Queen Elizabeth's death, James "did by inherent birthright and lawful and undoubted succession" become king, as "lineally, justly, and lawfully next and sole heir of the blood royal." Much of this phrasing, particularly the idea that James was the "sole heir," responds to and shuts the door on the succession critique of the 1590s.

---

[4] Buc was a substantial, completely loyal figure, recently knighted by James, deputy Master of the Revels under Edmund Tilney, and succeeding him in that office in 1608.

[5] **pretermit:** omit.

[6] See Ashley, Bingham, Donaldson, and Pittock for the actual historical origins of the house of Stuart.

Shakespeare's *Macbeth*, as we have noted, embodies virtually every issue of the succession controversy in the four paradigms of kingship within the play. While the play does represent the line of Banquo, stretching out to the crack of doom, it also leaves us with two significant gaps in the *"show of eight Kings and Banquo last"* (4.1.111sd) — there should be nine kings, but James's mother, Mary Queen of Scots, is missing from the sequence, and at the end of the play Fleance is missing, unseen and unmentioned, as if he had never existed.

Finally, Shakespeare also engages the mystique of blood in a graphic, even specular way. The king's blood, Duncan's "golden blood" (2.3.106) — a single drop of which could, in theory, guarantee royal succession — proves to be horrifyingly inexhaustible, in a kind of mockery of the king's traditional plenitude: it is like a river ("I am in blood / Stepped in so far that, should I wade no more, / Returning were as tedious as go o'er" [3.4.137–39]) or a whole ocean (the blood on Macbeth's hands will "The multitudinous seas incarnadine, / Making the green one red" [2.2.66–67]). Denied succession to the kingship by blood relation, Macbeth can only shed blood, marvelling, as Lady Macbeth does, "Yet who would have thought the old man to have had so much blood in him?" (5.1.31–32).

→ R. DOLEMAN [ROBERT PARSONS]

From A Conference about the Next Succession to the Crown of England
1595

Robert Parsons (1546–1610) — sometimes spelled Persons — was a remarkable man. He was perhaps the most indefatigable English proponent of Catholicism and author of one of the most controversial political works of the period — *A Conference about the Next Succession to the Crown of England.* A political intriguer deeply involved in direct negotiations with kings and popes — a "broker of kingdoms," in the words of one of his contemporary critics[1] — he was also a learned man and a prolific writer — his surviving written works number thousands of pages.

Apparently brought up as a Protestant, Parsons took his BA and MA at Oxford and briefly became bursar and dean of Balliol College. Parsons left the

---

[1] The historian William Camden; quoted in Hurstfield, 378.

R. Doleman [Robert Parsons], *A Conference about the Next Succession to the Crown of England, Divided into Two Parts* (N. [Antwerp], 1594 [actually appeared in 1595]) B4–B5, 34–35, 73, 109–17, 258–63.

FIGURE 10 *The genealogy of the English descent produced by the Jesuit priest* ➤ *Robert Parsons in* A Conference about the Next Succession to the Crown of England, *published under a pseudonym, "R. Doleman," in 1595. Parsons supported the legitimacy of Mary: his genealogy, and the book which explains and supports it, was designed to undermine the claims of James, whom he saw as a Protestant threat, as well as other claimants (in favor of the Catholic daughter of Philip II of Spain). Part of this strategy may be seen simply in the number of possible claimants; the neat genealogical lines of Figure 2 (p. 7)are multiplied into confusion here.*

college in 1574; the causes alleged for his departure are unclear — he may have begun promoting Catholic doctrine, he may have fallen out of favor with the master, he may have been too strict with his students, and he does seem to have been exposed as of illegitimate birth. In any event, Parsons left England to study medicine at Padua, but soon found himself in Louvain (in what is now Belgium) — where he probably declared his Catholicism — and then in Rome. Except for an interval of a year and a half, he never returned to England.

Parsons entered the Society of Jesus — the Jesuit order — in 1575, and within a few years was a high-ranking figure. In 1580, he was sent, along with the priest Edmund Campion, into England in disguise (as a soldier). For eighteen months, he moved around the country, energizing the faithful — even dispatching a priest to Scotland, at Mary, Queen of Scot's, request, to attempt to convert the young King James VI (then thirteen years old); it would not be the last time Parsons attempted to cross James's destiny. Governmental decrees against harboring priests made Parsons's situation quite dangerous, but he proceeded to set up a secret printing press, which frequently changed locations; with it he produced books and pamphlets advancing the Catholic cause. The government was not amused. Campion was betrayed, captured, and eventually executed, but Parsons escaped to France late in 1581, never (as far as we know) to return. But his name and influence continued.

From various posts in Europe, Parsons pressed the Catholic cause through written and diplomatic efforts; at various times, he urged the deliverance of Mary, Queen of Scots (now imprisoned by Elizabeth), the Spanish invasion of England, and the personal political involvement of the pope against England. Parsons also had time to become rector of the English College in Rome, and there and elsewhere helped train many Jesuits. He was prominent enough as an opponent of Protestant England that Queen Elizabeth denounced him by name in 1591; Parsons responded with yet another pamphlet, this time declaring that the pope's power to depose kings and queens was an article of faith.

His already great notoriety would soon drastically increase. Although Parsons had supported Mary, Queen of Scots, as the rightful Scottish monarch, he saw her son, James, a Protestant, as a threat to the Catholic cause. In 1595, he published the work excerpted here, *A Conference upon the Succession*, which not only contested the validity of James's claim to the throne, but disputed the whole

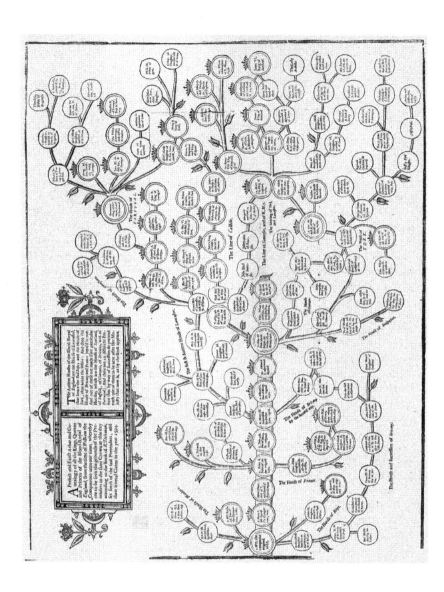

concept of the strictly hereditary kingship and advanced the claim of the Spanish Infanta, the daughter of Philip II, to the English crown.[2] The genealogical chart which accompanied the book (see Figure 10) aims not only to help the reader follow the various hereditary lines, but also, in representing the great proliferation of claimants, to minimize what James would say was his unique claim. The book inspired a number of written responses, some nearly hysterical in tone, even *after* James had succeeded to the English crown. Well into James's reign, and well after Parsons's death, Parsons and his book were still being denounced.

A Conference infuriated Elizabeth's government, as might be expected, for its open speculations on Elizabeth's death and successors; since the so-called Statute of Silence early in Elizabeth's reign, it had been forbidden to discuss who would be the queen's successor. The book also infuriated James and his supporters, as might be expected, since it argued that even under the rules of a hereditary monarchy, James was disqualified as Elizabeth's successor. But it may come as a surprise to many modern readers that *A Conference* also infuriated many Catholics, both English and European, for its intrusions into the political relations between France, Spain, and England, and the delicate religious relations among all groups. The book's reception should remind us that there was no monolithic Catholic political position in this period. Among the great strengths of Parsons's book, which his opponents found most annoying (as indicated in the excerpt from Constable, p. 201), is his calm tone of dispassionate rationality — his willingness to put every assertion to the test, as well as his powers of logic and his detailed knowledge of English monarchical history. Some responses to *A Conference,* such as Hayward's (p. 203) argued against it point by point, chapter by chapter; others could only launch into sputtering, abusive attacks on Parsons's motives, appearance, and illegitimacy. A potentially even more controversial work by Parsons — the *Memorial for the Reformation of England* — suggested what measures might be taken, such as the establishment of the Inquisition, when England was restored to Catholic rule; it was presented to the Infanta in 1601 but not printed until 1690.

After James VI succeeded to the English throne, against Parsons's predictions and desires, Parsons seems to have accepted James as the monarch by possession, if not by hereditary right; Parsons was not involved in the Gunpowder Plot, and at the time was arguing against rebellion. But Parsons did not abandon his fundamental cause — the restoration of Catholicism to England — and continued writing controversial works until his death in 1610.

---

[2] The book was published under the pseudonym "R. Doleman" (some critics mocked the name as dole [i.e. woeful] man), but Parsons's authorship was instantly known, as the title of Constable's work (printed below) indicates. There is some question whether Parsons was the sole author of the book (see Hicks, and Nenner [264 n.51]), but he was certainly taken for the sole author at the time. In addition to disguising himself when he returned to England, Parsons used other pseudonyms ("John Howlet," "Philopater" [i.e. 'love of the father']) and false places of publication on the title pages of his published works.

A Conference about the Next Succession

I. The Plan of the Book[1]

Your succession, said the Civilian [lawyer], includeth also an election or approbation of the common wealth and so doth the succession of all kings in Christendom besides, as well appeareth by the manner of their new admission at their coronations, where the people are demanded again, *if they be content to accept such a man for their King:* though his title of nearness by blood, be never so clear. And therefore much more it is like to be in this case of English pretenders now, where their lawful nearness in blood is so doubtful as you have signified, and so I do come to confirm your former proposition, of the doubtfulness of the next successor in England, with another reason besides that which you have alleged of the ambiguity of their true propinquity in blood: for I say further, that albeit the nearness of each man's succession in blood were evidently known, yet were it very uncertain (as things now stand in England and in the rest of Christendom round about) who should prevail, for that it is not enough for a man to be next only in blood, thereby to pretend a crown, but that other circumstances also must concur, which if they want,[2] the bare propinquity or ancestry of blood may justly be rejected, and he that is second, third, fourth, fifth or last, may lawfully be preferred before the first, and this by all law both divine and human, and by all reason, conscience, and custom of all nations, Christian.

To this said the Temporal lawyer, You go further, sir, than I had meant to do or did conceive of the matter, for my meaning only was to show how many pretenders there be to the English crown at this day, and how doubtful the pretensions of divers of the chief of them be, in respect of the many exclusions, stops and bars that their adversaries or fellow competitors do lay against them; and now you do add further, that albeit these stops were taken away, and their propinquity in blood were manifest, yet for other considerations the course of their next succession by birth may be justly altered, upon such considerations as you insinuate, that the English may have in the

---

[1] The *Conference* is written, like many works of the time, in the form of a dialogue between two speakers — the Civilian (or Civil) lawyer and the Temporal lawyer, who speaks for the tradition of common law. ("Civil law" refers to any system of law having its origin in Roman law; here, it also implies law as defined by parliamentary statute. "Common law" refers to the system of laws based on court decisions, on the doctrines implicit in those decisions, and on customs and usage.) The book is divided into two parts. In the first part, the Civilian lawyer discourses on more philosophical questions, such as the origin of the state, the nature of kingship, and the rights of the commonwealth; he argues that succession by blood relation is not a law of nature and historically has often been rightly disregarded in various countries. The second part of the book is the Temporal lawyer's analysis of the claims of the several pretenders to the English crown.   [2] **want:** lack.

admission of their next king or queen, after her Majesty that now is, which indeed (if it be true) maketh the matter of succession much more doubtful than I pretended, which I confess I have not so much studied or thought of, for that our common law goeth no further ordinarily, than to the next successor in blood, to consider whether he be lawfully descended or no, thereby to give him the crown.

I confess, said the Civilian, that ordinarily neither your law, nor ours doth go any further, especially in those realms where the government goeth by succession of blood, which I think to be the best of all other ways, but yet there may happen out such extraordinary cases sometimes, against this ordinary rule, as your common law must needs take also consideration of them, except it will be contrary to all other law and reason, both divine and human, as for example, if it should fall out that the next in blood should be a natural fool or a madman: if he should be taken by Turks or Moors in his infancy and brought up in their religion and would maintain the same in your country, with all his forces, and other like urgent cases, wherein it is not probable, but that your common law must needs have further consideration, than of the bare propinquity of blood only, for that otherwise it should be a very imperfect law, that hath not provided for accidents so weighty and important, as these are, for saving and conserving of your common wealth.

At this speech, the residue of the company began to smile, to see the two lawyers grow into some heat and comparison of their professions. But yet for that both their asseverations[3] did tend to prove one thing, which was the first proposition set down, to wit, *that the next successor of England must needs be very doubtful*: they requested them both with very great instance, that each one would be content to prove his assertion apart, to wit, the Temporal lawyer to show that the titles and pretensions of all those ten or eleven families of the English blood royal, which remain at this day, are ambiguous and doubtful, according to the common laws of England; and the Civilian to declare that albeit their titles by succession were clear, yet that as things stand now in that realm, and other countries near adjoining, there may be a great doubt which of them shall prevail.

This I say, was the request of the whole company, and the lawyers were content to take it upon them.

II. Sovereign Authority and the Subject's Obedience

I am of opinion, that whatsoever a Prince's title be, if once he be settled in the crown, and admitted by the common wealth (for of all other holds I

---

[3] **asseverations**: assertions.

esteem the tenure of a crown) if so it may be termed (the most irregular and extraordinary) every man is bound to settle his conscience to obey the same, in all that lawfully he may command, and this without examination of his title, or interest, for that (as I have said) God disposeth of kingdoms and worketh His will in Princes' affairs as He pleaseth, and this by extraordinary means, oftentimes so that if we should examine the titles at this day, of all the Princes of Christendom, by the ordinary rule of private men's rights, successions or tenures, we should find so many knots and difficulties, as it were hard for any law to make the same plain, but only the supreme law of God's disposition, which can dispense in what He listeth.

This is my opinion in this behalf for true and quiet obedience, and yet on the other side, as far off am I from the abject and wicked flattery of such as affirm Princes to be subject to no law or limitation at all, either in authority, government, life, or succession, but as though by nature they had been created kings from the beginning of the world, or as though the common wealth had been made for them and not they for the common wealth, or as though they had begotten or purchased or given life to the wealpublic,[4] and not that the wealpublic had exalted them or given them their authority, honor and dignity: so these flatterers do free them from all obligation, duty, reverence or respect unto the whole body whereof they are the heads, nay expressly they say and affirm that: *all men's goods, bodies and lives are the Princes', at their pleasures to dispose of: that they are under no law or accompt[5]-giving whatsoever, that they succeed by nature and generation only and not by any authority, admission or approbation of the common wealth, and that consequently no merit or demerit of their persons is to be respected, nor any considerations of their natures or qualities, to wit of capacity, disposition, or other personal circumstances, is to be had or admitted, and do they what they list, no authority is there under God, to chasten them.* . . . these [are] absurd paradoxes.[6]

III. Contract Theory

The power and authority which the Prince hath from the common wealth is in very truth, not absolute, but *potestas vicaria or deligata,* as we Civilians call it, that is to say, a power delegate, or power by commission from the common wealth, which is given with such restrictions, cautels[7] and conditions, yea, with such plain exceptions, promises and oaths of both parties (I mean between the king and common wealth at the day of his admission

---

[4] **wealpublic:** the public good.   [5] **accompt:** account.   [6] Parsons is here refuting the kind of claims for divine right and absolute authority made by the French philosopher Pierre du Bellay, but which would also be made by James, his son Charles, and their propagandists.   [7] **cautels:** precautions.

or coronation) as if the same be not kept, but willfully broken, on either part, then is the other not bound to observe his promise neither, though never so solemnly made or sworn, for that in all bargains, agreements and contracts, where one part is bound mutually and reciprocally to the other, by oath, vow or condition, there, if one side go from his promise, the other standeth not obliged to perform his: and this is so notorious by all law, both of nature and nations, and so conform to all reason and equity, that it is put among the very rules of both the Civil and canon law.

IV. The Validity of James VI's Claim to the Crown of England

For the King of Scots, those that do favor his cause (whereof I confess that I have not found very many in England) do allege, that he is the first and chiefest pretender of all others, and next in succession, for that he is the first person that is descended (as you see) of the eldest daughter of King Henry the Seventh, and that in this descent there can no bastardy or other lawful impediment be avowed, why he should not succeed according to the priority of his pretension and birth. And moreover secondly they do allege that it would be greatly for the honor and profit of England, for that hereby the two realms of England and Scotland should come to be joined, a point long sought for, and much to be wished, and finally such as are affected to his religion do add, that hereby true religion will come to be more settled also and established in England, which they take to be a matter of no small consequence, and consideration, and this in effect is that which the favorers of this prince do allege in his behalf.

But on the other side, there want not many[8] that do accompt this pretence of the King of Scots neither good nor just, nor any way expedient for the state of England, and they do answer largely to all the allegations before mentioned in his behalf.

And first of all, as concerning his title, by nearness of succession, they make little accompt thereof, both for that in itself (they say) it may easily be overthrown, and proved to be of no validity, as also for that if it were never so good, yet might it for other considerations be rejected, and made frustrate, as our friend the Civil lawyer, hath largely and learnedly proved these days in our hearing.

To begin then to speak first of the King of Scots' title by nearness of blood, these men do affirm, that albeit there be not alleged any bastardy in

---

[8] **there want not many:** i.e., there are many.

his descent from King Henry the Seventh his daughter, as there is in her second marriage against the lady Arbella, yet are there other reasons enough to frustrate and overthrow this claim and pretension, and first of all, for that he is not (say these men) of the house of Lancaster by Lady Blanch the only true heir thereof, as before hath in part been shown, and shall be afterward more largely, but only by Catherine Swinford, whose children being unlawfully begotten, and but of the half blood, whether they may by that legitimation of Parliament that was given them, be made inheritable unto the crown before the lawful daughter of the whole blood, shall be discussed afterward in place convenient, when we shall talk of the house of Portugal: but in the mean space, these men do presume that the King of Scots is but only of the House of York, and then affirming further that the title of the House of Lancaster, is better than that of York, as by many arguments the favorers of Lancaster have endeavored to show in the former chapter, they do insert that this is sufficient, to make void all claim of the King of Scots, that he may pretend by nearness of blood, especially seeing there want not at this day pretenders enough of the other House of Lancaster to claim their right, so as the House of York shall not need to enter for fault of true heirs, and this is the first argument which is made against the Scottish King and all the rest of his lineage, by the favorers and followers of the said House of Lancaster.

A second argument is made against the said King's succession not by them of Lancaster, but rather by those of his own House of York, which is founded upon his foreign birth, by which they hold that he is excluded, by the common laws of England, from succession to the crown, for that the said laws do bar all strangers[9] born out of the realm, to inherit within the said land . . . [Parsons summarizes the responses to these arguments by supporters of James's right.]

[Among the other reasons to exclude the King of Scots from the English crown, one is] grounded upon a certain testament[10] of King Henry the Eighth as before hath been touched, by which testament the said House of Suffolk, that is to say, the heirs of the Lady Francis, and of the Lady Eleanor, nieces to King Henry the Eighth, by his second sister Mary, are appointed to succeed in the crown of England, before the heirs of Margaret the first sister, married in Scotland, if King Henry's own children should come to die without issue, as now they are all like to do, and this testament had both the King's hand or stamp unto it, and divers witnesses' names besides, and was enrolled in the Chancery and was authorized by two acts of

---

[9] **strangers**: foreigners.   [10] **testament**: will.

Parliament, to wit, in the 28th and 35th years of King Henry, in which Parliament's authority was given to the said King, to dispose and ordain of this point of succession, as he and his learned Council should think best for the weal public. [Parsons summarizes one response to this objection by James's supporters.]

. . . A fourth argument is made against the King of Scots' succession by all the other competitors jointly, and it seemeth to them, to be an argument that hath no solution or reply, for that it is grounded upon a plain fresh statute, made in the Parliament held in the 27th year (if I err not) of her Majesty that now is, wherein is enacted and decreed, that whosoever shall be convinced to conspire, attempt, or procure the death of the Queen, or to be privy or accessary to the same, shall lose all right, title, pretence, claim or action that the same parties or their heirs have or may have, to the crown of England. Upon which statute, seeing that afterward the Lady Mary Queen of Scotland, mother of this King, was condemned and executed by the authority of the said Parliament, it seemeth evident, unto these men, that this King who pretendeth all his right to the crown of England by his said mother, can have none at all.

V. Predictions

First of all (said he) my opinion is, that this affair [of determining the succession] cannot possibly be ended by any possibility moral, without some war, at leastwise, for some time at the beginning. . . . My second proposition and conjecture is, that this matter is not like to come easily to any great or main battle, but rather to be ended at length, by some composition, and general agreement. . . . My third and last conjecture is (and for a mere conjecture only, I would have you to hold it) that seeing there be two sorts of pretenders, which stand for this preferment, the one stranger, the other English, my opinion is, that of any one foreign prince that pretendeth, the Infanta of Spain is likest to bear it away, or some other by her title, laid upon him by her father the King's good will, and on the other side, of any domestical competitors, the second son of the Earl of Hartford, or of the issue of the Countess of Darby, carrieth much show to be preferred.

→ HENRY CONSTABLE

From A Discovery of a Counterfeit Conference   *1600*

Henry Constable (1562–1613) became a Catholic at an early age and spent considerable time in France before finally returning to England in 1604. He is best known today as a minor poet; his verse was quoted in Sir Philip Sidney's *Apology for Poetry* (1595) and in the well-known collection *England's Helicon* (1600), among other places, and he was ranked highly by critics of the time, such as Francis Meres. Like many Catholics at the end of the century, he supported James's claim to the English throne because he believed that James would, at the least, reduce or eliminate the legal strictures against Catholics in England and, at best, might be persuaded to convert to Catholicism himself. Not only was James's mother, Queen Mary, Catholic, but his wife, Queen Anne, had converted to Catholicism, and James had made vague, verbal assurances to European Catholic leaders about his intentions. Like many Catholics, too, Constable was outraged by Robert Parsons's attack on James's claim to the English throne. Constable's reaction indicates some of the divisions within the world of Catholics at the time.

I. On Parsons's Method of Argument

Moreover every man's pretence of claim to the Crown must seem just, and his allegations true, for none must be discouraged to stir questions and doubts; yea the matter is so handled, that every one which is of kin to the Crown, how far off so ever it be, shall be allowed and encouraged to pretend and claim a title, both men and women, to make the matter much more doubtful, as the number of pretenders increaseth more and more; though in very deed these lawyers intend that none of them shall be able to prevail, except one [of] two, at the most they care not which. . . . Beside all this, these lawyers will protest indifference to all, though they show themselves friends to none but to one alone, which in their conceits will be able to rule the time. And some persons and their cause must be covertly abased, whose renown other whiles these men have magnified, as some others must be extolled above the skies whom in other times they would have blotted forth of their books. As also the late Queen of Scots Mary of famous memory, and consequently her heirs must be rejected with indignities, and impudently spotted with infamy of treason and other crimes to please the time, though

Henry Constable, *A Discovery of a Counterfeit Conference Held at a counterfeit place, by counterfeit travellers, for the advancement of a counterfeit title, and invented, printed, and published by one (PERSON) that dare not avow his name* (Collen, 1600) 45–47, 75, 90–92.

when time served they thought otherwise of her, or else they were most odible[1] dissemblers.

[They claim that] every lawful king is deposable for or without cause, if the common wealth dislike him; and every quarrel is a sufficient cause to depose a king if the common wealth so esteem it, and every king shall be accompted[2] a tyrant, an heretic, an infidel, or incapable otherways and unfit, and consequently deposable, because the public state here called a common wealth holdeth him so to be and is the only judge of all causes in this case of a king's state and of all commission that must proceed from a king, for no other judge is appointed in these men's text, a plain contradiction to their own doctrine.

II. Parsons a Catholic?

And it seemeth strange to wise and virtuous people that this author and disguised lawyers making show to be Catholics, and to advance God's cause, follow not the pattern and example of His holiness and predecessors who have ever held mild and modest courses towards the King of Scotland, most agreeable to the Apostolic, Roman Catholic Church, which is a sweet Mother esteeming it the best and readiest way to draw and gain such princes to the right and true religion as be out of the said Church especially not of malice but by education. And yet these phantastical author and lawyers would have all violent and furious courses exercised against the said King, as deprivation of his own realm and right to the crown of England, if it lay in their power. Though they see by daily experience that both princes and other particular persons of great quality that fall from the Catholic Church, being once in it, and were accompted as desperate persons for ever returning, yet since have reconciled themselves with great repentance and have done notable services by their examples, in procuring and hastening others of principal rank to be reconciled, as namely the most Christian King of France hath done, for the which he deserveth immortal fame.

---

[1] **odible**: odious, hateful.   [2] **accompted**: accounted, considered.

→ **SIR JOHN HAYWARD**

From An Answer to the First Part of a Certain Conference   *1603*

Sir John Hayward (1564?–1627) is best known to Renaissance scholars and historians as the author of *The First Part of the Life and Reign of Henry the IIII* (1599), for which he was imprisoned in the Tower for a period. Hayward's alleged sin in *The First Part* was to have more or less vindicated Henry IV's deposition of Richard II, although several writers of the time, including Francis Bacon, could find no trace of treason in the book. But Hayward had dedicated the book to the Earl of Essex, and Essex's enemies at court may have been behind the accusations against Hayward. A year or so after *The First Part* appeared, in February 1601, however, Essex led an abortive rebellion against Queen Elizabeth; the night before the planned action, members of his group paid Shakespeare's company to put on a performance of *Richard II* (though not necessarily Shakespeare's version), supposedly to energize the idea of monarchical deposition. Hayward was released from prison after Essex's execution.

Aside from this brush with the queen's displeasure, however, Hayward was openly royalist in his statements and received royal appointments from James. In addition to the work excerpted here, rebutting Parsons and defending James's claim to the throne, Hayward wrote many other religious and political works, including a long argument in favor of James's proposal to unite legally the two kingdoms of England and Scotland.

Learn then, heavy-headed Cloisterer,[1] unable to manage these mysteries of state: learn of me, I say, for I owe this duty to all Christians: the Prophets, the Apostles, Christ Himself hath taught us, to be obedient to Princes, though both tyrants and infidels. This ought to stand with us for a thousand reasons to submit ourselves to such kings, as it pleaseth God to send unto us, without either judging or examining their qualities. Their hearts are in God's hand; they do His service, sometimes in preserving, sometimes in punishing us; they execute His judgment both ways, in the same measure which He doth prescribe. If they abuse any part of their power, we do not excuse, we do not extenuate it; we do not exempt them from punishment: let them look unto it, let them assuredly expect, that God will dart His vengeance against them with a most stiff and dreadful arm. In the mean season, we must not oppose our selves, otherwise than by humble suits and

---

[1] **Cloisterer**: i.e., one who lives in a monastery; addressed to Robert Parsons, a Jesuit priest.

Sir John Hayward, *An Answer to the First Part of a Certain Conference, Concerning Succession, Published not long since under the name of R. Dolman* (London, 1603) N3r–v, N4r–O, O3.

prayers: acknowledging that those evils are always just for us to suffer, which are many times unjust for them to do. If we do otherwise, if we break into tumult and disorder, we resemble those Giants of whom the Poets write, who making offer to scale the skies, and to pull Jupiter out of his throne, were overwhelmed in a moment with the mountains which they had heaped together. Believe it, Cloisterer; or ask any man who is both honest and wise, and he will tell you: It is a rule in reason, a trial in experience, an authority confirmed by the best, that rebellion produceth more horrible effects than either the tyranny or insufficiency of any Prince. . . .

For your device in joining election to succession, whereby one of them should remedy the difficulties of the other, it is a mere utopical[2] conceit: what else shall I term it? An imposture of state, a dream, an illusion, fit only to surprise the judgment of the weak and ignorant multitude. These toys are always hatched by the discursive[3] sort of men, rather than the active, being matters more in imagination than in use: and herein two respects do principally oppose against you.

The first is, for that in most nations of the world, the people have lost all power of election; and succession is firmly settled in one descent, as before I have declared.

The second is, for that more fiery factions are hereby kindled, than where succession or election are mere[4] without mixture. For where one claimeth the crown by succession, and another possesseth it by title of election, there, not a disunion only of the people, not a division in arms, but a cruel throat-cutting, a most immortal and merciless butchery doth usually ensue. It is somewhat inconvenient (I grant) to be governed by a Prince either impotent or evil, but it is a greater inconvenience, by making a breach into this high point of state, to open a way to all manner of ambitions, perjuries, cruelties and spoil: whereto the nature of the common people would give a great furtherance, who being weak in wisdom, violent in will; soon weary of quiet, always desirous of change, and most especially in matters of state, are easily made serviceable to any man's aspiring desires. . . . But so soon as the king departeth out of life, the royalty is presently transferred to the next successor, according to the laws and customs of our realm. All writs go forth in his name, all course of justice is exercised, all offices are held by his authority, all states, all persons, are bound to bear to him allegiance: not under supposal of approbation[5] when he shall be crowned, according to your dull and drowsy conjecture, but as being the true Sovereign King of the realm.

---

[2] **utopical:** utopian, fanciful.   [3] **discursive:** i.e. men who think and write, rather than the "active."   [4] **mere:** absolutely, completely.   [5] **approbation:** approval, being shown favor.

→ *From* Succession Act   *1604*

A most joyful and just recognition of the immediate, lawful,
and undoubted Succession, Descent, and Right of the Crown

Great and manifold were the benefits, most dread and most gracious Sovereign, wherewith Almighty God blessed this kingdom and nation by the happy union and conjunction of the two noble Houses of York and Lancaster, thereby preserving this noble realm, formerly torn and almost wasted with long and miserable dissension and bloody civil war; but more inestimable and unspeakable blessings are thereby poured upon us because there is derived and grown from and out of that union of those two princely families a more famous and greater union, or rather a reuniting, of two mighty, famous, and ancient kingdoms (yet anciently but one) of England and Scotland under one Imperial Crown in your most Royal Person, who is lineally, rightfully, and lawfully descended of the body of the most excellent Lady Margaret, eldest daughter of the most renowned King Henry the Seventh and the high and noble Princess, Queen Elizabeth[1] his wife, eldest daughter of King Edward the Fourth, the said Lady Margaret being eldest sister of King Henry the Eighth, father of the high and mighty Princess of famous memory, Elizabeth,[2] late Queen of England: In consideration whereof, albeit we your Majesty's loyal and faithful subjects, of all estates and degrees, with all possible and public joy and acclamation, by open proclamations within five hours after the decease of our late Sovereign Queen, acknowledging thereby with one full voice of tongue and heart that your Majesty was our only lawful and rightful liege[3] Lord and Sovereign, by our unspeakable and general rejoicing and applause at your Majesty's most happy Inauguration and Coronation, by the affectionate desire of infinite numbers of us of all degrees to see your Royal Person, and by all possible outward means have endeavoured to make demonstration of our inward love, zeal, and devotion to your most excellent Majesty our undoubted rightful liege Sovereign Lord and King. . . . It may be published and declared in this High Court of Parliament, and enacted by authority of the same, that we (being bounden thereunto both by the laws of God and man) do recognise and acknowledge (and thereby express our unspeakable joys) that immediately

---

[1] **Queen Elizabeth his wife**: not Shakespeare's Queen Elizabeth I.   [2] **Elizabeth, late Queen of England**: Queen Elizabeth I.   [3] **liege**: lord or sovereign; a term from feudal law that implies the king's ownership of the land.

Excerpt from the "Succession Act" of 1604. Printed in *Statutes of the Realm*, 4.1017 (*1 Jac. I, c. 1:* i.e., the first year of the reign of James [Latin: *Jacobus*] the First [official documents usually were dated by reference to the year of the monarch's reign]; "c. 1" refers to the location of the particular Act in the volume [here, chapter 1]).

upon the dissolution and decease of Elizabeth, late Queen of England, the Imperial Crown of the realm of England, and of all the kingdoms, dominions, and rights belonging to the same, did by inherent birthright and lawful and undoubted succession descend and come to your most excellent Majesty, as being lineally, justly, and lawfully next and sole heir of the blood royal of this realm as is aforesaid, and that by the goodness of God Almighty and lawful right of descent under one Imperial Crown your Majesty is of the realms and kingdoms of England, Scotland, France, and Ireland the most potent and mighty King, and by God's goodness more able to protect and govern us your loving subjects in all peace and plenty than any of your noble progenitors; and thereunto we most humbly and faithfully do submit and oblige ourselves, our heirs and posterities, for ever, until the last drop of our bloods be spent.

The Jacobean Theory of Kingship

It is admittedly an oversimplification to attempt to describe *the* Jacobean theory of kingship, for James's positions on many issues shifted over the years, and some of his positions, perhaps, were never clear to begin with. Nevertheless, James and his followers frequently asserted several key ideas, which were generally understood by his contemporaries. We should note that the nature and ground of authority of the kingship (represented in such contradictory ways in *Macbeth*) was controversial in Shakespeare's England; the theory described below derives from what might be termed "official discourse" — the writings of James himself and his followers, who believed in and hoped to impose on others a particular set of ideas. As even these documents attest, however, a strongly felt and well-argued discourse contrary to James's positions flourished at the same time. Given the hindsight of history, in fact, one can say that the Jacobean position eventually lost out, as evidenced most spectacularly in the deposition and execution of James's son, Charles I.

James was an unusual monarch in that he wrote and spoke so much about the nature of kingship; Elizabeth, by contrast, wrote very little and

FIGURE 11 *A portrait of James in 1605, now King James VI and I, attributed to* ➤ *John de Critz the Elder. The jewel in his hat symbolizes the unity of the kingdoms. This portrait depicts James, early in his English reign, as relatively young and vigorous. Within a few years, many portraits show a much more aged James, often sitting rather than standing.*

seemed to work effectively by keeping her beliefs ambiguous. In two major works published in Scotland before he was king of England, James articulated many essential theoretical positions. *The True Law of Free Monarchies* (1598) is a systematic attempt to define the grounds of kingly authority and royal prerogative — that is, the powers belonging to the king alone, rather than to Parliament or some other institution — while *Basilikon Doron* (The King's Testament), written in 1598, is the king as father giving practical advice to his son, Prince Henry, toward the day when he will become king.[1] When James became king of England in 1603, both works were reprinted in London, in several successive editions, as the English sought to find out as much as possible about their new, foreign, and relatively unknown king. *Basilikon Doron* was phenomenally popular, with perhaps as many as nine versions printed in London in 1603 alone, totaling more than twelve thousand copies.[2] *True Law* and *Basilikon Doron* were directed toward a Scottish audience, but many readers in England took them as signs of what James would do as king of England. But what was successful in ruling Scotland would not necessarily succeed in England as well.

In these two works written before 1603, and in his famous speech of 1610 (also excerpted below), James articulated three key points, which had been or would be contested by others. First, the king is God's lieutenant on earth. Only God has the power to exalt or depose a king; if a people chafes under their king, they must suffer his misrule until God removes the king. Thus the king's *right* to the throne does not derive from man, but from God; hence, the kingship cannot be elected or chosen, but can only be inherited, in a chain that goes back to the Bible (see pp. 185–91 on succession theory in the period). Second, the king is not bound by the law, for the king came before the law; here James invokes both biblical and Scottish precedents. Thus, Parliament cannot "make any kind of law or statute, without [the king's] scepter be to it, for giving it the force of a law" (*True Law*). (James would soon find that the English Parliament was far less passive and quiescent than the Scottish Parliament had been.) The king possesses many powerful "prerogatives" (a term that became controversial) that cannot be abridged; what they are, and how far they extended, were sources of contention throughout James's reign. Third, it follows that the king cannot be lawfully deposed, or his power restricted, by any act of Parliament, or by any uprising of the people. Even a tyrannical king must be obeyed by his people (see Chapter 3 for discussion of this concept).

---

[1] Henry died in 1612, before becoming king; his brother Charles became King Charles I upon James's death in 1625.

[2] For more on the printing history as well as the political context, see Wormald (especially 150).

The king's right to the throne was said to be absolute, and his powers also absolute. This term, which was initially a wholly positive concept — *absolute* meaning perfect, complete, unrestricted, or unimprovable — eventually also became a term of negative judgment, suggesting "too much," and finally virtually a synonym for "tyranny."[3] Some writers made the kind of distinction that Sir Thomas Smith did in *De republica Anglorum* (1583), when he asserted that the king "hath absolutely in his power the authority of war and peace, to defy what Prince it shall please him, and to bid him war, and again to reconcile himself and enter into league or truce with him at his pleasure or the advice only of his privy council" (bk. 2, ch. 3), though he also noted that "in time of peace, the same [absolute power] is very dangerous, as well to him that doth use it, and much more to the people upon whom it is used," because man's imperfect nature is soon corrupted by such power, which turns into tyranny (bk. 1, ch. 8). In England, moreover, "the most high and absolute power of the realm of England consisteth in the Parliament" (bk. 2, ch. 1), not in the king. The "king-in-Parliament" was, in the English tradition that James inherited, the ultimate power.

In his speech to Parliament in 1610, after several years of conflict, James tries to have it both ways, asserting his divine right and absolute power, but allowing that every king who is not a tyrant will willingly submit himself to the laws of the land — even though he is above those laws. In the end, James will permit others to discuss *why* he did something, but "I will not be content that my power be disputed upon." This speech was in response to a petition protesting James's attempt to exclude Parliament from discussing "impositions" (i.e., a particular tax) because they were his "prerogative"; for Parliament, it was a matter of free speech. James eventually conceded the point, but his 1610 speech only exacerbated the controversy, as John Chamberlain noted in a letter to Sir Ralph Winwood of May 24, 1610. The king, he said, had made a speech to both houses of Parliament,

> but so little to their satisfaction, that I hear it bred generally much discomfort; to see our monarchical power and regal prerogative strained so high and made so transcendent every way, that if the practise should follow the positions, we are not like to leave to our successors that freedom we received from our forefathers, nor make account of any thing we have longer than they list that govern. Many bold passages have been since [spoken] in the lower house, and among the rest a wish that this speech might never come in print: but what issue this business now in hand will come unto, God knows. (Chamberlain 2: 301)

---

[3] On the idea of absolute monarchy in the seventeenth century, and the shifting implications of the word *absolute*, see Daly.

Chamberlain's frank disapproval of James's claims, and his concern for the subject's traditional freedoms, follows from a long line of political discourse at odds with such Jacobean assertions. This tradition is perhaps best exemplified in Sir John Ponet's *A Short Treatise of Politic Power* (1556): "Kings and princes ought, both by God's law, the law of nature, man's laws, and good reason, to be obedient and subject to the positive laws of their country, and may not break them. And that they be not exempt from them, nor may dispense with them, unless the makers of the laws give them express authority so to do" (Ponet, qtd. in Hodgdon 187).

James's claim of divine right, evident in the Act of Succession (see p. 205) among other places, was not only important to his claim of succession to the throne, but, as we see here, essential to his assertions of power. English monarchs had claimed some form of divine right for many years, yet no prior monarch had made the doctrine so central to his identity and authority as James. But this claim, too, made some uneasy; as another letter writer observed, "the most strictly religious [members of James's audience for the 1610 speech] could have wished that his Highness would have been more sparing in using the Name of God, and comparing the Deity with Princes' sovereignty."[4]

Jacobean claims of power also appealed to the law of nature, as is evident in the following excerpts, particularly through the interlinking metaphors of the king as father to a family, and as head to a body. An equation between the body politic and the human body, long a staple of political discourse, received renewed emphasis in James's writings, and is perfectly represented in the selection below from Sir Robert Filmer's *Patriarcha* (c. 1630). Filmer's work was not published in his lifetime, but it effectively sums up the royalist theory of kingship, defining it throughout in terms of patriarchal theory. The titles of some of Filmer's other works — *The Anarchy of a Limited or Mixed Monarchy, The Necessity of the Absolute Power of All Kings* — should be considered along with their date of publication — 1648. Like these works, *Patriarcha* was a strongly prescriptive text, offering a nostalgic vision of the absolute powers of the kingship, which were under severe attack at that moment. Charles I's execution occurred only a year later, in 1649.

---

[4] John More to Sir Ralph Winwood, March 24, 1610 (Winwood 3: 141–42).

From Basilikon Doron   *1598*

I. On the Role of a King

It is a true old saying, that a king is as one set on a stage, whose smallest actions and gestures, all the people gazingly do behold: and therefore although a king be never so precise in the discharging of his office, the people, who seeth but the outward part, will ever judge of the substance, by the circumstances; and according to the outward appearance, if his behavior be light or dissolute, will conceive pre-occupied conceits of the king's inward intention: which although with time (the trier of all truth), it will evanish, by the evidence of the contrary effects, yet *interim patitur iustus*[1]; and prejudged conceits will, in the meantime, breed contempt, the mother of rebellion and disorder. And besides that, it is certain, that all the indifferent actions and behavior of a man, have a certain holding and dependence, either upon virtue or vice, according as they are used or ruled: for there is not a middes[2] betwixt them, no more than betwixt their rewards, heaven and hell.

Be careful then, my Son, so to frame all your indifferent actions and outward behavior, as they may serve for the furtherance and forth-setting of your inward virtuous disposition.

II. Advice

And for conclusion of this my whole treatise, remember my Son, by your true and constant depending upon God, to look for a blessing to all your actions in your office: by the outward using thereof, to testify the inward uprightness of your heart; and by your behavior in all indifferent things, to set forth the vive[3] image of your virtuous disposition; and in respect of the greatness and weight of your burden, to be patient in hearing, keeping your heart free from preoccupation, ripe in concluding, and constant in your resolution. For better it is to bide at your resolution, although there were some defect in it, than by daily changing, to effectuate nothing: taking the pattern thereof from the microcosm of your own body; wherein ye have two eyes, signifying great foresight and providence, with a narrow looking in all

---

[1] **interim . . . iustus:** meanwhile the just man suffers.   [2] **middes:** mean, balance.   [3] **vive:** living.

King James I, *Basilikon Doron. Or His Majesty's Instructions To His Dearest Son, Henry the Prince* (Edinburgh, 1603; reprinted London 1603 [several editions]. Written 1598; seven copies printed privately 1599. This text is taken from James's collected *Works* of 1616) bk. 3, 180, 188–89.

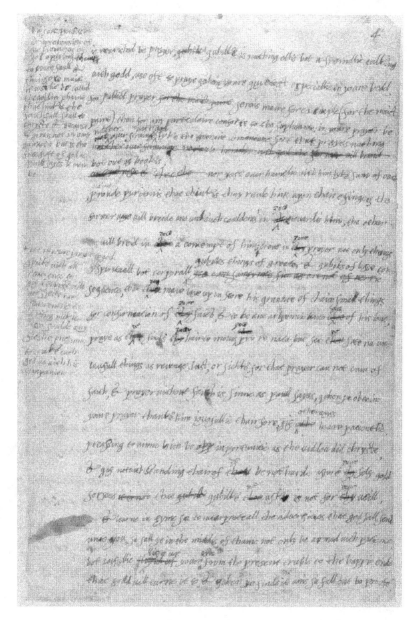

FIGURE 12 *A page, in James's handwriting, from the manuscript of* Basilikon Doron.

things; and also two ears, signifying patient hearing, and that of both the parties. But ye have but one tongue, for pronouncing a plain, sensible, and uniform sentence; and but one head, and one heart, for keeping a constant and uniform resolution, according to your apprehension: having two hands and two feet, with many fingers and toes for quick execution, in employing all instruments meet for effectuating your deliberations.

But forget not to digest ever your passion, before ye determine upon anything, since *Ira furor brevis est*:[4] uttering only your anger according to the Apostle's rule, *Irascimini, sed ne peccetis*:[5] taking pleasure, not only to reward, but to advance the good, which is a chief point of a king's glory (but make none over-great, but according as the power of the country may bear) and punishing the evil; but every man according to his own offence: not punishing nor blaming the father for the son, nor the brother for the brother; much less generally to hate a whole race for the fault of one: for *noxa caput sequitur*. . . .[6]

And being content to let others excell in other things, let it be your chiefest earthly glory, to excell in your own craft.

---

[4] Ira . . . est: anger is a short-lived madness.   [5] Irascimini . . . peccetis: be ye angry, and sin not.   [6] noxa . . . sequitur: the crime follows the head.

→ KING JAMES I

From The True Law of Free Monarchies   *1598*

I. On the Relation between the King and the Law

For as our Chronicles bear witness, this isle, and especially our part of it, being scantly inhabited, but by very few, and they as barbarous and scant of civility, as number, there comes our first King Fergus,[1] with a great number with him, out of Ireland, which was long inhabited before us, and making himself master of the country, by his own friendship, and force, as well of the Irelandmen that came with him, as of the countrymen that willingly fell to him, he made himself King and Lord, as well of the whole lands, as of the

---

[1] **Fergus**: legendary king, supposed to have ruled in third century B.C.E.

King James I, *The True Law of Free Monarchies: Or the Reciprock and Mutual Duty Betwixt a Free King, and His Natural Subjects* (Edinburgh, 1598; reprinted London 1603. This text is taken from James's collected *Works* of 1616) 201–02, 203, 204.

◄ FIGURE 13 *The frontispiece, by Reynald Elstrack, to the collected writings of King James, published in 1616. The two statues represent Religion (standing victorious over death) and Peace (standing victorious over the implements of war), and James's crown rises above all to the heavens.*

whole inhabitants within the same. Thereafter he and his successors, a long while after their being kings, made and established their laws from time to time, and as the occasion required. So the truth is directly contrary in our state to the false affirmation of such seditious writers, as would persuade us, that the laws and state of our country were established before the admitting of a king: where by the contrary ye see it plainly proved, that a wise king coming in among barbarians, first established the estate and form of government, and thereafter made laws by himself, and his successors according thereto.

The kings therefore in Scotland were before any estates or ranks of men within the same, before any Parliaments were holden, or laws made: and by them was the land distributed (which at the first was whole theirs), states erected and decerned,[2] and forms of government devised and established. And so it follows of necessity, that the kings were the authors and makers of the laws, and not the laws of the kings. . . . [T]he King is *Dominus omnium bonorum*,[3] and *Dominus directus totius Dominii*,[4] the whole subjects being but his vassals, and from him holding all their lands as their over-lord, who according to good services done unto him, changeth their holdings from tack[5] to few, from ward to blanch,[6] erecteth new Baronies, and uniteth old, without advice or authority of either Parliament or any other subaltern[7] judicial state. . . . [W]e daily see that in the Parliament (which is nothing else but the head court of the king and his vassals) the laws are but craved by his subjects, and only made by him at their rogation,[8] and with their advice. For albeit the king make daily statutes and ordinances, enjoining such pains thereto as he thinks meet, without any advice of Parliament or estates, yet it lies in the power of no Parliament, to make any kind of law or statute, without his scepter be to it, for giving it the force of a law.

---

[2] **decerned**: decreed by judicial sentence. [3] **Dominus . . . bonorum**: lord of all goods. [4] **Dominus . . . Dominii**: direct lord of the whole dominion. [5] **tack**: holding property by lease. [6] **ward to blanch**: from guardianship to merely renting; i.e., the king has power to change the forms of land ownership at will. [7] **subaltern**: subordinate, inferior. [8] **rogation**: formal request.

II. The King's Power

And as ye see it manifest, that the king is over-lord of the whole land, so is he master over every person that inhabiteth the same, having power over the life and death of every one of them. For although a just prince will not take the life of any of his subjects without a clear law, yet the same laws whereby he taketh them, are made by himself, or his predecessors, and so the power flows always from himself; as by daily experience we see, good and just princes will from time to time make new laws and statutes, adjoining the penalties to the breakers thereof, which before the law was made, had been no crime to the subject to have committed. Not that I deny the old definition of a king, and of a law, which makes the king to be a speaking law, and the law a dumb[9] king: for certainly a king that governs not by his law, can neither be countable to God for his administration, nor have a happy and established reign. For albeit it be true that I have at length proved, that the king is above the law, as both the author and giver of strength thereto, yet a good king will not only delight to rule his subjects by the law, but even will conform himself in his own actions thereunto, always keeping that ground, that the health of the commonwealth be his chief law. And where he sees the law doubtsome or rigorous, he may interpret or mitigate the same, lest otherwise *Summum ius* be *summa iniuria*.[10] And therefore general laws, made publicly in Parliament, may upon known respects to the king by his authority be mitigated, and suspended upon causes only known to him.

III. The King as Father and Head

And the agreement of the law of nature in this our ground with the laws and constitutions of God, and man, already alleged, will by two similitudes easily appear. The king towards his people is rightly compared to a father of children, and to a head of a body composed of divers members: for as fathers, the good princes and magistrates of the people of God acknowledged themselves to their subjects. And for all other well-ruled commonwealths, the style of *Pater patriae*[11] was ever, and is commonly used to kings. And the proper office of a king towards his subjects agrees very well with the office of the head towards the body, and all members thereof: for from the head, being the seat of judgment, proceedeth the care and foresight of guiding, and preventing all evil that may come to the body or any part thereof. The head cares for the body, so doth the king for his people. As the discourse and direction flows from the head, and the execution according thereunto

---

[9] **dumb**: silent.   [10] *Summum . . . iniuria:* the most extreme ("highest") laws be extreme injustice.   [11] *Pater patriae:* father of the fatherland.

belongs to the rest of the members, every one according to their office, so it is betwixt a wise prince, and his people. As the judgment coming from the head may not only employ the members, every one in their own office, as long as they are able for it; but likewise in case any of them be affected with any infirmity must care and provide for their remedy, in case it be curable, and if otherwise, gar cut them off [12] for fear of infecting the rest: even so is it betwixt the prince, and his people.

[12] **gar cut them off:** have them cut off.

→ KING JAMES I

From A Speech to the Lords and Commons of the Parliament at Whitehall *March 21, 1610*

The state of monarchy is the supremest thing upon earth. For kings are not only God's lieutenants upon earth, and sit upon God's throne, but even by God Himself they are called gods. There be three principal similitudes that illustrate the state of monarchy: one taken out of the word of God, and the two other out of the grounds of policy[1] and philosophy. In the Scriptures kings are called gods, and so their power after a certain relation compared to the divine power. Kings are also compared to fathers of families, for a king is truly *Parens patriae,*[2] the politic father of his people. And lastly, kings are compared to the head of this microcosm[3] of the body of man.

Kings are justly called gods, for that they exercise a manner or resemblance of divine power upon earth. For if you will consider the attributes to God, you shall see how they agree in the person of a king. God hath power to create, or destroy, make, or unmake at His pleasure, to give life, or send death, to judge all, and to be judged nor accomptable[4] to none; to raise low things, and to make high things low at His pleasure, and to God are both soul and body due. And the like power have kings: they make and unmake their subjects; they have power of raising, and casting down; of life, and of death; judges over all their subjects and in all causes, and yet accomptable to none but God only. They have power to exalt low things, and abase high

[1] **policy:** political theory.   [2] *Parens patriae:* parent of the fatherland.   [3] **microcosm:** a small world within the larger world.   [4] **nor accomptable:** not accountable.

King James I, "A Speech to the Lords and Commons of the Parliament at Whitehall, On Wednesday the XXI. of March. Anno 1609" (i.e., 1610 New Style). (This text is taken from James's collected *Works* of 1616, 527–31.)

things, and make of their subjects like men at the chess, a pawn to take a bishop or a knight, and to cry up,[5] or down any of their subjects, as they do their money. And to the king is due both the affection of the soul, and the service of the body of his subjects. . . . [In addition to confirming a king's godlike claim on his subjects, James says that he would also conclude] as an Englishman, showing this people, that as in general all subjects were bound to relieve their king, so to exhort them, that as we lived in a settled state of a kingdom which was governed by his[6] own fundamental laws and orders, that according thereunto, they were now (being assembled for this purpose in Parliament) to consider how to help such a king as now they had; and that according to the ancient form, and order established in this kingdom, putting so, a difference between the general power of a king in divinity, and the settled and established state of this crown, and kingdom. . . .

As for the father of a family, they had of old under the law of nature *Patriam potestatem*,[7] which was *Potestatem vitae & necis*,[8] over their children or family (I mean such fathers of families as were the lineal heirs of those families whereof kings did originally come). For kings had their first original from them, who planted and spread themselves in colonies through the world. Now a father may dispose of his inheritance to his children at his pleasure: yea, even disinherit the eldest upon just occasions, and prefer the youngest, according to his liking: make them beggers, or rich at his pleasure; restrain, or banish out of his presence, as he finds them give cause of offense, or restore them in favor again with the penitent sinner. So may the king deal with his subjects.

And lastly, as for the head of the natural body, the head hath the power of directing all the members of the body to that use which the judgment in the head thinks most convenient. It may apply sharp cures, or cut off corrupt members, let blood[9] in what proportion it thinks fit, and as the body may spare, but yet is all this power ordained by God *Ad aedificationem, non ad destructionem*.[10] For although God have power as well of destruction, as of creation or maintenance, yet will it not agree with the wisdom of God, to exercise His power in the destruction of nature, and overturning the whole frame of things, since His creatures were made, that His glory might thereby be the better expressed. So were he a foolish father that would disinherit or destroy his children without a cause, or leave off the careful education of them. And it were an idle head that would in place of physic[11] so

---

[5] **cry up:** to proclaim (a thing or person) to be excellent.   [6] **his:** its.   [7] *Patriam potestatem:* fatherly power.   [8] *Potestatem . . . necis:* the power of life and death.   [9] **let blood:** to bleed, with leeches or heated cups, in order to purge the body of disease.   [10] *Ad . . . destructionem:* for constructive, not destructive, use.   [11] **physic:** medicine.

poison or phlebotomize[12] the body as might breed a dangerous distemper or destruction thereof.

But now in these our times we are to distinguish between the state of kings in their first original, and between the state of settled kings and monarchs, that do at this time govern in civil kingdoms. For even as God, during the time of the Old Testament, spake by oracles, and wrought by miracles, yet how soon it pleased Him to settle a Church which was bought, and redeemed by the blood of His only Son Christ then was there a cessation of both,[13] He ever after governing His people and Church within the limits of His revealed will. So in the first original of kings, whereof some had their beginning by conquest, and some by election of the people, their wills at that time served for law; yet how soon kingdoms began to be settled in civility and policy, than did kings set down their minds by laws,which are properly made by the king only; but at the rogation[14] of the people, the king's grant being obtained thereunto. And so the king became to be *Lex loquens,*[15] after a sort, binding himself by a double oath to the observation of the fundamental laws of his kingdom: tacitly, as by being a king, and so bound to protect as well the people, as the laws of his kingdom; and expressly, by his oath at his coronation. So as every just king in a settled kingdom is bound to observe that paction[16] made to his people by his laws, in framing his government agreeable thereunto, according to that paction which God made with Noah after the deluge, *Hereafter seedtime, and harvest, cold and heat, summer and winter, and day and night shall not cease, so long as the earth remains.*[17] And therefore a king governing in a settled kingdom, leaves to be a king, and degenerates into a tyrant, as soon as he leaves off to rule according to his laws. In which case the king's conscience may speak unto him, as the poor widow said to Philip of Macedon: either govern according to your law, *Aut ne Rex sis.*[18] And though no Christian man ought to allow any rebellion of people against their prince, yet doth God never leave kings unpunished when they transgress these limits. For in that same Psalm where God saith to kings, *Vos Dii estis,*[19] he immediately thereafter concludes, *But ye shall die like men.* The higher we are placed, the greater shall our fall be . . . the taller the trees be, the more in danger of the wind; and the tempest beats sorest upon the highest mountains. Therefore all kings that are not tyrants, or perjured, will be glad to bound themselves within the limits of their laws; and they that persuade them the contrary, are vipers, and pests, both against them and the commonwealth. For it is a great difference between a king's

---

[12] **phlebotomize:** to bleed.   [13] **both:** i.e., oracles and miracles.   [14] **rogation:** formal request.   [15] *Lex loquens:* a speaking law.   [16] **paction:** pact, contract.   [17] *Hereafter . . . remains:* Genesis 8:22.   [18] *Aut . . . sis:* or may you be no king.   [19] *Vos . . . estis:* you are gods (Psalm 82:6).

government in a settled state, and what kings in their original power might do in *Individuo vago*.[20] As for my part, I thank God, I have ever given good proof, that I never had intention to the contrary. And I am sure to go to my grave with that reputation and comfort, that never king was in all his time more careful to have his laws duly observed, and himself to govern thereafter, than I.

I conclude then this point touching the power of kings, with this axiom of divinity, that as to dispute what God may do, is blasphemy, but *quid vult Deus*,[21] that divines may lawfully, and do ordinarily dispute and discuss; for to dispute *a posse ad esse*[22] is both against logic and divinity, so is it sedition in subjects, to dispute what a king may do in the height of his power. But just kings will ever be willing to declare what they will do, if they will not incur the curse of God. I will not be content that my power be disputed upon, but I shall ever be willing to make the reason appear of all my doings, and rule my actions according to my laws.

[20] *in Individuo vago:* as an unrestrained individual.   [21] *quid . . . Deus:* what God wants.
[22] *a posse ad esse:* from what may be to what is.

→ SIR ROBERT FILMER

From Patriarcha: Or the Natural Power of Kings   *c. 1630*

I. On the Claim of the People's Liberty

Since the time that school divinity began to flourish, there hath been a common opinion maintained, as well by divines[1] as by divers other learned men, which affirms: *Mankind is naturally endowed and born with freedom from all subjection, and at liberty to choose what form of government it please, and that the power which any one man hath over others was at first bestowed according to the discretion of the mulititude.*

This tenet was first hatched in the schools,[2] and hath been fostered by all succeeding papists for good divinity. The divines also of the Reformed churches[3] have entertained it, and the common people everywhere tenderly embrace it as being most plausible to flesh and blood, for that it prodigally distributes a portion of liberty to the meanest[4] of the multitude, who magnify

[1] **divines:** theologians.   [2] **schools:** medieval Catholic universities.   [3] **Reformed churches:** i.e. Protestant churches.   [4] **meanest:** the lowest.

Sir Robert Filmer, *Patriarcha: Or The Natural Power of Kings* (c. 1630; published London, 1680) 3–5, 22–24.

liberty, as if the height of human felicity were only to be found in it — never remembering that the desire of liberty was the first cause of the fall of Adam.

But howsoever this vulgar opinion hath of late obtained great reputation, yet it is not to be found in the ancient Fathers and doctors of the primitive church.[5] It contradicts the doctrine and history of the Holy Scriptures, the constant practice of all ancient monarchies, and the very principles of the law of nature. It is hard to say whether it be more erroneous in divinity or dangerous in policy.

Yet upon the ground of this doctrine both Jesuits and some over-zealous favorers of the Geneva discipline[6] have built a perilous conclusion, which is, *that the people or multitude have power to punish, or deprive, the prince if he transgress the laws of the kingdom.* Witness Parsons[7] and Buchanan.[8] The first, under the name of Doleman . . . labors to prove that kings have been lawfully chastised by their commonwealths. The latter in his book *De Jure Regni apud Scotos* maintains a liberty of the people to depose their prince. . . .

This desperate assertion, whereby kings are made subject to the censures and deprivations of their subjects, follows (as the authors of it conceive) as a necessary consequence of that former position of the supposed natural equality and freedom of mankind, and liberty to choose what form of government it please.

And though Sir John Hayward[9] . . . and some others have learnedly confuted both Buchanan and Parsons, and bravely vindicated the right of kings in most points, yet all of them, when they come to the argument drawn from the *natural liberty and equality of mankind,* do with one consent admit it for a truth unquestionable, not so much as once denying or opposing it. Whereas if they did but confute this first erroneous principle, the whole fabric of this vast engine of popular sedition would drop down of itself.

The rebellious consequence which follows this prime article of the *natural freedom of mankind* may be my sufficient warrant for a modest examination of the original truth of it. Much hath been said, and by many, for the affirmative. Equity requires that an ear be reserved a little for the negative.

II. On the King as Father

In all kingdoms or commonwealths in the world, whether the prince be the supreme father of the people or but the true heir of such a father, or whether

---

[5] **primitive church:** the original early church, after Jesus's death but before the consolidation of Catholicism; by implication, a purer, less corrupted time.   [6] **Geneva discipline:** followers of John Calvin, i.e. radical Protestants of the day.   [7] **Parsons:** see p. 191.   [8] **Buchanan:** see p. 128.
[9] **Hayward:** see p. 203.

he come to the crown by usurpation, or by election of the nobles or of the people, or by any other way whatsoever, or whether some few or a multitude govern the commonwealth, yet still the authority that is in any one, or in many, or in all of these, is the only right and natural authority of a supreme father. There is, and always shall be continued to the end of the world, a natural right of a supreme father over every multitude, although, by the secret will of God, many at first do most unjustly obtain the exercise of it.

To confirm this natural right of regal power, we find in the Decalogue[10] that the law which enjoins obedience to kings is delivered in the terms of *Honor thy father* as if all power were originally in the father. If obedience to parents be immediately due by a natural law, and subjection to princes but by the mediation of an human ordinance, what reason is there that the law of nature should give place to the laws of men, as we see the power of the father over his child gives place and is subordinate to the power of the magistrate?

If we compare the natural rights of a father with those of a king, we find them all one, without any difference at all but only in the latitude or extent of them. As the father over one family, so the king, as father over many families, extends his care to preserve, feed, clothe, instruct and defend the whole commonwealth. His war, his peace, his courts of justice and all his acts of sovereignty tend only to preserve and distribute to every subordinate and inferior father, and to their children, their rights and privileges, so that all the duties of a king are summed up in an universal fatherly care of his people.

[10] **Decalogue**: the Ten Commandments.

Royal Charisma and the King's Touch

Two-thirds of the way through the long scene 3 of act 4, after the exiled Malcolm has tested Macduff's loyalty, and before Ross enters to tell Macduff that his family has been murdered by Macbeth, Shakespeare stops the action to allow Malcolm to offer an account of the English king, Edward the Confessor, who has given him sanctuary. The English doctor has reported that "a crew of wretched souls / That stay his cure" are outside; their "malady . . . at his touch" is cured. Macduff asks, "What's the disease he means?" and Malcolm answers:

> 'Tis called the evil.
> A most miraculous work in this good king,
> Which often, since my here-remain in England,
> I have seen him do. How he solicits heaven
> Himself best knows; but strangely-visited people,

All swoll'n and ulcerous, pitiful to the eye,
The mere despair of surgery, he cures,
Hanging a golden stamp about their necks
Put on with holy prayers; and 'tis spoken,
To the succeeding royalty he leaves
The healing benediction. With this strange virtue
He hath a heavenly gift of prophecy,
And sundry blessings hang about his throne
That speak him full of grace.   (lines 147–60)

The disease, the "evil," was scrofula, or *struma* in Latin; it was also known as the King's Evil. A condition marked by swelling glands (particularly in the neck), lymphatic infection, and a predisposition to tuberculosis, scrofula was believed curable by the touch of the monarch alone, when other medical remedies had failed.[1] English historians traced this attribute of sovereign power back to the reign of Edward the Confessor, as Holinshed notes:

> [H]e seemed wholly given to a devout trade of life, charitable to the poor, and very liberal, namely to hospitals and houses of religion . . . As hath been thought he was inspired with the gift of prophecy, and also to have had the gift of healing infirmities and diseases. He used to help those that were vexed with the disease, commonly called the king's evil, and left that virtue as it were a portion of inheritance unto his successors the kings of this realm. (Holinshed 1: 754)

John Speed added, in his *History of Great Britain* (1611), that Edward's successors hold this power by virtue of their very sovereignty, "by the touch of those gracious hands who have held the Scepter, as God's Vicegerents[2] of this most blessed and happy kingdom" (Speed 401).[3] It would be difficult to specify exactly *how* this power worked, however, since, according to Protestant beliefs, all miracles had ceased with the coming of Christ. It could not be claimed that the monarch possessed the power in his or her own person — it was God's power, after all — but the power somehow flowed through them, or was energized by them. And just as Edward's possession of the power stemmed from his own holiness, so later monarchs were understood to be "full of grace," like Shakespeare's Edward.

Queen Elizabeth had developed the ritual of healing into a highly formalized practice, as the excerpts from William Tooker and William Clowes

---

[1] The term *scrofula* seems to have been used to describe almost any kind of lesion in the neck area.

[2] **Vicegerents**: applied to rulers as representatives of God.

[3] As Bloch and others point out, the ceremony of the royal touch had also existed in France for centuries, and was not a purely English phenomenon; see also Crawfurd.

reveal. Throughout her reign, Elizabeth had mastered the art of separating herself from Catholic images and rituals, while at the same time appropriating and reinscribing them for her own purposes. Catholic worship of the Virgin Mary might be proscribed, for example, but an analogous idealization of the Virgin Queen was officially encouraged. So too the ritual of healing the King's Evil became yet another demonstration of Elizabeth's personal sanctity and, not incidentally, certain proof of her legitimacy as monarch, since she possessed the power handed down "to the succeeding royalty." As Keith Thomas has shown, simultaneous with the development of the royal ceremony was the legal banishment of such activities among the people of the kingdom — the cunning women and itinerant magicians of the countryside (197–211). Thus, all forms of charismatic healing power were centralized and reserved as attributes of sovereign power. In the excerpt from his sermon (below), John Howson links, in quite typical fashion, the divinity of the monarch and the power to heal with "power absolute without limitation accountable only to God."

Given the clear ideological function of the royal touch, one could logically assume that King James would have readily welcomed it as an institution. It represented, at a minimum, another guarantee of *his* legitimacy as monarch, which had been much in question, and additional argument for sovereign power. Yet James was evidently too much the Protestant to accept the ceremony, as a dispatch from the Venetian ambassador (June 4, 1603) makes clear; in it he notes that James had objected to using the Catholic custom of the sign of the cross, which even Queen Elizabeth used in the ceremony of the royal touch (see the excerpt from Tooker that follows): "and he says that neither he nor any other King can have power to heal scrofula, for the age of miracles is past, and God alone can work them. However, he will have the full ceremony, so as not to lose this prerogative, which belongs to the Kings of England as Kings of France" (*CSP* Ven. 10: 44).[4] The calculation in James's adoption of the ceremony, in spite of his religious objections to it, is clear in a letter of October 8, 1603, in the Vatican archives:

> At this time the King began to take interest in the practice pertaining to certain ancient customs of the kings of England respecting the cure of persons suffering with the King's Evil. So when some of these patients were presented to him in his ante-chamber, he first had a prayer offered by a Calvinist minister, and then remarked that he was puzzled as to how to act. From one point of view he did not see how the patient could be cured without a

---

[4] James, however, dispensed with crossing, and actually touching the sore, in the ceremony; see Crawfurd 85–87.

miracle, and nowadays miracles had ceased and no longer happened: so he was afraid of committing a superstitious act. From another point of view, however, inasmuch as it was an ancient usage and for the good of his subjects, he resolved to give it a trial, but only by way of prayer, in which he begged all present to join him, and then he touched the sick folk.

It was observed that when the King made this speech, he several times turned his eyes towards the Scotch ministers around him, as though he expected their approval of what he was saying, having first conferred with them.[5]

Court records throughout James's reign describe him frequently presiding over the ceremony, yet his skepticism about its efficacy remained well known. The Duke of Saxe-Weimar, visiting the court on September 19, 1613, reported that "The ceremony of healing is understood to be very distasteful to the King, and it is said he would willingly abolish it," which of course he never did (Rye 151). As one of James's least sympathetic contemporary biographers, Arthur Wilson, put it, James knew the royal touch was "a device, to aggrandize the virtue of kings, when miracles were in fashion; but he let the world believe it, though he smiled at it in his own reason, finding the strength of the imagination a more powerful agent in the cure, than the plasters his chirurgions[6] prescribed for the sore" (289).

Returning to *Macbeth* now, we might well ask how including the reference to healing the King's Evil can be understood as another effort to "please" James, as some readers in the past have argued.[7] James's skepticism seems to have been widely known throughout his reign, and particularly at the beginning of it, when Catholic issues were highly sensitive.[8] Moreover, James was not alone in his skepticism about the efficacy of the royal touch; other writers of the period — generally, those not associated with or indebted to the sovereign — expressed opinions ranging from politely ambiguous doubt to complete disbelief. The Puritan jailers of King Charles I mocked his continuation of the ritual while in prison, even nicknaming him "Stroker" (Thomas 197).

Certainly Shakespeare wants us to see that the disease, referred to by Malcolm only as "the evil," is on the one hand scrofula, curable only by the king of England, and on the other hand Macbeth himself, curable only with the help of the king of England (and the "ten thousand men" he is sending

[5] Translated by Crawfurd 83.

[6] **chirurgions**: surgeons.

[7] Cf. Paul 383; Bloch 192.

[8] James's personal aversion to disease and physical unpleasantness, and to crowds generally, may also have been part of his resistance.

along). The contrast between the holy king and the evil king is thus made clear; moreover, the physical disease described by the English doctor can be cured, while the disease described by the Scottish doctor in act 5, scene 1 — Lady Macbeth's sleepwalking and "sorely charged" heart — is, he says, "beyond my practice" (5.1.47). Macbeth will later ask the doctor,

> Canst thou not minister to a mind diseased,
> Pluck from the memory a rooted sorrow,
> Raze out the written troubles of the brain,
> And with some sweet oblivious antidote
> Cleanse the stuffed bosom of that perilous stuff
> Which weighs upon the heart? (5.3.42–47)

They are ostensibly talking about Lady Macbeth, but Macbeth's description is too full of personal knowledge, of pain and guilt, and the doctor's response — "Therein the patient / Must minister to himself" (5.3.47–48) — shifts the pronoun from the feminine to its implied male subject, Macbeth himself.

In further contrast to the English king, moreover, Macbeth does not have a "heavenly gift of prophecy," but rather has had to invoke demonic powers of prophecy, which he cannot read properly in any event. Nor will Macbeth be able to leave "To the succeeding royalty . . . / The healing benediction," or anything else, for that matter, since he and Lady Macbeth have no children.

The healing powers of the royal touch were possessed by the English king, not the Scottish one. Therefore Malcolm — whose moral nature is confusingly under interrogation in the first part of this scene — will not possess it either, nor will Banquo's son Fleance. James may have ultimately claimed descent and royal blood on the English side, but to the extent that he is a Scottish king, he too could only observe the power from a distance. The purity of it, as it is embodied in Shakespeare's Edward the Confessor, reminds us of James's ultimately hypocritical appropriation of the ritual. James's position as the foreign king coming to claim the English throne, finally, does not parallel but contrasts with Edward the Confessor's position as the last British king before the invasion by the foreigner, William of Normandy. The historical context of the ceremony of the king's touch was quite complex, then, and the ritual itself remained a flashpoint in later disputes about the nature of sovereign power.[9]

---

[9] The last English monarch to have employed the royal touch seems to have been Queen Anne, who last performed the ritual on April 27, 1714 (Bloch 220); among her patients had been the young Samuel Johnson.

→ WILLIAM TOOKER

From The Divine Power or Gift of Healing   *1597*

[Tooker quotes "The Office of Healing" for Queen Elizabeth, which consists of readings of biblical passages interspersed with descriptions of the Queen's actions. The biblical passages are omitted here.]

The Chaplain shall read the Gospel written in the sixteenth chapter of St. Mark at verse 14 . . . While these words are repeated, her most serene Majesty lays her hands on each side of them that are sick and diseased with the evil, on the jaws, or the throat, or the affected part, and touches the sore places with her bare hands, and forthwith heals them: and after their sores have been touched by her most healing hands the sick persons retire a while, till the rest of the ceremony is finished: then the Chaplain makes an end of the Gospel. . . .

The Chaplain shall then say the second Gospel written in the first chapter of John. . . . At which words Her Majesty rises, and as each person is summoned and led back singly, and receives a golden coin of the value of ten shillings, bored and slung on a ribbon, she makes the sign of the cross on the part diseased: so with a prayer for the health and happiness of each and with a blessing, they are bidden to retire a while till the rest of the gospel is finished. . . . When this [reading of John] is ended, Her Majesty, along with the whole congregation, meekly kneeling upon her knees, prays. . . . These common prayers being ended, there followeth a special prayer, that is not found in the Book of daily Prayers, yet is above all things needful. . . .

[Tooker offers personal assurances as to the efficacy of the ceremony:] How often have I seen her most Serene Majesty prostrate on her knees, body and soul wrapped in prayer, calling upon God and beseeching the Savior Christ for such as these: how often have I seen her with her exquisite hands, whiter than whitest snow, boldly and without disgust pressing their sores and ulcers and handling them to health, not merely touching them with her finger-tips: how often have I seen her worn with fatigue, as when in one single day during the preparation for the last Passover she healed eight and thirty persons of the struma . . . some at once, some more, some less quickly and after a longer interval, most of them [whom the Queen had

---

William Tooker, *Charisma sive donum sanationis* (London, 1597; English translation by Raymond Crawfurd, *The King's Evil* [Oxford: Clarendon Press, 1911]) 72–75.

touched] arrived safe and sound at an excellent state of body and a permanent condition of good health.

→ WILLIAM CLOWES

From A Right Fruitful and Approved Treatise   *1602*

Amongst an infinite number (which I have known daily cured by her Highness, of the foresaid Evil) this cure following is worthy of great admiration. There came into my hands not many years past, a certain stranger, born (as he said) in the Land of Gulicke near unto Cleveland. This stranger had been in cure a long time before he came unto me, with diverse skillful chirurgians,[1] both English and strangers,[2] being then greatly molested and sore troubled with diverse pernicious cancerous fistulous[3] ulcers in certain places of his body; likewise he had many knotty swellings or abscessions, gathered together upon heaps in the fore part of his neck, near unto the windpipe, and some in the hinder part of the neck: and also amongst the principal and notable vessels, viz. the great sinews, veins and arteries, and therefore could not without great peril and danger be safely taken away, either by lance[4] or caustick[5] remedies, by reason of their near knitting together, and were also very unfit, to be brought to suppuration.[6] The cause was, they were for the most part engendered of dull and slow or tough slimy matter, for the which I craved now and then the advice and counsel of diverse learned and expert physicians and chirurgians, only to prevent and avoid those pernicious dangers that oftentimes do follow. Howbeit (in conclusion), notwithstanding all our turmoiling, much care, industry and diligence, with the application of most excellent medicines (very remediable and appropriate for that cure) yet was his grief rather the worse than better. For look what way soever we took with approved medicines, some mild, some vehement, and some stronger (which by natural reason and common sense, were very good and commendable), yea, and which brought oftentimes all his ulcers to be very near whole: yet upon a sudden (without any just cause to us known), his sores did putrefy and break forth again, with

---

[1] **chirurgians:** surgeons.   [2] **strangers:** foreigners.   [3] **fistulous:** hollow; like an abscess.   [4] **lance:** surgical instrument; like the scalpel.   [5] **caustick:** a substance that burns living tissue upon contact.   [6] **suppuration:** formation or discharge of pus.

William Clowes, *A Right Fruitful and Approved Treatise, for the Artificial Cure of that Malady called in Latin* Struma, *and in English, the* Evil, *cured by Kings and Queens of England* (London, 1602) 48–50.

much loathsome filthiness, so that I feared his ulcers would gangrenize, by reason of the concursion[7] and vigor of the unexpected accidents, so that his disease wearied us all. In the end, after he had been twelve or thirteen months in my cure, perceiving we all missed of our expected hope and purpose for the curing of this infirmity, and likewise himself being overtired with extreme pains and grief, so that oftentimes he bewailed his own great misery and wretchedness: for which cause he went his ways, and came no more unto me for any cure, but by the counsel of some of his own countrymen and friends, made means (unknown to me) unto other of my fellows the Queen's Majesty's Chirurgians, which are in place of preferment before me. Who pitying his miserable estate, upon a time (amongst many others) he was then presented unto our most sacred and renowned Prince the Queen's most excellent Majesty, for the cure of the said Evil: which through the gift and power of Almighty God, by her Grace's only means laying of her blessed and happy hands upon him, she cured him safely within the space of six months. Hereby it appeareth it is a more divine than human work, so afterwards upon a time I did meet with him by chance in London, but I did not well know him, his color and complexion was so greatly altered and amended. And being in very comely manner attired, otherwise than before I had seen him, and he told me who he was. Then I asked him how he did with his grief? He answered me, I thank God and the Queen of England, I am by her Majesty perfectly cured and healed; and after her Grace had touched me, I never applied any medicine at all, but kept it clean, with sweet and fresh clean clothes, and now and then washed the sore with white wine: and thus all my griefs did consume and waste clean away. And that I should credit him the more, he shewed me the Angel of gold[8] which her Majesty did put about his neck, truly a cure (as I have said) requireth divine honor and reverence. And here I do confidently affirm and steadfastly believe, that (for the certain cure of this most miserable malady) when all arts and sciences do fail, her Highness is the only Daystar,[9] peerless and without comparison: for whose long life, much happiness, peace and tranquillity, let us all (according to our bounden duties) continually pray unto the Almighty God, that he will bless, keep and defend her Sacred person, from the malice of all her known and unknown enemies, so that she may for ever reign over us (if it please the Lord God), even unto the end of the world, still to cure and heal many thousands more, than ever she hath yet done. Amen.

---

[7] **concursion**: running or rushing together.   [8] **Angel of gold**: gold coin, known as an "angel" because it bore an image of the archangel Michael on one side.   [9] **Daystar**: the sun; i.e., the source of all light.

From A Sermon Preached at St. Mary's in Oxford, the 17. Day of November, 1602

And surely God is very jealous of the honor of princes, and lest we should in any sort despise them and be disobedient unto them, because we be all made of one mould of the earth, as the days of the year of one sun in the firmament, and therefore are all *pares in esse natura,* equal one to another in nature; that there might be a difference *in esse morali,* in civil being, God honoreth princes with His own name, so that they are called *Gods,* and *God's anointed,* and the *sons of the most high.* . . .

For there is *divinatio in labii regis,* divination in the lips of the king, Proverbs 16, so that they do often foresee, forespeak, and foretell things to come, and it is noted in the first kings that ever God instituted. . . .

Secondly, there is a certain *depth in the heart of a king. Which none can seek out, even higher than the heaven, and deeper than the earth.* Proverbs 25.

Thirdly, they have gifts of healing incurable diseases, which is miraculous and above nature, so that when Vespasian[1] was seen to perform such a cure, the people concluded he should be Emperor, as Tacitus notes.

Fourthly, they have power absolute without limitation accountable only to God for their actions.

Fifthly, they have authority to bless their dutiful and loyal subjects, and they are blessed; and authority to curse their subjects disobedient, and they are cursed with temporal curse. . . .

And as God is jealous of their honor, so much more of their safeties, and therefore he sets a *guard of Angels about them. He keepeth them as the apple of His eye.* Psalms 17. *He hides them under the shadow of His wings*: he will not have them touched. . . .

Finally, He revengeth their wrongs before His own, treasons against them before blasphemies against Himself.

---

[1] **Vespasian**: Roman emperor 69–79 C.E.

John Howson, *A Sermon Preached at St. Mary's in Oxford, the 17. Day of November, 1602.* 2nd ed. (Oxford, 1603) 26–27.

CHAPTER 3

Treason and Resistance

>‹

Resistance in Theory

In reading historical material from the early modern period, some readers inevitably privilege certain documents over others; for example, it is logical to focus more closely on pronouncements by the monarch than on, say, the diary of an anonymous merchant. But the *truth* of either document is not necessarily a reflection of its status. The English monarch, his court, and their followers had, relatively speaking, a vast propaganda machine at their disposal, as well as the ability to suppress publications of which they disapproved. *An Homily against Disobedience and Willful Rebellion* (excerpted below), for example, was issued in 1570, as a response to the so-called Northern Rebellion, an uprising largely in support of Mary, Queen of Scots; two authorized texts of collections of such homilies were placed in every Anglican church in the kingdom, along with the Bible and the *Book of Common Prayer*.[1] In many churches, the sermons preached were simply these homilies. The *Homily against Disobedience and Willful Rebellion* asserts a natural

---

[1] The first collection was published in 1547, the second in 1563; the *Homily against Disobedience and Willful Rebellion*, published in 1570, was added later. By 1640, the first collection had been reprinted thirty-nine times, the second twenty-two times.

and inevitable connection between religious and political obedience, reinforcing the ideology of political order argued by Tudor and Stuart monarchs
alike. Nevertheless, subversive material was often readily available, printed
in Scotland or in Catholic Europe and smuggled into England, or printed
on secret presses within England and given false places of publication on
their title pages.

The *Homily* and the texts in Chapter 2 on the Jacobean theory of royal
power amply demonstrate the kind of claims made on behalf of sovereign
power, ranging from the immodest to the grandiose (the godlike nature of
the king, for example). Such claims became ever more strident and absolute
as the Stuart monarchy lost more and more of its power and influence, until
the deposition of Charles I in 1649. Long before the Stuarts succeeded to
the English throne, however, a European-wide discourse argued the limited
nature of kingship and promoted the right of resistance to tyranny; this discourse justified the overthrow of even rightfully enthroned kings if necessary. As is evident in James's *True Law of Free Monarchies* and his Speech to
Parliament in 1610, such a doctrine was understood to be an enormous
threat; the alleged right of the people to set aside a lawful king, either
directly or through their representatives, struck at the very heart of Stuart
royal ideology.

Proponents of resistance argued the theory on different grounds in different countries, but most premised their arguments on local or national traditions of popular rights, written or unwritten, and on appeals to natural
law. Although a long history of resistance theory preceded the Reformation,
many of the most compelling arguments were made in the context of Protestant radicalism.[2] John Ponet's *A Short Treatise of Politic Power* (excerpted
below), for example, published in 1556, was in effect a justification for the
deposition of the then Catholic monarch, Queen Mary of England; Ponet
had been exiled to the continent at the time. His argument for resistance
rests on the principles of God's absolute sovereignty, the traditional duties
and limitations of a monarch in England, and the right of individual
judgment.

The most insistent of these resistance texts were written in the immediate aftermath of the St. Bartholomew Day's massacre of Protestants
throughout France in 1572.[3] The classic Huguenot[4] resistance treatises
appeared soon afterward: François Hotman, *Francogallia*, published in 1573;
Theodore de Beza, *Du droit des magistrats* (The right of magistrates over

---

[2] As amply demonstrated by Skinner (2: 189–358), among others.

[3] Christopher Marlowe's play, *The Massacre at Paris* (c. 1593), stages these events.

[4] "Huguenot" refers generally to any French Protestant of the sixteenth and seventeenth
centuries.

their subjects), published in French in 1574 and in Latin in 1576; the anonymous works *Le Reveille-Matin* (1574), *Le Politique* (1574), and *Le Tocsain* (1577), among many others; and perhaps the most important (or notorious, depending on one's point of view) text of them all, the *Vindiciae contra tyrannos* ("A Defence of Liberty against Tyrants"), by Stephano Junio Bruto Celta (Stephanus Junius Brutus, the Celt), first published in 1579.

The authorship of the *Vindiciae* still remains unclear; the title page pseudonym recalls, in part, the legendary Brutus.[5] The *Vindiciae* was attributed by contemporaries to both Hubert Languet[6] and Philippe du Plessis Mornay; the work's most recent editor concludes that "we can only say that the most likely scenario is some form of close collaboration" between the two (Garnett lxxvi). There is no doubt, however, of the popularity of the *Vindiciae*, as gauged by its publishing history, with another nine editions in Latin by 1622 (in many cases, as a supplement to the works of Machiavelli), as well as translations into French and Dutch in the 1580s. The "Fourth Question" of the *Vindiciae* was translated into English and published in 1588 as *A Short Apology for Christian Soldiers*. The entire work was translated into English and printed twice in the next hundred years, both times in years linked to revolutionary political events: 1648 (from which the excerpt below is taken) and 1689.[7]

The entire controversy is too complex to outline here, but it is safe to say that virtually all of these Huguenot "monarchomachs" ("king-killers," according to one of their opponents[8]) argued that the cynical political principles of Niccolò Machiavelli were the guiding principles of royal government; resistance to such tyranny was justified on both political and religious grounds. Hence, Machiavelli and his ideas were systematically demonized — as atheistical, vicious, and false — with significant implications, eventually, for Elizabethan and Jacobean drama in England.[9]

---

[5] Brutus was the legendary founder of the British race; a great-grandson of Aeneas, he gathered Trojan survivors and brought them to England (supposed then to have been uninhabited except for a few giants). This Brutus is often conflated with Lucius Junius Brutus, the legendary first consul of Rome, who led the Romans to overthrow the tyranny of Tarquinius Superbus, and establish a republic; Shakespeare tells this story in his poem of 1593, "The Rape of Lucrece."

[6] Languet was for a time a kind of senior mentor to Sir Philip Sidney, who had met him on one of his trips to the Continent.

[7] See the complete textual history outlined by Garnett lxxxiv–lxxxviii.

[8] Skinner 301.

[9] Christopher Marlowe, for example, brings Machiavelli onto the stage in his play, *The Jew of Malta* (c. 1590), as the evil genius whose soul has now flown beyond the Alps to infect other countries. Many plays would use the character stereotype of the "Machiavel," the deceitful, scheming villain; Shakespeare's *Richard III* is one of the more extravagant examples. The terms "policy" and "politics" — synonymous with the Machiavel — became highly negative as a result.

The *Vindiciae* is divided into four questions, which are addressed in the four sections of the book. Simply listing the four questions will indicate how radical a text this must have seemed to royalist supporters — indeed, even to *ask* the questions was dangerous:

1. "Whether subjects are bound and ought, to obey princes, if they command that which is against the law of God."

2. "Whether it be lawful to resist a prince which doth infringe the law of God, or ruin His church, by whom, how, and how far it is lawful."

3. "Whether it be lawful to resist a prince which doth oppress or ruin a public State, and how far such resistance may be extended, by whom, how, and by what right, or law, it is permitted."

4. "Whether neighbor princes may by right, or are bound by law, to aid the subjects of other princes, persecuted for true religion, or oppressed by manifest tyranny."

The excerpts that follow indicate key concepts that James argued against in his own works: namely, that the people and the law are prior to any kings; that there is a right, even a duty, to resist a tyrant; that the relation between king and people is one of a contract, not a divine fiat; and that since contracts imply reciprocal obligations, one side (the people) may break it if the other side (the king) fails to honor his commitments.

We should by now not be surprised to find the name of George Buchanan in this context of resistance theory (see pp. 121–23). Buchanan's major text, *De jure regni apud Scotos* (1579), was written to provide a theoretical basis for and to justify the deposition of James's mother, Mary, Queen of Scots, and his history, the *Rerum Scoticarum historia,* offered a vision of Scottish history that supported his views.[10] The *De jure* was written sometime about 1567, shortly after Mary's forced abdication. It is in the form of a dialogue between Thomas Maitland (who represents the typical Scot who needs to be reassured that the deposition was right) and George Buchanan (who wins all the arguments and presents a case for the traditionalism of limited government in Scotland). The *De jure* had a tremendous influence on subsequent political

[10] The author of the *Vindiciae* had noted Mary's deposition as one of several precedents justifying his position, in addition to a well-known English example, later dramatized by Marlowe: "Elizabeth [Isabella], the wife of Edward the Second, king of England, assembled the parliament against her husband, who was there deposed, both because he tyrannized in general over his subjects, as also for that he cut off the heads of many noble men, without any just or legal proceeding. It is not long since Christierne lost the crown of Denmark, Henry that of Sweden, Mary Steward [James's mother, Mary, Queen of Scots] that of Scotland, for the same, or near resembling occasions" (125).

discourse, and after James came of age as King James VI of Scotland, the Scottish Parliament condemned the book and ordered all copies of it confiscated (Arrowood 16). Later writers would invariably link Buchanan and the Huguenot polemicists as part of the same antimonarchical movement.

Throughout *Macbeth*, questions of election, patrilineal succession, and the nature of sovereign power are in dispute. Shakespeare's awareness of resistance theory and the debates surrounding it is evident as well. Macbeth's soliloquy in act 1, scene 7 acknowledges, for example, that no claim can be made against Duncan as ruler to justify his overthrow: "this Duncan / Hath borne his faculties so meek, hath been / So clear in his great office, that his virtues / Will plead like angels, trumpet-tongued, against / The deep damnation of his taking-off" (1.7.16–20). But it is in act 4, scene 3, at the English court, that the rhetoric of resistance theory stands out; suddenly, the words *tyranny* and *tyrant* sound repeatedly.[11] The charge against Macbeth in this scene is not that he has murdered the good king Duncan, but that he has assaulted the body politic of the commonwealth: as Malcolm says, "I think our country sinks beneath the yoke; / It weeps, it bleeds, and each new day a gash / Is added to her wounds" (4.3.40–42). Malcolm looks to the day when he "shall tread upon the tyrant's head, / Or wear it on my sword" (46–47). When Malcolm "tests" Macduff's loyalty, he describes himself as potentially an even greater tyrant than Macbeth. Macduff, who shows himself willing to tolerate a surprising amount of lechery and avarice in a king, eventually revolts after Malcolm pushes his potential tyranny to a metaphysical extreme:

> MALCOLM: Nay, had I power, I should
> Pour the sweet milk of concord into hell,
> Uproar the universal peace, confound
> All unity on earth.
> MACDUFF: O Scotland, Scotland!
> MALCOLM: If such a one be fit to govern, speak.
> I am as I have spoken.
> MACDUFF: Fit to govern?
> No, not to live. O nation miserable,
> With an untitled tyrant bloody-sceptered,
> When shalt thou see thy wholesome days again,
> Since that the truest issue of thy throne
> By his own interdiction stands accurst
> And does blaspheme his breed?   (4.3.98–109)

---

[11] The words *tyrant, tyrant's,* or *tyranny* occur eighteen times in the play, eight of which are in act 4, scene 3; another eight are in the final act.

Here Macduff objects to Macbeth on two different, and not necessarily related, grounds: that he is "untitled," or without right to the title of king, and that he is a "tyrant bloody-sceptered." Malcolm, in an allusion to but not quite an assertion of hereditary succession, is "the truest issue of thy [Scotland's] throne," but has disqualified himself as equivalent to Macbeth. The contrast here, as it was in terms of charismatic royal power, is with the offstage English king: "sundry blessings hang about his throne / That speak him full of grace" (4.3.159–60).

By the end of the play, the word *tyrant* has effectively been attached to Macbeth as part of his proper name: "My name's Macbeth." "Thou liest, abhorrèd tyrant" (5.7.8,11); "Tyrant, show thy face!" (5.7.15); "The tyrant's people on both sides do fight" (5.7.26). Macduff has considered the proper generic punishment for Macbeth: "We'll have thee, as our rarer monsters are, / Painted upon a pole, and underwrit, / 'Here may you see the tyrant' " (5.8.25–27), as if Macbeth will not be just *a* tyrant, but the exemplary instance of all tyrants. Malcolm concludes the play by "calling home our exiled friends abroad / That fled the snares of watchful tyranny" (5.8.67–68). Macbeth's murder of Duncan has virtually vanished from men's memories, while his own overthrow — an act of regicide — floats on the rhetoric of tyrannicide. Moreover, Shakespeare has erased one of the most surprising facts about the Macbeth of the chronicle histories — his ten years of enlightened rule as king — to bring forward his tyranny as essentially simultaneous with his accession.[12] It is more than a little ironic that the destruction of Macbeth (the murderer of King James's supposed ancestor Banquo) and the restoration of legitimate order depend on arguments of resistance theory that James explicitly rejected.

---

[12] Holinshed said that Macbeth's turn to tyranny was caused by fear: "For the prick of conscience (as it chanceth ever in tyrants, and such as attain to any estate by unrighteous means) caused him ever to fear, lest he should be served of the same cup as he had ministered to his predecessor," while Buchanan suggested it came from simple guilt: "But when he had so strengthened himself with the aid and favor of the multitude, that he feared no force to disturb him; the murder of the king (as 'tis very probable) hurried his mind into dangerous precipices, so that he converted his government, got by treachery, into a cruel tyranny." Shakespeare does not accept either of these explanations by themselves.

→ JOHN PONET

From A Short Treatise of Politic Power 1556

But here ye see, the body of every state may (if it will) yea and ought to redress and correct the vices and heads of their governors. And forasmuch as ye have already seen whereof politic power and government groweth, and the end whereunto it was ordained. And seeing it is before manifestly and sufficiently proved, that kings and princes have not an absolute power over their subjects; that they are and ought to be subject to the law of God, and the wholesome positive laws of their country; and that they may not lawfully take or use their subjects' goods at their pleasure: the reasons, arguments and law that serve for the deposing and displacing of an evil governor, will do as much for the proof, that it is lawful to kill a tyrant, if they may be indifferently[1] heard. As God hath ordained magistrates to hear and determine private men's matters, and to punish their vices, so also will he, that the magistrates' doings be called to accompt and reckoning, and their vices corrected and punished by the body of the whole congregation or commonwealth. . . .

Kings, princes and governors have their authority of the people, as all laws, usages and policies do declare and testify.

For in some places and countries they have more and greater authority, in some places less. And in some the people have not given this authority to any other, but retain and exercise it themselves. And is any man so unreasonable to deny, that the whole may do as much as they have permitted one member to do? Or those that appointed an office upon trust, have not authority upon just occasion (as the abuse of it) to take away that they gave? . . .

But now to pose the latter of this question affirmatively, that it is lawful to kill a tyrant. . . . For it is no private law to a few or certain people, but common to all: not written in books, but graffed[2] in the hearts of men; not made by man, but ordained of God, which we have not learned, received, or read, but have taken, sucked and drawn it out of nature, whereunto we are not taught, but made, not instructed, but seasoned, and (as Saint Paul saith) man's conscience bearing witness of it.

This law testifieth to every man's conscience, that it is natural to cut away an incurable member, which (being suffered) would destroy the whole body.

---

[1] **indifferently**: without bias, impartially.   [2] **graffed**: i.e. grafted — set or fixed firmly in place.

John Ponet, *A Short Treatise of Politic Power, and of the true Obedience which subjects owe to kings and other civil Governors, with an Exhortation to all true natural Englishmen* (London, 1556) H3r–H7v.

Kings, princes and other governors, albeit they are the heads of a politic body, yet they are not the whole body. And though they be the chief members, yet they are but members: neither are the people ordained for them, but they are ordained for the people.

→ *From* An Homily against Disobedience and Willful Rebellion

1570

As God the Creator and Lord of all things appointed his angels and heavenly creatures in all obedience to serve and to honor His majesty, so was it His will that man, his chief creature upon the earth, should live under the obedience of his Creator and Lord: and for that cause, God, as soon as He had created man, gave unto him a certain precept and law, which he (being yet in the state of innocency, and remaining in Paradise) should observe as a pledge and token of his due and bounden obedience, with denunciation of death if he did transgress and break the said law and commandment. And as God would have man to be His obedient subject, so did He make all earthly creatures subject unto man, who kept their due obedience unto man, so long as man remained in his obedience unto God: in the which obedience if man had continued still, there had been no poverty, no diseases, no sickness, no death, nor other miseries wherewith mankind is now infinitely and most miserably afflicted and oppressed. So here appeareth the original kingdom of God over angels and man, and universally over all things, and of man over earthly creatures which God had made subject unto him, and with all the felicity and blessed state, which angels, man, and all creatures had remained in, had they continued in due obedience unto God their King. For as long as in this first kingdom the subjects continued in due obedience to God their king, so long did God embrace all His subjects with His love, favor, and grace, which to enjoy, is perfect felicity, whereby it is evident, that obedience is the principal virtue of all virtues, and indeed the very root of all virtues, and the cause of all felicity. But as all felicity and blessedness should have continued with the continuance of obedience, so with the breach of obedience and breaking in of rebellion, all vices and miseries did withal break in, and overwhelm the world. The first author of which rebellion, the root of all vices and mother of all mischiefs, was Lucifer, first God's most excellent creature and most bounden subject, who, by rebelling against the majesty of

An Homily against disobedience and willful rebellion (London, 1570) A1–B3.

God, of the brightest and most glorious angel is become the blackest and most foulest fiend and devil, and from the height of heaven is fallen into the pit and bottom of hell.

Here you may see the first author and founder of rebellion, and the reward thereof, here you may see the grand captain and father of all rebels, who, persuading the following of his rebellion against God their Creator and Lord, unto our first parents, Adam and Eve, brought them in high displeasure with God, wrought their exile and banishment out of Paradise, a place of all pleasure and goodness, into this wretched earth and vale of all misery, procured unto them sorrows of their minds, mischiefs, sickness, diseases, death of their bodies, and, which is far more horrible than all worldly and bodily mischiefs, he had wrought thereby their eternal and everlasting death and damnation, had not God by the obedience of His son Jesus Christ repaired that which man by disobedience and rebellion had destroyed, and so of His mercy had pardoned and forgiven him. Of which all and singular the premises the Holy Scriptures do bear record in sundry places. Thus you do see that neither heaven nor paradise could suffer any rebellion in them, neither be places for any rebels to remain in. Thus became rebellion, as you see, both the first and greatest, and the very root of all other sins, and the first and principal cause both of all worldly and bodily miseries, sorrows, diseases, sicknesses, and deaths, and, which is infinitely worse than all these, as is said, the very cause of death and damnation eternal also. After this breach of obedience to God, and rebellion against His majesty, all mischiefs and miseries breaking in therewith and overflowing the world, lest all things should come unto confusion and utter ruin, God forthwith, by laws given unto mankind, repaired again the rule and order of obedience thus by rebellion overthrown, and, besides the obedience due unto His Majesty, He not only ordained that in families and households the wife should be obedient unto her husband, the children unto their parents, the servants unto their masters, but also, when mankind increased and spread itself more largely over the world, He by His Holy Word did constitute and ordain in cities and countries several and special governors and rulers, unto whom the residue of His people should be obedient.

As in reading of the Holy Scriptures we shall find in very many and almost infinite places, as well of the Old Testament as of the New, that kings and princes, as well the evil as the good, do reign by God's ordinance, and that subjects are bounden to obey them; that God doth give princes wisdom, great power, and authority; that God defendeth them against their enemies, and destroyeth their enemies horribly; that the anger and displeasure of the prince is as the roaring of a lion, and the very messenger of death;

and that the subject that provoketh him to displeasure sinneth against his own soul; with many other things concerning both the authority of princes and the duty of subjects.

[Here the author quotes from Romans 13, and 1 Peter 2 on the divine authority of kings and the duty of obedience.]

By these two places of the Holy Scriptures, it is most evident that kings, queens, and other princes (for he speaketh of authority and power, be it in men or women) are ordained of God, are to be obeyed and honored of their subjects; that such subjects as are disobedient or rebellious against their princes disobey God and procure their own damnation, that the government of princes is a great blessing of God given for the commonwealth, specially of the good and godly; for the comfort and cherishing of whom God giveth and setteth up princes; and on the contrary part, to the fear and for the punishment of the evil and wicked. Finally, that if servants ought to obey their masters, not only being gentle, but such as be froward,[1] as well and much more ought subjects to be obedient, not only to their good and courteous, but also to their sharp and rigorous princes. It cometh therefore neither of chance and fortune (as they term it) nor of the ambition of mortal men and women climbing up of their own accord to dominion, that there be kings, queens, princes, and other governors over men being their subjects: but all kings, queens, and other governors are specially appointed by the ordinance of God. And as God Himself, being of an infinite majesty, power, and wisdom, ruleth and governeth all things in heaven and in earth, as the universal monarch and only king and emperor over all, as being only able to take and bear the charge of all: so hath He constituted, ordained, and set earthly princes over particular kingdoms and dominions in earth, both for the avoiding of all confusion, which else would be in the world if it should be without such governors, and for the great quiet and benefit of earthly men their subjects, and also that the princes themselves in authority, power, wisdom, providence, and righteousness in government of people and countries committed to their charge, should resemble His heavenly governance, as the majesty of heavenly things may by the baseness of earthly things be shadowed and resembled. . . .

What shall subjects do then? Shall they obey valiant, stout, wise, and good princes, and condemn, disobey, and rebel against children being their princes, or against undiscreet and evil governors? God forbid: for first, what a perilous thing were it to commit unto the subjects the judgment which

---

[1] **froward:** difficult to deal with, hard to please.

prince is wise and godly, and his government good, and which is otherwise. As though the foot must judge of the head, an enterprise very heinous, and must needs breed rebellion. For who else be they that are most inclined to rebellion, but such haughty spirits? From whom springeth such foul ruin of realms? Is not rebellion the greatest of all mischiefs? And who are most ready to the greatest mischiefs, but the worst men? Rebels therefore, the worst of all subjects, are most ready to rebellion, as being the worst of all vices, and furthest from the duty of a good subject. As on the contrary part, the best subjects are most firm and constant in obedience, as in the special and peculiar virtue of good subjects. . . . But whereas indeed a rebel is worse than the worst prince, and rebellion worse than the worst government of the worst prince that hitherto hath been: both are rebels unmeet ministers, and rebellion an unfit and unwholesome medicine to reform any small lacks in a prince, or to cure any little griefs in government, such lewd remedies being far worse than any other maladies and disorders that can be in the body of a commonwealth. But whatsoever the prince be, or his government, it is evident that for the most part those princes whom some subjects do think to be very godly and under whose government they rejoice to live, some other subjects do take the same to be evil and ungodly and do wish for a change. If therefore all subjects that mislike of their prince should rebel, no realm should ever be without rebellion. . . . [T]he Scriptures do teach, that God giveth wisdom unto princes, and maketh a wise and good king to reign over that people whom He loveth, and who loveth Him. Again, "If the people obey God, both they and their king shall prosper and be safe, else both shall perish," saith God by the mouth of Samuel.[2]

Here you see, that God placeth as well evil princes as good, and for what cause he doth both. If we therefore will have a good prince, either to be given us, or to continue, now we have such a one, let us by our obedience to God and to our prince, move God thereunto. If we will have an evil prince (when God shall send such a one) taken away, and a good in his place, let us take away our wickedness which provoketh God to place such a one over us, and God will either displace him, or of an evil prince, make him a good prince. So that we first will change our evil into good. . . . Nay, let us either deserve to have a good prince, or let us patiently suffer and obey such as we deserve.

---

[2] **Samuel:** in 1 Kings 12.

→ GEORGE BUCHANAN

From The Powers of the Crown in Scotland 1579

I. On Limited Kingship

MAITLAND: Do you not believe that the royal authority should be absolute and unlimited?

BUCHANAN: Emphatically, no! For I bear in mind that the ruler is not a king only, but is, as well, a man; mistaken in many cases through ignorance; doing wrong in many cases through wilfulness; acting in many cases under constraint. He is, in fact, an animal, easily moved by every breath of good or ill will; so that I have learned the truth of that exceedingly strong statement from one of the comedies, "Where there is license, everything goes from bad to worse."[1] It is for this reason that men of the keenest insight have made the law the King's associate; that it may show him the way when he is ignorant, and bring him back to it when he goes astray. . . . It is, therefore, reasonable to stand by the position we have announced from the first, that kings, initially, were set up to preserve justice. If they had been able to have kept their exercise of authority as they had received it — that is, released and made free under the laws — they might have kept it in perpetuity. But, as is always the case in human affairs, matters degenerated, and the authority, which was established to serve the public interest, became an arrogant overlordship. For — since the arbitrary will of kings supplanted the laws, and men invested with unlimited and undefined powers did not regulate their conduct by reason but allowed many things because of partiality, many because of prejudice, and many because of self-interest — the arrogance of kings made laws necessary. For this reason, therefore, laws were devised by the people, and kings were forced to employ the legal authority, conferred upon them by the people, and not their arbitrary wills, in deciding cases. The people had been taught by long experience that it is better to trust their liberty to the laws than to kings; for the latter can be drawn away from justice by a great variety of forces, but the former, being deaf to both entreaties and to threats, pursues the one, unbroken course. . . .

Our kings, when they are publicly consecrated, promise the entire people, with an oath, that they will preserve the laws and usages of their

---

[1] Quoted from the Roman dramatist Terence, *Hauton Timorumenos.*

George Buchanan, *De jure regni apud Scotos* (Edinburgh, 1579; English translation by Charles F. Arrowood, *The Powers of the Crown in Scotland* [Austin: U of Texas P, 1949]) 56–58, 107, 109–13, 124–25.

ancestors and our ancient institutions, and will use the same system of justice which they have received from their ancestors. The entire ceremonial and the first entry of a king into every city reflect it. From all of these instances it is easy to understand what sort of authority they have received from their ancestors; namely, that it is just this: Those who are elected by the suffrages of the people swear obedience to the laws. God gave this principle as the correct one for a kingdom to David and to his posterity; and promised that they would continue to reign just so long as they obeyed the laws which He had given them.

It is most probable then that this was actually what took place: Our kings received from our ancestors an authority which was not absolute, but which was limited within definite bounds. Confirmation, moreover, is supplied by immemorial usage and by the people's assumption, without objection being made, of certain rights — for no one has challenged this assumption by a public pronouncement.

II. On the Legitimacy of Resistance

BUCHANAN: If, therefore, the king breaks all the bonds of the laws, and clearly conducts himself as a public enemy, what do you think should be done with him?

MAITLAND: I am at a standstill. For, although the arguments you have presented seem to be sufficient to convince me that we should outlaw such a king, nevertheless, the strength of long-continued habit is such that, in my opinion, it has the force of a law. This bias is fixed so firmly in the minds of men that should it at any time lead to some wrong course of action, it would be better to endure that than to strive to cure an ailment which custom has rendered quite mild, and so to upset the entire public order. For such is the nature of some disorders that it is preferable to bear the pain which they occasion than to seek some hoped-for cure. For in experimenting with them, even though our efforts should, in some respects, prove successful, such intense suffering is occasioned in the course of the treatment that the cure does more harm than does the disease.

But what concerns me more is that I regard the government which you call a tyranny as the type established by the word of God; and that what you denounce as the destruction of the laws, God calls the law of the royal prerogative. The force of this point affects me more than all the arguments of the philosophers. Unless you can settle this problem, the inventions of men will not prevent me from confessing my defection to the opposition.

BUCHANAN: It appears to me that by appealing to tyranny to sanction tyranny, you have involved yourself in a false, but very generally accepted position, and one of serious importance. For there is no lack of experience in our own age to show . . . how great is the tyranny of custom. . . . although it is our duty to pray for bad princes, we ought not to conclude from this that their crimes ought not to be punished; they should no more be immune to punishment than are the robbers for whom we are commanded to pray. Nor does it follow from the fact that good rulers ought to be obeyed that the bad ones ought not to be resisted."

III. Scottish Precedents

BUCHANAN: I could name twelve, or even more, kings of Scotland who, on account of their crimes and disgraceful deeds, have either been condemned to life imprisonment or who have escaped the just punishment of their crimes by voluntary exile or suicide. . . . All the Estates of Scotland, in public assembly, gave judgment that James the Third was lawfully put to death, for his extreme cruelty toward his people and his shameful wickedness.[2] And they made sure that none of the persons who banded together, plotted, and contributed money or effort in connection with the slaying should suffer because of it. They judged this act, then, to have been right, and done with due regard to legal form; nor is there any doubt but that they wished to set a precedent for posterity.

[2] Buchanan tells the story in his *History of Scotland,* bk. 12.

→   PHILIPPE DU PLESSIS MORNAY

From A Defense of Liberty against Tyrants   *1648*

I. On the King's Relation to God

Now for that we see that God invests kings into their kingdoms, almost in the same manner that vassals are invested into their fees by their sovereign, we must needs conclude, that kings are the vassals of God, and deserve to be deprived of the benefit they receive from their lord if they commit felony, in

Vindiciae contra Tyrannos: A Defence of Liberty against Tyrants. Or, Of the lawful power of the Prince over the people, and of the people over the prince. Being a Treatise written in Latin and French by Junius Brutus, and translated out of both into English (London, 1648) 14, 46–47, 49–51, 96–97, 120, 102–03, 111–13, 121. *Vindiciae* was translated as "defense," but it also had more technical resonances associated with reclaiming disputed property; as Garnett notes, "it came to mean to liberate a people from oppressive rule" (lxxxiii).

the same fashion as rebellious vassals are of their estates. These premises being allowed, this question may be easily resolved; for if God hold the place of sovereign Lord, and the king as vassal, who dare deny but that we must rather obey the sovereign than the vassal? If God commands one thing, and the king commands the contrary, what is that proud man that would term him a rebel who refuseth to obey the king, when else he must disobey God? But, on the contrary, he should rather be condemned, and held for truly rebellious, who omits to obey God, or who will obey the king, when he forbids him to yield obedience to God. Briefly, if God calls us on the one side to enroll us in His service, and the king on the other, is any man so void of reason as he will not say we must leave the king, and apply ourselves to God's service: so far be it from us to believe, that we are bound to obey a king, commanding anything contrary to the law of God, that, contrarily, in obeying him we become rebels to God. . . .

II. KINGS ARE MADE BY THE PEOPLE

We have shewed before that it is God that doth appoint kings, who chooseth them, who gives the kingdom to them: now we say that the people establish kings, putteth the sceptre into their hands, and who with their suffrages, approveth the election. God would have it done in this manner, to the end that the kings should acknowledge, that after God they hold their power and sovereignty from the people, and that it might the rather induce them, to apply and address the utmost of their care and thoughts for the profit of the people, without being puffed with any vain imagination, that they were formed of any matter more excellent than other men, for which they were raised so high above others; as if they were to command our flocks of sheep, or herds of cattle. But let them remember and know, that they are of the same mould and condition as others, raised from the earth by the voice and acclamations, now as it were upon the shoulders of the people unto their thrones, that they might afterwards bear on their own shoulders the greatest burdens of the commonwealth. . . .

Briefly, for so much as none were ever born with crowns on their heads, and sceptres in their hands, and that no man can be a king by himself, nor reign without people, whereas on the contrary, the people may subsist of themselves, and were, long before they had any kings, it must of necessity follow, that kings were at the first constituted by the people; and although the sons and dependants of such kings, inheriting their fathers' virtues, may in a sort seem to have rendered their kingdoms hereditary to their offsprings, and that in some kingdoms and countries, the right of free election seems in a sort buried; yet, notwithstanding, in all well-ordered kingdoms, this custom is yet remaining. The sons do not succeed the fathers, before the people first have as it were anew established them by their new approbation: neither were they acknowledged in quality, as inheriting it from the dead; but approved and accounted kings then only, when they were invested with the kingdom, by receiving the sceptre and diadem from the hands of those who represent the majesty of the people. One may see most evident marks of this in Christian kingdoms, which are at this day esteemed hereditary; for the French king, he of Spain and England, and others, are commonly sacred, and, as it were, put into possession of their authority by the peers, lords of the kingdom, and officers of the crown, who represent the body of the people; no more nor less than the emperors of Germany are chosen by the electors, and the kings of Polonia, by the yawodes and palatines[1] of the kingdom, where the right of election is yet in force. . . . But lest the continued course of some successions should deceive us, we must take notice, that the estates of the kingdoms have often preferred the cousin before the son, the younger brother before the elder. . . . Nay, which is more by authority of the people [in France] . . . the crown has been transported (the lawful inheritors living) from one lineage to another. . . .

To conclude in a word, all kings at the first were altogether elected, and those who at this day seem to have their crowns and royal authority by inheritance, have or should have, first and principally their confirmation from the people. Briefly, although the people of some countries have been accustomed to choose their kings of such a lineage, which for some notable merits have worthily deserved it, yet we must believe that they choose the stock itself, and not every branch that proceeds from it; neither are they so tied to that election, as if the successor degenerate, they may not choose another more worthy, neither those who come and are the next of that stock, are born kings, but created such, nor called kings, but princes of the blood royal.

Now, seeing that the people choose and establish their kings, it follows that the whole body of the people is above the king.

III. ON THE CONTRACT BETWEEN THE KING AND THE PEOPLE

We have shewed already, that in the establishing of the king, there were two alliances or covenants contracted: the first between God, the king, and the people, of which we have formerly treated; the second, between the king

---

[1] **yawodes . . . palatines:** the first word is evidently the author's phonetic rendering of a Polish word that is equivalent to the English *palatines,* a lord of a county palatinate (a political territory or district) such as the counties of Durham, Lancaster, or Chester; these lords had royal powers.

and the people, of which we must now say somewhat. . . . It is certain, then, that the people by way of stipulation, require a performance of covenants. The king promises it. Now the condition of a stipulator is in terms of law more worthy than of a promiser. The people asketh the king, whether he will govern justly and according to the laws? He promiseth he will. Then the people answereth, and not before, that whilst he governs uprightly, they will obey faithfully. The king therefore promiseth simply and absolutely, the people upon condition: the which failing to be accomplished, the people rest according to equity and reason, quit from their promise.

In the first covenant or contract there is only an obligation to piety: in the second, to justice. In that the king promises to serve God religiously: in this, to rule the people justly. By the one he is obliged with the utmost of his endeavors to procure the glory of God: by the other, the profit of the people. In the first, there is a condition expressed, "if thou keep my commandments": in the second, "if thou distribute justice equally to every man." God is the proper revenger of deficiency in the former, and the whole people the lawful punisher of delinquency in the latter, or the estates,[2] the representative body thereof, who have assumed to themselves the protection of the people. . . .

If the prince fail in his promise, the people are exempt from obedience, the contract is made void, the right of obligation of no force.

IV. THE TYRANT

There is, therefore, a mutual obligation between the king and the people, which, whether it be civil or natural only, whether tacit or expressed in words, it cannot by any means be annihilated, nor by any law be abrogated, much less by force made void. And this obligation is of such power that the prince who wilfully violates it, is a tyrant. And the people who purposely break it, may be justly termed seditious.

Hitherto we have treated of a king. It now rests we do somewhat more fully describe a tyrant. We have shewed that he is a king who lawfully governs a kingdom, either derived to him by succession, or committed to him by election. It follows, therefore, that he is reputed a tyrant, which, as opposite to a king, either gains a kingdom by violence or indirect means, or being invested therewith by lawful election or succession, governs it not according to law and equity, or neglects those contracts and agreements, to the observation whereof he was strictly obliged at his reception. All which may very well occur in one and the same person. The first is commonly called a tyrant

---

[2] **estates**: an assembly of the governing classes or their representatives.

without title: the second a tyrant by practice. Now, it may well so come to pass, that he who possesseth himself of a kingdom by force, to govern justly, and he on whom it descends by a lawful title, to rule unjustly. But for so much as a kingdom is rather a right than an inheritance, and an office than a possession, he seems rather worthy the name of a tyrant, who unworthily acquits himself of his charge, than he who entered into his place by a wrong door.

V. The Right of Resistance

It now follows that we treat, how, and by whom a tyrant may be lawfully resisted, and who are the persons that ought to be chiefly actors therein, and what course is to be held, that the action may be managed according to right and reason. . . .

First, the law of nature teacheth and commandeth us to maintain and defend our lives and liberties, without which life is scant worth the enjoying, against all injury and violence. . . .

There is, besides this, the civil law, or municipal laws of several countries, which governs the societies of men. . . . If, therefore, any offer either by fraud or force to violate this law, we are all bound to resist him, because he wrongs that society to which we owe all that we have, and would ruin our country, to the preservation whereof all men by nature, by law and by solemn oath, are strictly obliged: insomuch that fear or negligence, or bad purposes, make us omit this duty, we may justly be accounted breakers of the laws, betrayers of our country, and contemners[3] of religion. Now as the laws of nature, of nations, and the Civil[4] commands us to take arms against such tyrants; so, is there not any manner of reason that should persuade us to the contrary; neither is there any oath, covenant, or obligation, public or private, of power justly to restrain us; therefore the meanest private man may resist and lawfully oppose such an intruding tyrant.

VI. The Duty of Councillors to Resist

It is therefore permitted the officers of a kingdom, either all, or some good number of them, to suppress a tyrant; and it is not only lawful for them to do it, but their duty expressly requires it; and, if they do it not, they can by no excuse color their baseness. For the electors, palatines, peers, and other officers of state, must not think they were established only to make pompous paradoes[5] and shows, when they are at the coronation of the king, habited in their robes of state, as if there were some masque or interlude to

---

[3] **contemners**: those who despise.   [4] **Civil**: i.e., the civil law.   [5] **paradoes**: parades.

be represented, or as if they were that day to act the parts of Roland, Oliver, or Renaldo,[6] and such other personages on a stage, or to counterfeit and revive the memory of the knights of the round table; and after the dismissing of that day's assembly, to suppose they have sufficiently acquitted themselves of their duty, until a recess of the like solemnity. Those solemn rites and ceremonies were not instituted for vain ostentation, nor to pass, as in a dumb show, to please the spectators, nor in children's sports as it is with Horace, to create a king in jest; but those grandees must know, that as well for office and duty, as for honor, they are called to the performance of those rites, and that in them, the commonwealth is committed and recommended to the king, as to her supreme and principal tutor and protector.

[6] **Roland . . . Renaldo:** famous chivalric heroes.

Resistance in Action

In an age filled with political plots, intrigue, and assassination attempts, perhaps the most spectacular single instance of such activity was the attempted regicide known as the Gunpowder Plot, or Powder Treason — the plan, by a small group of radical, alienated Catholics, to blow up Parliament and with it, the king, his family, most of the royal bureaucracy, all the members of Parliament, the chief judges of the kingdom, and more. It was an attempt to destroy at one stroke the entire state that had subjugated and persecuted Catholics. The day of discovery, November 5, 1605, has been forever after known in England as Guy Fawkes Day; it was celebrated thereafter as now, with bonfires, revelry, and the burning of an effigy of Guy Fawkes, the most notorious of the conspirators (though he was not one of the key leaders of the group). The Gunpowder Plot conspirators were captured and executed later that winter of 1605, just as Shakespeare had begun or was about to begin writing *Macbeth*; at one point in the play, which will be discussed shortly, Shakespeare alludes quite specifically to these events. *Macbeth*'s own politics of treason, hypocrisy, paranoia, and regicide must have seemed quite familiar to an audience of 1606.

The conspirators were Catholics who took no hope from James's reputation for religious tolerance, or from the fact of his wife's conversion to Catholicism. It had become clear, shortly after James's accession, that he would not himself convert to Catholicism, and in 1604 his government issued a new law against the activities of the Jesuits.[1] Worse, from the conspirators'

[1] On James's relations to Catholics, and the general tenor of anti-Catholic feeling at this time, see Fraser, Wiener, and Wormald, "Gunpowder," among many others.

FIGURE 14 *The frontispiece to John Vicars,* Mischief's Mystery: Or, Treason's ➤
Masterpiece, the Powder Plot *(1617). This image shows the miraculous delivery
of the Monteagle letter (hence the eagle bearing it) to Cecil, who then warned
James (already presciently reaching for it) of the Gunpowder Plot.*

point of view, James had, among his very first acts, sought to make peace
with Spain, which had been accomplished in 1604. For radical Catholics,
any hope of a Spanish — that is, Catholic — victory over England had disappeared, and with it, all hope for the official restitution of the Catholic
faith in England. As is often the case, when things look most hopeful to
moderates, they seem most desperate to radicals. In this climate, then,
Robert Catesby, Thomas Wintour, John Wright, and Thomas Percy began
to plot the great act that would strike the ultimate blow for their cause.
Among the thirteen men recruited as part of the plan was a mercenary soldier, Guy (or Guido) Fawkes.

Printed below is an account of the plot's discovery by Nicolo Molin, the
Venetian ambassador to England, written while some of the conspirators
were still at large. Molin's account varies from what we know of the historical record in some details, but is largely accurate in the sense that it provides
the official version of the story — one that emphasizes the wisdom and
penetrating insight of King James in his personal intervention and accepts
at face value the almost miraculous appearance of the infamous Monteagle
letter (see Figure 14).[2] Many historians, Catholic and non-Catholic alike,
have been suspicious of the Monteagle letter — its convenient, anonymous
appearance, the fact that Salisbury, James's chief minister, did not act on it
immediately, the king's godlike role in deciphering it — and some have suggested that it was a forgery by Salisbury himself.[3] It does seem as if Salisbury allowed the plot to go forward and to ripen, perhaps so as to capture
the plotters at a more critical and dramatic moment. But much remains
murky in the various accounts.

All the conspirators were quickly captured or killed while resisting arrest;
the survivors were publicly executed (see Figure 15). Fawkes and the others
who survived initial capture were tortured for the names of other conspirators and, of particular interest to the government, for the names of the Jesuit

---

[2] The official version of these events was enshrined in the *King's Book,* printed near the end of
November 1605; it included James's speech to Parliament, excerpted below, plus a revised version of Guy Fawkes's confession, and the confession of Thomas Wintour.

[3] A number of conspirators themselves have been argued as the author, as well as other prominent Catholics aware of but not part of the plot. At least one contemporary suspected Monteagle himself (Fraser 155).

MISCHEEFES
MYSTERIE:
OR,
Treasons Master-peece,
The Powder-plot.

Inuented by hellish Malice, preuented by heauenly
Mercy : truely related.

And from the Latine of the learned and reuerend Doctour
HERRING *translated, and very much dilated.*

By IOHN VICARS.

The gallant *Eagle*, soaring vp on high :
Beares in his beake, *Treasons* discouery.
MOVNT, noble EAGLE, with thy happy prey,
And thy rich *Prize* to th' *King* with speed conuay.

LONDON,
Printed by E. GRIFFIN, dwelling in the Little Olde
Bayly neere the signe of the Kings-head. 1617.

FIGURE 15 *A Dutch engraving of the key Gunpowder Plot conspirators and their fates. Each is named in the upper picture. The three lower frames depict stages in the execution process: being drawn through the streets on a hurdle; being hung, beheaded, and disembowelled; finally, the heads of traitors mounted on poles as warnings to others.*

priests who had aided them. The fact is that no Jesuit priests aided the conspirators, but at least one, Father Henry Garnet, apparently heard of the plot in confession from another priest; since he was bound by his religious oath not to reveal the contents of any confession, he could not warn the intended victims, though he seems to have attempted to dissuade those plotters he knew of from going forward. He may also not entirely have believed that they would go through with it. Still, the official torturers were efficient, and eventually enough "evidence" was manufactured to justify charges against several Jesuits, chiefly Garnet. He was soon captured, imprisoned, almost certainly tortured, and executed.

The discourse of treason must have seemed omnipresent at this time, in early 1606. The government was firmly in control of these particular conspirators, but remained noticeably jittery. Virtually all Catholics were more or less under suspicion for a time, and within a few years a new, more rigorous oath of allegiance would be required of all citizens. Although King James, as Molin's account notes, went out of his way to assert the innocence of all foreign governments — otherwise, there might have been war — he also singled out the Jesuits for particular blame. In this atmosphere, the trial of Father Garnet took place, and the notorious Jesuit doctrine of "equivocation" (saying one thing while meaning another) became part of the case against him — one of the obvious points of contact with Shakespeare's *Macbeth*, in which the Porter allows into Hell the "equivocator":

> Faith, here's an equivocator, that could swear in both the scales against either scale, who committed treason enough for God's sake, yet could not equivocate to heaven. O, come in, equivocator.   (2.3.6–8)

This passage seems quite clearly an allusion to Garnet; compare, for example, the similar reference by Dudley Carleton to John Chamberlain, in a letter of May 2, 1606: Carleton notes that Garnet had seemed surprised when told he was to die: lately, he has been found "shifting and faltering in all his answers, and it is looked he will equivocate at the gallows, but he will be hanged without equivocation" (80–81). Macbeth will go on to call the witches' prophecies "th' equivocation of the fiend / That lies like truth" (5.5.43–44).

The theory of equivocation was developed to allow Jesuit priests to mislead their interrogators without technically lying; it is, in essence, to say one thing while meaning another. It was elaborated by a large number of examples, including what became known as the "bloody question" — if the pope or another prince at his command invaded the realm, whose side would you take: the pope's or the king's? Even before the Gunpowder Plot, equivocation had already become synonymous with verbal trickery and deception. Hamlet (1601), usually the master of words but defeated by the punning of the gravedigger, tells Horatio that "we must speak by the card, or equivocation will undo us" (5.1.137–38). Still, the notoriety of the idea of equivocation increased a thousandfold after Garnet's trial. For many, then, there was a simple equation among the terms *Jesuit, traitor, hypocrite*, and *equivocator*. (See pp. 263–70 for a more detailed discussion of the concept.)

In *Macbeth*, Shakespeare uses part of this discourse, linking treason and false speaking. The concept of equivocation echoes throughout the play, not only in the double meanings of the witches' prophecies, but also in many of Macbeth's and Lady Macbeth's own speeches, even in their appearances, which are fair without but foul within. The idea of treason, too, spreads

Enclos'd with *Clouds* of *Ignorance* and *Error*,
Rome, *Hell* and *Spaine*, do threaten *Englands* terror:
The *Card'nall*, *Legate*, *Iesuite*, impious *Fryers*
Homebred *Recusant*, *Britaines* bane desires;
Each *puffs* and *snuffs* with *envy*, all in vaine,
At *Christs* pure *Gospell*, which shall still remaine.

MIS·

FIGURE 16 *From John Vicars,* Michief's Mystery: Or, Treason's Masterpiece, the Powder Plot *(1617). This image shows an England buffeted by enemies on all sides, such as "Recusancy and Rebellion." Most of the threats are associated with religion (the Pope's mitre is represented at the 10 o'clock position), but one goes all the way back to the attempted Spanish invasion, "The Armado in [15]88."*

throughout the play, from the obvious instances of the disloyal thanes, Cawdor and Macdonwald, and the treason of the Macbeths, to the Porter's equivocator, and on to a much more general sense of treason as self-betrayal, in Lady Macduff's comment to her son, as both have been abandoned by Macduff and will soon be killed by Macbeth's hired murderers. Ross has warned her of the murderers' approach — "cruel are the times when we are traitors / And do not know ourselves" (4.2.18–19) — and her son begins an ironic dialogue on the subject:

SON: Was my father a traitor, Mother?

LADY MACDUFF: Ay, that he was.

SON: What is a traitor?

LADY MACDUFF: Why, one that swears and lies.

SON: And be all traitors that do so?

LADY MACDUFF: Every one that does so is a traitor,
And must be hanged.

SON: And must they all be hanged that swear and lie?

LADY MACDUFF: Every one.

SON: Who must hang them?

LADY MACDUFF: Why, the honest men.

SON: Then the liars and swearers are fools, for there are liars and swearers enough to beat the honest men and hang up them. (4.2.45–57)

As James noted in his speech to Parliament (see p. 261) shortly after the Plot was foiled, this was not the first attempt on his life. He refers in that speech to his threatened murder when he was still in his mother's womb, and thanks God for his deliverance. But James's early life had several other threats in it, particularly from the Earl of Bothwell and his descendants. The most famous of these had occurred just three years before James's accession, in 1600, when he narrowly escaped — or so the official version went — murder at the hands of the Earl of Gowrie at his castle, who was then himself killed. His deliverance from the Gowrie conspiracy, as it became known, was celebrated by James every August 5, the date of his escape, and after 1605, Guy Fawkes Day was celebrated every November 5.[4] James's interest in ritualizing his miraculous salvation from treason did not generally extend as far as allowing such events to be dramatized; a play by Shakespeare's company entitled *The Tragedy of Gowrie* was performed twice

---

[4] Just two days after the Gunpowder Plot's discovery, John Chamberlain noted the connection: "Curious folks observe that this deliverance happened to the King the fifth of November answerable to the fifth of August, both Tuesdays, and this plot to be executed by Johnson [Fawkes's alias] as that at Johnstown [at Gowrie Castle]" (Chamberlain 1: 213). After James's death in 1625, the annual celebration of deliverance from the Gowrie conspiracy was discontinued, but November 5 continues to be observed as a holiday to the present.

in 1604 but then apparently censored.[5] One year later, Catesby, Wright, Fawkes, and the rest attempted a new act of treason.

[5] On December 18, 1604, John Chamberlain wrote to Ralph Winwood: "the tragedie of Gowrie with all the action and actors hath been twice represented by the King's players, with exceeding concourse of all sorts of people, but whether the matter or manner be not well handled, or that it be thought unfit that princes should be played on the stage in their life-time, I hear that some great counsellors are much displeased with it: and so is thought shall be forbidden" (Chamberlain 1: 199). No copy of the play has survived.

→ NICOLO MOLIN

Report to the Doge and Senate 1605

I. 16[6] NOVEMBER[1] 1605

The King came to London on Thursday evening, the 10th of this month, and made all preparations for opening Parliament on Tuesday, the 15th. This would have taken place had not a most grave and important event upset the arrangement. About six months ago a gentleman, named Thomas Percy, relation of the Earl of Northumberland and pensioner of the King, hired, by means of a trusty servant, some wine cellars under the place where Parliament meets, and stored in them some barrels of beer, the usual drink of this country, as well as wood and coal. He said he meant to open a tavern for the use of servants who attended their masters to Parliament. But among this beer, wood, and coals he introduced thirty-three barrels of gunpowder, besides four tuns,[2] the size of Cretan hogsheads, intending to make use of it at the right moment. About two months ago Lord Salisbury[3] received anonymous letters from France, warning him to be on his guard, for a great conspiracy was being hatched by priests and Jesuits; but, as similar information had been sent about a year ago by the English lieger in France, no great attention was paid to these letters, and they were attributed to the empty-headed vanity of persons who wished to seem more conversant with affairs than became them. Finally, on Monday last,[4] a letter was brought by an unknown person, for it was dark, about two o'clock of the night, to a servant

[1] **16[6] November:** the dates in Molin's reports are given according to the reformed, Gregorian calendar, which had not yet been adopted in England; the English, Julian calendar was ten days behind the Gregorian. Thus, James was to open Parliament on Tuesday, November 5. [2] **tuns:** very large casks to hold wine. [3] **Salisbury:** Robert Cecil. [4] **Monday last:** the Monteagle letter actually arrived on Saturday, October 26.

Nicolo Molin, Venetian Ambassador in England, *Calendar of State Papers, Venetian* (London: Her Majesty's Stationery Office, 1864–), vol. 10 (1605), 288–90, 293, 294–97.

of Lord Monteagle, who was standing at the door. The unknown said, "Please give this to your master: and tell him to reply at once, as I will come back in half an hour for the answer to carry to my master." The servant took the letter, and went upstairs and gave it to his master, who opened it and found it was anonymous, nor did he recognize the hand. The substance of the letter was this, that the writer, in return for the favors received at various times from Lord Monteagle, had resolved to warn him by letter that he should on no account attend Parliament the following morning, as he valued his life, for the good party in England had resolved to execute the will of God, which was to punish the King . . . and the Ministers for their bitter persecution employed against the poor [Catholics] . . . in such brief space . . . he could burn the letter, which he earnestly begged him to do. Lord Monteagle read the letter, and in great astonishment took it to the Earl of Salisbury, who at once carried it to the King, and under various pretexts ordered a search of all the neighboring houses to see if arms or anything of that sort, which might furnish a clue, were hidden there. Meantime the King read the letter, and in terrified amaze he said, "I remember that my father died by gunpowder.[5] I see the letter says the blow is to be struck on a sudden. Search the basements of the meeting place." The Chamberlain,[6] with three or four attendants, went straightaway to carry out this order. First he inquired who had hired the basements; then he caused the door to be opened and went in. He saw nothing but beer barrels, faggots[7] and coal. Meantime those who had searched the neighboring houses came back and reported that they had found nothing of any importance, and when the Chamberlain returned and reported that he, too, had seen nothing but the barrels, faggots and coal this increased the alarm and suspicions of the King, who said, "I don't like these faggots and coal. Go back and shift all the wood and all the coal and see what is underneath, and use all diligence to come to certainty in the matter." The Chamberlain went back, and after shifting the wood he found underneath some barrels of powder, and after shifting the coal he found more barrels. In confusion he returned to the King and told him; and orders were at once given to a certain knight to take a company with him and to set sentinels in various posts to watch who approached the door of the cellars. About two in the morning they saw a man approaching with a dark lantern, but not so well closed as to hide the light completely. The guards cunningly drew back and left him free passage to the cellars, the door of which had been securely fastened as it was at first. The man went in,

---

[5] **gunpowder**: James's father, Lord Darnley, was murdered when James was an infant. His house was blown up with gunpowder, though Darnley was apparently strangled. [6] **Chamberlain**: Lord Suffolk, the lord chamberlain (the chief administrative officer of the court).
[7] **faggots**: bundles of sticks or branches.

laid a train of powder and fitted a slow match,[8] the powder and the tinder reached the powder barrels. His intention was to fire the train in the morning. When he had finished his business, as he was coming out, he was surprised by the guard, who asked what [he was doing] at that hour at that place. [He replied] that he had come there, as he had a fancy to see his property. They saw a bag in his hand, and found in it little bits of slow match, and when they turned on the light they saw the train of powder. Thereupon they bound him and took him to the Palace, where some of the Council[9] were awake, waiting the issue of this affair. The man was brought into their presence, and at once confessed that he was servant to Thomas Percy,[10] who had left the evening before, he knew not where for, and was quite ignorant of these facts. He further confessed that it was his firm resolve to have set fire to the mine that morning while the King, Queen, Princes, Clergy, Nobility, and Judges were met in Parliament, and thus to purge the kingdom of perfidious heresies. His only regret was that the discovery of the plot had frustrated its due execution, though it was certain that God would not for long endure such injustice and iniquity. The rest in my next dispatch.

II. 17[7] NOVEMBER 1605

After the Lords of the Council had briefly examined the prisoner, they informed the Lord Mayor . . . so that he might place the whole City under arms, and keep a sharp lookout. This was done, and not only that night, but all next day, which was Tuesday, the citizens were kept under arms. The other Lords of the Council, who had gone home, were summoned, and two hours before dawn they all met at the Palace. The prisoner was then introduced under strict guard. When questioned he replied, "My Lords, I cannot and will not say more than I have already said, namely that I was resolved to obey the will of God, who wishes to punish severely in every way the King and the Ministers for the persecutions they employed and still employ against the poor afflicted Catholics. I am deeply pained that I have failed to carry out so pious and holy a work." Asked if there were many who were aware of this design, he replied that there were very many, but that he would never name them. That he knew quite well that he would suffer a martyrdom of most cruel torments, which he was resolved and ready to endure, but from his lips nothing should ever issue that might hurt or injure another. That he was guilty he confessed, but no further confession need be looked for from him. He was remanded under strict guard, and the Council went to

---

[8] **slow match:** a fuse.   [9] **Council:** the Privy Council, the chief administrative body of the kingdom.   [10] **Thomas Percy:** the man was actually Guy Fawkes, who claimed at first to be John Johnson, a servant to Thomas Percy (one of the other conspirators).

report to the King. His Majesty was amazed that so vast and so audacious a scheme should have been hatched in the mind of a man of such low and abject estate. "Let us go," he said, "not to Parliament, but to Church to thank God, who has saved me, my family, all you nobles and the whole kingdom from a great and terrible disaster. For, beyond a doubt, had the plot succeeded the kingdom would have been in such confusion that God only knows when it would have recovered. The city would have fallen a prey to these wild people, and all strangers, who are hated, would have been put to the sword. In short, had it been successful, it would have been the most stupendous and amazing event that ever was heard of."

III. 21[11] November 1605

The King had let it be known that he wished to have the Scots about his person, as he has not much confidence in the English, who know this and are greatly annoyed. The King is in terror; he does not appear nor does he take his meals in public as usual. He lives in the innermost rooms, with only Scotchmen about him. The Lords of the Council also are alarmed and confused by the plot itself and the King's suspicions; the city is in great uncertainty; Catholics fear heretics, and vice-versa; both are armed; foreigners live in terror of their houses being sacked by the mob that is convinced that some, if not all, foreign Princes are at the bottom of the plot. The King and Council have very prudently thought it advisable to quiet the popular feeling by issuing a proclamation, in which they declare that no foreign Sovereign had any part in the conspiracy. God grant this be sufficient, but as it is everyone has his own share of alarm.[11]

The suspicion about the Earl of Northumberland goes on growing every day rather than diminishing, for it seems impossible that so vast a plot should have been hatched unless some great Lord were interested in it, and there is not the smallest indication against anyone except against this nobleman.[12]

IV. 23[13] November 1605

On Saturday last the King was in Parliament, where he made a long speech about the plot . . . Although it appeared that religion was the cause of the conspiracy, yet in reality it had another object. All the conspirators were gentlemen, though of broken estate, which they hoped to better under the cloak of conscience, as one frequently sees nowadays, when every kind of

---

[11] **alarm:** this passage in italics was originally written in code, as being particularly sensitive matter. [12] **nobleman:** Northumberland was heavily fined and imprisoned in the Tower — where he lived in comfort and splendor — until 1621, when he was released.

FIGURE 17 *"The Execution of the Gunpowder Plot Conspirators," a print by Nicholas de Visscher. The print shows the various stages of the ritualized process of execution for a traitor: being drawn on a cart through the streets; being hung (but not to the point of death); being mutilated and disembowelled while still alive, then beheaded; being quartered; the parts of the body being burned. Large crowds, as here, usually gathered for such spectacles.*

iniquity is covered by the mantle of religion. He bore no ill-will against the Catholics as a body, for he knew very well that he had among them many faithful subjects. [Molin relates news of the capture of the chief remaining conspirators, Percy and Catesby, which resulted in Catesby's death, which has] caused profound satisfaction to the King and Council, for they think that there is no further cause for alarm, now that all the chiefs are either dead or prisoners. No other accomplices are discovered, though not a day passes but what someone is arrested or some Baron confined to his own house, or placed in the custody of others. This is merely a precautionary measure, because they are leading Catholics, and they arrest them till full light can be thrown on the whole affair. . . .

On Monday I had audience of his Majesty to congratulate him on the special protection which God had bestowed on his person and his kingdom, by which they had been saved from such ruin and peril. . . . [T]he King told me that he had discovered the person who administered the Sacrament to all the conspirators when they pledged their faith and the honor not to name each other; and although his Majesty did not tell me who this person is I hear from other quarters that it is thought he is a Jesuit,[13] nay, they say that the prisoner himself is one, though not a priest. All this, however, is very uncertain, and may have been invented by those who hate the Catholic religion and intend to give it a deadly blow, and thus complete its ruin, as is only too likely to happen, unless the Lord God stretch out His holy hand. . . . I asked if his Majesty had as yet discovered the real object of the conspirators, for it was probable they had made arrangements for governing the country when the King, Queen, Princes, nobles, judges had all been killed. His Majesty replied that their intention was to crown and proclaim as Queen his daughter, who is in the charge of a Baron, who lives about ten miles out of London. The draft of the proclamation, which they intended to publish immediately after explosion of the mine, has been found. It names her as Queen, and themselves as protectors and governors of her person and of the kingdom.

[13] **Jesuit:** Father Tesimond heard the confession of Catesby some months before the plot, and he in turn told Father Garnet in confession.

KING JAMES I

From A Speech to Parliament *November 9, 1605*

For although I confess, as all mankind, so chiefly kings, as being in the higher places like the high trees, or stayest mountains, and steepest rocks, are most subject to the daily tempests of innumerable dangers; and I amongst all other kings have ever been subject unto them, not only ever since my birth, but even as I may justly say, before my birth, and while I was yet in my mother's belly:[1] yet have I been exposed to two more special and greater dangers than all the rest.

The first of them, in the kingdom where I was born,[2] and passed the first part of my life: and the last of them here, which is the greatest. . . .

[1] **belly:** when Mary was six months pregnant with James, her secretary (and perhaps lover) David Riccio was murdered in her presence.　[2] **born:** James had several narrow escapes while King of Scotland; he may be referring here to the attempt on his life at Gowrie in 1600.

From King James I, "A Speech in the Parliament House, as Near The Very Words as Could Be Gathered at the Instant" (November 9, 1605; this text is taken from James's collected *Works* of 1616) 500, 501, 502, 503.

First, in the cruelty of the Plot itself, wherein cannot be enough admired the horrible and fearful cruelty of their device, which was not only for the destruction of my person, nor of my wife and posterity only, but of the whole body of the State in general; wherein should neither have been spared, or distinction made of young nor of old, of great nor of small, of man nor of woman: the whole Nobility, the whole reverend Clergy, Bishops, and most part of the good Preachers, the most part of the Knights and Gentry; yea, and if that any in this society were favorers of their profession, they should all have gone one way: the whole Judges of the land, with the most of the Lawyers, and the whole Clerks: And as the wretch[3] himself which is in the Tower, doth confess, it was purposely devised by them, and concluded to be done in this house; that where the cruel laws (as they say) were made against their religion, both place and persons should all be destroyed and blown up at once. . . .

And the wretch himself in hands doth confess, that there was no cause moving him or them, but merely and only religion. And specially that Christian men, at least so called, Englishmen, born within the country, and one of the specials of them my sworn servant in an honorable place,[4] should practice the destruction of their King, his posterity, their country and all: wherein their following obstinacy is so joined to their former malice, as the fellow himself that is in hand, cannot be moved to discover any signs or notes of repentance, except only that he doth not yet stand to avow, that he repents for not being able to perform his intent. . . .

When the letter[5] was shown to me by my Secretary,[6] wherein a general obscure advertisement was given of some dangerous blow at this time, I did upon the instant interpret and apprehend some dark phrases therein, contrary to the ordinary grammar construction of them (and in another sort than I am sure any divine, or lawyer in any university would have taken them) to be meant by this horrible form of blowing us up all by powder; and thereupon ordered that search to be made, whereby the matter was discovered, and the man apprehended. Whereas if I had apprehended or interpreted it to any other sort of danger, no worldly provision or prevention could have made us escape our utter destruction.

And in that also was there a wonderful providence of God, that when the party himself was taken, he was but new come out of his house from working, having his firework for kindling ready in his pocket, wherewith as he confesseth, if he had been taken but immediately before when he was in the house, he was resolved to have blown up himself with his takers. . . .

[3] **wretch:** Guy Fawkes, who had originally given his name as John Johnson, servant to Thomas Percy.   [4] **servant . . . place:** Thomas Percy was a relative and employee of the Earl of Northumberland.   [5] **letter:** the letter sent to Lord Monteagle.   [6] **Secretary:** Robert Cecil.

For although it cannot be denied, that it was the only blind superstition of their errors in religion, that led them to this desperate device; yet doth it not follow, that all professing that Romish religion were guilty of the same.

Equivocation

The theory of equivocation, though it has deep roots in scholastic thought, seems to have become first well known, or notorious, in England only in the 1590s, when the Jesuit priest-poet Robert Southwell defended the practice at his trial in 1595. Two years later, at the trial of another Jesuit, John Gerard, Attorney General Sir Edward Coke questioned Gerard to determine if he agreed with Southwell's comments, and "tried to show it countenanced lying and undermined social intercourse between men. Against this," Gerard reported in his *Autobiography*,

> I maintained that equivocation was different from lying. In equivocation the intention was not to deceive, which was the essence of a lie, but simply to withhold the truth in cases where the questioned party is not bound to reveal it. To deny a man what he has no claim to was not deception. I showed that this teaching in no way destroyed the bonds of society, or made human intercourse impossible. "Equivocation," I said, "could not be invoked in contracts, since every man is bound to give his neighbor even his smallest due, and in contracts truth is due to the contracting party. Nor could it be invoked in ordinary conversation to the prejudice of plain truth and Christian sincerity, and still less in matters falling under the lawful cognizance of the State. For instance, a man cannot deny a crime if he is guilty and lawfully interrogated." "What do you mean by lawful interrogation?" asked the Attorney General.

Coke was quick to see how this very interrogation might be heading in the wrong direction. Gerard claims that "they had practically no answer to make" to his reasoning (125–27). What particularly exercised Protestant opponents was the doctrine of "mental reservation," whereby part of a sentence could be withheld from verbal speech, and spoken only inwardly, and was not considered a lie.[1] Nor, as Coke noticed, was it a lie to withhold the truth from authorities who are not "legal."

Thus, English knowledge of the theory of equivocation seems to have originated in, and been closely associated with, treason trials of Jesuits in the 1590s. This equation received further confirmation when government authorities in 1605 searched the rooms of Francis Tresham, one of the Gunpowder

---

[1] See Perez Zagorin 186–214 for a history of the concept in this period.

Plot conspirators, and discovered two manuscript copies of *A Treatise against Lying and Fraudulent Dissimulation*; the original title, crossed through but still visible on the manuscript, was *A Treatise of Equivocation*, and it is by this title that the work was and is known.[2] The *Treatise* had been written by Father Henry Garnet by 1598, as a defense of Southwell's assertions; one copy was primarily in his own handwriting and the other in the handwriting of one of Tresham's servants, who had copied it.[3] The authorities eagerly used the *Treatise* as one more piece of evidence against Garnet, even though it had nothing to do with the Plot itself. Attorney General Coke quoted from it at Garnet's trial, though he seems never to have realized that Garnet was the *author*, not merely the owner and reviser, of the manuscript. The *Treatise* is without question one of the most controversial *unpublished* books in this period. Only a few people seem to have read it: Coke used it at the trial, and Thomas Morton read it, quoting liberally from it in his attacks, *Exact Discovery of Romish Doctrine* (1605) and *Full Satisfaction Concerning a Double Romish Iniquity* (1606). A third copy of the *Treatise* was smuggled out of England and eventually delivered to the exiled Jesuit priest Robert Parsons.

Parsons had already undertaken a defense of the doctrine of equivocation in *A Treatise Tending to Mitigation* (1607), quoted below, in response to Morton's attacks; Parsons was somewhat disadvantaged, as he said, in that he had not yet been able to read Garnet's work. Still, he managed to produce over 250 pages of rebuttal and defense, noting only on page 553 that "at that very instant" he had received a copy of Garnet's *Treatise*. Thus Garnet's work existed only secondarily, through allusion and partial quotation. Morton's and Parsons's works, however, were published and widely circulated. What follows, therefore, are excerpts from Coke's comments at Father Garnet's trial, Parsons's pamphlet, and Father Garnet's manuscript.

---

[2] The full original title of Garnet's manuscript illustrates the particular problem the Jesuits grappled with: *A treatise of equivocation wherein is largely discussed the question whether a Catholicke or any other person before a magistrate being demaunded uppon his oath whether a Prieste were in such a place may (not withstanding his perfect knowledge to the contrary) without Perjury and securely in conscience answere, No, with this secret meaning reserved in his mynde, that he was not there so that any man is bound to detect it.* The revised title noted that the manuscript was *published* [sic] *for the defence of innocency and the instruction of ignorants.*

[3] See Malloch for a full account of the *Treatise*'s textual history.

➔ **SIR EDWARD COKE**

From Speech at the Trial of Father Henry Garnet   *1606*

[Father Garnet is] a doctor of Jesuits, that is, a doctor of five DD's, as dissimulation, deposing of princes, disposing of kingdoms, daunting and deterring of subjects, and destruction.

Their dissimulation appeareth out of their doctrine of equivocation: . . . wherein, under the pretext of the lawfulness of a mixed proposition to express one part of a man's mind, and retain another, people are indeed taught not only simply lying, but fearful and damnable blasphemy. And whereas the Jesuits ask, why we convict and condemn them not for heresy; it is for that they will equivocate, and so cannot that way be tried or judged according to their words.

Now for the antiquity of equivocation, it is indeed very old, within little more than three hundred years after Christ, used by Arius the heretic, who having in a general council been condemned, and then by the commandment of Constantine the emperor sent into exile, was by the said emperor, upon instant intercession for him, and promise of his future conformity to the Nicene faith,[1] recalled again: who returning home, and having before craftily set down in writing his heretical belief, and put it into his bosom, when he came into the presence of the emperor, and had the Nicene faith propounded unto him, and was thereupon asked, whether he then did indeed, and so constantly would hold that faith, he (clapping his hand upon his bosom where his paper lay) answered and vowed that he did, and so would constantly profess and hold that faith (laying his hand on his bosom where the paper of his heresy lay) meaning fraudulently (by way of equivocation) that faith of his own, which he had written and carried in his bosom.

For these Jesuits, they indeed make no vow of speaking truth, and yet even this equivocating and lying is a kind of unchastity, against which they vow and promise: For as it hath been said of old, *"Cor linguae foederat naturae sanctio, veluti in quodam certo connubio: ergo cum dissonent cor et loquutio, sermo concipitur in adulterio."* That is, The law and sanction of nature, hath, as it were, married the heart and tongue, by joining and knitting of them together in a certain kind of marriage; and therefore when there is discord

---

[1] **Nicene faith:** the formal statement of Christian faith, particularly the doctrine of the Trinity, set forth by the Council of Nicaea in 325 C.E. The heresy of "Arius," or Arianism, denied the divinity of Jesus, saying that he was only the highest of created beings.

Sir Edward Coke (Attorney General), "Speech at the Trial of Father Henry Garnet," from *Cobbett's Complete Collection of State Trials*, vol. 2 (London, 1809), 234–35.

between them two, the speech that proceeds from them, is said to be conceived in adultery, and he that breeds such bastard-children offends against chastity.

From A Treatise of Equivocation   *c. 1598*

I. On Different Types of Equivocation

Besides these kinds of propositions which we have hitherto defended not to be lies [in earlier chapters], although by them always some truth is concealed, there be some other ways, whereby without a lie a truth may be covered,[1] which I will briefly set down.

1. First, we may use some equivocal word which hath many significations, and we understand it in one sense, which is true, although the hearer conceive the other, which is false . . . [as for example,] if one should be asked whether such a stranger lodgeth in my house, and I should answer, "he lieth not in my house," meaning that he doth not tell a lie there, although he lodge there.

2. Secondly, when unto one question may be given many answers, we may yield one and conceal the other. . . . So may it happen that one coming to a place to hear mass may answer them who ask the cause of his coming, that he came to dinner or to visit some person which is there, or with some other alleged cause satisfy the demanders.

3. Thirdly, the whole sentence which we pronounce, or some word thereof, or the manner of pointing or dividing the sentence, may be ambiguous, and we may speak it in one sense true for our own advantage. So it is recorded of St. Francis, that being asked of one who was sought for to death, whether he came not that way, he answered (putting his hand into his sleeve, or as some say into his ear), "he came not this way." . . .

4. To these three ways of concealing a truth by words if we add the other of which we spoke before, that is, when we utter certain words, which of themselves may engender a false conceit in the mind of the hearers, and yet with somewhat which we understand and reserve in our minds maketh a true proposition, then shall we have four ways how to conceal a truth without making of a lie.

[1] **covered:** concealed.

Henry Garnet, *A Treatise of Equivocation,* edited from the transcription of the manuscript by David Jardine (London, 1851), ch. 5, 48–52; ch. 8, 83–86.

II. On the Situation of the Catholic Subject

But to Her Majesty's more grave officers we will seek to give such satisfaction, as we hope may declare the innocency of our conscience, and content their upright and indifferent minds.

For although we bear them all manner of civil reverence, and acknowledge them as our liege and most dread Sovereign her lawful officers, and are ready to obey them in any thing not contrary to the laws of God, and the necessary means of our everlasting salvation, yet in this case we say we are not lawfully convented, nor so demanded for many respects that we are bound to answer directly. We say that in this case of religion, we are by God's laws exempted from all civil magistrates, and that that religion which both hath enjoyed and doth at this present enjoy perfect liberty under heathen princes and governors, ought much more to be favored of those which profess the most holy name of Christ. We say that the law which persecuteth Christ's priests, doth persecute Christ Himself, and that they are the very eyes of the mystical body whereof we are part, and that without them we cannot maintain our religion, no more than our corruptible bodies can exercise all necessary actions without the principal members thereof. And we persuade ourselves that we cannot doubt of the unjustice of this law except we would withal doubt of the most certain verity of our faith, and live like atheists and infidels in this world. [That we may say nothing of the invalidity of those parliaments wherein for the most part, in cases of religion, a small number beareth the sway, and with might and terror wrest out unwilling voices from the rest for the establishing of unjust laws.][2] We say that in case the law were never so just, yet are we convented[3] without order of law, and in such sort as neither thieves nor murderers are convented, no nor those neither who do justly deserve the names of traitors (although that name of late doth seem to be appropriated only unto us, how unjustly God shall once make known) — by violent irruptions into our houses, unjust oaths, and subtle examinations, without any other presumption than that we are Catholics. Besides the strange and barbarous torturing of men after they be apprehended, not for to utter any treason to our country, or danger to her Majesty's sacred person [who we wish with tears did know our loyal and most faithful hearts],[4] but only to wring out with diverse cruelties the names of Catholics, and such actions as may be subject unto penal statutes; a thing most contrary to the mildness of the common law, by which this realm hath

---

[2] This passage in brackets, attacking the tyranny of parliaments, was deleted (by crossing it out) by Garnet on the manuscript Coke found.   [3] **convented**: summoned before a judge or tribunal, for trial or interrogation.   [4] This passage in brackets was deleted by Garnet, who substituted the following phrase in the margin: "whose princely heart detesteth hard proceedings."

so many ages been maintained in all manner of felicity [and a ready way to bring in other manners of civil regiment never heard of within our realm, with manifest hazard of the subversion of the same; for there are no means more forceable to the maintenance of any state, than those by which it was first erected; and no way more ready to the overthrow thereof, than the neglecting and breach of their ancient customs].[5]

[5] This passage in brackets was deleted by Garnet.

→ **ROBERT PARSONS**

From A Treatise Tending to Mitigation towards Catholic Subjects in England   *1607*

I. On the Antiquity of the Doctrine of Equivocation

The judicious Reader [will remember] that this point of doctrine of *Amphibology*,[1] or doubtful speech in some cases to be admitted, and here objected unto us by this Minister,[2] under the odious titles *of heathenish and hellish Equivocation, license of lying and perjury, black art,* and the like, is no new doctrine invented of late against Protestants by Catholics, and much less by Jesuits . . . [Morton himself admits] that for the space of these last 400 years it hath been received for true, and lawful doctrine in our schools, and consequently practiced also throughout Christendom.

[1] **Amphibology**: a rhetorical term, defined by George Puttenham (*The Art of English Poesie* [London, 1589]) associated with prophecies and treason: "Then have ye one other vicious [figure of] speech . . . when we speak or write doubtfully and that the sense may be taken two ways, such ambiguous terms they call *Amphibologia*, we call it the *ambiguous*, or figure of sense incertain . . . in effect all our old British and Saxon prophecies be of the same sort, that turn them on which side ye will, the matter of them may be verified, nevertheless carrieth generally such force in the heads of fond people, that by the comfort of those blind prophecies many insurrections and rebellions have been stirred up in this realm, as that of *Jack Straw,* and *Jack Cade* in Richard the Second's time, and in our time by a seditious fellow in Norfolk calling himself Captain Kett and others in other places of the realm led altogether by certain prophetical rhymes, which might be [construed] two or three ways as well as to that one whereunto the rebels applied it" (217–18).   [2] **Minister**: Thomas Morton.

Robert Parsons, *A Treatise Tending to Mitigation towards Catholic-Subjects in England . . . [and] Against The seditious writings of Thomas Morton . . . Whose two false and slanderous grounds . . . concerning Rebellion and Equivocation, are overthrown, and cast upon himself* (1607) 279, 288–89, 484–85.

II. The "Bloody Question"

If their Princess then living, Queen Elizabeth, upon a sudden assault of insurrection against her, should be unjustly pursued by enemies . . . with intention to deprive her both of Crown and life, and that only Thomas Morton knowing where she were, should be demanded thereof, and this with such impetuosity and eagerness, as if he answered not directly to their demand, her life and state were utterly lost, what would he do, or what might he do in this case of his Princess's extreme distress? For to discover[3] her were against justice, and duty, in that she is his liege, and innocently pursued; to deny that he knoweth where she is, must be either a lie (which we all hold to be unlawful to be made, no not for the saving the temporal life of any . . .) or by some equivocation or doubtful speech (but yet such as is no lie) she must be covered,[4] and the persecutors deluded, which our Minister thinketh not lawful, but holdeth it for impious, yea hellish, heathenish, and sacrilegious also, if it be with an oath.

Well then, what will he do in this case? Will he discover and deliver unto traitors his innocent Princess? That were more impious and hellish, as before hath been declared . . . [and] suppose that Thomas Morton were taken and asked even at the very door of the house, where he had hidden his Queen, and that if he held his peace, or denied to answer, he should thereby discover her to be there, and consequently betray her, what could he do, or rather what might he do? Or what ought he to do in so great a necessity? For what he would do, I nothing doubt, to wit, that he either would betray her, or defend her with some notable lie.

III. Two Kinds of Equivocation

But now must we further distinguish the same [equivocation] into two different sorts or kinds, the one proper, according to the true nature of equivocation before defined, which though it may seem to have falsity in it, and sometimes also hath in deed, in respect of the words only or understanding of the hearer: yet always hath it truth in respect of the speaker's meaning. The other sort is improperly called equivocation, for that no way it is true, and therefore his[5] proper name indeed is a lie, though after a large and improper manner, it may be called also equivocation for the reason which after we shall declare.

---

[3] **discover:** reveal.   [4] **covered:** concealed.   [5] **his:** its.

Now then both of those kinds of equivocation are subdivided again each one into two sorts, for that true equivocation may be either verbal or mental. . . . Verbal is that, when any word or speech hath either naturally, or by peculiar custom of particular language, two or more significations. . . . Mental equivocation is, when any speech hath, or may have a double sense, not by any double signification, or composition of the words themselves, but only by some reservation of mind in the speaker, whereby his meaning is made different from that sense which the words that are uttered do bear, or yield without that reservation. And of both these sorts of equivocations that they are lawful, and free from falsity, and may be used without sin in certain cases before specified, we have now laid forth so many examples out of Scriptures and Fathers[6] in the precedent Chapters, as it were a needless work to name them here again.

Wherefore all our speech in this place shall be about the second kind of equivocation, which is false and lying, and thereby also ever unlawful; which though not properly, yet in a general manner may be called equivocation, as I have said, for that the hearer is always wrongfully deceived, or intended to be deceived by some falsity, which is known to be such by the speaker, and consequently is plain lying: and for that lying hath been shewed also before to be divided into two sorts, the one a material lie, when the thing spoken is false in itself, but not so understood by the speaker, the other a formal lie when the speaker doth know it, or think it to be false, and yet speaketh it. This kind of equivocation, which really is a lie, must have also the same subdivision, so as the one sort thereof may be called a material lying equivocation, and the other a formal: and so much worse, as a formal lie is in itself (which always is sin) than a material (which oftentimes may be without sin of the speaker) by so much is a formal lying equivocation worse, than a material.

[6] **Fathers**: theologians such as Augustine or Jerome.

CHAPTER 4

The Cultural Construction of Scotland

For most English men and women in this period, Scotland was a foreign country. Legally and politically, Scotland was entirely separate from and independent of England, with its own monarchy, parliament, history, and legal and cultural traditions. Yet even though the two countries shared a common border, a common language (more or less), and, since 1560, a common religion (again, more or less), Scotland remained foreign to the English in every sense of the term. It was thought to be a wild place, dominated by dangerous extremes of geography and weather, inhabited by a learned Protestant king, yes, but also by an ungovernable, clannish nobility that continually challenged (and even occasionally imprisoned) its monarch, and a near-barbarous populace descended from the Picts — the ancient, savage peoples (named "Picts," presumably, for being "painted" or tattooed) absorbed by the hardly-more-civilized invading Scots between the sixth and ninth centuries.

Scotland's proximity to England made it sometimes a potential ally, but more often a political and military threat. There had been many military skirmishes and incursions on both sides over the centuries, but the Scots had never been conquered, unlike the English, as they pointed out (to which the English often replied, Who would want Scotland?). Scotland's chief foreign policy connection, moreover, was with France, not England, and the chief Scottish intellectuals (an oxymoron, according to some English), such as Major and Buchanan, were educated, taught, or lived in France at various times. Finally, while James VI was a confirmed Protestant, his mother, Mary, Queen of Scots, had not only been a Catholic but, in the official English view, a traitor who had plotted the death of Queen Elizabeth and as a result had herself been executed in 1587.[1] In spite of James's descent from the daughter of Henry VII (see the discussion on the succession controversy beginning on p. 185), his claim to the throne of England was seriously undermined by his very Scottishness: as the son of a traitor, and as a non-English citizen, thereby disqualified from owning land in England.

English attitudes toward Scotland in the late sixteenth century were mixed, of course, but certainly anti-Scottish discourse predominated: suspicion, condescension, and contempt were widespread among English writers, most of whom had never ventured anywhere near Scotland. This anti-Scottish discourse was comprised of maps, legends, unreliable histories, and occasionally, narratives of travellers who had actually gone to Scotland. Much of the English attitude, it seems, derived from the English project of nation building and self-definition (see Helgerson) in the sixteenth century, in which the English nation was constructed, in part, by defining, and excluding, what it was *not*: England was not Scotland, not even Wales, and certainly not Ireland, yet by 1603, it ruled (not always successfully or efficiently) over all of them. Like these other countries, Scotland was constructed as a cultural Other, demonized as a place and people by those standing in the center — the English.

As it became clearer, before 1603, that James was the logical successor to Queen Elizabeth, pro- and anti-Scottish discourses intensified. Both Scottish and English writers noted that, on the positive side, James was learned, experienced as a monarch, and would not present succession problems at *his* death, since he had many children, including not one but (after 1600) two male heirs, Henry and Charles. Moreover, James VI of Scotland would, if he succeeded Elizabeth, unite the two countries, a possibility that most Scots and a few English welcomed. On the negative side, however, James was, well, Scottish, and the prospect of English union (implying equality) with an inferior nation was extremely distasteful to many. Upon James's accession to the English throne, English xenophobic anxieties continued to increase, particularly when James proposed to his first Parliament, in 1604, that the two kingdoms be united legally and politically, as well as through his person.[2]

---

[1] For her other indiscretions, Mary had been forced to abdicate as queen of Scotland in 1567, with her thirteen-month-old son, James, succeeding her.
[2] See Galloway and Lockyer for more on the Union question.

FIGURE 18 *A map of Scotland, in John Speed's* The Theatre of the Empire of Great Britain *(1611–12). The marginal pictures of James, Queen Anne, and their two sons indicate their possession of the kingdom. Speed's map also reflects the highly mountainous, unpopulated nature of the country.*

The Anglo-Scots Union Commission was established in 1604 and drew up provisions for the more formal union of the two countries, but the English Parliament declined to act on them, and James's proposals were eventually abandoned; formal union with Scotland did not in fact occur until 1707. Much of the resistance to the union proposals was simply anti-Scottish sentiment, but James did not help his own cause by instituting what seemed to many a hubristic imperialist agenda. His first coin as monarch, for example, depicted him as a Roman emperor, and against strong Parliamentary resistance, he began to describe his kingdom as "Great Britain," as if, it seemed to many, England was simply to disappear.

The new Jacobean court, finally, added to existing tensions and created new ones. It was no doubt understandable that the new King would want to bring some of his friends and colleagues from his Scottish court with him to England, but the English, after briefly tolerating this practice, almost immediately turned unsympathetic, and often bitterly resentful. The residue of courtiers from Queen Elizabeth's court who were never fully satisfied with appointments or favors was undoubtedly large, and fully expectant of some reward at last. These expectations, along with anti-Scottish condescension and James's own heavy-handedness and impolitic maneuvers, led within months of his ascension to anger and envy among many of the English. A Venetian diplomat, Giovanni Scaramelli, noted in 1603 that resentment was building not just over James's placement of high-ranking Scottish ministers,

> but because every day posts are taken from the English and given to the Scotch. All these changes the King carries out in that highhanded manner which was recommended to him by the English Lords themselves. Indeed they are charged with having sold England to the Scots, for no Englishman, be his rank what it may, can enter the Presence Chamber without being summoned, whereas the Scottish Lords have free entree of the privy chamber, and more especially at the toilette, at which time they discuss those proposals which after dinner are submitted to the Council, in so high and mighty a fashion that no one has the courage to raise opposition. . . . While advancing the Scotch and those English, to whom he says he is under obligation, the King shows small regard for the rest. . . . And as he is seen every day to deprive some one of his office, and never lets a day pass without lamenting that his mother's head fell, at the third stroke, by a villainous deed, all those who, even by relationship are stained with that blood, grow fearful, not merely lest they should lose their appointments but lest their end be a bloody one. (*CSP, Venetian* 10:33)

This account may be an overly negative one, too eager to find discord and fault in the English court. Yet English accounts hardly differ. Sir Francis

Osborne described the Scots at court as hanging "like horseleeches on" James, "till they could get no more, falling then off by retiring into their own country, or living at ease, leaving all chargeable attendance to the English" (1: 270). The crude personal habits now evident at court — slovenly appearances, excessive and disgusting eating and drinking — were blamed on the Scots, even, very quietly by some, on the King himself.[3]

Not only did James promote Scots over English courtiers in patronage positions that already existed, but he also presided over the greatest increase in honors and titles in the history of the English monarchy. While Queen Elizabeth had been notoriously parsimonious in distributing honors during her reign, James was almost absurdly profligate. At the end of Elizabeth's reign, for example, there were approximately 550 knights in the realm; James, on the other hand, created 237 new knights in his first *six weeks*, 934 in a single year, even 46 before breakfast one day (Stone 40–41). This gross inflation in numbers meant a devaluation in the honor itself, corresponding to the corruption of those who now held the rank, as James's unsympathetic early biographer Arthur Wilson noted:

> Many of the gentry that came out of Scotland with the King were advanced to honors, as well as those he found there, to shew the northern soil as fruitful that way as the southern. But knights swarmed in every corner; the sword ranged about, and men bowed in obedience to it, more in peace than in war. This airy title [of knight] blew up many a fair estate. The Scots naturally, by long converse, affecting the French vanity, drew on a garb of gallantry (meeting with a plentiful soil, and an openhanded prince). The English, excellent for imitation, loth to be exceeded in their own country, maintained their follies at their own charge.

James's aim, in Wilson's view, was a scheme of Machiavellian cleverness, "to subdue the greatness of the nobility," and his tactic, which ultimately backfired, Wilson says, was that "by [making] a multiplicity of them, [James] made them cheap and invalid in the vulgar opinion; for nothing is more destructive to monarchy than lessening the nobility: upon their decline the commons rise, and anarchy increases" (664–65). Wilson's hindsight casts a far more cynical light on James's profligacy and supposed cleverness than they probably deserve, but most English would have agreed that Scottish knights "swarmed" (the insect metaphor is typical) everywhere. In perhaps the most famous single example of such English attitudes, the playwrights Ben Jonson and George Chapman were briefly imprisoned (their fellow coauthor, John Marston, seems to have escaped somehow) for several

---

[3] See Wilson and Akrigg for accounts of James's personal slovenliness.

anti-Scottish sneers in their play of 1605, *Eastward Ho!*. The play includes sarcastic references to "thirty-pound knights" — the going price to purchase a knighthood — such as Sir Petronel Flash (4.1.168), and comic stage Scottish accents, as well as this description touting the virtues of Virginia by Captain Seagull:

> you shall live freely there, without sergeants, or courtiers, or lawyers, or intelligencers [spies]; only a few industrious Scots, perhaps, who indeed are dispersed over the face of the whole earth. But as for them, there are no greater friends to Englishmen and England, when they are out on't, in the world, than they are. And for my part, I would a hundred thousand of 'em were there; for we are all one countrymen now, ye know; and we should find ten times more comfort of them there than we do here. (3.3.36–45)

As Jonson reported, a Scottish courtier named Sir James Murray complained to the king, and their imprisonment was swift. It was also short-lived, as Jonson's and Chapman's appeals to high-placed friends resulted in their release, and no lasting harm to their literary careers at court.[4] Still, the censoring of this passage in subsequent printed editions, and the closing down of *The Tragedy of Gowrie* in 1604, reflect some of the Scottish-English tensions of the period.

Shakespeare's *Macbeth* complicates this nationalistic discourse by, on the one hand, depicting heroic Scottish thanes and James's supposed ancestors, but, on the other hand, representing the Scottish monarchy as inherently unstable, its principle of succession unclear, and its nobility unusually violent and susceptible to treason. The imaginary geography of the play represents a Scotland of crags and hollows, barren heaths, mists and storms, haunted by demonic spirits and supernatural forces, cannibalistic horses and strange screams in the night. The Scotland of *Macbeth* is, above all, the home of regicides and traitors. The England of the play, by contrast, is represented by the English court in which Malcolm has taken refuge, its values implicit in its saintly king, Edward the Confessor. The subjugation of the Scottish tyrant Macbeth by an English army led by Malcolm may have seemed an appropriate fate for both the character and the country.

The excerpts printed here reflect a wide range of pro- and anti-Scottish discourse. William Harrison's *Description of Scotland* is a translation of a translation of Hector Boece's commentary of 1527. Boece/Harrison offers up a standard English view of a wild country, with strange beasts and omens. This account also locates the beginning of a change in the character of the

---

[4] See Riggs's biography of Jonson for more on this incident.

Scots — a degeneracy — as occurring in the realm of Malcolm Canmore; now, he says, the Scots are too often drunken gluttons, licentious, and no longer capable of the military prowess that in an earlier day had made them such feared warriors and had constituted their honor. The discussion at court in Shakespeare's *Henry V* further extends the stereotype of the Scots as violent but not honorable — not only are they allied with France, which was true enough, but they engage in cowardly sneak attacks. Here England is personified as a weak, frightened, "open" female who "shook and trembled" at the violent inroads of the male Scots, who have penetrated England's defenses with "hot assays." These near-rapes have been averted by English virtue, of course, but the "weasel Scot" — now reduced to the most thieving, abject, and deceitful of animals — always still "comes sneaking, and so sucks her [England's] princely eggs."

Hundreds of similar anti-Scottish comments could easily be found in English texts. This residual prejudice became so intensified during the debates about uniting of 1603–07 that some pro-Scottish writers, such as Sir Thomas Craig, had not only to defend the Scots generally but also to rebut specific accusations. Perhaps the most notorious of the legends of the early Scots, still invoked as a way of discrediting the alleged savagery of the contemporary Scots, is an anecdote first related by Saint Jerome and repeated in virtually all the histories of Scotland, including those of John Major, John Leslie, and Boece/Harrison. Craig describes the slander succinctly:

> Our most determined opponents among the English, to leave no stone unturned, do not scruple to bring up against us the charge of Jerome, who declares that when he was a youth in Gaul he saw Scots, a British people, feeding on human flesh in the forests, though cattle were abundant; and that their dainties[5] were the buttocks of shepherds and the breasts of women. The reputation of its author has given this remark of Jerome's such currency that hardly a dictionary or work on national customs appears without the passage being quoted as if it were a Delphic[6] utterance. I propose therefore to devote some consideration to confuting it; for if it is not disposed of there will seem to be some argument to support those who accuse us of being savages, wild and barbarous; seeing that to eat human flesh is not only savage but worse than bestial. What people write of others, however, is not always true. (383)

Craig then indeed spends several pages attempting to erase this slander, quoting Erasmus on it, and even, on one of his visits to London, personally engaging the opinion of the great teacher and scholar William Camden

---

[5] **dainties**: choice delicacies.
[6] **Delphic**: i.e., utterance of truth by an oracle.

(Ben Jonson's tutor), who speculated that there had been an error of transcription in the manuscript.[7] Of such examples did the debate over the union of two sovereign nations (in part) consist.

This section of documents concludes with the descriptions of Scotland made by three English travellers in this period. Fynes Moryson made his trip in 1598, although his *Itinerary* was not published until 1617. Moryson travelled throughout Europe in the early 1590s and to Palestine and Lebanon in 1595. He wrote the *Itinerary* over a period of years, first in Latin, then translating it into English. Some parts of it remained unpublished until after his death in 1630. Sir Anthony Weldon wrote *A Perfect Description* during or just after he accompanied King James on his first visit back to Scotland after becoming king of England in 1603. Weldon, like several generations of his ancestors, held minor posts at court. The *Description* was not published until 1659, but the manuscript was discovered soon after it was written, and it led to Weldon's dismissal from service. Weldon eventually had his revenge on the Stuarts, however, as he became an extremist on the Parliamentary side during the Civil War and wrote a profoundly anti-Stuart biography and history called *The Court and Character of King James,* a work that in effect established the terms of the negative stereotyping of James for future historians. Even before his dismissal, as the *Description* makes clear, however, Weldon had nothing but contempt for the Scots. By contrast, John Taylor, whose *Penniless Pilgrimage* describes his journey in the year following Weldon, was a pro-Stuart Royalist, eager to please his monarch. Taylor (1580–1653), known as the "Water-Poet" because of his sometime trade as a waterman (one who rowed people back and forth across the Thames), wrote a number of occasional pieces, often a journey of one kind or another. He was a Royalist supporter during the Civil War and ran the Crown Inn in London from 1646 until his death.

Moryson, Weldon, and Taylor describe many of the same sights — each visits and describes Edinburgh, for example — and Weldon and Taylor

---

[7] Leslie did not dispute legends of early cannibalism, only confining it to those who lived in a certain area, and with the logical point that "the old cruelty of few should not be ascribed to the whole Scottish nation" (Leslie, *History* 100). Leslie spends more time on the story of a particular Scot seen to eat salmon raw. John Major, too, did not reject the story, given its saintly origin, but defended the Scots on two grounds: first, "even if all the Scots did so, 't would bring no stain on their posterity: the faithful in Europe are descended from the Gentile and the infidel; the guilt of an ancestor is no disgrace to his children when these have learned to live conformably with reason"; and second, "in their own island even the Scots did not generally live in such fashion" (Major 45), the proof of which is that Bede never mentions it in his history.

travelled within a year of one another. Yet these accounts often differ considerably, suggesting how each author imposes an ideological screen on what he is seeing. Weldon's savage satire is so predisposed to be negative that it can hardly be taken as an accurate guide; yet accurate or not, it helped form part of the image of Scotland known to the English. Taylor's description, on the other hand, is so positive about Scotland, so eager to please his monarch, that he feels he must apologize for it, defending himself in his epilogue from the charge of writing mere flattery. Taylor admiringly notes the inscription of the "unconquered" line of 106 kings, for example, just as the Scotsman Craig boasts that "there is no one who can boast the title 'Conqueror' over us!" Moryson seems to have had fewer axes to grind than either of the other writers, and the tone of his account falls somewhere in between theirs.

Shortly before Taylor set out for Scotland, a far more distinguished poet, Ben Jonson, set out to *walk* to Scotland. Jonson intended to gather legends, geographical descriptions, and various other antiquarian information in order to write a descriptive poem about Scotland, to be called *A Discovery* — a project that was never completed, in part no doubt because of a disastrous fire that destroyed Jonson's library in 1623. Jonson was well received on his journey, particularly in Edinburgh, and he was reported to have called Edinburgh "the heart of Scotland, Britain's other eye." The beauty of Scotland, it seems clear, lay in the eye of the beholder.[8]

---

[8] Jonson complained to William Drummond of Hawthornden that "Taylor was sent along here to scorn him" (Jonson 608), an opinion that Taylor evidently heard, because he denied it, unconvincingly, in his own work. Jonson had a low opinion of Taylor's poetry, using it as an example, in an incredulous tone, of how "a man cannot imagine that thing so foolish or rude but will find and enjoy an admirer . . . [even] the Sculler's poems have their applause" (Jonson 538). King James, however, Jonson claimed, admired Taylor's verses, while at the same time "the king said Sir P[hilip] Sidney was no poet" (Jonson 603). Unlike Sir Anthony Weldon, Jonson could keep to himself his opinions touching royal interests.

→ WILLIAM HARRISON

From The Description of Scotland   *1587*

I. On Highlanders

They are more hard of constitution of body, to bear off the cold blasts, to watch better, and abstain long, wherunto also it appeareth that they are bold, nimble, and thereto more skillful in the wars.

II. On the Borderers

[There] are many strong thieves, which often spoil the country, and exercise much cruel slaughter upon such as inhabit there, in any troublous time. These robbers (because the English do border upon their dry marches,[1] and are their perpetual enemies) do often make forceable rodes[2] into the English bounds, for their better maintenance and sustentation, or else they pilfer privily[3] from them, as men leading in the mean season a poor beggarly and very miserable life. In the time of peace also, they are so inured to theft and rapine,[4] that they cannot leave off to steal at home. And notwithstanding that they be often very sore handled therefore, yet they think it praiseworthy to molest their adversary, as they call the truer sort, whereby it cometh to pass, that many rich and fertile places of Scotland lie waste and void of culture for fear of their invasion.

III. Scottish Monstrosities

It was told me once by Doncan Campbell, a noble knight, that out of Garloll, one of the pools[5] of Argyle, there came a terrible beast, in the year of Grace 1510, which was of the bigness of a greyhound, and footed like a gander,[6] and issuing out of the water early in the morning about midsummer time, did very easily and without any visible force or straining of himself overthrow huge oaks with his tail, and thereunto killed three men outright that hunted him with three strokes of his said tail, the rest of them saving

---

[1] **marches:** tracts of land on the border of a country.   [2] **rodes:** i.e., inroads.   [3] **privily:** secretly.
[4] **rapine:** the seizure and removal by force of the property of others.   [5] **pools:** bodies of water.
[6] **footed like a gander:** i.e., with webbed feet.

William Harrison, *The Description of Scotland* in Raphael Holinshed, *The Chronicles of England, Scotland, and Ireland* (London, 1587; text from the edition printed in London, 1808), vol. 5, 3, 4, 6, 11, 25–27. Originally written in Latin by Hector Boece, "translated into the Scottish speech by John Bellenden . . . and now finally [translated] into English by W[illiam]. H[arrison]." . . .

themselves in trees thereabouts, whilest the foresaid monster returned to the water. Those that are given to the observations of rare and uncouth sights, believe that this beast is never seen but against some great trouble and mischief to come upon the realm of Scotland. . . .

In the said firth[7] [of Forth] are sundry fishes oftentimes seen of monstrous shape, with cowles hanging over their heads like unto monks, and in the rest resembling the body of man. They shew themselves likewise above the water to the navel, howbeit they never appear but against some great pestilence of men, or murrain[8] of cattle; wherefore their only[9] sight doth breed great terror unto the Scottish nation, who are very great observers of uncouth signs and tokens.

IV. On the Scottish Character in the Present

In process of time, therefore, and chiefly about the days of Malcolm Canmore, our manners began greatly to change and alter. For when our neighbors the Britons began, after they were subdued by the Romans, to wax idle and slothful, and thereupon driven out of their country into Wales by their enemies the Saxons, we began to have alliance (by proximity of the Romans) with Englishmen, specially after the subversion of the Picts, and through our daily trades and conversation with them, to learn also their manners, and therewithal their language, as I have said already. Hereby shortly after it came also to pass, that the temperance and virtue of our ancestors grew to be judged worthy of small estimation amongst us, notwithstanding that a certain idle desire of our former renown did still remain within us.

Furthermore as men not walking in the right path, we began to follow also the vain shadow of the German honor and titles of nobility, and boasting of the same after the English manner, it fell out yer[10] long, that whereas he in times past was accompted[11] only honorable, which excelled other men not in riches and possessions, but in prowess and manhood, now he would be taken most glorious that went loaden with most titles, whereof it came to pass, that some were named dukes, some earls, some lords, some barons, in which vain puffs they fixed all their felicity. Before time the noble men of Scotland were of one condition, and called by the name of Thanes, so much in Latin as *Quaestores regii*, gatherers of the king's duties, in English: and this denomination was given unto them after their desert and merit.

But how far we in these present days are swerved from the virtues and temperance of our elders, I believe there is no man so eloquent, nor indued

---

[7] **firth**: a long, narrow inlet of the sea.   [8] **murrain**: any pestilent or mortal disease in cattle.   [9] **only**: i.e., merely the sight of them.   [10] **yer**: archaic form of "ere"; i.e., before.   [11] **accompted**: judged, considered.

with such utterance, as that he is able sufficiently to express. For whereas they gave their minds to doughtiness,[12] we apply ourselves to drunkenness; they had plenty with sufficiency, we have inordinate excess with superfluity; they were temperate, we effeminate; and so is the case now altered with us, that he which can devour and drink most, is the noblest man and most honest companion, and thereto hath no peer if he can once find the vein, though with his great travail[13] to purvey[14] himself of the plentifullest number of new fine and delicate dishes, and best provoke his stomach to receive the greatest quantity of them, though he never make due digestion of it.

Being thus drowned in our delicate gluttony, it is a world to see, how we stuff ourselves both day and night, never ceasing to ingorge and pour in, till our bellies be so full that we must needs depart. Certes[15] it is not supposed meet[16] that we should now content ourselves with breakfast and supper only, as our elders have done before us, nor enough that we have added our dinners unto their aforesaid meals, but we must have thereto our beverages and rear suppers,[17] so that small time is spared wherein to occupy ourselves in any Godly exercise, sith[18] almost the whole day and night do scarcely suffice for the filling of our paunches. We have also our merchants, whose charge is not to look out, and bring home such things as necessarily pertain to the maintenance of our lives, but unto the furniture of our kitchen, and these search all the secret corners of our forests for venison, of the air for fowls, and of the sea for fish, for wine also they travel not only into France, whose wines do now grow into contempt, but also into Spain, Italy and Greece — nay, Africa is not void of our factors,[19] no nor Asia, and only for fine and delicate wines if they might be had for money.

In like sort they gad[20] over all the world for sweet and pleasant spices, and drugs (provokers unto all lust and licentiousness of behavior) as men that adventure their own lives to bring home poison and destruction unto their countrymen, as if the mind were not already sufficiently bereft of her image of the divinity, but must yet more be clogged and overladen with such a franked[21] case, therewithal to be extinguished outright, which already dwelleth or is buried rather in such an ugly sepulchre. The body likewise being oppressed with such a heap of superfluous food, although otherwise it be indued with an excellent nature, cannot be able to execute his office, nor keep himself upright, but must needs yield as overcome, and to be torn in pieces and rent with sundry maladies.

Hereof also it cometh to pass, that our countrymen travelling into the

---

[12] **doughtiness:** valiantness, valor.   [13] **travail:** labor, effort.   [14] **purvey:** provide.   [15] **Certes:** certainly.   [16] **meet:** appropriate.   [17] **rear suppers:** suppers coming after the evening meal, and hence very late.   [18] **sith:** since.   [19] **factors:** mercantile agents.   [20] **gad:** to roam about, ramble restlessly.   [21] **franked:** fattened (as a pig in a pen).

colder regions are nowadays contrary to their former usage taken sometime with fevers, whereby their inward parts do burn and parch as it were with continual fire, the only cause whereof we may ascribe unto those hot spices and drugs which are brought unto us from the hot countries. Others of them are so swollen and grown full of humors, that they are often taken suddenly, and die of vehement apoplexies, and although here and there one or two recover for a little while, yet are they but dead people, reviving again, leading the rest of their lives like shadows, and walking about as if they were buried already.

Our youth also following these unhappy steps of their parents, give themselves wholly to lust and licentiousness, having all virtue and knowledge in contempt, and eschewing the same as a pestilence and subversion of their pleasures, whereunto they apply themselves as unto the most excellent trade. But sithens[22] they are now inured, and as it were haunted with these vices, when time doth come of service, and that our country shall stand in need of manhood, these will become so effeminate, that they must now ride on horseback as clad in heavy armor, for on foot they cannot go by reason of their fatness which choketh up their vital forces, neither be able to perform any thing at all in comparison of the sovereign manhood and prowess of their elders. So soon also as they return home, because their possessions are not otherwise able to nourish them up in pleasure and pampering of their maws,[23] they must fall to covetous and greedy practices, thereby to enrich themselves, or else prove strong thieves, or finally sowers of dissension and discord among the noblemen, thereby to pray some commodity.

Certes these and other vices following them necessarily proceed generally from none other fountain than voluptuous life and intemperancy, the which if we would refrain, there is no region under the sun that would prove more wholesome, less subject to pestilence, nor more commodious and profitable for the sustentation[24] of her people. Certes I despair not of the redress of these things, but still hope that in short time these corrupt manners of my countrymen will be turned into better frame. We are not yet become impudent, neither altogether have cast off unshamefastness, sith that in a great many some remainder of our ancient soberness and manhood doth yet appear, and thereto newness of life with fervent devotion increase every day, through the working of the zeal of our Christian religion in us.

This also will I add, without offense unto other nations, that there was never people more steadfast to my knowledge in the Christian faith, nor more constant in their faithful promises, than the Scots have been since their first beginning. And for a conclusion I will say more, not only for their

---

[22] **sithens:** since.   [23] **maws:** stomachs, guts.   [24] **sustentation:** sustenance.

FIGURES 19 AND 20 *From Thomas Hariot*, A Brief and True Report of the New Found Land of Virginia *(Frankfurt am Main, 1590). The artist John White, with Hariot, accompanied Sir Walter Raleigh's 1585–86 expedition to what is now North Carolina; White turned his field sketches into finished watercolors when he returned to England. Hariot's* Report, *first published in 1588, was reprinted in 1590 with engravings by the Flemish publisher Theodore de Bry of White's illustrations. At the end of the volume of illustrations of New World Indians is a set of five illustrations: "Some picture of the Picts which in the old time did habit one part of the great Britain . . . [which] show how that the inhabitants of the great Britain have been in times past as savage as those of Virginia." To the English reading public, then, New World savages and the early inhabitants of Scotland (by way of Ireland) were equally primitive and un-English.*

From the 1590 caption for "The True Picture of One Pict" (FIGURE 19): *the Picts "did let their hair grow as far as their shoulders, saving those which hang upon their forehead, the which they did cut. They shaved all their beard except the mustaches; upon their breasts were painted the head of some bird, and about the paps as it were beams of the sun, upon the belly some fearful and monstrous face, spreading the beams very far upon the thighs. Upon the two knees some faces of*

lion, and upon their legs as it hath been shells of fish. Upon their shoulders griffins'
heads, and then they hath serpents about their arms. They carried about their
necks one iron ring, and another about the midst of their body, about the belly, and
the said [irons] hang on a chain, a scimitar or Turkish sword. They did carry in
one arm a target made of wood, and in the other hand a pick. . . . And when they
hath overcome some of their enemies, they did never fail to carry away their heads
with them."

 From the 1590 caption for "The True Picture of a Woman Pict" (FIGURE 20):
"The women of the Pict . . . were no worser for the wars than the men. And were
painted after the manner following, having their heads bare, did let their hair fly-
ing. About their shoulders were painted with griffin heads, the low parts and thighs
with lion faces, or some other beast as it comest best into their fancy, their breast hath
a manner of a half moon, with a great star, and four lesser in both the sides, their
paps painted in manner of beams of the sun, and among all this a great lightening
star upon their breasts. The said [stars] of some points or beams, and the whole belly
as a sun, the arms, thighs, and legs well painted, of diverse figures. They did also
carry about their necks an iron ring, as the men did, and such a girdle with the sword
hanging, having a pick or a lance in one hand, and two darts in the other."

praise, but also in exhorting them unto perseverance, that as our people now living do pass[25] their ancestors in sumptuous and curious[26] attire, so they are more neat and fine in their houses, better given to learning, and much more magnificent in building and decking of their churches. God grant them also to return to their former frugality, and that with speed, Amen.

[25] **pass**: surpass.   [26] **curious**: elaborate, fine.

→ WILLIAM SHAKESPEARE

Henry V, *Act 1, Scene 2*   *1600*

KING HENRY:
We must not only arm t' invade the French,
But lay down our proportions[1] to defend
Against the Scot, who will make road[2] upon us
With all advantages.[3]

CANTERBURY:
They of those marches,[4] gracious sovereign,   140
Shall be a wall sufficient to defend
Our inland from the pilfering borderers.

KING HENRY:
We do not mean the coursing snatchers[5] only,
But fear the main intendment[6] of the Scot,
Who hath been still[7] a giddy[8] neighbor to us.   145
For you shall read that my great-grandfather
Never went with his forces into France
But that the Scot on his unfurnished[9] kingdom
Came pouring like the tide into a breach
With ample and brim[10] fullness of his force,   150
Galling the gleaned land with hot assays,[11]

---

[1] **lay ... proportions**: allocate our forces.   [2] **road**: inroad, raid.   [3] **With all advantages**: whenever a good opportunity presents itself.   [4] **marches**: borderlands (here, in the north).   [5] **coursing snatchers**: mounted raiders.   [6] **intendment**: plan, hostile intent.   [7] **still**: always.   [8] **giddy**: unstable, fickle.   [9] **unfurnished**: unprovided with defense.   [10] **brim**: absolute, complete.   [11] **Galling ... assays**: worrying the land stripped of defenders with hot attacks.

William Shakespeare, *Henry V* (Quarto printed in London, 1600; Folio printed in London, 1623; text and annotations from the Bevington edition), 1.2.136–77. New York: HarperCollins, 1992.

Girding with grievous siege castles and towns;
That England, being empty of defense,
Hath shook and trembled at th' ill neighborhood.[12]

CANTERBURY:
She hath been then more feared[13] than harmed, my liege.   155
For hear her but exampled by herself:[14]
When all her chivalry[15] hath been in France
And she a mourning widow of her nobles,
She hath herself not only well defended
But taken and impounded as a stray[16]   160
The King of Scots, whom she did send to France[17]
To fill King Edward's fame with prisoner kings
And make her chronicle as rich with praise
As is the ooze and bottom of the sea
With sunken wrack[18] and sumless[19] treasuries.   165

A LORD:
But there's a saying very old and true:
  "If that you will France win,
  Then with Scotland first begin."
For once the eagle England being in prey,[20]
To her unguarded nest the weasel Scot   170
Comes sneaking, and so sucks her princely eggs,
Playing the mouse in absence of the cat,
To 'tame[21] and havoc[22] more than she can eat.

EXETER:
It follows then the cat must stay at home;
Yet that is but a crushed necessity,[23]   175
Since we have locks to safeguard necessaries
And pretty[24] traps to catch the petty thieves.

---

[12] **neighborhood:** neighborliness.   [13] **feared:** frightened.   [14] **hear . . . herself:** i.e., only listen how she can be instructed by an example from her own history.   [15] **chivalry:** knights.   [16] **impounded as a stray:** David II of Scotland was captured and imprisoned in 1346 while Edward III was in France.   [17] **to France:** Historically, David II was imprisoned in London, not sent to France.   [18] **wrack:** wreckage.   [19] **sumless:** inestimable.   [20] **in prey:** absent in search of prey.   [21] **'tame:** attame, break into.   [22] **havoc:** ravage.   [23] **crushed necessity:** forced conclusion.   [24] **pretty:** ingenious.

→ SIR THOMAS CRAIG

From A Treatise on the Union of the British Realms *1603/08*

The English historians, and particularly William of Newbury, Holinshed, and others of repute, have aspersed[1] the Scots as uncivilized, wild, and barbarous, strangers to the humanities and the study of them. We are therefore justified in employing our own weapons to repel these charges, lest our silence should appear to support them.

So long as the two countries were enemies, nothing that was Scottish ever found favor with our neighbors and their historians. The latter must not be too implicitly believed; though, being monks, inert and idle, ignorant of what was going on round them, their ears and pens receptive of rumor rather than truth, some excuse may be urged in their behalf. When I was in London as one of the Commissioners at the recent Conference,[2] I had a good deal of conversation with Englishmen on the association or incorporation of the two peoples in a single state. They frequently expressed themselves in a manner depreciatory of Scotland, and were frankly indignant that our countrymen should have equality in honors and employment, their own reputation and resources being so much the greater. . . .

And if this union is to be formed and be permanent, any disposition on the part of the richer to despise and look down upon the poorer partner must be avoided. Ours is a nation which cannot tolerate contempt. On that very ground we took immediate offense when the English objected that the union would attach them to a people weaker and poorer than themselves, in an alliance whose drawbacks were more patent than its advantages. . . . When I was in England I was told by a lawyer, a man of some importance in his own opinion, that although no English king had ever thought of conquering Scotland, yet that achievement might have been easily accomplished if England, with her superior power and resources, had set her mind upon it. He added, that there were no educated men in Scotland and no Universities, nor any laws other than those which had been borrowed from England and in the transfer had lost their original purity. But such state-

---

[1] **aspersed**: slandered.   [2] **Conference**: the Anglo-Scottish Union Commission of thirty-nine English and twenty-eight Scottish officials who, in October and November 1604, drew up an instrument of union between the two countries, to be considered in the House of Commons. The great majority of the provisions were never passed by the Commons.

Sir Thomas Craig, *De unione regnorum Britanniae tractatus* (1603–08), edited from the translation by C. Sanford Terry, *A Treatise on the Union of the British Realms* (Edinburgh: Edinburgh UP, 1909) 354–56, 416–17.

ments are as nothing by the side of Christopher Piggot's recent outburst.[3] He did not scruple to declare in Parliament that Scotland is the barrenest country in the world; that Scotsmen are the most perfidious and barbarous of all nations, devoid of an altar of faith, as the saying is, not to be tolerated in the courts of kings, and of a bloodthirsty and treacherous disposition; that the only possible relation between the two countries would be that of judge and thief, the one decreeing, the other undergoing the penalty; and that in public representations of comedy a Scotsman is always treated as a fitting subject of ridicule — a statement which is false. But, and this is quite beyond the bounds of patience, at a public meeting which ought rather to have promoted the cause of common fellowship and goodwill, our countrymen were libelled in a wild and virulent sermon at St. Paul's by one D. Robinson, a preacher of God's word, as a people poor, lying, and prone to all manner of treachery.

ON CONTEMPORARY SCOTLAND

Whatever may be said of our poverty, we can assert, as could the Lombards in days gone by, that we have held our own to this day against the richest and most puissant[4] peoples, not by truckling[5] to them, but by hard fighting and sheer endurance. There is no one who can boast the title "Conqueror" over us! Our women do not indulge themselves with wine, exotic foodstuffs, spices from distant lands, so hurtful to the womb. Therefore they do the more readily conceive. Hence we boast a teeming population not surpassed elsewhere. Indeed it is naught but the fecundity of our women which makes us poor, if poor we are. For when there are several children in a family the eldest succeeds to the real estate,[6] and the personalty[7] is divided among the other children. Though the latter may not be sufficient to support their position, which they consider in no whit inferior to that of the eldest, yet they refuse to apply themselves to handicrafts or trades, regarding them as beneath their dignity. Ages ago the same trait was noted in the Germans by those reliable historians Caesar and Tacitus, and is indeed a characteristic of proud-spirited nations. Therefore our people go out into foreign countries, where they do not find it derogatory to display their poverty. . . . But nowadays our countrymen have begun to accustom themselves to occupations and trade rather than to remain poor and idle. They have undoubted ability, and there is therefore reason to hope that the reproach may no longer apply

---

[3] **outburst**: Sir Christopher Piggot's virulent attack on things Scottish occurred in February 1607; he was expelled from the House and sent to the Tower. [4] **puissant**: powerful. [5] **truckling**: yielding weakly. [6] **real estate**: the immovable property, such as land and houses. [7] **personalty**: personal goods, personal estate.

to us. We lack nothing but industry and skilled workers to teach our poor men profitable trades. At any rate our poverty has never been a hardship to ourselves nor an inconvenience to other people. The pathway to eternal happiness is as easy in and from Scotland and is marked by fewer obstacles and rugged by-paths of vice than anywhere else, unless I am much mistaken.

Nowadays, to our great hurt, we are learning to condone and even to affect vicious[8] luxuries in the guise of civilization and good manners. . . . But there is no country in which a man can live more pleasantly and delicately than Scotland. Nowhere else are fish so plentiful; indeed unless they are freshly caught on the very day we refuse to eat them. We have meat of every kind. Nowhere else will you find more tender beef and mutton, or wildfowl more numerous and of greater variety, gratifying every whim of appetite and taste. We eat barley bread as pure and white as that of England and France. Our servants are content with oatmeal, which makes them hardy and long-lived.

[8] **vicious:** the adjective form of the word *vice.*

→ FYNES MORYSON

From An Itinerary *1617*

I. On Edinburgh

This city is high seated, in a fruitful soil and wholesome air, and is adorned with many noblemen's towers lying about it, and aboundeth with many springs of sweet waters. At the end towards the east is the King's palace joining to the monastery of the Holy Cross, which King David the first built, over which, in a park of hares, conies,[1] and deer, an high mountain hangs, called the chair of Arthur (of Arthur the Prince of the Britains, whose monuments famous among all ballad-makers, are for the most part to be found on these borders of England and Scotland). From the King's palace at the east, the city still riseth higher and higher towards the west, and consists especially of one broad and very fair street (which is the greatest part and sole ornament thereof), the rest of the side streets and allies being of poor building and inhabited with very poor people, and this length from the east to the west is about a mile, whereas the breadth of the city from the

[1] **conies:** rabbits.

Fynes Moryson, *An Itinerary* (London, 1617), pt. 1, bk. 3, 273; pt. 3, bk. 3, 154–55, 156.

north to the south is narrow, and cannot be half a mile. At the furthest end towards the west, is a very strong castle, which the Scots hold unexpugnable.[2] . . . And from this castle towards the west, is a most steep rock pointed on the highest top, out of which this castle is cut. But on the north and south sides without the walls, be plain and fruitful fields of corn.[3] In the midst of the foresaid fair street, the cathedral church is built, which is large and lightsome, but little stately for the building, and nothing at all for the beauty and ornament. In this church the King's seat is built some few stairs high of wood, and leaning upon the pillar next to the pulpit. And opposite to the same is another seat very like it, in which the incontinent[4] use to stand and do penance; and some few weeks past, a gentleman, being a stranger, and taking it for a place wherein men of better quality used to sit, boldly entered the same in sermon time, till he was driven away with the profuse laughter of the common sort, to the disturbance of the whole congregation. The houses are built of unpolished stone, and in the fair street good part of them is of free stone, which in that broad street would make a fair show, but that the outsides of them are faced with wooden galleries, built upon the second story of the houses; yet these galleries give the owners a fair and pleasant prospect, into the said fair and broad street, when they sit or stand in the same. The walls of the city are built of little and unpolished stones, and seem ancient, but are very narrow, and in some places exceeding low, in other, ruined.

II. On Scotland's Geography and Trade

Scotland reaching so far into the north, must needs be subject to excessive cold, yet the same is in some sort mitigated by the thickness of the cloudy air and sea vapors. And as in the northern parts of England, they have small pleasantness, goodness or abundance of fruits and flowers, so in Scotland they have much less, or none at all. And I remember, that coming to Berwick in the month of May, we had great storms, and felt great cold, when for two months before, the pleasant spring had smiled on us at London.

On the west side of Scotland are many woods, mountains, and lakes. On the east side towards the sea, I passed Fife, a pleasant little territory of open fields, without enclosures, fruitful in corn (as be all the parts near Berwick, save that they yield little wheat, and much barley and oats), and all a plain country, but it had no woods at all, only the gentlemen's dwellings were shadowed with some little groves, pleasant to the view.[5] Scotland abounds

---

[2] **unexpugnable**: cannot be taken by assault.   [3] **corn**: i.e., grain in general.   [4] **incontinent**: those lacking in self-restraint, particularly sexual.   [5] Many visitors to Scotland in this period commented on the lack of forestation.

with fish, and hath plenty of cattle, yet not so big as ours, and their horses are full of spirit, and patient of labor, but very little, so as the Scots then would give any price for one of our English geldings, which notwithstanding in Queen Elizabeth's time might not upon great penalty be sold unto them. . . . The inhabitants of the western parts of Scotland carry into Ireland and neighboring places red and pickled herrings, sea coals,[6] and aquavitae,[7] with like commodities, and bring out of Ireland yarn and cows' hides or silver. The eastern Scots carry into France coarse clothes, both linen and woolen, which be narrow and shrink in the wetting. They also carry thither wool, skins of goats, wethers,[8] and of conies, and divers kinds of fishes, taken in the Scottish sea, and near other northern islands, and after smoked, or otherwise dried and salted. And they bring from thence salt and wines. . . .

And in these kingdoms [France, Denmark, and Poland] they lived at this time in great multitudes, rather for the poverty of their own kingdom, than for any great traffic they exercised there, dealing rather for small fardels,[9] than for great quantities of rich wares.

III. On Scottish Drinking

The country people and merchants used to drink largely, the gentlemen somewhat more sparingly — yet the very courtiers, at feasts, by night meetings, and entertaining any stranger, used to drink healths not without excess, and (to speak truth without offense) the excess of drinking was then far greater in general among the Scots than the English. Myself being at the Court invited by some gentlemen to supper, and being forewarned to fear this excess, would not promise to sup with them, but upon condition that my inviter would be my protection from large drinking, which I was many times forced to invoke, being courteously entertained, and much provoked to garraussing,[10] and so for that time avoided any great intemperance. Remembering this, and having since observed in my conversation at the English Court with the Scots of the better sort, that they spend great part of the night in drinking, not only wine, but even beer, as myself will not accuse them of great intemperance, so I cannot altogether free them from the imputation of excess, wherewith the popular voice chargeth them.

---

[6] **sea coals**: i.e., mineral coal as opposed to charcoal.   [7] **aquavitae**: a general name for strong liquor.   [8] **wethers**: male sheep, especially castrated rams.   [9] **fardels**: small bundles.   [10] **garraussing**: carousing.

→ SIR ANTHONY WELDON

From A Perfect Description of the People and Country of Scotland
1617

First, for the country, I must confess it is good for those that possess it, and too bad for others, to be at the charge to conquer it. The air might be wholesome but for the stinking people that inhabit it. The ground might be fruitful had they wit to manure it.

Their beasts be generally small, women only excepted, of which sort there are none greater in the whole world. There is great store of fowl too, as foul houses, foul sheets, foul linen, foul dishes and pots, foul trenchers[1] and napkins. . . . They have good store of fish too, and good for those that can eat it raw; but if it come once into their hands, it is worse than if it were three days old. For their butter and cheese, I will not meddle withal at this time, nor no man else at any time that loves his life.

They have great store of deer, but they are so far from the place where I have been, that I rather believe than go to disprove it. I confess, all the deer I met withal, was dear[2] lodgings, dear horse-meat, and dear tobacco, and English beer.

As for fruit, for their grandsire Adam's sake they never planted any; and for other trees, had Christ been betrayed in this country (as doubtless he should, had he come as a stranger), Judas had sooner found the grace of repentance, than a tree to hang himself on.

They have many hills, wherein they say is much treasure, but they show none of it; nature hath only discovered to them some mines of coal, to show to what end he created them.

I saw little grass, but in their pottage.[3] The thistle is not given them of nought, for it is the fairest flower in their garden. The word hay is Heathen-Greek[4] unto them; neither man nor beast knows what it means.

Corn is reasonable plenty at this time; for since they heard of the king's coming, it hath been as unlawful for the common people to eat wheat, as it was in the old time for any but the priests to eat shew-bread.[5] They prayed much for his coming, and long fasted for his welfare. . . .

---

[1] **trenchers**: plates or platters of wood or metal.   [2] **dear**: expensive.   [3] **pottage**: porridge, soup.   [4] **Heathen-Greek**: i.e., unknown.   [5] **shew-bread**: the twelve loaves that were placed on a table beside the altar of incense every Sabbath; at the end of the week, they were eaten by the priests alone. i.e., Because of scarcity, wheat has been denied the people, so that the King and his party will have enough.

Sir Anthony Weldon, *A Perfect Description of the People and Country of Scotland* (1617; from the edition printed in London, 1659) 1–4, 8–9, 11–15, 16–17, 18–19, 21.

For his majesty's entertainment, I must needs ingenuously[6] confess, he was received in the parish of Edinburgh (for a city I cannot call it), with great shouts of joy, but no shows of charge for pageants; they hold them idolatrous things, and not fit to be used in so reformed[7] a place; from the castle they gave him some pieces of ordnance,[8] which surely he gave them since he was king of England; and at the entrance of the town they presented him with a golden bason,[9] which was carried before him on mens' shoulders to his palace, I think, from whence it came. . . .

Now I will begin briefly to speak of the people according to their degrees and qualities. For the lords spiritual, they may well be termed so indeed, for they are neither fish nor flesh, but what it shall please their earthly God, the king, to make them. Obedience is better than sacrifice, and therefore they make a mock at martyrdom, saying, That Christ was to die for them, and not they for him. They will rather subscribe than surrender, and rather dispense with small things than trouble themselves with great disputation; they will rather acknowledge the king to be their head than want wherewith to pamper their bodies.

They have taken great pains and trouble to compass their bishoprics, and they will not leave them for a trifle; for the deacons, whose defects will not lift them up to dignities, all their study is to disgrace them that have gotten the least degree above them; and because they cannot bishop, they proclaim they never heard of any. The scriptures, say they, speak of deacons and elders, but not a word of bishops.[10] Their discourses are full of detraction, their sermons nothing but railing, and their conclusions nothing but heresies and treasons. For the religion they have, I confess they hold it above reach, and, God willing, I will never reach for it.

They christen without the cross, marry without the ring, receive the sacrament without reverence, die without repentance, and bury without divine service; they keep no holy-days, nor acknowledge any saint but St. Andrew, who they said got that honor by presenting Christ with an oaten cake after his forty days fast. They say likewise, that he that translated the Bible was the son of a maltster, because it speaks of a miracle done by barley-loaves; whereas they swear they were oaten cakes, and that no other bread of that quantity could have sufficed so many thousands.

They use no prayer at all, for they say it is needless; God knows their minds without prattling, and what He doth, He loves to do it freely. Their

---

[6] **ingenuously**: frankly, openly.   [7] **reformed**: i.e., Calvinist, strict Protestant.   [8] **pieces of ordnance**: guns, cannons.   [9] **bason**: i.e., basinet, or helmet.   [10] **bishops**: the dispute over whether there could be bishops in the church proved a great divide between James and Puritan elements; he linked royal authority to their existence in his famous declaration in 1604, "No Bishop, No King."

Sabbath's exercise is a preaching in the forenoon, and a persecuting in the afternoon; they go to church in the forenoon to hear the law, and to the crags and mountains in the afternoon to louze[11] themselves.

They hold their noses if you talk of bear-baiting, and stop their ears if you speak of a play;[12] fornication they hold but a pastime, wherein man's ability is approved, and a woman's fertility is discovered; at adultery they shake their heads; theft they rail at; murder they wink at; and blasphemy they laugh at; they think it impossible to lose the way to heaven, if they can but leave Rome behind them. . . .

For the lords temporal and spiritual, [they are] temporizing gentlemen, if I were apt to speak of any, I could not speak much of them; only I must let you know they are not Scottishmen, for as soon as they fall from the breast of the beast their mother, their careful sire posts them away for France, which as they pass, the sea sucks from them that which they have sucked from their rude dams; there they gather new flesh, new blood, new manners, and there they learn to put on their clothes, and then return into their countries to wear them out. There they learn to stand, to speak, and to discourse, and congee,[13] to court women, and to compliment[14] with men. . . .

The country, although it be mountainous, affords no monsters but women, of which the greatest sort (as countesses and ladies) are kept like lions in iron gates; the merchants' wives are also prisoners, but not in so strong a hold; they have wooden cages, like our boar-franks,[15] through which, sometimes peeping to catch the air, we are almost choked with the sight of them. The greatest madness among the men is jealousy; in that they fear what no man that hath but two of his senses will take from them.

The ladies are of opinion, that Susanna[16] could not be chaste, because she bathed so often. Pride is a thing bred in their bones, and their flesh naturally abhors cleanliness. Their breath commonly stinks of pottage, their linen of piss, their hands of pig turds, their body of sweat, and their splay feet never offend in socks. To be chained in marriage with one of them, were to be tied to a dead carcass, and cast into a stinking ditch. . . .

And therefore to conclude, the men of old did no more wonder that the great Messiah should be born in so poor a town as Bethlehem in Judea, than I do wonder that so brave a prince as King James, should be born in so stinking a town as Edinburgh in lousy Scotland.

[11] louze: to remove lice.   [12] play: Puritan/Calvinist opposition to plays and other festivities was well known, particularly through plays such as Ben Jonson's *Bartholomew Fair* (1614) and anti-theatrical tracts.   [13] congee: ceremonial bow (part of courtly behavior).   [14] compliment: to employ ceremony or formal courtesy in acts and expressions.   [15] boar-franks: enclosures in which to feed hogs (i.e., Scottish women peered through the wooden bars on their windows as boars do).   [16] Susanna: Susanna was spied on by the elders, who then accused her of unchastity, while she was bathing; the story is told in one of the apocryphal books of the Old Testament.

→ JOHN TAYLOR

From The Penniless Pilgrimage, Or the Moneyless Perambulation   *1618*

I. On Visiting Edinburgh

[Taylor establishes contact with a stranger:] Presently the gentleman (being of a generous disposition) overtook me with unexpected and undeserved courtesy, brought me to a lodging, and caused my horse to be put into his own stable, whilst we discoursing over a pint of Spanish,[1] I related as much [of things] English to him, as made him lend me ten shillings (his name was Mr. John Maxwell), which money I am sure was the first that I handled after I came from out the walls of London: but having rested two hours and refreshed myself, the gentleman and I walked to see the city and the castle, which as my poor unable and unworthy pen can, I will truly describe.

The castle on a lofty rock is so strongly grounded, bounded, and founded, that by force of man it can never be confounded; the foundation and walls are unpenetrable, the rampiers[2] impregnable, the bulwarks invincible, no way but one to it is or can be possible to be made passable. In a word, I have seen many straits[3] and fortresses in Germany, the Netherlands, Spain, and England, but they must all give place to this unconquered castle, both for strength and situation.

Amongst the many memorable things which I was showed there, I noted especially a great piece of ordnance of iron;[4] it is not for battery, but it will serve to defend a breach, or to toss balls of wild-fire against any that should assail or assault the castle; it lies now dismounted. And it is so great within, that it was told me that a child was once gotten there, but I, to make trial, crept into it, lying on my back, and I am sure there was room enough and spare for a greater than myself.

So leaving the castle, as it is both defensive against any opposition, and magnifick for lodging and receipt,[5] I descended lower to the city, wherein I observed the fairest and goodliest street that ever mine eyes beheld, for I did never see or hear of a street of that length (which is half an English mile

---

[1] **Spanish**: wine from Spain.   [2] **rampiers**: i.e., ramparts — mounds of earth raised for the defense of a place.   [3] **straits**: a narrow, confined place or space.   [4] **ordnance of iron**: a huge cannon, called Mons Meg, on which many visitors to Scotland commented.   [5] **receipt**: the ordinary reception of strangers or travellers.

John Taylor, *The Penniless Pilgrimage, or the Moneyless Perambulation, of John Taylor, Alias the King's Majesty's Water-Poet* (London, 1618) D1v–D3, E4v–F2v, G2v.

from the castle to a fair port which they call the Nether-bow), and from that port, the street which they call the Kenny-hate is one quarter of a mile more, down to the King's palace, called Holy-rood-house, the buildings on each side of the way being all of squared stone, five, six, and seven stories high, and many by-lanes and closes[6] on each side of the way, wherein are gentlemen's houses, much fairer than the buildings in the high-street, for in the high-street the merchants and tradesmen do dwell, but the gentlemen's mansions and goodliest houses are obscurely[7] founded in the aforesaid lanes: the walls are eight or ten foot thick, exceeding strong, not built for a day, a week, or a month, or a year, but from antiquity to posterity, for many ages; there I found entertainment beyond my expectation or merit, and there is fish, flesh, bread and fruit, in such variety, that I think I may offenseless call it superfluity, or satiety. The worst was, that wine and ale was so scarce, and the people there such misers of it, that every night before I went to bed, if any man had asked me a civil question, all the wit in my head could not have made him a sober answer.

I was at His Majesty's palace, a stately and princely seat, wherein I saw a sumptuous chapel, most richly adorned with all appurtenances belonging to so sacred a place, or so royal an owner. In the inner court, I saw the King's arms cunningly carved in stone, and fixed over a door aloft on the wall, the red lion being the crest, over which was written this inscription in Latin, *"Nobis haec invicta miserunt 106 proavi."* I inquired what the English of it was. It was told me as followeth, which I thought worthy to be recorded: "106 fore-fathers have left this to us unconquered." This is a worthy and memorable motto, and I think few kingdoms or none in the world can truly write the like, that notwithstanding so many inroads, incursions, attempts, assaults, civil wars, and foreign hostilities, bloody battles, and mighty foughten fields, that maugre[8] the strength and policy of enemies, that royal crown and scepter hath from one hundred and seven descents, keep still unconquered, and by the power of the King of Kings (through the grace of the Prince of peace), is now left peacefully to our peaceful King, whom long in blessed peace, the God of peace defend and govern.

II. On Hunting in the Highlands

I rode with him [the Lord of Mar] from his house, where I saw the ruins of an old castle, called the castle of Kindroghit. It was built by King Malcolm

---

[6] **closes:** entries or passages leading to houses.   [7] **obscurely:** inconspicuously; darkly, dimly.
[8] **maugre:** in spite of.

Canmore (for a hunting house), who reigned in Scotland when Edward the Confessor, Harold, and Norman William[9] reigned in England. I speak of it, because it was the last house that I saw in those parts; for I was the space of twelve days after, before I saw either house, corn field, or habitation for any creature but deer, wild horses, wolves, and such like creatures, which made me doubt that I should never have seen a house again. . . . [M]y good Lord Erskine, he commanded that I should always be lodged in his lodging; the kitchen being always on the side of a bank, many kettles and pots boiling, and many spits turning and winding, with great variety of cheer — as venison baked, sodden,[10] roast, and stewed beef, mutton, goats, kid, hares, fresh salmon, pigeons, hens, capons, chickens, partridge, moorcoots, heathcocks, caperkellies and termagants;[11] good ale, sack,[12] white and claret, tent (or allegant)[13] with most potent *aquavitae*.[14]

All these and more than these, we had continually, in superfluous abundance, caught by falconers, fowlers, and fishers, and brought by my Lord's tenants and purveyors to victual[15] our camp, which consisted of fourteen or fifteen hundred men and horses. . . .

Being come to our lodgings [after the hunt], there was such baking, boiling, roasting, and stewing . . . and after supper a fire of firewood as high as an indifferent maypole. . . . For I dare affirm he [the Earl of Mar] hath as many [great fir trees] growing there, as would serve for masts (from this time to the end of the world) for all the ships, caracks, hoyes, galleys, drumlers, barks,[16] and watercrafts, that are now, or can be in the world these forty years.

This sounds like a lie to an unbeliever, but I and many thousands do know that I speak within the compass of truth: for indeed (the more is the pity), they do grow so far from any passage of water, and withal in such rocky mountains, that no way to convey them is possible to be passable either with boat, horse, or cart.

III. THE EPILOGUE

Yet had I wrote all things that there [in Scotland] I saw,
Misjudging censures would suppose I flatter,

---

[9] **Norman William**: William the Conqueror, of Normandy, who conquered England in 1066. [10] **sodden**: boiled. [11] **moorcoots . . . termagants**: all types of native birds; "termagant" was incorrectly believed to derive from "ptarmigan," a bird of the grouse family. [12] **sack**: general name for a class of white wines, formerly imported from Spain. [13] **tent (or allegant)**: tent was a Spanish "tincted" wine, one of a dark red color; allegant was any wine made in Alicante, a city on the southeast coast of Spain. [14] *aquavitae:* strong-tasting liquor. [15] **victual**: to feed. [16] **caracks . . . barks**: all types of ships, large and small.

And so my name I should in question draw;
Where asses bray, and pratling pies[17] do chatter.
Yet (armed with truth) I publish with my pen,
That there [in Scotland] th'Almighty doth his blessings heap,
In such abundant food for beasts and men,
That I ne'er saw more plenty or more cheap.

[17] **pies:** magpies.

CHAPTER 5

Witchcraft and Prophecy

⋊⋉

Discourses of Witchcraft

The history of witchcraft is long, violent, and terrible.[1] Witch hunts in
western Europe over the past five hundred years have led to the executions
of thousands of people, mostly women. From the earliest records in the
twelfth century up to the present day, a belief in witchcraft has led to, at best,
demonization and scapegoating and, at worst, state- or church-sanctioned
executions. Witches have always readily served to define the negative side of
culturally sanctioned boundaries of good versus evil, natural versus deviant,
and have been punished accordingly.

There were many references to witches and witchcraft in the Bible, from
the clear prohibition of Exodus 22:18 ("Thou shalt not suffer a witch to live")
to the story of the Witch of Endor, who raised up Samuel from death upon
Saul's request (1 Samuel 28).[2] Such Biblical references seemed to confirm

---

[1] There is a vast amount of scholarship on the subject of witchcraft; the following references
are only starting points. For the European phenomenon, see Briggs, Cohn, Ginzburg, and
Trevor-Roper. For England, see Clark, Macfarlane, *Witchcraft*, Thomas, Willis, and especially Purkiss. For Scotland, see Larner. For New England, see Demos and Karlsen.

[2] The Witch of Endor was often linked with a famous witch in classical literature, Medea. In
The Tempest, Prospero's "Ye elves of hills" speech (5.1.33–57) is virtually a quotation from
Ovid's version of Medea's invocation as she prepares to restore Aeson, Jason's father, to his

that witches did, at one time at least, exist. For those — believers or skeptics — who argued about whether witchcraft was real, the story of the Witch of Endor became a particular flashpoint.[3] Skeptics usually offered two lines of response: first, that it was not a witch, but the Devil (who can of course transform himself into an angel of light); and second, that even if it had been a witch, since the coming of Christ, all oracles, miracles, and other spiritual phenomena, such as witches, were banished, and so any contemporary demonstrations of such power were simply illusions.

Early modern witchcraft persecutions tended to coincide with the establishment of absolutist, Christian monarchs in Europe, and tended to recede as discourses of "enlightenment" and "empiricism" grew more dominant. Court prosecutions and royal prohibitions of witchcraft may have waned considerably in the seventeenth century, yet people did not cease to believe in witches at such times. It is perhaps safest to observe that a belief in witchcraft requires, or rests upon, an underlying cultural *structure* of belief in magical power — either Christian and/or folk and popular. Diane Purkiss has observed how a monarch, such as James, could appropriate either belief *or* skepticism in witchcraft for his own purposes: "Using the forensic discourses of interrogation and observation, and the nascent discourses of the medicalisation of hysteria, James tried to ground the monarch's authority in new science as well as old superstition" (Purkiss 201).[4]

The history and nature of witchcraft beliefs in the sixteenth and seventeenth centuries differed considerably by country. Persecutions on the Continent, particularly Germany, were vastly more virulent, widespread, and murderous than anything in England — which nevertheless had its own spectacular cases. In the seventeenth century, the craze spread to America, most notoriously to Salem. The late-sixteenth-century history of witchcraft in Scotland, moreover, differed in substantial ways from that of England, as we shall see.

In England, witchcraft was a crime, but witches were rarely tortured, and

---

youth (*Metamorphoses* bk. 7, 265–77). Ovid's version of Medea's speech became a touchstone for the power of witchcraft, quoted as a proof by Cornelius Agrippa and Bodin, among many others, but contemptuously dismissed by skeptics such as Scot (see p. 307), who refers to Ovid sarcastically as "Bodin's poet . . . whose *Metamorphosis* make so much for him" (bk. 5, ch. 5). The speech is also quoted in Middleton's *The Witch* (5.2).

[3] Reginald Scot (see below) took up the issue of the Witch of Endor (bk. 7, chs. 8–14); King James addressed the story within the first two pages of his work (see below), in the first chapter of book 1.

[4] Purkiss also argues that, in writing *Macbeth*, Shakespeare was well aware of James's ambivalent position, understanding "how discourses of scepticism could naturalise the king's absolutism as privileged spectator more naturally than discourses of paranoid belief" (Purkiss 211). As seen in his supposed insight into the meaning of the Monteagle letter (see p. 250), James prided himself on his ability to discover secrets and sniff out fraud.

legal distinctions were made between white and black magic; the beneficent magic practiced by cunning women in the villages, for example, was often highly regarded (as in the selection from George Gifford, below, in which a man goes to a cunning woman in order to be told he was bewitched by someone else).[5] Nor did English writers on witchcraft seem to be familiar with many of the more notorious characteristics of witches, as described by Continental writers — such as the idea of the demonic pact, the witches' coven, the "secret mark" or supposed "witch's teat."[6]

There was also, in England, a strong tradition of skepticism about witchcraft, even doubt about its very existence. Certainly the most famous doubter of all was Reginald Scot (c. 1538–1599), whose book, *The Discovery of Witchcraft* (see p. 307), achieved a European-wide notoriety and the explicit displeasure of King James VI of Scotland. Scot's campaign against belief in witchcraft and (in his view) its mistaken persecution seems to have begun through his interest in the witch trials in St. Osyth (in Essex), conducted by the justice of the peace Brian Darcy, in 1582. Scot thoroughly and relentlessly debunks belief in witchcraft, far transcending the specifics of the St. Osyth cases. For Scot, witchcraft is ultimately a species of deceit and counterfeiting. Like many skeptical writers of the period, as we will see, he also argued a link between the superstitions of witchcraft and the superstitious beliefs of the Catholic church. Scot's book is astonishingly encyclopedic — hundreds of pages of arguments, biblical citations, examples, even illustrations, of how people have been deluded into believing the claims of witchcraft; he offers explanations of how alleged witches came to "confess" their imaginary crimes and offers an example of classic scapegoating (in the excerpt below), which contemporary theorists might find exactly congruent with modern sociological explanations of the witchcraft phenomenon. Yet the *Discovery*'s very encyclopedic nature made it a kind of source book not just for skeptics, but for believers as well.

The selection from George Gifford that follows reveals a skepticism about the claims of logic and, above all, evidence of witchcraft accusations — in fact, the accusation itself seemed to be the chief piece of evidence; the accus-

---

[5] For the tradition of cunning men and women, see Thomas. Some writers, however, such as William Perkins, argued that "the blessing witch" as well as the evil ones should suffer the same penalty: "Death therefore is the just and deserved portion of the good witch" (quoted by Kittredge 292).

[6] "The portrait of the English witch that emerges from pamphlets between 1566 and 1618 has nothing to do with the Continental one" (Rosen 29). The witch's third teat, supposedly sucked by her familiar, is part of the antimaternal fantasy that helps construct the early modern witch: "the witch is the dark other of the early modern woman, expressing and acting on desires that other women must repress to construct their identities as mothers" (Purkiss 100). See also Willis for a related interpretation of witchcraft as the antimaternal.

ing friends and neighbors of Samuel in the dialogue reveal only their own prejudice and lack of charity.[7] An analogous example may be seen in a remarkable play of 1621 by William Rowley, Thomas Dekker, John Ford, and perhaps others, *The Witch of Edmonton.* Elizabeth Sawyer, an old village-woman, articulates the scapegoat theory of witch origins even as the play demonstrates it at work on her:

> And why on me? Why should the envious world
> Throw all their scandalous malice upon me?
> 'Cause I am poor, deformed and ignorant,
> And like a bow buckled and bent together
> By some more strong in mischiefs than myself,
> Must I for that be made a common sink
> For all the filth and rubbish of men's tongues
> To fall and run into? Some call me witch,
> And, being ignorant of myself, they go
> About to teach me how to be one, urging
> That my bad tongue, by their bad usage made so,
> Forspeaks their cattle, doth bewitch their corn,
> Themselves, their servants and their babes at nurse.
> This they enforce upon me, and in part
> Make me to credit it.   (2.1.1–15)

Later, she notes "I am shunned / And hated like a sickness" (lines 100–01) and " 'Tis all one / To be a witch as to be counted one" (118–19).[8] Then, as she calls for vengeance against her enemies, a black dog, her familiar (a demon), appears, and she in fact becomes a witch. The play has it both ways, then, for her status as a witch is both culturally constructed *and* real.

Elizabeth Sawyer, the unnamed woman in Gifford's story, and the witch in Scot's account all fulfill the stereotypical social profile of a witch in the early modern period: not only is the witch female, but she is an old, single, poor woman. The most common situation of witchcraft accusation, as Keith Thomas has noted, "was that in which the victim (or, if he were an infant, the victim's parents) had been guilty of a breach of charity of neighbourliness, by turning away an old woman who had come to the door to beg or borrow some food or drink, or the loan of some household utensil. . . . The overwhelming majority of fully documented witch cases fall into this simple pattern. The witch is sent away empty-handed, perhaps mumbling a malediction, and in due course something goes wrong with the household, for which she is immediately held responsible" (553–54). The two key features of

---

[7] Gifford, however, did not ultimately deny the existence of witches.

[8] Text from *Three Jacobean Witchcraft Plays,* ed. Peter Corbin and Douglas Sedge (Manchester: Manchester UP, 1983).

most allegations were therefore, first, "the occurrence of a personal misfortune for which no natural explanation was immediately forthcoming," and second, "an awareness on the victim's part of having given offence to a neighbour, usually by having failed to discharge some hitherto customary social obligation" (557). Such local occurrences of social trangression were all too frequently swept up into more wide-ranging kinds of accusations.[9]

A witch could, in theory, be either male or female, but something like nine of every ten prosecutions were of women. Skeptics and believers alike took note of this phenomenon and tried to account for it, as King James does in the excerpt below. Some recent writers have argued that the overwhelming predominance of women as the victims of such accusations is simply the product of the misogyny of a patriarchal society — that the categories of *deviant* and *feminine* merge in the collective anxieties of patriarchal discourse to create the largely female-gendered category of "the witch." Larner associates the witchcraft terror with an increasing trend to criminalize certain activities of women for the first time and suggests that "in the law-and-order crises generated by the new regimes of early modern Europe, women were a prime symbol of disorder" (86). She goes on to ask "why women appeared particularly threatening to patriarchal order at this time, and why they ceased to be so threatening about 1700 [when prosecutions declined]" (87), suggesting that witch hunting served to support the political ideology of Christianity, Catholic and Protestant alike.

Certainly the alleged moral weakness of women (a pure example of projection by male writers) was recognized as one cause of their susceptibility, as King James argued. Or, as the authors of the *Malleus maleficarum* (The hammer of witches, written in 1486) — the most important and influential Continental exposition of witchcraft in the early modern period — observed, there are more female witches than male because women are inherently wicked, more credulous (hence easier for the Devil to attack), and have slippery tongues (they "are unable to conceal from their fellow-women those things which by evil arts they know, and, since they are weak, they find an easy and secret manner of vindicating themselves by witchcraft" [120]). But the main, "natural reason is that she is more carnal than a man." Eve "was formed from a bent rib [from Adam], that is, a rib of the breast, which is bent as it were in a contrary direction to a man. And since through this defect she is an imperfect animal, she always deceives." In her disobedience to God's command in the Garden of Eden, therefore, Eve "showed that she

---

[9] Purkiss has recently challenged this reigning "social" explanation of witchcraft accusations, noting that its effect is to erase female agency; a master narrative of subjection and domination by patriarchal ideology, she argues, often runs counter to historical evidence (Purkiss 145–70).

doubted, and had little faith in the word of God. And all this is indicated by the etymology of the word; for *Femina* comes from *Fe* and *Minus* [i.e., without faith], since she is ever weaker to hold and preserve the faith" (121).[10] This astonishing etymological claim thus casts *all* women as inherently faithless, and thus potentially witches.[11]

The history of witchcraft in Scotland differs from that of England in several important ways, although both countries passed antiwitchcraft statutes in 1563. The turning point in the Scottish experience seems to have been King James's voyage to Denmark in 1589 to bring back his new queen, Anne. While in Denmark, James evidently first encountered the writings of Continental witchcraft theorists such as Jean Bodin, Hyperius, Henningius (whom he met), and Cornelius Agrippa, all of whom are acknowledged in the "Preface" to his *Daemonology,* published in 1597.[12] The other salient experience of this voyage was the great storms in the spring of 1590, which prevented the king's return to Scotland, forcing the ships back to Denmark until they subsided. These storms were blamed on witches, both in Copenhagen and later, as seen in the pamphlet *News from Scotland* (p. 312), in Scotland. Upon his return, James revealed a new, intense interest in witchcraft and began to involve himself directly in interrogations and trials. James himself seems to have brought Continental witchcraft theory — with its covens, secret marks, and demonic compacts — directly to Scotland and initiated a general witch hunt beginning in 1590.[13] Moreover, witchcraft theory merged all too easily with divine right theory in James's thinking, and as a result, witchcraft began to be understood as a species of treason as well. The true aim of witches was to assault the body of the king. James evidently believed that the North Berwick witches in the *News from Scotland* pamphlet were acting on the behest of his great enemy, the Earl of Bothwell who, one observer said, was "committed to Edinburgh Castle for conspiring the King's death by sorcery" (*CSP, Scot* 10: 510). Witchcraft thus became not only a crime of deviance, but *the* crime against the state and monarch. The personal nature of the threat was made evident to James by the accused witch, Agnes Sampson, who, as reported in *News from Scotland,* privately repeated to James "the very words which passed between the King's Majesty

[10] Text from *Witchcraft in Europe 1100–1700: A Documentary History,* ed. Alan C. Kors and Edward Peters.

[11] It is important to point out, however, that many, perhaps even a majority, of witchcraft accusations were made by women against other women.

[12] James's *Daemonology,* written in rebuttal of Scot and Wierus (see below), is not original in any way; it is important not only because the monarch wrote it, but because it disseminates Continental witchcraft ideas to a wide, English-reading audience.

[13] Whether James initiated the witchhunt or simply rode the crest of a popular panic is difficult to determine.

and his Queen at Upslo in Norway the first night of their marriage, with their answers each to other: whereat the King's Majesty wondered greatly, and swore by the living God, that he believed that all the devils in hell could not have discovered the same: acknowledging her words to be most true, and therefore gave the more credit to the rest." Given this scene — and other "evidence," such as her alleged plan to poison the king with toad venom — it is little wonder that James took the threat posed by these witches as a potential regicide.

When James came down to England in 1603, however, he found himself in a country that had a substantially different, more skeptical experience with witchcraft than the Scots had suffered. Although Parliament passed the new antiwitchcraft statute in 1604 — which slightly strengthened the penalties of the 1563 statute and added new sections against digging up dead bodies for use in sorcery, or consulting with evil spirits[14] — James's new countrymen were less inclined to credit unfounded accusations, particularly those of children. Even before 1603, James's enthusiasm for persecution had waned considerably, and he seems to have grown even more skeptical after his ascent to the English throne.[15] James personally intervened in several English witchcraft trials on the side of doubt and caution and was invariably skeptical about accusations by those said to be possessed, especially children.[16]

In 1605–06, then, when *Macbeth* was written, witchcraft was decidedly a prominent and controversial topic in London, in large part because of the new monarch's complex and evolving personal interests. The discourse of witchcraft intersected with many other controversial issues of the time, from the place of women and the nature of supernatural power, to treason and regicide. It is impossible to specify what Shakespeare's audience in 1605–06 "believed" about witchcraft. Clearly, though, they did not all believe the same thing. Some must have been skeptics like Scot, while some, probably the majority, must have been believers — and still others must have "believed" in witchcraft as a dramatic proposition that, like men dressed as ghosts or boys dressed as women, was simply another dramatic given that an audience had to grant to a play in order for it to work. To take some more recent examples, no one had to believe in the actual existence of witches to

[14] James has often been blamed for this new law, but it seems to have issued more from Parliament than from royal pressure.

[15] In the end, there was no increase in the number of executions for witchcraft during the twenty-two years of James's reign over the last twenty-two years of Elizabeth's reign (Kittredge 288). On the other hand, James allowed the *Daemonology* to be reprinted in the 1616 collection of his works.

[16] For useful accounts of James's evolving position, especially his interventions, see Larner, and Kittredge (276–328).

enjoy *The Witches of Eastwick* (1987); or believe in ghosts to enjoy *Ghost*, the most popular film of 1990; or believe in werewolves to enjoy *Wolf* (1994). Belief is a concept with many different levels — and some belief in witchcraft seems always to have existed.

→ REGINALD SCOT

From The Discovery of Witchcraft   *1584*

I. An Impeachment of Witches' Power

The fables of witchcraft have taken so fast hold and deep root in the heart of man, that few or none can (nowadays) with patience endure the hand and correction of God. For if any adversity, grief, sickness, loss of children, corn, cattle, or liberty happen unto them, by and by they exclaim upon witches. As though there were no God in Israel that ordereth all things according to His will, punishing both just and unjust with griefs, plagues, and afflictions in manner and form as He thinketh good,[1] but that certain old women here on earth, called witches, must needs be the contrivers of all men's calamities, and as though they themselves were innocents, and had deserved no such punishments. Insomuch as they stick not to ride and go to such, as either are injuriously termed witches, or else are willing so to be accounted, seeking at their hands comfort and remedy in time of their tribulation, contrary to God's will and commandment in that behalf, who bids us resort to Him in all our necessities.

Such faithless people (I say) are also persuaded, that neither hail nor snow, thunder nor lightning, rain nor tempestuous winds come from the heavens at the commandment of God: but are raised by the cunning and power of witches and conjurors; insomuch as a clap of thunder, or a gale of wind is no sooner heard, but either they run to ring bells, or cry out to burn witches; or else burn consecrated things, hoping by the smoke thereof, to

---

[1] Job 5.

Reginald Scot, *The Discovery of Witchcraft; Wherein the lewd dealing of witches and witchmongers is notably detected, the knavery of conjurors, the impiety of enchanters, the folly of soothsayers, the impudent falsehood of coseners, the infidelity of atheists, the pestilent practices of Pythonists, the curiosity of figurecasters, the vanity of dreamers, the beggerly art of Alchemistry, the abomination of idolatry, the horrible art of poisoning, the virtue and power of natural magic, and all the conveyances of Legerdemain and juggling are deciphered: and many other things opened, which have long lien hidden, howbeit very necessary to be known* (London, 1584), bk. 1, ch. 1, 1–2; bk. 1, ch. 3, 7–9; bk. 1, ch. 5, 11; bk. 15, ch. 30, 450; bk. 16, ch. 2, 471.

drive the devil out of the air, as though spirits could be frayed away with such external toys.

II. The Identity of Witches

One sort of such as are said to be witches, are women which be commonly old, lame, blear-eyed, pale, foul, and full of wrinkles; poor, sullen, superstitious, and papists; or such as know no religion: in whose drowsy minds the devil hath gotten a fine seat; so as, what mischief, mischance, calamity, or slaughter is brought to pass, they are easily persuaded the same is done by themselves; imprinting in their minds an earnest and constant imagination hereof. They are lean and deformed, showing melancholy in their faces, to the horror of all that see them. They are doting, scolds, mad, devilish; and not much differing from them that are thought to be possessed with spirits; so firm and steadfast in their opinions, as whosoever shall only have respect to the constancy of their words uttered, would easily believe they were true indeed.

These miserable wretches are so odious unto all their neighbors, and so feared, as few dare offend them, or deny them any thing they ask: whereby they take upon them, yea, and sometimes think, that they can do such things as are beyond the ability of human nature. These go from house to house, and from door to door, for a pot full of milk, yeast, drink, pottage,[2] or some such relief; without the which they could hardly live: neither obtaining for their service and pains, nor by their art, nor yet at the devil's hands (with whom they are said to make a perfect and visible bargain) either beauty, money, promotion, wealth, worship, pleasure, honor, knowledge, learning, or any other benefit whatsoever.

It falleth out many times, that neither their necessities, nor their expectation is answered or served, in those places where they beg or borrow; but rather their lewdness is by their neighbors reproved. And further, in tract of time the witch waxeth odious and tedious to her neighbors; and they again are despised and despited[3] of her: so as sometimes she curseth one, and sometimes another; and that from the master of the house, his wife, children, cattle, etc. to the little pig that lieth in the sty. Thus in process of time they have all displeased her, and she hath wished evil luck unto them all; perhaps with curses and imprecations made in form. Doubtless (at length) some of her neighbors die, or fall sick; or some of their children are visited with diseases that vex them strangely: as apoplexies, epilepsies, convulsions, hot fevers, worms, etc. Which by ignorant parents are supposed to be the vengeance of

---

[2] **pottage:** porridge, soup.   [3] **despited:** held in contempt.

witches. Yea and their opinions and conceits are confirmed and maintained by unskillful physicians. . . . Witchcraft and enchantment is [*sic*] the cloak of ignorance: whereas indeed evil humors, and not strange words, witches, or spirits are the causes of such diseases. Also some of their cattle perish, either by disease or mischance. Then they, upon whom such adversities fall, weighing the fame that goeth upon this woman (her words, displeasure, and curses meeting so justly with their misfortune) do not only conceive, but also are resolved, that all their mishaps are brought to pass by her only means.

The witch on the other side expecting her neighbor's mischances, and seeing things sometimes come to pass acccording to her wishes, curses, and incantations (for Bodin himself confesseth,[4] that not above two in a hundred of their witchings or wishings take effect) being called before a Justice, by due examination of the circumstances is driven to see her imprecations and desires, and her neighbors harms and losses to concur, and as it were to take effect: and so confesseth that she (as a goddess) hath brought such things to pass. Wherein, not only she, but the accuser, and also the Justice, are foully deceived and abused; as being through her confession and other circumstances persuaded (to the injury of God's glory) that she hath done, or can do that which is proper only to God Himself.

III. A CONFUTATION OF COMMON OPINION

But whatsoever is reported or conceived of such manner of witchcrafts, I dare avow to be false and fabulous (cosenage,[5] dotage, and poisoning excepted): neither is there any mention made of these kind of witches in the Bible. If Christ had known them, He would not have pretermitted[6] to inveigh against their presumption, in taking upon them His office: as, to heal and cure diseases; and to work such miraculous and supernatural things, as whereby He Himself was specially known, believed, and published to be God.

---

[4] **Bodin . . . effect:** in book 2, chapter 8 of Jean Bodin's *De la demonomanie des sorciers* (published in Paris in 1580), Bodin argued the reality of witches and urged severe punishments. His work was known by King James, who alludes to him with approval in his *Daemonology*, and probably became acquainted with his work when he traveled to Denmark in 1590. In 1581, Bodin visited England where, among other things, he attended the trial of the Jesuit priest Father Campion. In response to the radicalism of Huguenot resistance after the massacres of 1572 (see discussion in "Resistance in Theory" in the introduction to Chapter 3, p. 232), Bodin published his *Six Livres de la Republique* (*Six Books of the Commonweal*) in 1576, translated into English in 1580. The *Six Livres* became the foremost Continental exposition of the absolutist theory of sovereign power; Bodin urged the rejection of all theories of resistance and the acceptance of a strong monarchy. Bodin's political work was highly influential and, along with that of Machiavelli, became one of the central targets of resistance theorists.   [5] **cosenage:** deceit, trickery.   [6] **pretermitted:** overlooked, omitted.

IV. Witchcraft and Papistry

And still methinks papists[7] (of all others) which indeed are most credulous, and do most maintain the forces of witches' charms, and of conjurors' cosenages, should perceive and judge conjurors' doings to be void of effect. For when they see their own stuff, as holy water, salt, candles, etc. conjured by their holy bishop and priests; and that in the words of consecration or conjuration (for so their own doctors term them) they adjure the water etc. to heal, not only the soul's infirmity, but also every malady, hurt, or ache of the body; and do also command the candles, with the force of all their authority and power, and by the effect of all their holy words, not to consume: and yet neither soul nor body anything recover, nor the candles last one minute the longer: with what face can they defend the others' miraculous works, as though the witches' and conjurors' actions were more effectual than their own?

IV. Why the Common People Believe in Witchcraft

The common people have been so assotted[8] and bewitched, with whatsoever poets have feigned of witchcraft, either in earnest, in jest, or else in derision; and with whatsoever loud liars and cosenors for their pleasures herein have invented, and with whatsoever tales they have heard from old doting women, or from their mothers' maids, and with whatsoever the grandfool their ghostly[9] father, or any other morrow-mass[10] priest had informed them; and finally with whatsoever they have swallowed up through tract of time, or through their own timorous nature or ignorant conceipt,[11] concerning these matters of hags and witches: as they have so settled their opinion and credit thereupon, that they think it heresy to doubt in any part of the matter. . . .

Witchcraft is in truth a cosening art, wherein the name of God is abused, profaned and blasphemed, and His power attributed to a vile creature. In estimation of the vulgar people, it is a supernatural work, contrived between a corporal old woman, and a spiritual devil. The manner thereof is so secret, mystical, and strange, that to this day there hath never been any credible witness thereof. It is incomprehensible to the wise, learned or faithful; a probable matter to children, fools, melancholic persons, and papists.

---

[7] **papists**: a general pejorative used to refer to Catholics.   [8] **assotted**: made into a fool.   [9] **ghostly**: spiritual.   [10] **morrow-mass**: the first mass of the day.   [11] **conceipt**: understanding.

→ GEORGE GIFFORD

From A Dialogue Concerning Witches and Witchcrafts

1593

SAMUEL: I was of a jury not many years past, when there was an old woman arraigned for a witch. There came in eight or ten which gave evidence against her. I do not remember every particular but the chief, for some things were of small value. One woman came in and testified upon her oath that her husband upon his death-bed took it upon his death that he was bewitched, for he pined a long time. And he said further, he was sure that woman had bewitched him. He took her to be naught,[1] and thought she was angry with him because she would have borrowed five shillings of him and he denied to lend it her. The woman took her oath also, that she thought in her conscience that the old woman was a witch, and that she killed her husband. There came in a man that halted; he told a shrewd tale. "I once" said he "had both my legs sound. This old woman and I fell out and did chide; she said she would be even with me. Within three days after I had such a pain in my knee that I could not stand. And ever since I go halting of it, and now and then feel some pain." There came in another, a little fellow that was very earnest — methinks I see him yet. He took his oath directly that she was a witch: "I did once anger her," said he, "but I did repent me, for I looked somewhat would follow. And the next night I saw the ugliest sight that ever I saw; I awaked suddenly out of my sleep and there was, methought, a great face, as big as they use to set up in the sign of the Saracen's Head, looked full in my face. I was scarce my own man two days after." Another came in, a woman; and her child died with grievous pain, and she took her oath that in her conscience she [the witch] killed her child. Then followed a man, and he said he could not tell, but he thought she was once angry with him because she came to beg a few pot-herbs and he denied her; and presently after he heard a thing, as he thought, to whisper in his ear "Thou shalt be bewitched!" The next day he had such a pain in his back that he could not sit upright. He said he sent to a cunning woman, she told him he was bewitched, and by a woman that came for pot-herbs. But she said he should recover of it, and so he said he did within some

---

[1] **naught**: wicked.

George Gifford, *A Dialogue concerning Witches and Witchcrafts. In which is laid open how craftily the Devil deceiveth not only the Witches but many other and so leadeth them awry into many great errors* (London, 1593) L3–L4.

ten days. Then came in two or three grave honest men which testified that she was by common fame accounted a witch. We found her guilty, for what could we do less? She was condemned and executed, and upon the ladder she made her prayer and took it upon her death she was innocent, and free from all such dealings. Do you think we did not well?

DANIEL: Nay, what think you? Are you sure she was a witch? May it not be she was innocent, and you upon your oaths shed innocent blood?

SAMUEL: If she were innocent, what could we do less? We went according to the evidence of such as were sworn; they swore that they in their conscience took her to be a witch, and that she did those things.

DANIEL: If other take their oath that in their conscience they think so, is that sufficient to warrant men upon mine oath to say it is so?

SAMUEL: Nay, but you see what matters they brought, which persuaded them to think so.

DANIEL: Might not both you and they be deceived in your thinking, or may you upon matters which induce you to think so, present upon your oath that you know it is so? . . . [I]s this a good proof, the Devil appeareath to a man after he hath displeased a woman, therefore she sent him? Doth not Satan haunt all men continually, and would if he could get leave from God terrify them with such illusions when men are afraid, and have strong imaginations? What reason did the woman show, which took it upon her conscience that the old woman killed her child, to prove that it was so? If she thought so in her conscience, and ten thousand more with her upon bare imagination, was that a warrant for you to swear solemnly that it was so? As for the testimony of the cunning woman that he was bewitched which had the pain in his back upon the denial of pot-herbs, it was the testimony of the Devil, as I showed before. And what is common fame grounded upon imagination?

✦ News from Scotland
1591

The complete text of the pamphlet *News from Scotland* is printed here, with most of the original woodcuts.

TO THE READER.

The manifold untruths which is spread abroad, concerning the detestable actions and apprehension of those witches whereof this history following truly entreateth, hath caused me to publish the same in print: and the rather for that sundry written copies are lately dispersed thereof, containing, that the said witches were first discovered, by means of a poor peddler traveling to the town of Tranent, and that by a wonderful manner he was in a moment conveyed at midnight, from Scotland to Bordeaux in France (being places of no small distance between) into a merchant's cellar there, and after, being sent from Bordeaux into Scotland by certain Scottish merchants to the King's Majesty, that he discovered those witches and was the cause of their apprehension: with a number of matters miraculous and incredible: all which in truth are most false. Nevertheless to satisfy a number of honest minds, who are desirous to be informed of the verity and truth of their confessions, which for certainty is more stranger than the common report runneth, and yet with more truth I have undertaken to publish this short treatise, which declareth the true discourse of all that hath happened, and as well what was pretended by those wicked and detestable witches against the King's Majesty, as also by what means they wrought the same.

All which examinations (gentle Reader) I have here truly published, as they were taken and uttered in the presence of the King's Majesty, praying thee to accept it for verity, the same being so true as cannot be reproved.

A true discourse, Of the apprehension of sundry witches lately taken in Scotland: whereof some are executed, and some are yet imprisoned. With a particular recital of their examinations, taken in the presence of the King's Majesty.

God by His omnipotent power, hath at all times and daily doth take such care, and is so vigilant, for the weal[1] and preservation of His own, that

---

[1] **weal**: welfare, general good.

News from Scotland. Declaring the Damnable life and death of Doctor Fian, a notable Sorcerer, who was burned at Edinburgh in January last, 1591. Which Doctor was register to the Devil that sundry times preached at North Berwick Kirk,° to a number of notorious Witches. With the true examinations of the said Doctor and Witches, as they uttered them in the presence of the Scottish King. Discovering how they pretended to bewitch and drown his Majesty in the Sea coming from Denmark, with such other wonderful matters as the like hath not been heard of at any time. Published according to the Scottish Copy (London, 1591). (**Kirk**: church.)

FIGURE 21 *From* News from Scotland *(1591). Several scenes from the narrative are simultaneously depicted, such as the storm that threatened James's ship and the miraculous conveyance of the peddler from Scotland to a wine cellar in Bordeux.*

thereby He disappointeth the wicked practises and evil intents of all such as by any means whatsoever, seek indirectly to conspire any thing contrary to His holy will: yea and by the same power, He hath lately overthrown and hindered the intentions and wicked dealings of a great number of ungodly creatures, no better than Devils: who suffering themselves to be allured and enticed by the Devil whom they served, and to whom they were privately sworn, entered into the detestable art of witchcraft, which they studied and practised so long time, that in the end they had seduced by their sorcery a number of others to be as bad as themselves: dwelling in the bounds of Lothian, which is a principal shire or part of Scotland, where the King's Majesty useth to make his chiefest residence or abode: and to the end that their detestable wickedness which they privily[2] had pretended against the King's Majesty, the commonweal of that country, with the nobility and subjects of the same, should come to light: God of his unspeakable goodness did reveal and lay it open in very strange sort, thereby to make known unto

---

[2] **privily**: secretly.

the world, that their actions were contrary to the law of God, and the natural affection which we ought generally to bear one to another: the manner of the revealing whereof was as followeth:

Within the town of Tranent in the kingdom of Scotland, there dwelleth one David Seaton, who being deputy bailiff[3] in the said town, had a maidservant called Gillis Duncan, who used secretly to be absent and to lie forth of her master's house every other night: this Gillis Duncan took in hand to help all such as were troubled or grieved with any kind of sickness or infirmity: and in short space did perform many matters most miraculous, which things forasmuch as she began to do them upon a sudden, having never done the like before, made her master and others to be in great admiration,[4] and wondered thereat: by means whereof the said David Seaton had his maid in some great suspicion, that she did not those things by natural and lawful ways, but rather supposed it to be done by some extraordinary and unlawful means.

Whereupon, her Master began to grow very inquisitive, and examined her which way and by what means she were able to perform matters of so great importance: whereat she gave him no answer, nevertheless, her master to the intent that he might the better try and find out the truth of the same, did with the help of others, torment her with the torture of the pilliewinks[5] upon her fingers, which is a grievous torture, and binding or wrenching her head with a cord or rope, which is a most cruel torment also, yet would she not confess any thing, whereupon they suspecting that she had been marked by the Devil (as commonly witches are) made diligent search about her, and found the enemy's mark to be in her fore-crag[6] or fore-part of her throat: which being found, she confessed that all her doings was done by the wicked allurements and enticements of the Devil, and that she did them by witchcraft.

After this her confession, she was committed to prison, where she continued for a season, where immediately she accused these persons following to be notorious witches, and caused them forthwith to be apprehended one after an other, viz. Agnes Sampson the eldest witch of them all, dwelling in Haddington, Agnes Tompson of Edinburgh, Doctor Fian, alias John Cunningham, master of the school at Saltpans in Lothian, of whose life and strange acts, you shall hear more largely in the end of this discourse: these were by the said Gillis Duncan accused, as also George Mott's wife dwelling in Saltpans, Robert Grierson skipper, and Janet Bandilands, with the porter's wife of Seaton, the smith at the Bridge Halls[7] with innumerable others in that parts, and dwelling in those bounds aforesaid: of whom some

---

[3] **bailiff:** an officer of justice under a sheriff.   [4] **admiration:** astonishment.   [5] **pilliewinks:** thumbscrews; also known as "pinniwinks".   [6] **fore-crag:** front part.   [7] **Bridge Halls:** market area.

FIGURE 22 *From* News from Scotland *(1591). James interrogates the witches himself.*

are already executed, the rest remain in prison, to receive the doom of judgment at the King's Majesty's will and pleasure.

The said Gillis Duncan also caused Euphemia McCalzean to be apprehended, who conspired and performed the death of her godfather, and who used her art upon a gentleman being one of the lords and justices of the Session,[8] for bearing good will to her daughter: she also caused to be apprehended one Barbara Napier, for bewitching to death Archibald, last Earl of Angus, who languished to death by witchcraft and yet the same was not suspected, but that he died of so strange a disease, as the physician knew not how to cure or remedy the same: but of all other the said witches, these two

---

[8] **Session:** i.e., the law court.

last before recited, were reputed for as civil honest women as any that dwelled within the city of Edinburgh, before they were apprehended. Many other besides were taken dwelling in Leith, who are detained in prison, until his Majesty's further will and pleasure be known: of whose wicked doings you shall particularly hear, which was as followeth:

This aforesaid Agnes Sampson which was the elder witch, was taken and brought to Holyrood House[9] before the King's Majesty and sundry other of the nobility of Scotland, where she was straitly[10] examined, but all the persuasions which the King's Majesty used to her with the rest of his council, might not provoke or induce her to confess any thing, but stood stiffly in the denial of all that was laid to her charge: whereupon they caused her to be conveyed away to prison, there to receive such torture as hath been lately provided for witches in that country: and forasmuch as by due examination of witchcraft and witches in Scotland, it hath lately been found that the Devil doth generally mark them with a privy mark, by reason the witches have confessed themselves, that the Devil doth lick them with his tongue in some privy part of their body, before he doth receive them to be his servants, which mark commonly is given them under the hair in some part of their body, whereby it may not easily be found out or seen, although they be searched: and generally so long as the mark is not seen to those which search them, so long the parties that hath the mark will never confess anything. Therefore by special commandment this Agnes Sampson had all her hair shaven off, in each part of her body, and her head thrawen[11] with a rope according to the custom of that country, being a pain most grievous, which she continued almost an hour, during which time she would not confess any thing until the Devil's mark was found upon her privities,[12] then she immediately confessed whatsoever was demanded of her, and justifying those persons aforesaid to be notorious witches.

Item, the said Agnes Tompson was after brought again before the King's Majesty and his council, and being examined of the meetings and detestable dealings of those witches, she confessed that upon the night of All Hallow's Even[13] last, she was accompanied as well with the persons aforesaid, as also with a great many other witches, to the number of two hundred: and that all they together went by sea each one in a riddle or sieve[14] and went in the same very substantially with flagons[15] of wine making merry and drinking by the way in the same riddles or sieves, to the Kirk[16] of North Berwick in

---

[9] **Holyrood House**: the royal palace in Edinburgh.   [10] **straitly**: strictly, rigidly.   [11] **thrawen**: twisted.   [12] **privities**: genitals.   [13] **All Hallow's Even**: Halloween (October 31).   [14] **riddle or sieve**: a "riddle" is a coarse-meshed utensil that separates chaff from corn, sand from gravel, etc.; a "sieve" has the same function, but is more finely meshed. Sailing in a sieve was a traditional impossible task overcome by a witch's powers.   [15] **flagons**: large bottles.   [16] **Kirk**: church.

Lothian, and that after they had landed, took hands on the land and danced this reel or short dance, singing all with one voice.

Commer[17] go ye before, commer go ye,
If ye will not go before, commer let me.

At which time she confessed, that this Gillis Duncan did go before them playing this reel or dance upon a small trump, called a Jew's trump,[18] until they entered into the Kirk of North Berwick.

These confessions made the King in a wonderful admiration, and sent for the said Gillis Duncan, who upon the like trump did play the said dance before the King's Majesty, who in respect of the strangeness of these matters, took great delight to be present at their examinations.

Item, the said Agnes Tompson confessed that the Devil being then at North Berwick Kirk attending their coming in the habit or likeness of a man, and seeing that they tarried over long, he at their coming enjoined them all to a penance, which was, that they should kiss his buttocks, in sign of duty to him: which being put over the pulpit bare, every one did as he had enjoined them: and having made his ungodly exhortations, wherein he did greatly inveigh against the King of Scotland, he received their oaths for their good and true service towards him, and departed: which done, they returned to sea, and so home again.

At which time the witches demanded of the Devil why he did bear such hatred to the King, who answered, by reason the King is the greatest enemy he hath in the world: all which their confessions and depositions are still extant upon record.

Item, the said Agnes Sampson confessed before the King's Majesty sundry things which were so miraculous and strange, as that his Majesty said they were all extreme liars, whereat she answered, "she would not wish his Majesty to suppose her words to be false, but rather to believe them, in that she would discover such matter unto him as his Majesty should not any way doubt of."

And thereupon taking his Majesty a little aside, she declared unto him the very words which passed between the King's Majesty and his Queen at Oslo in Norway the first night of their marriage, with their answer each to other: whereat the King's Majesty wondered greatly, and swore by the living God, that he believed that all the Devils in hell could not have discovered the same: acknowledging her words to be most true, and therefore gave the more credit to the rest which is before declared.

---

[17] **Commer:** one who comes, visitor.   [18] **Jew's trump:** a small musical instrument with a metal frame and projecting steel tongue that is held between the teeth when played; also known as a Jew's harp.

Touching this Agnes Tompson, she is the only woman, who by the Devil's persuasion should have intended and put in execution the King's Majesty's death in this manner.

She confessed that she took a black toad, and did hang the same up by the heels, three days, and collected and gathered the venom as it dropped and fell from it in an oyster shell, and kept the same venom close covered, until she should obtain any part or piece of foul linen cloth, that had appertained to the King's Majesty, as shirt, handkerchief, napkin or any other thing[19] which she practised to obtain by means of one John Kerrs, who being attendant in his Majesty's chamber, desired him for old acquaintance between them, to help her to one or a piece of such a cloth as is aforesaid, which thing the said John Kerrs denied to help her to, saying he could not help her to it.

And the said Agnes Tompson by her depositions since her apprehension saith, that if she had obtained any one piece of linen cloth which the King had worn and fouled,[20] she had bewitched him to death, and put him to such extraordinary pains, as if he had been lying upon sharp thorns and ends of needles.

Moreover she confessed that at the time when his Majesty was in Denmark, she being accompanied with the parties before specially named, took a cat and christened it, and afterward bound to each part of that cat, the chiefest parts of a dead man, and several joints of his body, and that in the night following the said cat was conveyed into the midst of the sea by all these witches sailing in their riddles or sieves as is aforesaid, and so left the said cat right before the town of Leith in Scotland: this done, there did arise such a tempest in the sea, as a greater hath not been seen: which tempest was the cause of the perishing of a boat or vessel coming over from the town of Burnt Island to the town of Leith, wherein was sundry jewels and rich gifts, which should have been presented to the now Queen of Scotland, at her Majesty's coming to Leith.

Again it is confessed, that the said christened cat was the cause that the King's Majesty's ship at his coming forth of Denmark, had a contrary wind to the rest of his ships then being in his company, which thing was most strange and true, as the King's Majesty acknowledgeth, for when the rest of the ships had a fair and good wind, then was the wind contrary and altogether against his Majesty: and further the said witch declared, that his Majesty had never come safely from the sea, if his faith had not prevailed above their intentions.

[19] **other thing**: as in voodoo, objects close to a person were thought to be equivalent to the person, and hence whatever was done to the object would be felt by the person. [20] **fouled**: gotten dirty.

Moreover the said witches being demanded how the Devil would use them when he was in their company, they confessed that when the Devil did receive them for his servants, and that they had vowed themselves unto him, then he would carnally use them, albeit to their little pleasure, in respect of his cold nature: and would do the like at sundry other times.

As touching the aforesaid Doctor Fian, alias John Cunningham, the examination of his acts since his apprehension, declareth the great subtlety of the devil, and therefore maketh things to appear the more miraculous: for being apprehended by the accusation of the said Gillis Duncan aforesaid, who confessed he was their register, and that there was not one man suffered to come to the Devil's readings but only he, the said doctor was taken and imprisoned, and used with the accustomed pain, provided for those offenses, inflicted upon the rest as is aforesaid.

First by thrawing of his head with a rope, whereat he would confess nothing.

Secondly, he was persuaded by fair means to confess his follies, but that would prevail as little.

Lastly he was put to the most severe and cruel pain in the world, called the boots,[21] who after he had received three strokes, being inquired if he would confess his damnable acts and wicked life, his tongue would not serve him to speak, in respect whereof the rest of the witches willed to search his tongue, under which was found two pins thrust up into the head, whereupon the witches did say, "Now is the charm stinted," and showed that those charmed pins were the cause he could not confess anything: then he was immediately released of the boots, brought before the King, his confession was taken, and his own hand willingly set thereunto, which contained as followeth:

First, that at the general meetings of those witches, he was always present: that he was clerk to all those that were in subjection to the Devil's service, bearing the name of witches, that always he did take their oaths for their true service to the Devil, and that he wrote for them such matters as the Devil still pleased to command him.

Item, he confessed that by his witchcraft he did bewitch a gentleman dwelling near to the Saltpans, where the said doctor kept school, only for being enamored of a gentlewoman whom he loved himself: by means of which his sorcery, witchcraft, and devilish practises, he caused the said gentleman that once in 24 hours he fell into a lunacy and madness, and so continued one whole hour together, and for the verity of the same, he caused

---

[21] **boots**: wooden or metal "boots," into which wedges were hammered, thus crushing the feet and lower legs of the victim.

the gentleman to be brought before the King's Majesty, which was upon the 24th day of December last, and being in his Majesty's chamber, suddenly he gave a great screetch and fell into a madness, sometime bending himself, and sometime capering so directly up, that his head did touch the ceiling of the chamber, to the great admiration of his Majesty and others then present: so that all the gentlemen in the Chamber were not able to hold him, until they called in more help, who together bound him hand and foot: and suffering the said gentleman to lie still until his fury were past, he within an hour came again to himself, when being demanded of the King's Majesty what he saw or did all that while, answered that he had been in a sound sleep.

Item, the said doctor did also confess that he had used means sundry times to obtain his purpose and wicked intent of the same gentlewoman, and seeing himself disappointed of his intention, he determined by all ways he might to obtain the same, trusting by conjuring, witchcraft and sorcery to obtain it in this manner.

It happened this gentlewoman being unmarried, had a brother who went to school with the said doctor, and calling his scholar to him, demanded if he did lie with his sister, who answered he did, by means whereof he thought to obtain his purpose, and therefore secretly promised to teach him without stripes,[22] so he would obtain for him three hairs of his sister's privities at such time as he should spy best occasion for it: which the youth promised faithfully to perform, and vowed speedily to put it in practise, taking a piece of conjured paper of his master to lap[23] them in when he had gotten them: and thereupon the boy practised nightly to obtain his master's purpose, especially when his sister was asleep.

But God who knoweth the secrets of all hearts, and revealeth all wicked and ungodly practises, would not suffer the intents of this devilish doctor to come to that purpose which he supposed it would, and therefore to declare that he was heavily offended with his wicked intent, did so work by the gentlewoman's own means, that in the end the same was discovered and brought to light: for she being one night asleep, and her brother in bed with her, suddenly cried out to her mother, declaring that her brother would not suffer her to sleep, whereupon her mother having a quick capacity, did vehemently suspect Doctor Fian's intention, by reason she was a witch of herself, and therefore presently arose, and was very inquisitive of the boy to understand his intent, and the better to know the same, did beat him with sundry stripes, whereby he discovered the truth unto her.

The mother therefore being well practised in witchcraft, did think it most convenient to meet with the doctor in his own art, and thereupon took

---

[22] **stripes**: strokes, i.e. beating him. [23] **lap**: wrap.

the paper from the boy, wherein he should have put the same hairs, and went to a young heifer which never had born calf nor gone to the bull, and with a pair of shears, clipped off three hairs from the udder of the cow, and wrapped them in the same paper, which she again delivered to the boy, then willing him to give the same to his said Master, which he immediately did.

The schoolmaster so soon as he had received them, thinking them indeed to be the maid's hairs, went straight and wrought his art upon them: But the doctor had no sooner done his intent to them, but presently the heifer or cow whose hairs they were indeed, came unto the door of the church wherein the schoolmaster was, into the which the heifer went, and made towards the schoolmaster, leaping and dancing upon him, and following him forth of the church and to what place soever he went, to the great admiration of all the townsmen of Saltpans, and many other who did behold the same.

The report whereof made all men imagine that he did work it by the Devil, without whom it could never have been so sufficiently effected: and thereupon, the name of the said Doctor Fian (who was but a very young man) began to grow so common among the people of Scotland, that he was secretly nominated for a notable conjurer. All which although in the beginning he denied, and would not confess, yet having felt the pain of the boots (and the charm stinted,[24] as aforesaid) he confessed all the aforesaid to be most true, without producing any witnesses to justify the same, and thereupon before the King's Majesty he subscribed the said confessions with his own hand, which for truth remaineth upon record in Scotland.

After that the depositions and examinations of the said Doctor Fian *alias* Cunningham was taken, as already is declared, with his own hand willingly set thereunto, he was by the master of the prison committed to ward, and appointed to a chamber by himself, where forsaking his wicked ways, acknowledging his most ungodly life, showing that he had too much followed the allurements and enticements of Satan, and fondly practised his conclusions by conjuring, witchcraft, enchantment, sorcery, and such like, he renounced the devil and all his wicked works, vowed to lead the life of a Christian, and seemed newly connected towards God.

The morrow after, upon conference had with him, he granted that the devil had appeared unto him in the night before, apparelled all in black, with a white wand in his hand, and that the Devil demanded of him if he would continue his faithful service, according to his first oath and promise made to that effect. Whom (as he then said) he utterly renounced to his face, and said unto him in this manner, "Avoid Satan, avoid, for I have listened too much unto thee, and by the same thou hast undone me, in respect whereof I

---

[24] **stinted:** ended.

FIGURE 23 *From* News from Scotland *(1591). Scenes from Doctor Fian's life.*

utterly forsake thee." To whom the Devil answered, "That once ere thou die thou shalt be mine." And with that (as he said) the Devil brake the white wand, and immediately vanished forth of his sight.

Thus all the day this Doctor Fian continued very solitary, and seemed to have care of his own soul, and would call upon God, showing himself penitent for his wicked life, nevertheless the same night he found such means, that he stole the key of the prison door and chamber in the which he was, which in the night he opened and fled away to the Saltpans, where he was always resident, and first apprehended. Of whose sudden departure when the King's Majesty had intelligence, he presently commanded diligent inquiry to be made for his apprehension, and for the better effecting thereof, he sent public proclamations into all parts of his land to the same effect. By means of whose hot and hard pursuit, he was again taken and brought to prison, and then being called before the King's Highness, he was reexamined as well touching his departure, as also touching all that had before happened.

But this doctor, notwithstanding that his own confession appeareth remaining in record under his own handwriting, and the same thereunto fixed in the presence of the King's Majesty and sundry of his council, yet did he utterly deny the same.

Whereupon the King's Majesty perceiving his stubborn willfulness, conceived and imagined that in the time of his absence he had entered into new conference and league with the Devil his master, and that he had been again newly marked, for the which he was narrowly searched, but it could not in any wise be found, yet for more trial of him to make him confess, he was commanded to have a most strange torment which was done in this manner following.

His nails upon all his fingers were riven[25] and pulled off with an instrument called in Scottish a Turkas,[26] which in England we call a pair of pincers, and under every nail there was thrust in two needles over even up to the heads. At all which torments notwithstanding the doctor never shrunk any whit, neither would he then confess it the sooner for all the tortures inflicted upon him.

Then was he with all convenient speed, by commandment, conveyed again to the torment of the boots, wherein he continued a long time, and did abide so many blows in them, that his legs were crushed and beaten together as small as might be, and the bones and flesh so bruised, that the blood and marrow spouted forth in great abundance, whereby they were made unserviceable forever. And notwithstanding all these grievous pains and cruel torments he would not confess any thing, so deeply had the Devil entered into his heart, that he utterly denied all that which he had before avouched, and would say nothing thereunto but this, that what he had done and said before, was only done and said for fear of pains which he had endured.

Upon great consideration therefore taken by the King's Majesty and his council, as well for the due execution of justice upon such detestable malefactors, as also for example sake, to remain a terror to all others hereafter, that shall attempt to deal in the like wicked and ungodly actions, as witchcraft, sorcery, conjuration, and such like, the said Doctor Fian was soon after arraigned, condemned, and adjudged by the law to die, and then to be burned according to the law of that land, provided in that behalf. Whereupon he was put into a cart, and being first strangled, he was immediately put into a great fire, being ready provided for that purpose, and there burned in the Castle Hill of Edinburgh on a Saturday in the end of January last past 1591.

[25] **riven:** split, torn apart. [26] **Turkas:** pincers; the name may derive from the ethnic stereotype of the Turks, legendary in Elizabethan England for their cruelty.

The rest of the witches which are not yet executed, remain in prison, till further trial, and knowledge of his Majesty's pleasure.[27]

This strange discourse before recited, may perhaps give some occasion of doubt to such as shall happen to read the same, and thereby conjecture that the King's Majesty would not hazard himself in the presence of such notorious witches, lest thereby might have ensued great danger to his person and the general state of the land, which thing in truth might well have been feared. But to answer generally to such, let this suffice: that first it is well known that the King is the child and servant of God, and they but servants to the Devil, he is the Lord's anointed, and they but vessels of God's wrath: he is a true Christian, and trusteth in God, they worse than infidels, for they only trust in the Devil, who daily serve them, till he have brought them to utter destruction. But hereby it seemeth that his Highness carried a magnanimous and undaunted mind, not feared with their enchantments, but resolute in this, that so long as God is with him, he feareth not who is against him. And truly the whole scope of this treatise doth so plainly lay open the wonderful providence of the Almighty, that if he had not been defended by His omnipotence and power, his Highness had never returned alive in his voyage from Denmark, so that there is no doubt but God would as well defend him on the land as on the sea, where they pretended their damnable practice.

FINIS.

[27] According to the trial records, all the other accused witches, except Barbara Napier, were burned to death.

➔ KING JAMES I

From Daemonology, In Form of a Dialogue   *1597*

I. FROM THE PREFACE

The fearful abounding at this time in this country, of these detestable slaves of the Devil, the witches or enchanters, hath moved me (beloved reader) to dispatch in post, this following treatise of mine, not in any wise (as I protest) to serve for a show of my learning and ingine,[1] but only (moved of conscience) to press thereby, so far as I can, to resolve the doubting hearts of many; both

[1] **ingine**: genius, intellect.

King James VI, *Daemonology, In Form of a Dialogue* (Edinburgh, 1597) A2–A2v, D3v–D4, G2–G2v, G3–G4, H1v, K4–K4v, L2, L3–L3v.

that such assaults of Satan are most certainly practiced, and that the instruments thereof, merits most severely to be punished: against the damnable opinions of two principally in our age, whereof the one called Scot, an Englishman, is not ashamed in public print to deny, that there can be such a thing as witchcraft. . . . The other called Wierus,[2] a German physician, sets out a public apology for all these craftsfolks, whereby, procuring for their impunity, he plainly betrays himself to have been one of that profession.

II. MIRACLES

EPISTEMON:[3]   For that is the difference betwixt God's miracles and the Devil's, God is a creator, what He makes appear in miracle, it is so in effect. As Moses' rod being casten down, was no doubt turned in a natural serpent: whereas the Devil (as God's ape) counterfeiting that by his magicians, made their wands to appear so, only to men's outward senses.

III. WOMEN AS WITCHES

PHILOMATHES: What can be the cause that there are twenty women given to that craft, where there is one man?

EPISTEMON: The reason is easy, for as that sex is frailer than man is, so is it easier to be entrapped in these gross snares of the Devil, as was over well proved to be true, by the serpents' deceiving of Eve at the beginning.

IV. THE POWERS OF WITCHES

EPISTEMON: They can make men or women to love or hate other. . . . They can lay the sickness of one upon another. . . . They can be-witch and take the life of men or women, by roasting of the pictures. . . . They can raise storms and tempests in the air, either upon sea or land, though not universally, but in such a particular place and prescribed bounds, as God will permit them so to trouble. . . . They can make folks to become frantic or manic. . . . They can make spirits either to follow and trouble persons, or haunt certain houses, and affray[4] oftentimes the inhabitants. . . . And

---

[2] **Wierus**: Johan Weyer (1515–1588) — the Continental predecessor of Reginald Scot — author of *De praestigiis daemonum* (1563), an encyclopedic compendium of witchcraft lore, which exposes superstition and deceit, but also credits many beliefs that Scot, the greater skeptic, rejected: hence James's reference to Wierus as parallel to Scot but still "one of that profession" himself. Scot made direct use of Wierus's book.   [3] **Epistemon**: as in most dialogues, one speaker (here, Philomathes) represents the reasonable (but mistaken) point of view, asking questions that the other speaker (Epistemon), representing the author's point of view, easily and completely answers.   [4] **affray**: frighten.

likewise they can make some to be possessed with spirits, and so to become very demoniacs.

. . . .

PHILOMATHES: But what is their power against the magistrate?

EPISTEMON: Less or greater, according as he deals with them. For if he be slothful towards them, God is very able to make them instruments to waken and punish his sloth. But if he be the contrary, he according to the just law of God, and allowable law of all nations, will be diligent in examining and punishing of them: God will not permit their master to trouble or hinder so good a work.

IV. On Those Possessed

EPISTEMON: It is known so many of them to be counterfeit, which while the [Catholic] clergy invents for confirming of their rotten religion.[5] The next is, that by experience we find that few, who are possessed indeed, are fully cured by them, but rather the Devil is content to release the bodily hurting of them, for a short space, thereby to obtain the perpetual hurt of the souls of so many that by these false miracles may be induced or confirmed in the profession of that erroneous religion.

V. On Prophecy

PHILOMATHES: But what say ye to their fore-telling the death of sundry persons, whom they allege to hath seen in these places? That is, a sooth-dream (as they say) since they see it walking.

EPISTEMON: I think that either they have not been sharply enough examined, that gave so blunt a reason for their prophecy, or otherways, I think it likewise as possible that the Devil may prophesy to them when he deceives their imaginations in that sort, as well as when he plainly speaks unto them at other times for their prophesying, is but by a kind of vision, as it were, wherein he commonly counterfeits God.

V. On the Punishment of Witches

PHILOMATHES: What form of punishment think ye merits these magicians and witches? For I see that ye account them to be all alike guilty?

---

[5] **rotten religion:** James was suspicious of most claims of the power of exorcism, as here, even before he turned more skeptical about witchcraft beliefs in general. Like most Protestant writers, he invariably associated fraudulence and superstition with Catholic practices.

EPISTEMON: They ought to be put to death according to the law of God, the civil and imperial law, and municipal law of all Christian nations.

PHILOMATHES: But what kind of death, I pray you?

EPISTEMON: It is commonly used by fire, but that is an indifferent thing to be used in every country, according to the law or custom thereof.

PHILOMATHES: But ought no sex, age nor rank to be exempted?

EPISTEMON: None at all (being so used by the lawful magistrate), for it is the highest point of idolatry, wherein no exception is admitted by the law of God.

PHILOMATHES: Then bairns[6] may not be spared?

EPISTEMON: Yea, not a hair the less of my conclusion. For they are not that capable of reason as to practice such things. And for any being in company and not revealing thereof, their less and ignorant age will no doubt excuse them. . . . But in the end to spare the life [of an adult], and not to strike when God bids strike, and so severely punish in so odious a fault and treason against God, it is not only unlawful, but doubtless no less sin in that magistrate.

[6] **bairns:** children.

→ # An Act against Conjuration, Witchcraft, and Dealing with Evil and Wicked Spirits   *1604*

Be it enacted by the King our sovereign Lord, the Lords spiritual and temporal, and the Commons in this present Parliament assembled, and by the authority of the same, That the Statute made in the fifth year of the reign of our late sovereign lady of most famous and happy memory Queen Elizabeth, entitled "An Act against Conjurations, Enchantments and Witchcrafts,"[1] be from the Feast of St. Michael the Archangel next coming,[2] for and concerning all offences to be committed after the same Feast, utterly repealed. And for the better restraining the said offences, and more severe punishing the same, be it further enacted by the authority aforesaid, That if any person or persons, after the said Feast of St. Michael the Archangel next coming, shall use, practise, or exercise any invocation or conjuration of any

[1] *5 Eliz., c.16* (1563).   [2] **Feast . . . coming:** i.e., the next September 29 (many documents were dated by reference to saint's days or other holidays).

An Act against Conjuration, Witchcraft, and dealing with evil and wicked Spirits. I Jac. I, c.12 [in the first year in the reign of James I, chapter 12] (London, 1604).

evil and wicked spirit, or shall consult, covenant with, entertain, employ, feed, or reward any evil and wicked spirit to or for any intent or purpose; or take up any dead man, woman, or child out of his, her, or their grave, or any other place where the dead body resteth, or the skin, bone, or any other part of any dead person, to be employed or used in any manner of witchcraft, sorcery, charm, or enchantment; or shall use, practise, or exercise any witchcraft, enchantment, charm, or sorcery, whereby any person shall be killed, destroyed, wasted, consumed, pined, or lamed in his or her body, or any part thereof; that then every such offender or offenders, their aiders, abetters and counsellors, being of any [of] the said offences duly and lawfully convicted and attainted, shall suffer pains of death as a felon or felons, and shall lose the privilege and benefit of clergy and sanctuary.

And further, to the intent that all manner of practise, use, or exercise of witchcraft, enchantment, charm, or sorcery, should be from henceforth utterly avoided, abolished and taken away, Be it enacted by the authority of this present Parliament, That if any person or persons shall, from and after the said Feast of St. Michael the Archangel next coming, take upon him or them by witchcraft, enchantment, charm, or sorcery, to tell or declare in what place any treasure of gold or silver should or might be found or had, in the earth or other secret places, or where goods or things lost or stolen should be found or become; and to the intent to provoke any person to unlawful love, or where any chattel or goods of any person shall be destroyed, wasted, or impaired, or to hurt or destroy any person in his or her body, although the same be not effected and done; that then all and every such person and persons so offending, and being thereof lawfully convicted, shall for the said offence suffer imprisonment by the space of one whole year, without bail or mainprise,[3] and once in every quarter of the said year, shall in some market town, upon the market day, or at such time as any fair shall be kept there, stand openly upon the pillory[4] by the space of six hours, and there shall openly confess his or her error and offence. And if any person or persons being once convicted of the same offence as is aforesaid, do eftsoons[5] perpetrate and commit the like offence, that then every such offender, being of any the said offences the second time lawfully and duly convicted and attainted[6] as is aforesaid, shall suffer pains of death as a felon or felons, and shall lose the benefit and privilege of clergy and sanctuary. Saving to the wife of such person as shall offend in any thing contrary to

---

[3] **mainprise:** suretyship; responsibility or obligation of one person undertaken on behalf of another. [4] **pillory:** a wooden framework on a post, with holes for the head and hands, in which offenders were locked to be exposed to public scorn as punishment. [5] **eftsoons:** again, soon after. [6] **attainted:** proven guilty.

this Act, her title of dower; and also to the heir and successor of every such person, his or their titles of inheritance, succession and other rights, as though no such attainder[7] of the ancestor or predecessor had been made. Provided always, that if the offender in any [of] the cases aforesaid shall happen to be a peer of the realm,[8] then his trial therein to be had by his peers, as it is used in cases of felony or treason and not otherwise.

[7] **attainder:** the process of attainting (see note 6).   [8] **peer . . . realm:** i.e., a member of the House of Lords.

Prophecy

In early modern England, prophecy was not inherently something wicked, or necessarily associated with witchcraft; indeed, prophecy is an essential aspect of Biblical history, as William Perkins indicates in the excerpt below. But just as miracles were said to have ceased with the coming of Christ, so too were prophecies supposed to have ceased, as Reginald Scot argues (see p. 337). Thus, the prophecies made in the present time were understood either as generated by the devil (usually through witches), or were lucky guesses by ordinary men, or were simply a species of fraud perpetrated upon the gullible. *True* prophecy, the real foreknowledge of things to come, was a power reserved to God alone.

For many educated men of the time, a belief in prophecy was a form of popular superstition. The historian John Major recounted a supposed prophecy that came true, then remarked, "Our writers assure us that Thomas often foretold this thing and the other, and the common people throughout Britain give no little credence to such stories, which for the most part — and indeed they merit nothing else — I smile at. For that such persons foretold things purely contingent before they came to pass I cannot admit; and if only they use a sufficient obscurity of language, the uninstructed vulgar will twist a meaning out of it somehow in the direction that best pleases them" (190–91). In the essays excerpted below, two of the most powerful thinkers of the early modern period, Michel de Montaigne and Francis Bacon, make similarly skeptical arguments, with varying degrees of contempt for those who believe in prophecies.

But clearly many people, whether educated or not, did believe in prophecies, or at least understood them to be potentially dangerous. William Perkins (1558–1602), the distinguished and extremely well-educated Puritan theologian, wrote his *Discourse* sometime in the 1590s (it was published after his death, in 1608). His purpose was to argue against those (such as Reginald Scot) who claimed that witchcraft was nothing more than an illusion and that witches were only deluded or fraudulent people. Perkins meticulously responds to these arguments, pointing out in detail how prophecy stems from the Devil, through witches; in his account, the Devil has many advantages over mortals, and so, to less knowledgeable men, only *seems* to know the future. But even ordinary men, if they are highly observant, can make educated guesses which virtually amount to prophecies. The Devil's "fourth way" of being able to prophesy seems particularly relevant to *Macbeth:* "having therefore first brought into the mind of man a resolution to do some evil, he [the devil] goes and reveals it to the witch, and by force of persuasion upon the party tempted, he frames the action intended to the time foretold."

More than infecting popular gullibility, however, prophecies represented another kind of danger, one which the government of Elizabeth I officially addressed in 1563 (following similar acts by Henry VIII and Edward VI), in the Parliamentary Act against prophecies (see below). Prophecies were frequently associated with political rebellion, as this *Act* makes clear. There was a very long tradition of political prophecy, dating back to Geoffrey of Monmouth's *The Book of Merlin* in the twelfth century.[1] The so-called Galfridian (the adjectival form of Geoffrey) prophecy typically used animal names or types in a thinly-veiled allegorical narrative. As the 1563 act indicates, prophecies occurred in many different forms, both written and oral; they seem to have been primarily an aspect of what we would today call popular culture, though there are many sophisticated written collections. In 1603, for example, *The Whole Prophecy of Scotland* was published, with prophecies attributed to such (mostly legendary) figures as Merlin, Bede, Thomas the Rymer, Sibylla, and so forth; many deal with important events in Scottish history. There are many similar collections in England and elsewhere. The Fool in *King Lear* offers such a prophecy at the end of act 3, scene 2, in which some of the elements have already come true, while the rest will never come true (as in "When every case in law is right"); the result in both cases is politically disastrous — "Then shall the realm of Albion / Come to great confusion" — but then it already is. In an ironic anachronism, the Fool says "This prophecy Merlin shall make, for I live before his time" (3.2.81–96).

Prophecy's link to sedition is evident in the case of Henry Howard, the earl of Northampton, who wrote his *Defensative against the Poison of Supposed Prophecies* (excerpted below) in part to analyze how two members of his own family, including his son, had been executed, and in part to dissociate

---

[1] See Taylor, Thomas, and Dobin on the prophetic tradition in England.

himself from similar suspicions (Thomas 405). A few years later, John Harvey published his *A Discursive Problem Concerning Prophecies* (1588) in part to address the "terrible threatenings, and menaces, peremptorily denounced against the kingdoms and states of the world, this present famous year, 1588, supposed the great, wonderful, and fatal year of our age" (title page). The year of the Spanish Armada, 1588 was one of those special dates, like 1603, which called forth a host of apocalyptic prophecies (as the end of the second millenium is doing at present). Harvey is apoplectic in describing the gullibility of a populace that listens to rumors and prophecies:

> Must we resort to wizards, or soothsayers, or sorcerers, or conjurors, or witches, or gypsies, or shepherds, or any like private prophets of basest condition, and silliest[2] intelligence, in highest occurrences of state [?] . . . Were it not a needless, or bootless labor, to make a special analysis, either of their abcedary[3] and alphabetical spells, or of their characteristical and polygraphical subtleties, or of their acrostic and anagrammatic devices, or of their steganographical[4] and hieroglyphical mysteries, or of their hyperbolical metaphors, fantastical allegories, and heraldical illusions, or of their ambiguous equivocations, interdeux[5] amphibologies[6] and enigmatical riddles, or finally of any their other colorable[7] glosses, and hypocritical subornations,[8] in some like prestigiatory[9] and sophistical vein?

Harvey goes on to ask: can anyone imagine a more "ludicrous or ridiculous spectacle . . . than to see a wretched company of such woeful wights and miserable creatures, scarcely worth the ground they tread upon, and hardly deserving their daily bread, suddenly presented on a theater, or comical stage, in their threadbare liveries and stale gaberdines, of antique shape, and forlorn fashion? Is not their whole habit and gesture too notorious?" (64–66). The false spectacle they present is, not surprisingly, linked to the fabrications and illusions of the theater, as claims of demonic possession often were; perhaps Harvey is even thinking of a specific play. Harvey's objection is partly class-based, too, as he associates this power with the vulgar and poor. A large final section of his work is devoted specifically to the inflammatory prophecies circulated in 1588.

Tudor and Stuart governments opposed the circulation of prophecies because they were believed to cause or at least exacerbate political rebellion.

---

[2] **silliest**: most simple, foolish.   [3] **abcedary**: a table or book containing the alphabet.   [4] **steganographical**: the art of secret writing; cryptography.   [5] **interdeux**: i.e., just between two people in the know.   [6] **amphibologies**: ambiguous or equivocal words.   [7] **colorable**: leading to deceit.   [8] **subornations**: inducing a person to commit an evil act.   [9] **prestigiatory**: deceptive, deluding.

As Keith Thomas has shown, however, political prophecies were usually employed *after* the fact of political radicalism, as a means of justification: "at the heart of the belief in prophecies," he notes, "there lay an urge to believe that even the most revolutionary doings of contemporaries had been foreseen by the sages of the past. For what these predictions did was to demonstrate that there was a link between contemporary aspirations and those of remote antiquity. Their function was to persuade men that some proposed change was not so radical that it had not been foreseen by their ancestors. This had the effect of disguising any essentially revolutionary step by concealing it under the sanction of past approval" (423). There was, as might be expected, a huge increase in prophetic activities, particularly by women, in the period just before and then during the Civil War.[10]

When prophecies served the monarch's interests, of course, they were encouraged; thus the coming of King James to the English throne was interpreted as the fulfillment of virtually every Scottish prophecy, and therefore mysteriously inevitable. When James and his court journeyed to Oxford and witnessed an academic play by Matthew Gwinn on August 29, 1605, a few months before the Gunpowder Plot and the writing of *Macbeth*, they were greeted after the play with a brief, staged prophecy that fused James's claims of succession from Banquo and his (and his offspring's) destined success in the future, while anticipating the prophecies of Shakespeare's witches in *Macbeth*. "Three (as it were) Sibyls" greeted the monarch "as if from a wood":

FIRST SIBYL: Fame says the fatal Sisters once foretold
     Power without end, great Monarch, to thy stock.
     One greeted Banquo, proud Lochaber's Thane:
     Not to thee Banquo, but to thy descendants
     Eternal rule was promised by immortals,
     Hid in a glade as Banquo left the Court.
     We three same Fates so chant to thee and thine
     As, watched by all, from fields thou near'st the City;
     And thus we greet thee: Hail, whom Scotland serves!
SECOND SIBYL: Whom England, hail!
THIRD SIBYL: Whom Ireland serves, all hail!
FIRST SIBYL: Whom France gives titles, lands besides, all hail!
SECOND SIBYL: Hail, whom divided Britain join'st in one!
THIRD SIBYL: Hail, mighty Lord of Britain, Ireland, France!

---

[10] As Thomas notes, "the prominence of women among the religious prophets of this period is partly explained by the fact that . . . recourse to prophecy was the only means by which most women could hope to disseminate their opinions on public events" (138).

FIRST SIBYL: Hail Anne, of Kings the mother, sister, wife
   And daughter too!
SECOND SIBYL: Hail Henry, Prince and Heir![11]
THIRD SIBYL: Duke Charles, and lovely Polish princess, hail![12]
FIRST SIBYL: We set no times nor limits to the fates;
   In worldly rule fame's goal may be the stars.
   Thou dost restore the fourfold glory of Canute,[13]
   Great ancestor, his crowns and royal thrones.
   Nor shall we bear wars, slaughter, anxious hearts,
   Or fury 'gainst ourselves; but we'll grow warm
   With love and peace through prompting,

the speaker continues, of the spirit of the founder of St. John's College, the site of the prophecy.[14] The monarchy not only tolerated prophecies such as Gwinn's, but rewarded them.

The widespread skepticism about prophecies, and their appropriation for various political ends, might seem to suggest equal limitations in literature, but such is not the case. In drama, particularly, prophecies invariably come true: Oedipus *will* sleep with his mother and murder his father; the English civil wars, as Carlisle prophesies in Shakespeare's *Richard II*, *will* occur as a result of Richard's deposition; the oracle's prediction in *The Winter's Tale* *will* come true. Many, perhaps most, prophecies come in the form of a riddle, one whose solution is clear to the audience but obscure to the protagonist involved; but of the fulfillment of the prophecy, there is rarely any doubt at all. Hence the truth of the witches' prophecies in *Macbeth* is quickly demonstrated — Macbeth has already been named Thane of Cawdor and does not know it yet. Banquo's reaction to the news — "What, can the devil speak true?" (1.3.107) — is exactly the question often debated, and he provides one of the possible answers himself a few lines later: "oftentimes to win us to our harm / The instruments of darkness tell us truths, / Win us with honest trifles, to betray's / In deepest consequence" (123–26). As Bacon and Montaigne noted, one believes what one wants, however, and Macbeth's misreading of the second set of prophecies comes to a spectacular

---

[11] Prince Henry, James's oldest son, who would die in 1612.

[12] Prince Charles, later King Charles I, James's second son and successor. The "Polish princess" has not been identified.

[13] **Canute:** the King of England (and Denmark) when Macbeth defeated Canute's brother, Sweno of Norway.

[14] The text is quoted from Bullough, in his translation, 7.471. The play's title was *Vertumnus Sive Annus Recurrens* ("Vertumnus [the god of changing seasons], or the Returning Year"). One scholar, H. N. Paul, has argued that Shakespeare must have been present in Oxford with the king's party to hear these speeches, but there is no evidence that he was; the witches' prophecies were of course present in Holinshed's *Chronicles* (see p. 135).

disaster when he learns that Birnam Wood is coming to Dunsinane, and he begins, he says, "To doubt th' equivocation of the fiend / That lies like truth" (5.5.43–44). This reference to equivocation returns us to the earlier section on treason and equivocation (Chapter 3), and we see how, in *Macbeth*, Shakespeare too has associated prophecy with treason and witchcraft.

→ *From* An Act against Fond and Fantastical Prophecies   *1563*

F orasmuch as since the expiration and ending of the statute made in the time of King Edward the Sixth, entitled "An Act against fond and fantastic prophecies," diverse evil disposed persons, inclined to the stirring and moving of factions, seditions and rebellions within this realm, have been the more bold to attempt the like practice in feigning, imagining, inventing and publishing of such fond and fantastical prophecies, as well concerning the Queen's Majesty as diverse honorable personages, gentlemen and others of this realm, as was used and practised before the making of the said statute, to the great disquiet, trouble and peril of the Queen's Majesty, and of this her realm. For remedy whereof: Be it ordained and enacted by the authority of this present Parliament, That if any person or persons, after the first day of May next coming, do advisedly and directly advance, publish and set forth by writing, printing, singing or any other open speech or deed to any person or persons, any fond, fantastical or false prophecy, upon or by the occasion of any arms, fields, beasts, badges or such other like things accustomed in arms, cognizances or signets, or upon or by reason of any time, year or day, name, bloodshed or war to the intent thereby to make any rebellion, insurrection, dissension, loss of life or other disturbance within this realm or [of] other the Queen's dominions — that then every such person being thereof lawfully convicted according to the due course of the laws of this realm, for every such offense shall suffer imprisonment of his body by the space of one year, without bail or mainprise,[1] and shall forfeit for every such offense the sum of ten pounds. And if any such offender do after such conviction eftsoons[2] offend in any of the premises, and be thereof lawfully

---

[1] **mainprise**: suretyship; responsibility or obligation of one person undertaken on behalf of another.   [2] **eftsoons**: again, soon after.

At the Parliament holden at Westminster the xii of January, in the fifth year of the reign of our Sovereign Lady, Elizabeth by the grace of God, of England, France, and Ireland, Queen, defender of the faith etc. To the high pleasure of Almighty God, and the weal public of this Realm, were enacted as followeth (London, 1563), ca. xv (51v–52r).

convicted, as is aforesaid, that then every such offender shall for his second offence and conviction as is aforesaid, suffer imprisonment of his body without bail or mainprise during his life, and shall forfeit all his goods and chattels, reals and personals.[3]

[3] chattels . . . personals: property, real (i.e., land) and personal belongings

HENRY HOWARD

From A Defensative against the Poison of Supposed Prophecies
1583

[Among the seven explanations for the supposed power of prophecy:] the last branch or mean, whereby the contagion of unlawful prophecies is conveyed into the minds of mortal men, is conference with damned spirits or familiars, as commonly we call them. . . .

Where their hands are once laid on, sure hold is had, and the end of that man (as the text itself reporteth) is worse than the beginning. They pry, they watch, they search, they carry, and are ever at our elbow, not only to observe our steps, and how right we tread: but to suggest ungodly counsels in the secrets of our bosom. . . . But how painted, colorable, delicate, or fine soever their abuses be, methinks men should be wiser than to apply their ears, when they know beforehand, or at least may be instructed by most sound authority, that neither Satan nor his angels understand *Ex scientia propria,*[1] what shall come to pass, or know more than is in working at that present when they speak, though men by frailty and by shallowness of sense, be not so well able as they (by their subtlety) to sound the bottom of concealed mysteries. . . . [I]t is impossible to understand, or search out the mighty works of God, and again, future accidents can be revealed by no messenger, much less by these sly pages of Apollo's court,[2] who are as true in these days, when they cover and conceal the poison of their art, and only labor to

[1] **Ex . . . propria:** from their own knowledge.   [2] **these . . . court:** i.e., those contemporary writers who fabricate prophecies.

Henry Howard, *A Defensative against the Poison of Supposed Prophecies: Not hitherto confuted by the pen of any man, which being grounded, either upon the warrant and authority of old painted books, expositions of Dreams, Oracles, Revelations, Invocations of damned spirits, Judicials of Astrology, or any other kind of pretended knowledge whatsoever, De futuris contingentibus: have main causes of great disorder in the commonwealth, and chiefly among the simple and unlearned people: very needful to be published at this time, considering the late offence which grew by most palpable and gross errors in Astrology* (London, 1583) Y1–Y4.

recover credit in the world, as they were in old time, when they bleared and abused all the world with oracles. . . .

I was present myself when diverse gentlemen and noblemen, which undertook to descry the finest sleights that Scotto the Italian[3] was able to play by legerdemain[4] before the Queen: were notwithstanding no less beguiled than the rest, that presumed less upon their own dexterity and skill in those matters. Wherefore if jugglers may cast a veil before our eyes, whose stratagems are in comparison but plain and gross, by how much more fine and nimble may we deem familiars to be, which hover in a cloud and cannot be discerned?

---

[3] **Scotto the Italian:** a skilled Italian actor, juggler, and magician of the sixteenth century; he came to England in 1576 and appeared before Queen Elizabeth and her court. His name became synonymous with clever deceit.   [4] **legerdemain:** sleight of hand, trickery.

→ REGINALD SCOT

From The Discovery of Witchcraft   1584

THAT THE GIFT OF PROPHECY IS CEASED

That witches, nor the woman of Endor, nor yet her familiar or devil can tell what is to come, may plainly appear by the words of the prophet, who saith: "Show what things are to come, and we will say you are gods indeed."[1] According to that which Solomon saith: "Who can tell a man what shall happen [to] him under the sun?" "Marry, that can I" (saith the witch of Endor to Saul).[2] But I will rather believe Paul and Peter, which say, that prophecy is the gift of God, and no worldly thing.[3] . . .

Indeed we read that Samuel could tell where things lost were strayed, etc., but we see that gift also ceased by the coming of Christ, according to the saying of Paul. At sundry times, and in diverse manners, God spake in the old times by our fathers the prophets; [but] in these last days He hath spoken unto us by His son, etc. And therefore I say that gift of prophecy,

---

[1] Isaiah 41:23.   [2] 1 Samuel 28.   [3] 1 Corinthians 12:10; 1 Peter 1:12.

Reginald Scot, *The Discovery of Witchcraft, Wherein the lewd dealing of witches and witchmongers is notably detected, the knavery of conjurors, the impiety of enchanters, the folly of soothsayers, the impudent falsehood of coseners, the infidelity of atheists, the pestilent practices of Pythonists, the curiosity of figurecasters, the vanity of dreamers, the beggerly art of Alchemistry, the abomination of idolatry, the horrible art of poisoning, the virtue and power of natural magic, and all the conveyances of Legerdemain and juggling are deciphered: and many other things opened, which have long lien hidden, howbeit very necessary to be known* (London, 1584), bk. 8, ch. 2, 158–60.

wherewith God in times past endued his people, is also ceased, and counterfeits and coseners[4] are come in their places, according to this saying of Peter: "There were false prophets among the people, even as there shall be false teachers among you, etc."[5] . . .

The words of the prophet Zacariah are plain, touching the ceasing both of the good and bad prophet, to wit: "I will cause the prophets and unclean spirits to depart out of the land, and when any shall yet prophesy, his parents shall say to him, Thou shalt not live, for thou speakest lies in the name of the Lord. And his parents shall thrust him through when he prophesieth," etc. No, no: the foretelling of things to come, is the only work of God, who disposeth all things sweetly, of whose counsel there hath never yet been any man. And to know our labors, the times and moments God hath placed in His own power. . . .

But put the case, that one in our commonwealth should step up and say he were a prophet (as many frantic persons do), who would believe him, or not think rather that he were a lewd[6] person? See the statutes *Elizab.* 5,[7] whether there be not laws made against them, condemning their arrogancy and cosenage: see also the canon laws to the same effect.

---

[4] **coseners**: tricksters, deceivers.   [5] a paraphrase of 2 Peter 2:1.   [6] **lewd**: vulgar; ignorant; wicked.   [7] i.e., the Elizabethan statute against prophecy, excerpted above.

→ WILLIAM PERKINS

From A Discourse of the Damned Art of Witchcraft   *1608*

Divination is a part of witchcraft, whereby men reveal strange things, either past, present, or to come, by the assistance of the devil.

If it be here demanded, how the devil, being a creature, should be able to manifest and bring to light things past, or to foretell things to come, I answer, first generally, that Satan in this particular work, transforms himself into an angel of light, and takes upon him the exercise of these things in an ambitious (though false) imitation of divine revelations and predictions, made and used by God in the times of the prophets and apostles. And this he doth (as much as in him lieth) to obscure the glory of God, and to make himself great in the opinion of ignorant and unbelieving persons. Again, though Satan be but a creature, yet there be sundry ways whereby he is able to divine.

William Perkins, *A Discourse of the Damned Art of Witchcraft; So Far Forth as it is revealed in the Scriptures, and manifested by true experience* (Cambridge, 1608), ch. 3, 56–65.

First, by the Scriptures of the Old and New Testament, wherein are set down sundry prophecies concerning things to come. In the Old Testament are recorded many prophecies concerning the state of God's Church, from the first age of the world, till the coming of Christ. In the New Testament likewise are recorded others, touching the self same thing, from the coming of Christ in the latter days, to the end of the world. Now the devil being acquainted with the history of the Bible, and having attained unto a greater light of knowledge in the prophecies therein contained, than any man hath; by stealing divinations out of them, he is able to tell of many strange things, that may in time fall out in the world, and answerably may show them ere they come to pass. . . .

The second means, whereby the devil is furnished for his purpose, is his own exquisite knowledge of all natural things; as of the influences of the stars, the constitutions of men and other creatures, the kinds, virtues, and operations of plants, roots, herbs, stones, etc. which knowledge of his, goeth many degrees beyond the skill of all men, yea even of those that are most excellent in this kind, as philosophers and physicians. No marvel, therefore, though out of his experience in these and such like, he is able aforehand to give a likely guess at the issues and events of things, which are to him so manifestly apparent in their causes.

A third help and furtherance in this point is his presence in the most places: for some devils are present at all assemblies and meetings, and thereby are acquainted with the consultations and conferences both of princes and people; whereby knowing the drift and purpose of men's minds, when the same is manifested in their speeches and deliberations, they are the fitter to foretell many things, which men ordinarily cannot do. And hence it is apparent, how witches may know what is done in other countries, and whether one nation intends war against another, namely, by Satan's suggestion, who was present at the consultation, and so knew it, and revealed it unto them. . . .

The fourth way, is by putting into men's minds wicked purposes and counsels; for after the league once made, he laboreth with them by suggestions, and where God gives him leave, he never ceaseth persuading, till he hath brought his enterprise to pass. Having therefore first brought into the mind of man a resolution to do some evil, he goes and reveals it to the witch, and by force of persuasion upon the party tempted, he frames the action intended to the time foretold, and so finally deludes the witch his own instrument, foretelling nothing, but what himself hath compassed and set about.

The fifth help is the agility of Satan's nature, whereby he is able speedily to convey himself from place to place, yea to pass through the whole world in a short time. For God hath made him by nature a spirit, who by the gift of his creation, hath attained the benefit of swiftness, not only in dispatching his affairs, but also in the carriage of his person with great expedition for the present accomplishment of his own desires.

Lastly, God doth often use Satan as His instrument, for the effecting of His intended works, and the executing of His judgments upon men; and in these cases manifesteth unto him, the place where, the time when, and the manner how such thing should be done. Now all such things as God will have effected by the devil, he may foretell before they come to pass, because he knows them beforehand by revelation and assignment[1] from God. Thus by the Witch of Endor he foretold to Saul the time of his death and of his sons, and the ruin of his kingdom. . . . And these be the ordinary means and helps whereby the devil may know and declare strange things, whether past, present, or to come.

Neither may this seem strange, that Satan by such means should attain unto such knowledge, for even men by their own observations may give probable conjectures of the state and condition of sundry things to come. Thus we read, that some by observation have found out probably, and foretold the periods of families and kingdoms. For example, that the time and continuance of kingdoms is ordinarily determined at 500 years, or not much above; and that great families have not gone beyond the sixth and seventh generation. And as for special and private things, the world so runs (as it were) in a circle, that if a man should but ordinarily observe the course of things, either in the weather, or in the bodies of men, or otherwise, he might easily foretell beforehand what would come after. And by these and such like instances of experiences, men have guessed at the alterations and changes of estates and things in particular. Now if men, which be but of short continuance, and of a shallow reach in comparison, are able to do such things, how much more easily may the devil, having so great a measure of knowledge and experience, and being of so long continuance, having also marked the course of all estates, be able to foretell many things which are to come to pass? . . .

If it be here alleged, that divination is a prerogative to God Himself, and a part of His glory incommunicable to any creature, Isaiah 41:23, I answer, things to come must be considered two ways: either in themselves, or in their causes and signs, which either go with them, or before them. To foretell things to come, as they are in themselves, without respect unto their signs or causes, is a property belonging to God only; and the devil doth it not by an direct and immediate knowledge of things simply considered in

---

[1] **assignment:** a pointing out, specification.

themselves, but only as they are present in their signs or causes. Again, God foretelleth things to come certainly, without the help of any creature, or other means out of Himself; but the predictions of Satan are only probable and conjectural; and when he foretelleth any thing certainly, it is by some revelation from God, as the death of Saul; or by the Scripture . . . or by some special charge committed unto him, for the execution of God's will upon some particular places or persons.

→ MICHEL DE MONTAIGNE

From Of Prognostications   *1603*

As touching oracles it is very certain, that long before the coming of our Savior Jesus Christ,[1] they had begun to lose their credit: for we see that Cicero laboreth to find the cause of their declination . . . as for other prognosticks,[2] that were drawn from the anatomy of beasts in sacrifice, to which Plato doth in some sort ascribe the natural constitution of the internal members of them, of the scraping of chickens, of the flight of birds . . . and others, upon which antiquity grounded most of their enterprises, as well public as private: our religion hath abolished them. . . . [T]here remain yet amongst us some means of divination in the stars, in spirits, in shapes of the body, in dreams, and elsewhere a notable example of the mad and fond curiosity of our nature, amusing itself to preoccupate future things, as if it had not enough to do to digest the present.

[Montaigne then recounts several examples of misleading prophecies, including Francis Marquis of Saluzzo, who was led to an act of treason against the French king in spite of all the omens of the constellations: he "was drawn unto it as a man encompassed and beset by divers passions" and was destroyed.]

I see some that study, plod, and gloss their almanacks, and in all accidents allege their authority. A man were as good to say, they must needs speak truth and lies. *Quis est enim qui totum diem iaculans, non aliquando conlineet?*[3] *For who is he that shooting all day, sometimes hits not the white?* I think not the

---

[1] Protestant doctrine asserted that miracles had ceased with the coming of Christ; Montaigne was not a Protestant, but was skeptical in general.   [2] **prognosticks**: prophecies.   [3] A quotation (translated in the text) from the Roman writer Cicero, *De divinatione.*

Michel de Montaigne, "Of Prognostications," in *The Essays Or Moral, Politic and Military Discourses of Michael Lord of Montaigne*, trans. John Florio (London, 1603), bk. 1, 19–21.

better of them, though what they say prove sometimes true. It were more
certain, if there were either a rule or a truth to lie ever. Seeing no man
recordeth their fables, because they are ordinary and infinite; and their predictions are made to be of credit, because they are rare, incredible and prodigious. . . . This have I seen with mine own eyes, that in public confusions,
men amazed at their own fortune, give themselves headlong, as it were, to
all manner of superstition, to search in heaven the causes and ancient threats
of their ill-luck; and in my time are so strangely successful therein, as they
have persuaded me, that it is an amusing of sharp and idle wits, that such as
are inured to this subtlety, by folding and unfolding them, may in all other
writings be capable to find out what they seek after. But above all, their dark,
ambiguous, fantastical, and prophetical gibberish, mends the matter much,
to which their authors never give a plain sense, that posterity may apply
what meaning and construction it shall please unto it.

→ FRANCIS BACON

From Of Prophecies   *1625*

I mean not to speak of divine prophecies, nor of heathen oracles, nor of natural predictions, but only of prophecies that have been of certain memory
and from hidden causes. [Bacon recounts dreams reported by classical
authors, including Homer, Plutarch, Seneca, and Tacitus, and then turns to
more recent accounts.] Henry the Sixth of England said of Henry the Seventh, when he was a lad, and gave him water, *This is the lad that shall enjoy the
crown for which we strive.* When I was in France, I heard from one Dr. Pena
that the Queen Mother, who was given to curious arts, caused the King[1] her
husband's nativity to be calculated under a false name; and the astrologer
gave a judgment, that he should be killed in a duel, at which the Queen
laughed, thinking her husband to be above challenges and duels, but he was
slain upon a course at tilt, the splinters of the staff of Montgomery going in
at his beaver.[2] The trivial[3] prophecy which I heard when I was a child and
Queen Elizabeth was in the flower of her years, was, "When hempe is spun
/ England's done": whereby it was generally conceived that after the princes

---

[1] Henry II of France, accidentally killed in a tournament in 1559, as described.   [2] **beaver:** lower
portion of the face-guard of a helmet.   [3] **trivial:** common.

Francis Bacon, "Of Prophecies," from *The Essays or Counsels, Civil and Moral* (London, 1625)
212–17.

had reigned which had the principial[4] letters of that word *hempe* (which were Henry, Edward, Mary, Philip, and Elizabeth), England should come to utter confusion, which, thanks be to God, is verified only in the change of the name, for that the King's style is now no more of England, but of Britain.[5] There was also another prophecy before the year of eighty-eight, which I do not well understand: "There shall be seen upon a day, / Between the Baugh and the May, / The black fleet of Norway. / When that that is come and gone, / England build houses of lime and stone, / For after wars shall you have none." It was generally conceived to be meant of the Spanish fleet that came in eighty-eight, for that the king of Spain's surname, as they say, is Norway. . . . There are numbers of the like kind, especially if you include dreams and predictions of astrology. But I have set down these few only of certain credit, for example. My judgment is that they ought all to be despised, and ought to serve but for winter talk by the fireside. Though when I say *despised*, I mean it as for belief, for otherwise, the spreading or publishing of them is in no sort to be despised. For they have done much mischief, and I see many severe laws made to suppress them. That, that hath given them grace and some credit, consisteth in three things. First, that men mark when they hit, and never mark when they miss, as they do generally also of dreams. The second is, that probable conjectures or obscure traditions many times turn themselves into prophecies while the nature of man, which coveteth divination, thinks it no peril to foretell that which indeed they do but collect. . . . The third, and last (which is the great one), is that almost all of them, being infinite in number, have been impostors, and by idle and crafty brains merely contrived and feigned, after the event past.

---

[4] **principial**: initial.   [5] King James had begun using the name "Britain" or (more controversially) "Great Britain," rather than merely "England," as a way of denoting the extent and power of his kingdom; thus the name "England," not England itself, was "done."

CHAPTER 6

Discourses of the Feminine

———————————— ›‹ ————————————

Many of the topics we have already considered concern the nature or role of women: whether a woman could be monarch; whether succession to the monarchy could go through a woman; why treason was so often linked to women; why most witches were women, and why women were particularly disposed to the seduction of the devil; why women were associated with prophecy; and so on. In the materials on witchcraft, the constitution of the feminine itself — the "Fe minus" — was at the heart of the controversy. In this chapter, however, we will turn our attention to an even more concrete issue: the female body. The "feminine" is supposedly an attribute of what is "female"; many recent critics and theorists have argued, however, that the "feminine" is something that is culturally defined, while the "female" is more naturally or biologically defined — or, to use the current terminology of distinction, "gender" is cultural, "sex" is biological. Yet even this distinction, useful as it is, is not quite satisfactory since, as recent work in the history of science and anatomy has shown, early modern descriptions and anatomies of the female body are hardly biological or scientific in our senses of those terms.[1] Rather, early modern writers (overwhelmingly male) describe the

---

[1] See the work of Laqueur, Paster, and Sawday on early modern biological accounts of the body. Much contemporary feminist theory calls into question the entire nature/culture

female body and its operations in ways that are heavily inflected by the ide-
ologies of patriarchy and masculinity. Thus, the female sexual organs,
according to most writers, were simply inferior, inverted versions of the
male sexual organs; both men and women were thus said to have phalluses,
but the woman's was smaller, and inferior because incapable of generation.
Both men and women were said to generate seed, but male seed was said to
be more powerful, and so on. Even after the anatomical descriptions of
Vesalius, and the beginning of a general turn away from the medical writings of Aristotle and Galen — for whom empirical observation was to some
extent unnecessary — male writers continued to describe in minute detail
aspects of the female body that were merely fictions and dreams. Still, the
period beginning in the sixteenth century marks a turning point — fairly
soon to be a revolution — in medical knowledge of the human body, particularly the female body.[2]

In *Macbeth*, the female body is represented in two primary ways: as
demonic, and as maternal; the distinction between the two collapses at key
moments, particularly in the character of Lady Macbeth. The demonic
body, first represented in the witches, is deeply disturbing to Banquo, when
he and Macbeth first meet them on the heath. They are "so withered and so
wild in their attire, / That [they] look not like th' inhabitants o' th' earth /
And yet are on't" (1.3.40–42). They do not respond to Banquo, but, he notes,

> You seem to understand me
> By each at once her chappy finger laying
> Upon her skinny lips. You should be women,
> And yet your beards forbid me to interpret
> That you are so.   (1.3.43–47)

Beyond their wild and disordered appearance, their apparent androgyny —
women with male characteristics, such as beards — marks them as perverse
and "deviant," to use Larner's term.[3] In the excerpt from John Sadler below,
we learn that a woman with a beard may not be a witch at all, but simply
a woman with a specific medical problem, like Phaetusa, whose "voice
changed, and had a beard, with a countenance like a man." Thus the category of the metaphysical could also be explained by the discourse of the

---

binary opposition, arguing that bodies are never simply biologically "there," but are themselves always constituted by discourse. See, among many others, Judith Butler.

[2] Two landmarks in medical history published in this period: Andreas Vesalius's anatomies, *De
humani corporis fabrica* (1543), and William Harvey's account of the circulation of the blood,
De motu cordis (1628; translated into English in 1653).

[3] Note, too, Macduff's reference to Duncan's murdered body as "a new Gorgon" (2.3.65) — one
of the mythical three female monsters (Medusa is the most famous) with snakes for hair;
anyone who looked upon them was turned to stone.

medical. As we know from the witchcraft documents in Chapter 5, of course, it was exactly such women — and the sort suffering from melancholy, in Scot's description (see p. 352) — who were accused of witchcraft in the first place, and so we find a familiar circular logic to such definitions.

The specific medical problem suffered by the women in Sadler's and Scot's descriptions was the "retention of the months," or retention of menstrual blood (known scientifically as amenorrhea); such retention was believed to lead to a wide number of female diseases, as outlined in the excerpts from Sadler and Barrough, among a host of writers on the subject. Perhaps the most serious of these diseases, and the most notorious, was the "suffocation or strangling of the womb," also known as "suffocation of the mother" or "hysterica passio"; the suffocation or strangling effect was one of the chief symptoms, a choking or tightness in the throat. This disease was potentially fatal, always disturbing, and inherently female, as the selections from Barrough and Sadler indicate.[4]

Many medical writers in the early modern period discuss the suffocation of the mother, but by far the most famous is Edward Jorden, who wrote *A Brief Discourse of a Disease Called the Suffocation of the Mother*, printed in London in 1603. Jorden was a noted physician, as were other writers, but his short book is important not because of the medical knowledge it imparted — Jorden did little more than summarize what was already widely known in medical circles — but because his book held an important polemical position in a wide-ranging religious and political struggle of the time. Jorden's book was written specifically to counter beliefs in witchcraft possession, which had been the substance of the recent, spectacular trial of Elizabeth Jackson, accused of witchcraft by the young girl, Mary Glover, and her followers; as Michael MacDonald has argued, "the disturbed antics of a fourteen-year-old girl had become a contest of power between the church and the criminal courts of the City of London" (MacDonald xlii).[5] In the long run, in controversies over alleged exorcisms which came to a head in 1605, these disputes reached the attention, in different ways, of both Shakespeare and King James. Jorden's task in his book was to explain that Mary

---

[4] In *King Lear*, however, Shakespeare gives the affliction to Lear himself: "O, how this mother swells up toward my heart! / *Hysterica passio*, down, thou climbing sorrow! / Thy element's below" (2.4.55–57); see Adelman and Kahn for suggestive critical readings of this moment. Samuel Harsnett somewhat contemptuously, or sarcastically, notes that Richard Mainy "had a spice of the *Hysterica passio*, as seems, from his youth; he himself terms it the Mother . . . which a thousand poor girls in England had worse than ever Master Mainy had" (Brownlow 223). Complicating the *Lear* reference, moreover, is the fact that in both Quarto and Folio, Lear actually says "*Historica passio*"; see Halpern (215–69) for an interpretation of this reading.

[5] For lucid and compact accounts of these controversies, see Paul (90–130) and, especially, MacDonald (vii–lxiv).

Glover's signs of possession had a wholly *natural*, not a supernatural, cause; the possibility that she was counterfeiting some of the symptoms was also raised, but Jorden wanted to establish the natural basis of the symptoms. As a result, his argument helps to broaden the range of somatic disturbances that might be explained by reference to this disease. His skepticism about possession was part of the more general process leading to a relative decline in witchcraft beliefs.

The diseased, deviant, or demonic female body is known in part through its defined difference from the healthy, fertile maternal body; represented throughout *Macbeth* as a natural norm, the image of the maternal body structures the audience's perception of its perversion, particularly through the character of Lady Macbeth. In her great speech in act 1, scene 5, she seeks to undo what Shakespeare's audience would have understood as her essential femininity, particularly her maternal, or potentially maternal, characteristics. Her speech is by turns shocking, autoerotic, and blasphemous, linking her not only with the witches, but with all forms of darkness and evil:

> The raven himself is hoarse
> That croaks the fatal entrance of Duncan
> Under my battlements. Come, you spirits
> That tend on mortal thoughts, unsex me here
> And fill me from the crown to the toe top-full
> Of direst cruelty! Make thick my blood;
> Stop up th' access and passage to remorse,
> That no compunctious visitings of nature
> Shake my fell purpose, nor keep peace between
> Th' effect and it! Come to my woman's breasts
> And take my milk for gall, you murdering ministers,
> Wherever in your sightless substances
> You wait on nature's mischief! Come, thick night,
> And pall thee in the dunnest smoke of hell,
> That my keen knife see not the wound it makes,
> Nor heaven peep through the blanket of the dark
> To cry "Hold, hold!" (1.5.34–50)

What Lady Macbeth asks for here is nothing less than a reversal of nature itself: she beckons not her lover, but "murdering ministers"; she seeks to turn her maternal milk to gall;[6] she seeks to eliminate all pity from her body, and literally replace it with cruelty; she seeks to "make thick" her own blood, so that it can no longer flow as it should. And most bizarrely, she seeks to bring

---

[6] There are two ways of reading this line: (1) turn my milk, literally, into gall; (2) treat my milk *as* gall — that is, find poison in my milk.

to a halt her monthly menstrual flow, to eliminate the "compunctious visitings of nature" by stopping up — literally blocking — the "access and passage" to the womb. In the usual gender stereotyping, the feminine is soft, weak, and sympathetic, while the male is hard, strong, and pitiless; whatever is feminine is thus liable to pity and remorse. Blocking the womb, for Lady Macbeth, would be blocking remorse. While reproducing this gender distinction, though, Shakespeare also undermines it, since in this version being male means nothing more than being a murderer.

Lady Macbeth's plea for a self-induced amenorrhea is in effect an attack on her own womb — and it is exactly her womb that is in question in the play. The Macbeths are childless, without an heir — as Macbeth laments, "Upon my head they placed a fruitless crown / And put a barren scepter in my grip, / Thence to be wrenched with an unlineal hand, / No son of mine succeeding" (3.1.62–65). While this passage seems to suggest that the sterility is Macbeth's — his "barren scepter" produces no seed — the play also shows us a Lady Macbeth who resists everything maternal about her own body; it is no slip or fault of historical knowledge that Shakespeare never names Lady Macbeth's son by a previous marriage, Lulach.[7] What Shakespeare leaves his audience with is the sterility of the Macbeths, the self-willed suffocation of her womb.

Perhaps even more shocking than Lady Macbeth's speech in act 1, scene 5 is her challenge to Macbeth, in trying to rally and seduce him into murdering Duncan:

> What beast was't, then,
> That made you break this enterprise to me?
> When you durst do it, then you were a man;
> And, to be more than what you were, you would
> Be so much more the man. Nor time nor place
> Did then adhere, and yet you would make both.
> They have made themselves, and that their fitness now
> Does unmake you. I have given suck, and know

---

[7] In Holinshed's account, Lugtake (Lulach) is set up, after Macbeth's death, as a rival to Malcolm:

> Thus whilst Malcolm was busied in setting orders amongst his subjects, tidings came that one Lugtake surnamed the fool, being either the son, or (as some write) the cousin of the late mentioned Macbeth, was conveyed, with a great number of such as had taken part with the said Macbeth, unto Scone, and there by their support received the crown, as lawful inheritor thereto. To appease this business, was Macduff Earl [his new title, granted by Malcolm] of Fife sent with full commission in the king's name, who encountering with Lugtake at a village called Essen in Bogdale, slew him, and discomfited his whole power, ordering the matter with them in such wise, that afterwards there was no more trouble attempted in that behalf. (Holinshed 5: 278)

How tender 'tis to love the babe that milks me;
I would, while it was smiling in my face,
Have plucked my nipple from his boneless gums
And dashed the brains out, had I so sworn as you
Have done to this.   (1.7.48–60)

Here Lady Macbeth indicates that she *has* given birth to a child and nursed it — "I have given suck" — producing the play's paradox that the Macbeths are childless parents, or anti-parents.[8]

Lady Macbeth's vision of "the babe that milks me" connects to a whole host of interrelated images of children, milk, blood, and violence — and more.[9] When Lady Macbeth first hears of the witches' prophecies in act 1, scene 5, she immediately fears that Macbeth will not be cruel or violent enough to seize the opportunity by killing Duncan: "Yet do I fear thy nature; / It is too full o' the milk of human kindness / To catch the nearest way" (1.5.12–14). And in act 4, scene 3, when Malcolm is testing Macduff by claiming to possess absolutely none of the "king-becoming graces" — by claiming to be a Macbeth, in short — he too invokes the maternal metaphor to describe the depths of his supposed perversion:

Nay, had I power, I should
Pour the sweet milk of concord into hell,
Uproar the universal peace, confound
All unity on earth.   (4.3.98–101)

Mother's milk, then, figures as the opposite of male-gendered violence and cruelty. Men produce blood, and women (should) produce milk.

But women of course also produce blood, and several of the selections that follow describe the early modern biological understanding of the relationship between a woman's menstrual flow and her milk — "for the milk is nothing but the menstruous blood made white in the breasts," Sadler notes. Moreover, there is a special "sympathy" or biological connection between the womb — source of virtually all of women's ills, or so the accounts here seem to suggest — and various parts of the body, but above all, the breasts, as Crooke argues. The play's imagery of milk, blood, and breasts therefore hovers over a coherent set of theories of early modern biology and gynecology.[10]

---

[8] See the famous note on this question in Bradley, and L. C. Knights's rebuttal of such character analysis.

[9] See Cleanth Brooks's famous essay on the play's imagery; also see Adelman for a psychoanalytic explanation of it.

[10] Two essential works on early modern gynecology and obstetrics are Eccles and Crawford, "Attitudes"; see also Fox and La Belle for more specific reference to *Macbeth*.

This is not to suggest that Shakespeare's audience would simply have seen Lady Macbeth as suffering from the malign symptoms of womb suffocation as a result of amenorrhea; rather, it is that Shakespeare associates all of these things with Lady Macbeth's unnatural turn to violence. Her sleepwalking and other somatic afflictions seem an apt illustration of Jorden's haunting conclusion that the "perturbations of the mind" often cause the suffocation of the mother and other diseases: "For seeing we are not masters of our own affections, we are like battered cities without walls, or ships tossed in the sea, exposed to all manner of assaults and dangers, even to the overthrow of our own bodies."

It is also significant that Lady Macbeth claims to have suckled her own child herself, for in the early modern period upper-class or noble women overwhelmingly sent their children to a wet nurse for breast-feeding.[11] The excerpt below from *The Countess of Lincoln's Nursery* reveals the powerful but minority view of the virtues of breast-feeding in aristocratic women; the pathos and virtually modern sentimentalism of Elizabeth Clinton's exhortation are intensified by her painful admission that she herself did not suckle her own children, to her everlasting regret. One can only imagine what a woman like Elizabeth Clinton might have felt upon hearing Lady Macbeth's violent vow about "the babe that milks me."

The tradition of breast feeding in Scotland — at least in the ancient Scotland that William Harrison surveys in his *Description of Scotland* — was perhaps different, for there the warrior women

> slept moreover either upon the bare floor or pallets of straw, teaching their children even from their infancy to eschew ease, and practice the like hardness; and sith[12] it was a cause of suspicion of the mother's fidelity toward her husband, to seek a strange nurse for her children (although her milk failed), each woman would take intolerable pains to bring up and nourish her own children. They thought them furthermore not to be kindly fostered, except they were so well nourished after their births with the milk of their breasts, as they were before they were born with the blood of their own bellies, nay they feared lest they should degenerate and grow out of kind, except they gave them suck themselves, and eschewed strange milk.

These Scottish warrior women, moreover, "marched as well in the field as did the men," and "they slew the first living creature that they found, in whose blood they not only bathed their swords, but also tasted thereof with their mouths. . . . When they saw their own blood run from them in the fight, they waxed never a whit astonished with the matter, but rather

---

[11] See Crawford, "The Sucking Child," and Paster.
[12] **sith**: since.

doubling their courages, with more eagerness they assailed their enemies" (Holinshed 5:23–24). These warrior women, their milk and blood issuing almost simultaneously in this account, proving their fidelity and insuring the health of the line of inheritance, represent what Lady Macbeth would turn herself into — the terrifying spectacle of the mother who kills.

One recent critic, Janet Adelman, has shown how the play turns on a masculine fear of contamination by the maternal. The key to escaping this contamination is manifested in the character of Macduff, who is the embodiment of the second apparition's prophecy, "for none of woman born / Shall harm Macbeth" (4.1.80–81); Macduff tells Macbeth, just before he slays him, that he "was from his mother's womb / Untimely ripped" (5.8.15–16) — that is, he was born by caesarean section, and thus never passed through the maternal genital area, and so is uncontaminated. Malcolm also claims, in a related way, to be pure when he assures Macduff that he is good after all: "I am yet / Unknown to woman" (4.3.126–27), that is, a virgin. Thus, the only escape for men from the demonized maternal, it seems, is either never to be born, or, if born, never to "know" women sexually. At the end of the play, these two "innocent" men are the only significant male survivors.

What did a caesarean birth mean in early modern England? It meant, above all, that the mother was dead. As the selection from Guillimeau's *Childbirth* makes clear, a caesarean section was an operation only to be performed on an already-dead mother, as a means of rescuing the baby (at least to baptize it while it still lived).[13] Performing this procedure on a living woman was simply fatal to her, if not immediately, then once infection set in. Guillimeau refers to the medical controversy surrounding the operation, and here and elsewhere dismisses the anecdotes about women who survived the operation. The reference to the procedure in *Macbeth*, moreover, makes the mother's death even more inevitable, for Macduff was "ripped" from her womb; the word "untimely" may also suggest that he was born before the end of term.

As Blumenfeld-Kosinski notes, moreover, the caesarean procedure was the key event in the marginalization of women in the practice of obstetrics. The statutes of the Guild of Surgeons specified that "no carpenter, smith, weaver, or woman shall practice surgery,"[14] and the midwife, formerly the chief medical figure presiding over obstetrical practice, is now banished to being merely an assistant to the male surgeon, as Guillimeau's account makes clear.[15] A caesarean section was therefore a surgical procedure on a woman's body performed by a male surgeon. The result was inevitably a maternal corpse. The cesarean section is thus for a woman the equivalent of

---

[13] See Blumenfeld-Kosinski for the historical background.
[14] Quoted from Blumenfeld-Kosinski 99.
[15] The Scottish doctor in act 5 of *Macbeth*, like his English counterpart in act 4, scene 3, is male.

ripping open the male body on the battlefield, as Macdonwald was "unseamed . . . from the nave to th' chops" (1.2.22).

Macbeth does present an alternative paradigm of the maternal in contrast to Lady Macbeth's self-willed demonism: that of Lady Macduff and her children. As seen in the selections from Davenant's revision of the play (p. 162), the narrative line of Lady Macduff and her children has been seen as a more positive image of the maternal; Davenant's additions emphasize the domestic side of both women. Yet even the Macduff family seems dysfunctional — there are children (though we see only the son), to be sure, but Macduff has abandoned them, and Lady Macduff bitterly accuses him of not loving them. And just as Macduff is not of woman born, so his son, soon to be murdered, suffers a strange kind of paternity: "Fathered he is, and yet he's fatherless" (4.2.27). Positive image or not, the entire family is slaughtered, and Lady Macduff wonders, "Why then, alas, / Do I put up that womanly defense, / To say I have done no harm?" (4.2.78–80). The second apparition's prophecy was that none of woman born "Shall harm Macbeth" (4.1.81), and Banquo knows that "oftentimes to win us to our harm / The instruments of darkness tell us truths" (1.3.123–24). "Harm" is generated by the witches and visited by men upon the play's single productive maternal body. The struggle in *Macbeth* is supposedly resolved in the final tableau, in which Macduff salutes Malcolm — the two men unknown to women — as King of Scotland in an eerie echo of the witches' language ("Hail, King of Scotland!" [5.8.59]), as if succession could take place without the female body at all.

→ REGINALD SCOT

From The Discovery of Witchcraft   *1584*

How Melancholy Abuseth Old Women, and of the Effects Thereof by Sundry Examples

If any man advisedly mark their words, actions, cogitations, and gestures, he shall perceive that melancholy abounding in their head, and occupying their brain, hath deprived or rather depraved their judgments, and all their senses: I mean not of cosening[1] witches, but of poor melancholic women, which are themselves deceived. For you shall understand, that the force which melancholy hath, and the effects that it worketh in the body of a man, or rather of

---

[1] **cosening:** deceitful.

Reginald Scot, *The Discovery of Witchcraft* (London, 1584), bk. 3, ch. 9, 52–54.

a woman, are almost incredible. For as some of these melancholic persons imagine, they are witches and by witchcraft can work wonders, and do what they list: so do other, troubled with this disease, imagine many strange, incredible, and impossible things. . . . Now, if the fancy of a melancholic person may be occupied in causes which are both false and impossible; why should an old witch be thought free from such fantasies, who (as the learned philosophers and physicians say) upon the stopping of their monthly melancholic flux or issue of blood, in their age must needs increase therein, as (through their weakness both of body and brain) the aptest persons to meet with such melancholic imaginations: with whom their imaginations remain, even when their senses are gone.

→ PHILIP BARROUGH

From The Method of Physic   *1596*

OF STOPPING OF MENSTRUIS

Moreover stubborn carefulness, immoderate fear and great sorrow do stop the menstruis. There followeth suppression and stopping of the menstruis, heaviness of the whole body, desire to vomit, abhorring of meat, and certain terrible discursions, such as chance to those that have conceived. Moreover there be pains about the loins, thighs, neck, the hinder part of the eyes, and the forepart of the head. Also there follow continual fevers, and blackish urine, with certain red after, and filth in them, even like as one should mix soot with the water wherein new killed flesh hath lately been washed. Also to many either the urine doth come forth difficultly or else it is stopped altogether. The diversity of causes is known partly by the disposition of the whole body, and partly also and for the most part, by the telling of the patient. Women may know a cold distempure[1] in themselves, by these signs specially, because they be more sleepy and slower to all kind of moving, and whiter of color, and as it were of a leady color. Moreover their urine is watery and such like signs appear, which are often rehearsed before. The tokens of hot distempure are clean contrary to these signs of a cold distempure before rehearsed. Signs of fullness, besides those that may be gathered out of the former chapters, are wont[2] specially to be these: that women, that are vexed

---

[1] **distempure**: i.e., distemperature; disorder or ailment.   [2] **are wont**: are usually.

Philip Barrough, *The Method of Physic, Containing the Causes, Signs, and Cures of Inward Diseases in Man's Body from the Head to the Foot.* 3rd ed. (London, 1596), bk. 3, 186, 191–92.

therewith, are grieved most in the time of menstruis, and they feel vehement pain, about the loins and the privy members,[3] and their veins are swollen up very great.

Of Strangling of the Womb

Suffocation or strangling of the womb, is nothing else, but a drawing back of it up to the upper parts. It is caused through stretching out of it, which is engendered of fullness, that followeth after the retention and stopping of menstruis. . . . They that are vexed with this disease, when the fit is nigh, there followeth heaviness of mind, slowness, weakness of the legs, paleness of face, and a sorrowful countenance. But when the suffocation and strangling is now present there followeth disposition to sleep, doting, a withholding of the instruments of the senses, the voice doth wax dumb, and the legs are drawn up together. The pulses are small and weak. Also oftentimes they are altogether stopped. Also in many the breath that should come out at the mouth and nostrils, is stopped altogether, and yet that which is in the arteries, doth remain still. When the evil doth cease, the balls of the cheeks begin to wax red, and the eyes be lifted up and opened. . . . This kind of disease engendereth in all seasons, but specially in winter and autumn: and most commonly young folk, and such as be prone to lechery, and barren, specially if they be made so by medicines, be most taken with this disease.

[3] privy members: i.e., the genitals.

→ EDWARD JORDEN

From A Brief Discourse of a Disease Called the Suffocation of the Mother   *1603*

That this disease doth oftentimes give occasion unto simple and unlearned people, to suspect possession, witchcraft, or some such like supernatural cause.

The passive condition of womankind is subject unto more diseases and of other sorts and natures than men are, and especially in regard of that part from whence this disease which we speak of doth arise. For as it hath more

Edward Jorden, *A Brief Discourse of a Disease Called the Suffocation of the Mother. Written upon occasion which hath been of late taken thereby, to suspect possession of an evil spirit, or some such like supernatural power. Wherein is declared that diverse strange actions and passions of the body of man, which in the common opinion, are imputed to the Devil, have their true natural causes, and do accompany this disease* (London, 1603) B1r–v, C1r–v, F3v, G2v–G3.

variety of offices belonging unto it than other parts of the body have, and accordingly is supplied from other parts with whatsoever it hath need of for those uses: so it must needs thereby be subject unto more infirmities than other parts are, both by reason of such as are bred in the part itself, and also by reason of such as are communicated unto it from other parts, with which it hath correspondence. And as those offices in their proper kinds are more excellent than other; so the diseases whereby they are hurt or depraved, are more grievous. But amongst all the diseases whereunto that sex is obnoxious,[1] there is none comparable unto this which is called *The Suffocation of the Mother,* either for variety, or for strangeness of accidents.[2] For whatsoever strange accident may appear in any of the principal functions of man's body, either animal, vital, or natural, the same is to be seen in this disease, by reason of the community and consent which this part hath with the brain, heart, and liver, the principal seats of these three functions; and the easy passage which it hath unto them by the veins, arteries, and nerves. And whatsoever humor in other parts may cause extraordinary effects, by reason of the abundance or corruption of it, this part will afford the like in as plentiful a manner, and in as high a degree of corruption: and with this advantage, that whereas in the other, some one or two of the faculties only one are hurt (as in apoplexies, epilepsies, syncopies,[3] subversions of the stomach, etc.) and not all (unless as in syncopies by consent, where the vital function ceasing, all the rest must needs cease), in this case all the faculties of the body do suffer; not as one may do from another, but all directly from this one fountain, in such sort as you shall oftentimes perceive in one and the same person diverse accidents of contrary natures to concur at once.

And hereupon the symptoms of this disease are said to be monstrous and terrible to behold, and of such a variety as they can hardly be comprehended within any method or bounds. Insomuch as they which are ignorant of the strange affects which natural causes may produce, and of the manifold examples which our profession of physic doth minister in this kind, have sought above the moon for supernatural causes: ascribing these accidents either to diabolical possession, to witchcraft, or to the immediate finger of the Almighty.

What this disease is, and by what means it causeth such variety of symptoms

This disease is called by diverse names amongst our authors. *Passio Hysterica, Suffocatio, Praefocatio,* and *Strangulatus uteri, Caducus matricis, etc.* In English "the Mother," or "the Suffocation of the Mother," because most

---

[1] **sex . . . obnoxious:** i.e., which are harmful to the female sex.   [2] **accidents:** i.e., the symptoms.
[3] **syncopies:** failures of the heart's action, resulting in unconsciousness.

There may be made a fumigation of spices to be received up into the wombe, which, that it may be the easier done, the wombe may be held open by putting in this instrument here described into the neck thereof. Let it be made of gold, silver or latin into the forme of a pessary; at the one end thereof, that is to say, that end which goeth up into the necke of the wombe, let there be made many holes on each side, but at the lower end let it be made with a spring, that it may open and shut as you wil have it. Also it must have two laces or bands by which it must be made fast unto a swathe or girdle tyed about the patients belly.

The forme of a Pessary to be put into the neck of the wombe to hold it open.

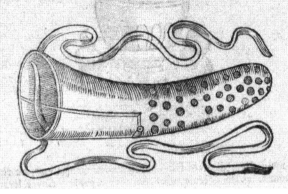

FIGURE 24 *From Helkiah Crooke,* Microcosmographia: A Description of the Body of Man *(1615). The plate shows a typical "cure" for womb disease, a pessary (suppository), intended to bring fresh air into the diseased womb.*

commonly it takes them with choking in the throat: and it is an effect of the Mother or womb wherein the principal parts of the body by consent do suffer diversely according to the diversity of the causes and diseases wherewith the matrix[4] is offended.

Of the causes of this disease

And as the want and scarcity of blood may procure this grief, so the abundance and excess thereof doth more commonly cause it, where the patients do want those monthly evacuations which should discharge their bodies of this superfluity: as we see in strong and lusty maidens, who having ease and good fare enough, have their veins filled with plenty of blood, which wanting[5] sufficient vent distendeth them in bulk and thickness, and so contracteth them in their length, whereby the matrix is drawn upwards or

[4] **matrix**: uterus.   [5] **wanting**: lacking.

sidewards, according as the repletion is, whereupon followeth a compression of the neighbor parts, as of the midriff which causeth shortness of breath, by straightening the instruments of respiration of their due scope.

But if this blood wanting his proper use do degenerate into the nature of an excrement, then it offendeth in quality as well as in excess, and being detained in the body, causeth diverse kinds of symptoms, according to the quality and degree of the distemperature thereof. . . .

Lastly, the perturbations of the mind are oftentimes to blame both for this and many other diseases. For seeing we are not masters of our own affections, we are like battered cities without walls, or ships tossed in the sea, exposed to all manner of assaults and dangers, even to the overthrow of our own bodies.

→ JOHN SADLER

From The Sick Woman's Private Looking-Glass   *1636*

I. The Menstruals

Now, touching the menstruals: they are defined to be a monthly flux of excrementitious[1] and unprofitable blood.

In which we are to note, that the matter flowing forth is excrementitious, which is to be understood of the superplus or redundancy of it: for it is an excrement in quantity, [but] in quality being pure and incorrupt, like unto the blood in the veins.

And that the menstruous blood is pure, and simply of itself, all one in quality with that in the veins, is proved two ways: First, from the final cause of this blood, which is the propagation and conservation of mankind: that man might be conceived; and being begotten, he might be comforted and preserved, both in the womb, and out of the womb. And all will grant it for a truth, that the child, while it is in the matrice,[2] is nourished with this blood; and it is as true, that being out of the womb, it is still nourished with the same; for the milk is nothing but the menstruous blood made white in the breasts; and I am sure woman's milk is not thought to be venomous, but of a nutritive quality, answerable to the tender nature of an infant. Secondly,

---

[1] **excrementitious:** waste, worthless.   [2] **matrice:** uterus, womb.

John Sadler, *The Sick Woman's Private Looking-Glass, Wherein methodically are handled all uterine affects, or diseases arising from the Womb. Enabling Women to inform the physician about the cause of their grief* (London, 1636) 8–21.

FIGURE 25 *The frontispiece to John Sadler,* The Sick Woman's Private Looking-Glass *(1636), typical of the medical pamphlets of the period. The fruits of the garden are being tended to the left, just as a woman's fertility had to be managed. The male physician and the midwife are shown together, but the doctor is central, and superior.*

it is proved to be pure from the generation of it, it being the superfluity of the last aliment[3] of the fleshy parts. . . . [Sadler recounts the supposed "venomous effects" of menstrual blood, then turns to the act of conception:] now in the act of conception, there must be an agent and a patient, for if they be

[3] **aliment**: that which nourishes or feeds.

both every way of one constitution, they cannot propagate; man therefore is hot and dry, woman cold and moist: he is the agent, she the patient, or weaker vessel, that she should be subject unto the office of the man. It is necessary likewise that woman should be of a cold constitution, because in her is required a redundancy of matter for the infant depending on her; for otherwise, if there were not a superplus of nourishment for the child, more than is convenient for the mother, then would the infant detract and weaken the principal parts of the mother; and like unto the viper, the generation of the infant would be the destruction of the parent. These monthly purgations continue from the 15th year, to the 46th or 50th. Yet often there happens a suppression, which is either natural, or morbifical.[4] They are naturally suppressed in breeding[5] women, and such as give suck. The morbifical suppression falls now into our method to be spoken of.

II. OF THE RETENTION OF THE MONTHS

The suppression of the terms is an interception of the accustomary evacuation of the blood, which every month should come from the matrice, proceeding from the instrument or matter vitiated. The part affected is the womb, and that of itself, or by consent.

Cause

The cause of this suppression is either external or internal. The external cause may be heat or dryness of the air, immoderate watching, great labor, vehement motion, and the like, whereby the matter is so consumed, and the body so exhaust[ed], that there is not a superplus remaining to be expelled; as is recorded of the Amazonites,[6] who being active, and always in motion, had their fluxions very little, or not at all. Or it may be caused by cold, which is most frequent, making the blood viscous and gross, condensing and binding up the passages, that it cannot flow forth.

The internal cause is either instrumental or material, in the womb or in the blood.

In the womb it may be diverse ways: by apostems,[7] tumors, ulcers, by the narrowness of the veins and passages, or by the *omentum* or kell[8] in fat bodies, pressing the neck of the matrice. . . . By overmuch cold or heat, the one vitiating the action, and the other consuming the matter. By an evil

---

[4] **morbifical:** producing disease.   [5] **breeding:** pregnant.   [6] **Amazonites:** the Amazons were a legendary nation of female warriors (see Jackson and Shepherd for the tradition in the Renaissance); the term was applied generically to any tall, vigorous, aggressive — and hence, masculinized — woman.   [7] **apostems:** deep-seated abcesses.   [8] *omentum* **or kell:** fatty membrane investing the intestines.

composition of the uterine parts; by the neck of the womb being turned aside; and sometimes, though rarely, by a membrane or excrescence of flesh growing about the mouth or neck of the womb. The blood may be in fault two ways, in quantity or in quality. In quantity, when it is so consumed, that there is not a superplus left, as in viragoes[9] and virile women, who through their heat and strength of nature, digest and consume all their last nourishment; as Hippocrates[10] writes of Phaetusa, who being exiled by her husband Pythea, her terms were suppressed, her voice changed, and had a beard, with a countenance like a man. But these I judge rather to be Anthropophagae,[11] women-eaters, than women-breeders, because they consume one of the principles of generation, which gives a being to the world, viz. the menstruous blood. The blood likewise may be consumed, and consequently, the terms stayed, by bleeding of the nose, by a flux of the hemorrhoids, by a dysentery, commonly called the bloody flux, by many other evacuations, and continual and chronical diseases. Secondly, the matter may be vicious[12] in quality; as suppose it be sanguineous, phlegmatical, bilious, or melancholious, every one of these, if they offend in grossness, will cause an obstruction in the veins.

Signs

Signs manifesting the disease, are pains in the head, neck, back, and loins; weariness of the whole body, but especially of the hips and legs, by reason of a concinnity[13] which the matrix[14] hath with these parts: trembling of the heart. Particular signs are these: if the suppression proceeds of cold, she is heavy, sluggish, of a pale color, and hath a slow pulse, Venus combats[15] are neglected, the urine is crude, waterish, and much in quantity; the excrements of the guts usually are retained. If [the suppression proceeds] of heat, the signs are contrary to those even now recited. If the retention be natural, and come of conception, this may be known by drinking of hydromel, that is water and honey, after supper going to bed, and by the effect which it worketh; for, after the taking of it, if she feels a beating pain about the navel and lower parts of the belly, it is a sign she hath conceived,[16] and that the suppression is natural. If not, that is it vicious, and ought medicinally to be taken away.

---

[9] **viragoes**: man-like women; female warriors. [10] **Hippocrates**: see note 1 of Crooke, *Microcosmographia* (p. 361). [11] **Anthropophagae**: man-eaters, cannibals; cf. *Othello* 1.3.146. [12] **vicious**: causing harm. [13] **concinnity**: harmonious fitting together of individual parts. [14] **matrix**: uterus, womb. [15] **Venus combats**: i.e., sexual activities. [16] **conceived**: become pregnant.

Prognostics

With the evil quality of the womb the whole body stands charged, but especially the heart, the liver, and the brain; and betwixt the womb and these three principal parts, there is a singular consent.

First, the womb communicates to the heart by the mediation of those arteries which come from aorta; hence the terms being suppressed, will ensue faintings, swoonings, intermission of pulse, cessation of breath.

Secondly, it communicates to the liver by the veins derived from the hollow vein; hence will follow obstructions, cachexies,[17] jaundice, dropsies,[18] hardness of the spleen.

Thirdly, it communicates unto the brain, by the nerves and membranes of the back; hence will arise epilepsies, apoplexies, frenzies, melancholy passions, pain in the after parts of the head, fearfulness, inability of speaking. Well therefore may I conclude with Hippocrates, if the months be suppressed, many dangerous diseases will follow.

---

[17] **cachexies:** depraved condition of the body, in which nutrition is everywhere defective.
[18] **dropsies:** areas swollen by the accumulation of watery fluid.

→ HELKIAH CROOKE

From Microcosmographia: A Description of the Body of Man *1615*

Of the wonderful consent between the womb and almost all the parts of women's bodies

Concerning the wonderful sympathy that is between the womb and almost all the parts of women's bodies, that place of Hippocrates[1] in his book *De locis in homine* is most remarkable, where he sayeth, "That the wombs of women are the causes of all diseases": that is to say, the womb being affected, there follow manifest signs of distemper in all the parts of the body, as the brain, the heart, the liver, the kidneys, the bladder, the guts, the share-bones:[2]

---

[1] Hippocrates was a physician in fifth-century B.C.E. Athens; virtually none of the works that bear his name can be definitively attributed to him. This group of texts and its authors — known as the Hippocratics — were however considered the founders of modern medicine; their medical and surgical books were in use into the eighteenth century.   [2] **share-bones**: the pubis.

Helkiah Crooke, *Microcosmographia: A Description of the Body of Man. Together with the Controversies and Figures Thereto Belonging* (London, 1615), bk. 4, 252–54.

and in all the faculties, animal, vital, and natural; but above all, the sympathy between the womb and the breasts is most notable. . . .

Between the brain and the womb there is very great consent, as well by the nerves as by the membranes of the marrow of the back: hence in affects of the mother[3] come the pains which some women often feel in the back-parts of their head, their frenzies or frantic fits, their dumb silence and indeed inability to speak, their strange fearfulness, sometimes loathing their lives yet fearing beyond measure to die; their convulsions, the caligation[4] or dimness of their sight, the hissing of their ears, and a world of such like and of unlike accidents.

[Crooke then expounds the connections between the womb and the heart, liver, kidneys, bladder, and gut.] But above all other consents is that sympathy between the womb and the breasts which exceedeth even admiration itself, and is diversely manifested by the frequent translation of humors out of the breasts into the womb, and out of the womb into the breasts; by the signs of the womb affected which are taken from the inspection of the breasts; from the usual cures of the diseases of both parts; and finally from the knowledge we have by the breasts, of the condition of the infant yet contained in the womb. . . .

Amatus Lusitanus[5] reporteth, that he saw two women, who upon the suppression of their courses did avoid[6] blood out of the nipples of their breasts at certain and set times and returns, imagine shortly after the usual time of their courses. And Hippocrates it appeareth had seen the like, for he writeth in the 40th Aphorism of the fifth section, that those women who have blood gathered about their breasts are in danger to grow mad and raging. Brassavolus reporteth, that he saw a woman out of whose breasts issued blood instead of milk; and this may well be, for we all know that nurses[7] have their courses stopped, because the blood returneth from the womb unto the breasts, where it is turned into milk usually; that in this example the blood came out unturned, that was the rarity. We have seen also on the contrary many women in childbed who have avoided by the womb and the bladder great quantities of milk. This translation of humors therefore is ordinary. Sometimes the blood goeth other ways, as I have known an ancient maid in Lincolnshire, who ever about the time she should have her courses, for many days together hath found in her mouth in the morning when she awaked, the quantity of four or five ounces of blood more or less,

---

[3] **the mother:** i.e., the disease of the mother, or womb.   [4] **caligation:** dimness or mistiness of sight.   [5] **Amatus Lusitanus:** sixteenth-century Italian anatomist, contemporary with Vesalius.
[6] **avoid:** to make empty; excrete.   [7] **nurses:** i.e., wet nurses — women, usually of a lower class, hired to breast feed the children of other women, especially those of aristocratic rank.

ΜΙΚΡΟΚΟΣΜΟΓΡΑΦΙΑ.

DESCRIPTION
of the Body of Man.

TOGETHER

WITH THE CONTROVERSIES
and Figures thereto belonging.

Collected and Translated out of all the Best Authors of Anatomy, Especially out of Gasper Bauhinus, and Andreas Laurentius. By HELKIAH CROOKE Doctor in Physicke, Phisition to His Maiesty, and His Highnesse PROFESSOR in Anatomy and Chirurgery.

Published by the Kings Maiesties especiall Direction and Warrant, according to the first integrity, as it was Originally written by the AVTHOR.

―――――― *Etiam Parnassia Laurus*
Parua, sub ingenti matris se subijcit vmbra.

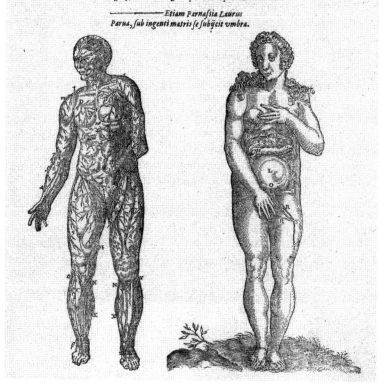

FIGURE 26 *The title page to Helkiah Crooke,* Microcosmographia: A Description of the Body of Man *(1615). Crooke was James's physician. The two figures reflect the relatively new art of dissection and anatomization.*

and most part of it caked as it is in a saucer after blood letting, and this continued with her for many years together, but her teeth rotted foully with it, her breath grew noisome, and she faint[ed] at those times, but without any other disease.

→ ELIZABETH CLINTON

From The Countess of Lincoln's Nursery   *1622*

Because it hath pleased God to bless me with many children and so caused me to observe many things falling out to mothers and to their children, I thought it good to open my mind concerning a special matter belonging to all childbearing women seriously to consider of, and, to manifest my mind the better, even to write of this matter so far as God shall please to direct me: in sum the matter I mean is the duty of nursing due by mothers to their own children.

In setting down whereof, I will first show that every woman ought to nurse her own child; and secondly I will endeavor to answer such objections as are used to be cast out against this duty to disgrace the same.

The first point is easily performed. For it is the express ordinance of God that mothers should nurse their own children and, being His ordinance, they are bound to it in conscience. . . .

I beseech all godly women to remember how we elder ones are commanded to instruct the younger to love their children: now, therefore, love them so as to do this office to them when they are born, more gladly for love's sake than a stranger, who bore them not, shall do for lucre's sake.[1] Also I pray you set no more so light by God's blessing[2] in your own breasts, which the Holy Spirit ranketh with other excellent blessings; if it be unlawful to trample underfeet a cluster of grapes, in which a little wine is found; then how unlawful is it to destroy and dry up those breasts, in which your own child (and perhaps one of God's very elect, to whom to be a nursing father is a king's honor; and to whom to be a nursing mother is a queen's honor) might find food of sincere milk, even from God's immediate providence, until it were fitter for stronger meat? I do know that the Lord may

---

[1] **for lucre's sake:** for the sake of money.   [2] **set . . . blessing:** i.e., do not dismiss so easily God's blessing.

Elizabeth Clinton, *The Countess of Lincoln's Nursery* (Oxford, 1622) 1–2, 17–21.

deny some women, either to have any milk in their breasts at all, or to have any passage for their milk, or to have any health, or to have a right mind: and so they may be letted[3] from this duty by want, by sickness, by lunacy, etc. But I speak not to these: I speak to you, whose consciences witness against you, that you cannot justly allege any of those impediments [which she has already articulated, such as that it is troublesome, that it makes one look old, etc.].

Therefore be no longer at the trouble and at the care to hire others to do your own work; be not so unnatural to thrust away your own children; be not so hardy as to venture a tender babe to a less tender heart; be not accessory to that disorder of causing a poorer woman to banish her own infant for the entertaining of a richer woman's child, as it were bidding her unlove her own to love yours. We have followed Eve in transgression, let us follow her in obedience. When God laid the sorrows of conception, of breeding, of bringing forth and bringing up her children upon her, and so upon us in her loins, did she reply any word against? Not a word; so I pray you all mine own daughters, and others that are still childbearing, reply not against the duty of suckling them when God hath sent you them. . . .

Think always that, having the child at your breast and having it in your arms, you have God's blessing there. For children are God's blessings. Think again how your babe crying for your breast, sucking heartily the milk out of it, and growing by it, is the Lord's own instruction: every hour, and every day that you are suckling it, instructing you to show that you are his new born babes, by your earnest desire after his word and the sincere doctrine thereof, and by your daily growing in grace and goodness thereby, so shall you reap pleasure and profit. Again you may consider that when your child is at your breast, it is a fit occasion to move your heart to pray for a blessing upon that work, and to give thanks for your child and for ability and freedom unto that, which many a mother would have done and could not, who have tried and ventured their health and taken much pains and yet have not obtained their desire. But they that are fitted every way for this commendable act have certainly great cause to be thankful: and I much desire that God may have glory and praise for every good work, and you much comfort that do seek to honor God in all things. Amen.

---

[3] **letted**: prevented.

→ JAMES GUILLIMEAU

From Childbirth, Or
the Happy Delivery of Women   *1612*

The means how to take forth a child, by the caesarean section

It now remains only, that I speak of the last kind of delivery, which must be practiced after the mother's decease, that thereby the child may be saved, and receive baptism. This birth is called caesarean . . . in imitation of Caesar, who was ripped out of his mother's womb, at the very instant she died.[1] The which ought to be observed in every well-governed commonwealth. . . . The lawyers judge them worthy of death, who shall bury a great-bellied woman that is dead, before the child be taken forth, because together with the mother, they seem to destroy the hope of a living creature. . . .

But before the chirurgion[2] come to this work, he must observe diligently, and be certainly assured, that the woman is dead, and that her kinsfolks, friends, and others that are present, do all affirm and confess, that her soul is departed. And then he must come presently to the handywork, because the deferring of it might cause the child's death, and so make the work unprofitable.

All the while that the woman lies in her pain and agony, the midwife, or else some other woman, shall hold their hand within the neck of the matrice,[3] to keep it as open, as may be possible: for though we know, that while the child is in the mother's womb, he breathes only by her arteries, yet notwithstanding, the air that may enter therein, doth not only not hurt, but doth very much good.

Now, to know certainly, and to be assured that the woman hath yielded up her last breath, you shall lay upon her lips, and about her nose, some light feathers; for if she breathe never so little, they will fly away.

[Guillimeau then describes the incisions to be made and surgical procedure for the operation.]

Some hold, that this caesarean section, may and ought to be practiced (the woman being alive) in a painful and troublesome birth: which for mine

---

[1] See Blumenfeld-Kosinski (143–53) for an account of the historical and etymological tradition that links Julius Caesar to this medical procedure.   [2] **chirurgion**: surgeon.   [3] **matrice**: uterus.

James Guillimeau, *Childbirth, Or The Happy Delivery of Women. Wherein is set down the government of women in the time of their breeding child; of their travail, both natural and contrary to nature; and of their lying in, together with the diseases, which happen to women in those times, and the means to help them* (London, 1612), bk. 2, ch. 25, 185–88.

Chap.1. *The expert Midwife.* 45

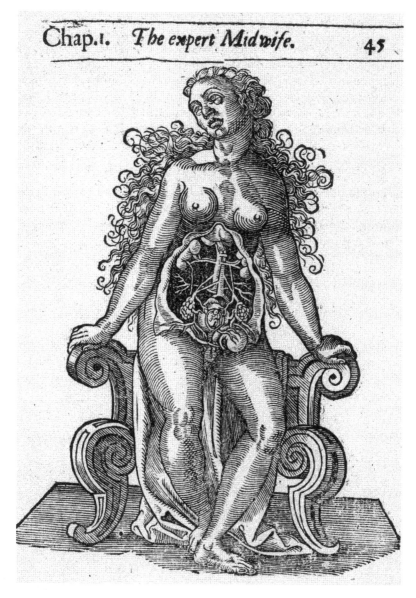

FIGURE 27 *From Jacob Rueff,* The Expert Midwife *(1637). A typical self-displaying "anatomized" view of the female reproductive organs.*

own part, I will not counsel anyone to do, having twice made trial of it myself, in the presence of Monsieur Paraeus,[4] and likewise seen it done by Monsieur Viart, Brunet, and Charbonnet, all excellent chirurgions, and men of great experience and practice, who omitted nothing, to do it artificially and methodically. Nevertheless, of five women, in whom this hath been practiced, not one hath escaped. I know that it may be alleged, that there be some have been saved thereby. But though it should happen so, yet ought we rather to admire it, than either practice or imitate it; for, one swallow makes not a spring, neither upon one experiment only, can one build a science.

After Monsieur Paraeus had caused us to make trial of it, and seen that the success was very lamentable and unfortunate, he left off, and disallowed this kind of practice, together with the whole College of Chirurgions of Paris: as likewise the discreeter sort, of the Regent Doctors in the faculty of Physic, at Paris.

---

[4] **Monsieur Paraeus**: the distinguished French surgeon, Ambroïse Paré, whose major works were translated into English by Thomas Johnson and published in 1634 (his name is given in English as "Parey"). Paré was Guillimeau's teacher and colleague. Guillimeau refers here to a general controversy in French medical circles in the 1580s, prompted by the claims of François Rousset that the caesarean procedure could safely be practiced on healthy, living women. Paré, Guillimeau, and others roundly attacked this view, disparaging in particular Rousset's claims about specific cases. Guillimeau himself, according to Blumenfeld-Koskinski, "seems to have checked up on some of Rousset's eye-witnesses and . . . found them to be lying" (45).

Bibliography

⇥⇤

Primary Sources

An Act against Conjuration, Witchcraft, and dealing with evil and wicked Spirits. London, 1604.

At the Parliament holden at Westminster the xii of January, in the fifth year of the reign of our Sovereign Lady, Elizabeth . . . were enacted as followeth. London, 1563.

Aubrey, John. *Aubrey's Brief Lives.* Ed. Oliver L. Dick. London: Secker, 1950.

Bacon, Francis. *The Essays or Counsels, Civil and Moral.* London, 1625.

Barrough, Philip. *The Method of Physic, Containing the Causes, Signs, and Cures of Inward Diseases in Man's Body from the Head to the Foot.* 3rd ed. London, 1596.

Beaumont, Francis. *The Knight of the Burning Pestle.* Ed. John Doebler. Lincoln: U of Nebraska P, 1967.

Boece, Hector. *The Chronicles of Scotland, compiled by Hector Boece, Translated into Scots by John Bellenden.* 1540? Edinburgh: Scottish Text Society, 1938.

Buc, Sir George. *Daphis Polystephanos. An Eclog treating of Crowns, and of Garlands.* London, 1605.

Buchanan, George. *Rerum Scoticarum historia [History of Scotland.]* Trans. T. Page. London, 1690.

———. *Powers of the Crown in Scotland.* Trans. Charles F. Arrowood. Austin: U of Texas P, 1949. Trans. of *De Jure Regni apud Scotos.* Edinburgh, 1579.

Bullough, Geoffrey, ed. *Narrative and Dramatic Sources of Shakespeare.* Vol. 7. New York: Columbia UP, 1975.

Calendar of State Papers and Manuscripts, Scottish.

Calendar of State Papers and Manuscripts, Venetian.

Carleton, Dudley. *Dudley Carleton to John Chamberlain 1603–1624. Jacobean Letters.* Ed. Maurice Lee, Jr. New Brunswick: Rutgers UP, 1972.

Chamberlain, John. *The Letters of John Chamberlain.* Ed. N. E. McClure. Philadelphia: American Philosophical Society, 1939.

Chambers, E. K. *The Elizabethan Stage.* 4 vols. Oxford: Clarendon, 1923.

———. *William Shakespeare: A Study of Facts and Problems.* 2 vols. Oxford: Clarendon, 1930.

Clinton, Elizabeth. *The Countess of Lincoln's Nursery.* Oxford, 1622.

Clowes, William. *A Right Fruitful and Approved Treatise, for the Artificial Cure of that Malady called in Latin* Struma, *and in English, the* Evil, *cured by Kings and Queens of England.* London, 1602.

Coke, Edward. Speech at the Trial of Father Henry Garnet. *Cobbett's Complete Collection of State Trials.* Ed. T. B. Howell. Vol. 2. London, 1809.

A Collection of Divers and Remarkable Stories. Tragical and Comical. 1670. Folger Shakespeare Library V.a.81.

Colman, Morgan. *The Genealogies of King James I, and Queen Anne, his wife, from the Conquest.* [London?] 1608.

Constable, Henry. *A Discovery of a Counterfeit Conference* . . . Collen, 1600.

Craig, Sir Thomas. *A Treatise on the Union of the British Realms.* Trans. C. Sanford Terry. Edinburgh: Edinburgh UP, 1909. Trans. of *De unione regnorum Britanniae tractatus.* c. 1603–08.

Crooke, Helkiah. *Microcosmographia: A Description of the Body of Man. Together with the Controversies and Figures Thereto Belonging.* London, 1615.

Davenant, William. *Macbeth, A Tragedy. With all The Alterations, Amendments, Additions, and New Songs.* London, 1674.

Doleman, R. See Parsons, Robert.

Duffett, Thomas. *Epilogue. Being a new Fancy after the old, and most surprising way of Macbeth, Perform'd with new and costly Machines.* Epilogue to *The Empress of Morocco. A Farce.* London, 1674.

Filmer, Sir Robert. *Patriarcha: Or The Natural Power of Kings.* c. 1630. London, 1680.

Forman, Simon. *The Book of Plays and Notes hereof and Formans for Common Policy.* Chambers, *Shakespeare* 2:337–38.

Garnet, Henry. *A Treatise of Equivocation.* c. 1598. Ed. David Jardine. London, 1851.

Garrick, David. *Macbeth, A Tragedy, by Shakespeare.* London, 1774.

Gerard, John. *The Autobiography of a Hunted Priest.* Trans. Philip Caraman. New York: Pellegrini & Cudahy, 1952.

Gifford, George. *A Dialogue concerning Witches and Witchcrafts* . . . London, 1593.

Guillimeau, James. *Childbirth Or The Happy Delivery of Women. Wherein is set down the government of women* . . . London, 1612.

Harington, Sir John. *A Tract on the Succession to the Crown (A.D. 1602)*. London: Roxburghe Club, 1880.

Harrison, William. "The Description of Scotland." In *The Chronicles of England, Scotland, and Ireland* by Raphael Holinshed. 1587. London, 1808.

Harry, George Owen. *The Genealogy of the High and Mighty Monarch, James*. London, 1604.

Harvey, John. *A Discursive Problem Concerning Prophecies*. London, 1588.

Hayward, John. *An Answer to the First Part of a Certain Conference, Concerning Succession, Published not long since under the name of R. Dolman*. London, 1603.

Heylyn, Peter. *Microcosmus*. Oxford, 1636.

Holinshed, Raphael. *The Chronicles of England, Scotland, and Ireland*. 1587. 6 vols. London, 1808.

An Homily against disobedience and willful rebellion. London, 1570.

Howard, Henry. *A Defensative against the Poison of Supposed Prophecies . . .* London, 1583.

Howson, John. *A Sermon Preached at St. Mary's in Oxford, the 17. Day of November, 1602 . . .* 2nd ed. Oxford, 1603.

King James I, *Basilikon Doron. Or His Majesty's Instructions To His Dearest Son, Henry the Prince*. Edinburgh, 1603. James, *Works*.

——. *Daemonology, In Form of a Dialogue*. Edinburgh, 1597.

——. "A Speech as it was Delivered in the Upper House of the Parliament to the Lords Spiritual and Temporal, and to the Knights, Citizens and Burgesses there Assembled, On Monday the XIX Day of March 1603." 1604. James, *Works*.

——. "A Speech in the Parliament House, as Near The Very Words as Could Be Gathered at the Instant." November 9, 1605. James, *Works*.

——. "A Speech to the Lords and Commons of the Parliament at Whitehall, On Wednesday the XXI. of March. Anno 1609." 1610. James, *Works*.

——. *The True Law of Free Monarchies: Or the Reciprock and Mutual Duty Betwixt a Free King, and His Natural Subjects*. Edinburgh, 1598. James, *Works*.

——. *The Works of the Most High and Mighty Prince, James*. London, 1616.

Jonson, Ben. *Ben Jonson*. Ed. Ian Donaldson. New York: Oxford UP, 1985.

Jonson, Ben, George Chapman, and John Marston. *Eastward Ho!* Ed. C. G. Petter. London: Benn, 1973.

Jorden, Edward. *A Brief Discourse of a Disease Called the Suffocation of the Mother . . .* London, 1603.

Kempe, Will. *Kempe's Nine Days' Wonder*. London, 1600.

Leslie, John. *A defence of the honor of . . . Mary Queen*. 1569.

——. *The History of Scotland*. Trans. Father James Dalrymple (1596). Ed. E. G. Cody. Edinburgh: Blackwood, 1888.

Major, John. *A History of Greater Britain*. 1521. Trans. Archibald Constable. Edinburgh: Scottish History Society, 1892.

Malleus Maleficarum. Trans. Montague Summers. In *Witchcraft in Europe 1100–1700: A Documentary History*. Ed. Alan C. Kors and Edward Peters. Philadelphia: U of Pennsylvania P, 1972.

Middleton, Thomas. *A Critical Edition of Thomas Middleton's* The Witch. Ed. Edward J. Esche. New York: Garland, 1993.

——. *The Witch.* Ed. W. W. Greg and F. P. Wilson. Oxford: Oxford UP, 1950.

——. *The Witch.* Ed. Elizabeth Schafer. London: Black, 1994.

Milton, John. *Complete Prose Works of John Milton.* Ed. Don M. Wolfe. Vol. 4. New Haven: Yale UP, 1966.

Molin, Nicolo. *Calendar of State Papers, Venetian.* Vol. 10 (1605). London, 1864.

Montaigne, Michel de. *The Essays Or Moral, Politic and Military Discourses of Michael Lord of Montaigne.* Trans. John Florio. London, 1603.

Moryson, Fynes. *An Itinerary.* London, 1617.

Munro, John, ed. *The Shakspere Allusion-Book.* 1909. London: Oxford UP, 1932.

News from Scotland. London, 1591.

Osborne, Francis. *Traditional Memoirs on the Reign of King James the First. The Secret History of the Court of James I.* Ed. Sir Walter Scott. Edinburgh, 1811.

Paré, Ambroïse. *The Works of that famous Chirurgion, Ambrose Parey.* Trans. Thomas Johnson. London, 1634.

[Parsons, Robert] Doleman, R. *A Conference about the Next Succession to the Crown of England, Divided into Two Parts.* N. [Antwerp], 1594 [actually appeared in 1595].

——. *A Treatise Tending to Mitigation towards Catholic-Subjects in England . . . Against The seditious writings of Thomas Morton . . . concerning Rebellion and Equivocation, are overthrown, and cast upon himself.* 1607.

Pepys, Samuel. *The Diary of Samuel Pepys.* Ed. Robert Latham and William Matthews. Berkeley: U of California P, 1970–83.

Perkins, William. *A Discourse of the Damned Art of Witchcraft; So Far Forth as it is revealed in the Scriptures, and manifested by true experience.* Cambridge, 1608.

Ponet, John. *A Short Treatise of Politic Power, and of the true Obedience which subjects owe to kings and other civil Governors, with an Exhortation to all true natural Englishmen.* London, 1556.

Puttenham, George. *The Art of English Poesie.* London, 1589.

Rowley, William, Thomas Dekker, John Ford, etc. *The Witch of Edmonton. Three Jacobean Witchcraft Plays.* Ed. Peter Corbin and Douglas Sedge. Manchester: Manchester UP, 1986.

Rye, W. B., ed. *England as Seen by Foreigners in the Days of Elizabeth and James the First.* 1865. New York: Bloom, 1967.

Sadler, John. *The Sick Woman's Private Looking-Glass, Wherein methodically are handled all uterine affects, or diseases arising from the Womb . . .* London, 1636.

Scot, Reginald. *The Discovery of Witchcraft . . .* London, 1584.

Shakespeare, William. *The Complete Works of Shakespeare.* Ed. David Bevington. 4th ed. New York: HarperCollins, 1992.

——. *Macbeth.* Ed. Nicholas Brooke. Oxford: Oxford UP, 1990.

——. *Macbeth.* Ed. A. R. Braunmuller. Cambridge: Cambridge UP, 1997.

——. *Macbeth.* Ed. Kenneth Muir. London: Methuen, 1951. Rev. ed. 1984.

Smith, Sir Thomas. *De Republica Anglorum: A Discourse on the Commonwealth of England.* Ed. L. Alston. 1906. Shannon: Irish UP, 1972.

Speed, John. *The History of Great Britain.* London, 1611.

"Succession Act" of 1604. *A Most Joyful and just recognition of the immediate, lawful, and undoubted Succession, Descent, and Right of the Crown. Statutes of the Realm,* 4. 1017.

Taylor, John. *The Penniless Pilgrimage, or The Moneyless Perambulation, of John Taylor, Alias the King's Majesty's Water-Poet.* London, 1618.

Tooker, William. *Charisma sive donum sanationis.* [*The Divine Power or Gift of Healing.*] London, 1597. Raymond Crawfurd. *The King's Evil.* Oxford: Clarendon, 1911.

Vindiciae contra Tyrannos: A Defence of Liberty against Tyrants. Or, Of the lawful power of the Prince over the people, and of the people over the prince. Being a Treatise written in Latin and French by Junius Brutus, and translated out of both into English. London, 1648.

Weldon, Sir Anthony. *A Perfect Description of the People and Country of Scotland.* 1617. London, 1659.

Wentworth, Peter. *A Treatise containing M. Wentworth's Judgment Concerning the Person of the true and lawful successor to these Realms of England and Ireland.* London, 1598.

Wilson, Arthur. *The Life and Reign of James the First, King of Great Britain. A Complete History of England with the Lives of all the Kings and Queens Hereof.* Ed. White Kennett. London, 1719.

Wilson, Thomas. *The State of England A.D. 1600.* Ed. F. J. Fisher. Camden Miscellany, 3rd ser., lii.

Winwood, Sir Ralph. *Memorials of Affairs of State in the Reigns of Queen Elizabeth and King James I.* London, 1725.

Secondary Sources

Adelman, Janet. *Suffocating Mothers: Fantasies of Maternal Origin in Shakespeare's Plays,* Hamlet *to* The Tempest. New York: Routledge, 1992.

Akrigg, G. P. V. *Jacobean Pageant Or The Court of King James I.* Cambridge: Harvard UP, 1962.

Amussen, Susan Dwyer. *An Ordered Society: Gender and Class in Early Modern England.* New York: Blackwell, 1988.

Arrowood, Charles F. *The Powers of the Crown in Scotland.* Austin: U of Texas P, 1949.

Ashley, Maurice. *The House of Stuart: Its Rise and Fall.* London: Dent, 1980.

Axton, Marie. *The Queen's Two Bodies: Drama and the Elizabethan Succession.* London: Royal Historical Society, 1977.

Bartholomeusz, Dennis. '*Macbeth*' *and the Players.* London: Cambridge UP, 1969.

Bingham, Caroline. *The Stewart Kingdom of Scotland 1371–1603.* London: Weidenfeld, 1974.

Birch, Thomas. *The Court and Times of James the First.* 2 vols. London, 1849.

Bloch, Marc. *The Royal Touch: Sacred Monarchy and Scrofula in England and France.* 1923. London: Routledge, 1973.

Blumenfeld-Kosinski, Renate. *Not of Woman Born: Representations of Caesarean Birth in Medieval and Renaissance Culture.* Ithaca: Cornell UP, 1990.

Bradley, A. C. *Shakespearean Tragedy.* 1904. London: St. Martin's, 1985.

Briggs, Robin. *Witches and Neighbors: The Social and Cultural Context of European Witchcraft.* New York: Viking, 1996.

Brooks, Cleanth. "The Naked Babe and the Cloak of Manliness." *The Well Wrought Urn.* New York: Harcourt, 1947.

Brownlow, F. W. *Shakespeare, Harsnett, and the Devils of Denham.* Newark: U of Delaware P, 1993.

Butler, Judith. *Bodies That Matter: On the Discursive Limits of "Sex."* New York: Routledge, 1993.

Clark, Stuart. "Inversion, Misrule, and the Meaning of Witchcraft." *Past & Present* 87 (1980): 98–127.

Cohn, Norman. *Europe's Inner Demons: An Enquiry Inspired by the Great Witch-Hunt.* New York: Basic, 1975.

Cook, Ann Jennalie. *Making a Match: Courtship in Shakespeare and His Society.* Princeton: Princeton UP, 1991.

Crawford, Patricia. "Attitudes to Menstruation in Seventeenth-Century England." *Past & Present* 91 (1981): 47–73.

——. "The Sucking Child: Adult Attitudes to Child Care in the First Year of Life in Seventeenth-Century England." *Continuity and Change* 1 (1986): 23–52.

Crawfurd, Raymond. *The King's Evil.* Oxford: Clarendon, 1911.

Daly, James. "The Idea of Absolute Monarchy in Seventeenth-Century England." *Historical Journal* 21 (1978): 227–50.

Demos, John. *Entertaining Satan: Witchcraft and the Culture of Early New England.* Oxford: Oxford UP, 1983.

Dobin, Howard. *Merlin's Disciples: Prophecy, Poetry, and Power in Renaissance England.* Stanford: Stanford UP, 1990.

Donaldson, Gordon. *Scottish Kings.* London: Batsford, 1977.

Eagleton, Terry. *William Shakespeare.* New York: Blackwell, 1986.

Eccles, Audrey. *Obstetrics and Gynaecology in Tudor and Stuart England.* Kent, OH: Kent State UP, 1982.

Fox, Alice. "Obstetrics and Gynecology in *Macbeth.*" *Shakespeare Studies* 12 (1979): 127–41.

Fraser, Antonia. *The Gunpowder Plot: Terror and Faith in 1605.* London: Weidenfeld, 1996.

Galloway, Bruce. *The Union of England and Scotland 1603–1608.* Edinburgh: Donald, 1986.

Garnett, George, ed. *Vindiciae, Contra Tyrannos.* Cambridge: Cambridge UP, 1994.

Gatherer, W. A., ed. *The Tyrannous Reign of Mary Stewart.* Edinburgh: Edinburgh UP, 1958.

Ginzburg, Carlo. *The Night Battles: Witchcraft and Agrarian Cults in the Sixteenth and Seventeenth Centuries.* Baltimore: Johns Hopkins UP, 1983.

Halpern, Richard. *The Poetics of Primitive Accumulation: English Renaissance Culture and the Genealogy of Capital.* Ithaca: Cornell UP, 1991.

Helgerson, Richard. *Forms of Nationhood: The Elizabethan Writing of England.* Chicago: U of Chicago P, 1992.

Hicks, Leo. "Father Robert Persons S. J. and *The Book of Succession.*" *Recusant History* 4 (1957): 104–37.

Hodgdon, Barbara, ed. *The First Part of King Henry the Fourth: Texts and Contexts.* Boston: Bedford, 1997.

Houlbrooke, Ralph. *The English Family, 1450–1700.* London: Longman, 1984.

Hurstfield, Joel. "The Succession Struggle in Late Elizabethan England." *Elizabethan Government and Society.* Ed. S. T. Bindoff, J. Hurstfield, and C. H. Williams. London: Athlone, 1961.

Jackson, Gabriele Bernhard. "Topical Ideology: Witches, Amazons, and Shakespeare's Joan of Arc." *English Literary Renaissance* 18 (1988): 40–65.

Kahn, Coppelia. "The Absent Mother in *King Lear.*" *Rewriting the Renaissance: The Discourses of Sexual Difference in Early Modern Europe.* Chicago: U of Chicago P, 1986.

Karlsen, Carol F. *The Devil in the Shape of a Woman: Witchcraft in Colonial New England.* New York: Norton, 1987.

Kittredge, George Lyman. *Witchcraft in Old and New England.* Cambridge: Harvard UP, 1929.

Kliman, Bernice W. *Shakespeare in Performance:* Macbeth. Manchester: Manchester UP, 1992.

Knights, L. C. "How Many Children Had Lady Macbeth?" *Explorations.* London: Chatto, 1946.

La Belle, Jenijoy. "'A Strange Infirmity': Lady Macbeth's Amenorrhea." *Shakespeare Quarterly* 31 (1980): 381–86.

Laqueur, Thomas. *Making Sex: Body and Gender from the Greeks to Freud.* Cambridge: Harvard UP, 1990.

Larner, Christina. *Witchcraft and Religion: The Politics of Popular Belief.* New York: Blackwell, 1984.

Levine, Mortimer. *Tudor Dynastic Problems 1460–1571.* London: Allen, 1973.

Lockyer, Roger. *The Early Stuarts: A Political History of England 1603–1642.* London: Longman, 1989.

MacDonald, Michael, ed. *Witchcraft and Hysteria in Elizabethan London.* New York: Routledge, 1991.

Macfarlane, Alan. *Marriage and Love in England: Modes of Reproduction, 1300–1840.* New York: Blackwell, 1986.

——. *Witchcraft in Tudor and Stuart England: A Regional and Comparative Study.* New York: Harper, 1970.

McFarlane, I. D. *Buchanan*. London: Duckworth, 1981.

Malloch, A. E. "Father Henry Garnet's Treatise of Equivocation." *Recusant History* 15 (1981): 387–95.

Moretti, Franco. "'A Huge Eclipse': Tragic Form and the Deconsecration of Sovereignty." *The Power of Forms in the English Renaissance*. Ed. Stephen Greenblatt. Norman: Pilgrim, 1982.

Mullaney, Steven. "Lying Like Truth: Riddle, Representation and Treason in Renaissance England." *ELH* 47 (1980): 32–47.

Nenner, Howard. *The Right to Be King: The Succession to the Crown of England 1603–1714*. Chapel Hill: U of North Carolina P, 1995.

Norbrook, David. "*Macbeth* and the Politics of Historiography." *Politics of Discourse: The Literature and History of Seventeenth-Century England*. Ed. Kevin Sharpe and Steven N. Zwicker. Berkeley: U of California P, 1987.

Paster, Gail Kern. *The Body Embarrassed: Drama and the Disciplines of Shame in Early Modern England*. Ithaca: Cornell UP, 1993.

Paul, Henry N. *The Royal Play of* Macbeth. New York: Macmillan, 1950.

Pittock, Murray G. H. *The Invention of Scotland: The Stuart Myth and the Scottish Identity, 1638 to the Present*. London: Routledge, 1991.

Purkiss, Diane. *The Witch in History: Early Modern and Twentieth-Century Representations*. New York: Routledge, 1996.

Riggs, David. *Ben Jonson: A Life*. Cambridge: Harvard UP, 1989.

Rosen, Barbara, ed. *Witchcraft in England, 1558–1618*. 1969. Amherst: U of Massachusetts P, 1991.

Rosenberg, Marvin. *The Masks of 'Macbeth.'* Berkeley: U of California P, 1978.

Sawday, Jonathan. *The Body Emblazoned: Dissection and the Human Body in Renaissance Culture*. London: Routledge, 1995.

Shepherd, Simon. *Amazons and Warrior Women: Varieties of Feminism in Seventeenth-Century Drama*. New York: St. Martin's, 1981.

Skinner, Quentin. *The Foundations of Modern Political Thought*. 2 vols. Cambridge: Cambridge UP, 1978.

Stallybrass, Peter. "*Macbeth* and Witchcraft." *Focus on Macbeth*. Ed. John Russell Brown. London: Routledge, 1982.

Stone, Lawrence. *The Crisis of the Aristocracy 1558–1641*. Abr. ed. Oxford: Oxford UP, 1967.

——. *The Family, Sex and Marriage in England 1500–1800*. London: Weidenfeld, 1977.

Taylor, Rupert. *The Political Prophecy in England*. New York: Columbia UP, 1911.

Thomas, Keith. *Religion and the Decline of Magic*. New York: Scribner's, 1971.

Trevor-Roper, H. R. *The European Witch-Craze of the Sixteenth and Seventeenth Centuries*. New York: Harper, 1969.

Wain, John, ed. *Shakespeare:* Macbeth: *A Casebook*. London: Macmillan, 1969.

Wells, Stanley, and Gary Taylor. *William Shakespeare: A Textual Companion*. Oxford: Clarendon, 1987.

Wiener, Carol Z. "The Beleaguered Isle: A Study of Elizabethan and Early Jacobean Anti-Catholicism." *Past & Present* 51 (1971): 27–62.

Willis, Deborah. *Malevolent Nurture: Witch-Hunting and Maternal Power in Early Modern England.* Ithaca: Cornell UP, 1995.

Willson, D. H. *King James VI and I.* New York: Oxford UP, 1956.

Woodbridge, Linda. *Women and the English Renaissance: Literature and the Nature of Womankind, 1540–1620.* Urbana: U of Illinois P, 1986.

Wormald, Jenny. "Gunpowder, Treason, and Scots." *Journal of British Studies* 24 (1985): 141–68.

———. "James VI and I, *Basilikon Doron* and *The Trew Law of Free Monarchies:* The Scottish Context and the English Translation." *The Mental World of the Jacobean Court.* Ed. Linda Levy Peck. Cambridge: Cambridge UP, 1991.

Zagorin, Perez. *Ways of Lying: Dissimulation, Persecution, and Conformity in Early Modern Europe.* Cambridge: Harvard UP, 1990.

Acknowledgments

Macbeth from Bevington, David. THE COMPLETE WORKS OF SHAKE-SPEARE, 4th Edition, © 1992. Reprinted by permission of Pearson Education, Inc., Upper Saddle River, NJ.

CHAPTER 1

Figure 4. The genealogy of the Scottish descent from Banquo in *De origine, moribus, et rebus gestis Scotorum* by John Leslie (1578). DA 775 L4 1578 copy 1. By permission of the Folger Shakespeare Library.

Figure 5. "A sergeant at arms, slain by the rebels," from *The Chronicles of England, Scotland, and Ireland* by Raphael Holinshed (1577). STC 13567.8. By permission of the Folger Shakespeare Library.

Figure 6. "Macdonwald slayeth his wife and children, and lastly himself," from *The Chronicles of England, Scotland, and Ireland* by Raphael Holinshed (1577). STC 13567.8. By permission of the Folger Shakespeare Library.

Figure 7. "Macbeth, Banquo, and the Three Weird Sisters," from *The Chronicles of England, Scotland, and Ireland* by Raphael Holinshed (1577). STC 13567.8. By permission of the Folger Shakespeare Library.

Figure 8. "Macbeth usurpeth the crown," from *The Chronicles of England, Scotland, and Ireland* by Raphael Holinshed (1577). STC 13567.8. By permission of the Folger Shakespeare Library.

CHAPTER 2

Figure 9. A genealogy of the contemporary Scottish descent in *De origine, moribus, et rebus gestis Scotorum* by John Leslie (1578). By permission of the Henry E. Huntington Library, San Marino, California.

Figure 10. The genealogy of the English descent in *A Conference About the Next Succession to the Crown of England* by R. Doleman. STC 19398. By permission of the Folger Shakespeare Library.

Figure 11. Portrait of King James attributed to John de Critz the elder. By permission of the Trustees of Dulwich Picture Gallery.

Figure 12. James VI, *Basilikon Doron*, autograph page. By permission of the British Library. Royal MS 18 B xv.

Figure 13. Frontispiece to *Works* by James I (1616). STC 14344. By permission of the Folger Shakespeare Library.

CHAPTER 3

Figure 14. Frontispiece to *Mischief's Mystery: Or, Treason's Masterpiece, the Powder Plot* by John Vicars (1617). STC 13247. By permission of the Folger Shakespeare Library.

Figure 15. Gunpowder Plot Conspirators. By permission of the Mary Evans Picture Library.

Figure 16. *Mischief's Mystery: Or, Treason's Masterpiece, the Powder Plot* by John Vicars (1617). STC 13247. By permission of the Folger Shakespeare Library.

Figure 17. "The Execution of the Gunpowder Plot Conspirators." Printed by Nicholas de Visscher. Art File G976 #2. By permission of the Folger Shakespeare Library.

CHAPTER 4

Figure 18. Map of Scotland in *The Theatre of the Empire of Great Britain* by John Speed. STC 23040. By permission of the Folger Shakespeare Library.

Figure 19. Thomas Hariot, "The True Picture of One Pict," *A Brief and True Report of the New Found Land of Virginia* (London, 1590). STC 12786, E3r. By permission of the Folger Shakespeare Library.

Figure 20. Thomas Hariot, "The True Picture of a Woman Pict," *A Brief and True Report of the New Found Land of Virginia* (London, 1590). STC 12786, E4r. By permission of the Folger Shakespeare Library.

Henry V, 1.2.136-77, from *The Complete Works of Shakespeare.* 4th ed. Ed. David Bevington. Copyright © 1992 by HarperCollins College Publishers, Inc. Reprinted by permission of Addison-Wesley Educational Publishers, Inc.

CHAPTER 5

Figure 21. Incidents from *News from Scotland* (1591). Shelfmark Douce F.210. C2v. By permission of the Bodleian Library, University of Oxford.

Figure 22. King James interrogates the witches from *News from Scotland* (1591). Shelfmark Douce F.210. B1. By permission of the Bodleian Library, University of Oxford.

Figure 23. Cow and men riding double from *News from Scotland* (1591). Shelfmark Douce F.210. C4v. By permission of the Bodleian Library, University of Oxford.

CHAPTER 6

Figure 24. Pessary for cure of Suffocation of the Mother from Helkiah Crooke, *Microcosmographia: A Description of the Body of Man* (1615). By permission of the Henry E. Huntington Library, San Marino, California.

Figure 25. Frontispiece to *The Sick Woman's Private Looking-Glass* by John Sadler (1636). By permission of the Henry E. Huntington Library, San Marino, California.

Figure 26. Title page to Helkiah Crooke, *Microcosmographia: A Description of the Body of Man* (1615). STC 6062.2. By permission of the Folger Shakespeare Library.

Figure 27. Illustration from *The Expert Midwife* by Jacob Rueff (1637). STC 21442. By permission of the Folger Shakespeare Library.

Index